+HX531 .M3 1984

50664000141343
Marx, Karl, 1818-188/On literature and a
HX531 .M3 1984 C.1 STACKS 1984

Workers of All Countries, Unite!

Marx Engels

On Literature and Art

PROGRESS Publishers · Moscow

PUBLISHERS' NOTE

This collection is compiled on the basis of two books published in Russian: Marx and Engels, *On Art* (Moscow, 1967) and Marx and Engels, *On Literature* (Moscow, 1958).

It also includes other material, such as an excerpt from Engels' manuscript "Slavic Languages and Philology", "Critical Articles" by Marx's wife Jenny, etc.

The collection is divided into sections according to subjects. The headings and subheadings have been supplied by the editors.

Some of the translations have been taken from various collections of Marx's and Engels' works put out by Progress Publishers. All other items have been translated from the German, unless otherwise indicated.

REQUEST TO READERS

Progress Publishers would be glad to have your opinion of this book, its translation and design and any suggestions you may have for future publications.

Please send your comments to 17, Zubovsky Boulevard, Moscow, U.S.S.R.

К. МАРКС и Ф. ЭНГЕЛЬС

О ЛИТЕРАТУРЕ И ИСКУССТВЕ

На английском языке

Copyright © Progress Publishers, Moscow, 1976

Second printing 1978
Third printing 1984

Published in the Union of Soviet Socialist Republics

МЭ $\frac{0101010000-137}{014(01)-84}$ без объявл.

Contents

PREFACE 15

MATERIALIST CONCEPTION OF THE HISTORY OF CULTURE

Social Being and Social Consciousness 41
   1 41
   2 42
Natural Conditions and Development of Culture 45
Landscapes 48
Against Vulgarisation of Historical Materialism 57
   1 57
   2 58
   3 58
   4 60
   5 61
Engels About Mehring's *The Lessing Legend* 63
   1 63
   2 63
   3 Engels to Franz Mehring 64
Class Relations and Class Ideology 70
   1 70
   2 73
Scientific and Vulgar Conceptions of Class Ideology 75
   Engels to Paul Ernst 75
Historical Continuity and Its Contradictions 79
   1 79
   2 79
Uneven Character of Historical Development and Questions of Art   82

GENERAL PROBLEMS OF ART

Ideological Content and Realism 87
    1. Engels to Minna Kautsky 87
    2. Engels to Margaret Harkness in London 89
    3 92
The Tragic and the Comic in Real History 94
    1 94
    2 95
    3 95
    4 96
    5 96
Problems of Revolutionary Tragedy 98
    Marx and Engels to Ferdinand Lassalle on his Drama *Franz von Sickingen* 98
    1. Marx to Ferdinand Lassalle 98
    2. Engels to Ferdinand Lassalle 101
Miscellaneous Items 108
    Language and Literature 108
        1 108
        2 108
    Improvisation and Poetry 109
    On Literary Style 110
        1 110
        2 111
        3 112
        4 112
    On Literary Polemics 113
        1 113
        2 114
        3 114
        4 115
        5 116
    On Translation 116
        1 116
        2 117
        3 118
        4 119
        5 119
        6 121
        7 122

ART IN CLASS SOCIETY

The Origin of Art 125
    Historical Development of the Artistic Sense 125

 1 125
 2 126
 3 126
The Role of Labour in the Origin of Art 128
Artistic Creation and Aesthetic Perception 129

Social Division of Labour 130
 Division of Labour and Social Consciousness 130
 Estrangement of Labour and the Condition of the Working
 People in Capitalist Society 132
Money and World Culture 134
 The Distorting Power of Money 134

Capitalism and Spiritual Production 140
 Relation of Art and Poetry to the Capitalist Mode of Production 140
 Bourgeois Taste and Its Evolution 141
 The Work of the Artist in Capitalist Society 142
  1 142
  2 144
  3 145

 Freedom of the Press and of Artistic Creation 146
  1 146
  2 146
  3 147
  4 148
  5 150
 Asceticism and Enjoyment 151
 Work and Play 153
 Bourgeois Civilisation and Crime 154

Historical Mission of the Working Class 157
 The Proletariat and Wealth 157
 The Working Class and the Progressive Development of Society 159
  1 159
  2 160
 The Working Class and Culture 161
  1 161
  2 162
  3 163
  4 163
  5 165
  6 166

Proletarian Revolution and the Vandalism of the Bourgeoisie . . 167
 1 167
 2 169

ART AND COMMUNISM

Criticism of Egalitarian Communism 173
    1 173
    2 175
Individuality and Society 177
    1 177
    2 179
    3 180
The Kingdom of Freedom and Material Labour 182
    1 182
    2 183

HISTORY OF SOCIAL THOUGHT, LITERATURE AND ART ANTIQUITY, MIDDLE AGES AND RENAISSANCE

Antiquity 187
  The Dawn of Human Culture 187
  The Beginnings of Mythology and Epos 188
  Epic Tradition of the Semites 189
  Ancient Greek Society in Homer's Poems 190
    1 190
    2 191
  Greek Tragedy 192
    1 192
    2 194
  Position of Women in Greece According to Ancient Writers . 195
  Ancient Slavery and World Culture 199
    1 199
    2 200
  The Plastic Element in Greek Arts 201
    1 201
    2 202
  Greek Enlightenment 203
    1 203
    2 204
  Religion and Culture in the Ancient World 205
  Philosophical Trends in the Epoch of the Decline of the Ancient World 207
  Lucretius Carus 208
    1 208
    2 208
  Horace 210
  Persius' Satire 210
  Lucian 211

CONTENTS

Middle Ages 212
  Germanic Culture 212
  Love in the Literature of Antiquity and the Middle Ages . . 215
  Wagner and Germanic Epos 217
  Legend of Siegfried and the German Revolutionary Movement 218
  Ancient Irish Literature 220
    1 220
    2 222
    3 225
    4 225

  Ancient Scandinavian Epos 227
  Early Medieval Danish Poetry 228
  The Chanson de Roland 230
  Provençal Literature 232
    1 232
    2 232
  Chivalrous Love Poetry 233
  Peasant Equalitarian Ideas in England. John Ball. William
  Langland's "Complaint of Piers the Ploughman" 234
  German *Volksbücher* 235

Renaissance 246

  Difference Between the Situation at the End of the Ancient
  World, *ca.* 300—and at the End of the Middle Ages—1453 . . 246
  Italian Culture from Dante to Garibaldi 247
    1 247
    2 248
  Dante 248
  Petrarch 249
  Boccaccio 251
  Great Renaissance 251
  Titian 254
  Grobian Literature of the Reformation Period 254
  Historical Significance of the Reformation 256
  Thomas More 257
    1 257
    2 257
    3 258
    4 258
  Shakespeare 259
    1 259
    2 260
    3 260
    4 261

Calderón	262
1	262
2	263
3	263
Cervantes	264
1	264
2	265

HISTORY OF SOCIAL THOUGHT AND LITERATURE
THE MODERN PERIOD

Three Unities of Classical Drama	269
La Rochefoucauld	269
Historic Significance of the Enlightenment	270
The Materialism of the Encyclopedists	272
1	272
2	272
The Enlightenment and Dialectics	274
Utilitarian Philosophy of the Enlightenment	275
Voltaire	277
1	277
2	278
Diderot	279
1	279
2	279
3	281
Rousseau	281
1	281
2	283
Sentimentalism as a Reaction to the Revolutionary and Rationalist Trends of the Enlightenment	283
The Crisis of Enlightenment Ideals	284
Transition from the Enlightenment to Romanticism	286
Criticism of Capitalist Progress from the Point of View of the Past	287
Feudal Socialism	287
Petty-Bourgeois Criticism of Capitalism	288
Restoration Writers	289
French Literature	291
Abbé Prévost	291
Chateaubriand	291
1	291
2	292
Alexandre Dumas	292

Lamartine	293
1	293
2	293
3	294
Victor Hugo	295
1	295
2	295
3	296
4	296
Eugène Sue	297
From Critical Analysis of Sue's *Mystères de Paris*	298
1	298
2	299
3	302
Balzac	313
1	313
2	313
3	314
4	314
5	314
Pierre Dupont	315
Arthur Ranc	315
Renan	316
1	316
2	316
Zola	317
Maupassant	317
English and Irish Literature	318
Daniel Defoe	318
1	318
2	318
Swift	319
Pope	320
Shelley and Byron	320
Walter Scott	321
William Cobett's Social Writings	321
English Working-Class Poet Mead	324
Thomas Carlyle	325
1	325
2	326
English Realists of the Mid-Nineteenth Century	339
Carleton	340
Bernard Shaw	340
Aveling	341
1	341

2	341
William Morris	341
German Literature	343
Situation of Germany and German Culture from the Mid-Seventeenth to the Early Nineteenth Century	343
1	343
2	346
Schiller. Shortcomings of His Poetry	348
Goethe	349
1	349
2	349
3	349
4	350
5	350
6 Karl Grün, *Über Göthe vom Menschlichen Standpunkte.* Darmstadt, 1846	351
Heine	374
1	374
2	375
3	376
4	377
5	377
6	378
"Young Germany"	378
Alexander Jung	379
German, or "True" Socialism	383
1	383
2	386
Karl Beck, *Lieder vom Armen Mann,* or the Poetry of True Socialism	387
1	387
2	388
3	389
4	389
Gottfried Kinkel	390
1	390
2	390
Freiligrath	395
1. [Editorial Statement Concerning the Reappearance of the *Neue Rheinische Zeitung*]	395
2	395
3	397
4	398
5	399
6	400

7	401
8	401
9	401
Weerth	402
Outstanding Personalities in the Working-Class Movement. Johann Philipp Becker	405
1	405
2	406
3	407
Russian Literature	408
The Russian Language	408
1	408
2	408
3	409
The Lay of Igor's Host	409
Lomonosov. Slavic Languages and Philology	410
Derzhavin	412
Pushkin	413
Chernyshevsky and Dobrolyubov	414
1	414
2	414
3	415
Chernyshevsky as a Scholar and Critic	415
Chernyshevsky and the Russian Village Commune	416
1	416
2	416
Chernyshevsky as a Revolutionary	420
1	420
2	420
3	421
4	421
5	421
Shchedrin	422
Flerovsky	422

REVOLUTIONARY AND SATIRICAL FOLK POETRY OF THE PAST

Herr Tidmann	427
Folk Songs on Stenka Razin	428
The Vicar of Bray	429
German Revolutionary Songs	431
Weavers' Song	433

Songs of the German Revolution of 1848 434
    1 434
    2 434
Satirical Folk Song Against Louis Bonaparte 435

CONFESSIONS OF MARX AND ENGELS 436

Karl Marx. Confessions 436
Frederick Engels. Confessions 437

FROM REMINISCENCES OF MARX AND ENGELS 438

From Reminiscences of Marx 438
  Paul Lafargue 438
    1 438
    2 438
    3 439
  Eleanor Marx-Aveling 440
  Franzisca Kugelmann 442
  Anselmo Lorenzo 444
From Reminiscences of Engels 445
  N. S. Rusanov 445
  Fanni Kravchinskaya 447

Critical Articles by Jenny Marx 449
    1. From London's Theatre World 449
    2. The London Season 453
    3. Shakespearean Studies in England 456
    4. Shakespeare's *Richard III* in London's Lyceum Theatre . 461
    5. From the London Theatre 465
Notes 471
Name Index 493
Index of Literary and Mythological Names 516

Preface

This volume offers the reader a selection of both excerpts and complete works and letters by Karl Marx and Frederick Engels, giving their views on art and its place in society. Though it contains far from all that was written by the founders of scientific communism on this subject, it will nevertheless acquaint the reader with Marx's and Engels' most important ideas about artistic work.

Karl Marx and Frederick Engels had an excellent knowledge of world art and truly loved literature, classical music, and painting. In their youth both Marx and Engels wrote poetry; in fact Engels at one time seriously contemplated becoming a poet.

They were well acquainted not only with classical literature, but also with the works of less prominent and even of little known writers both among their contemporaries and those who lived and worked in more distant times. They admired Aeschylus, Shakespeare, Dickens, Fielding, Goethe, Heine, Cervantes, Balzac, Dante, Chernyshevsky and Dobrolyubov, and mentioned many other less famous people who had also made their mark in the history of literature. They also displayed a great love for popular art, for the epics of various nations and other types of folklore: songs, tales, fables and proverbs.

Marx and Engels made extensive use of the treasures of world literature in their own works. Their repeated references to literary and mythological figures, and use of aphorisms, comparisons and direct quotations, masterfully woven into their works, are a distinctive feature of their style. The writings of Marx and Engels are notable not only for profundity of content, but also for their exceptional artistic merits. Wilhelm Liebknecht gave high praise to Marx's style, citing his *The Eighteenth Brumaire of Louis Bonaparte* as an example. "If ever hatred, scorn and passionate love of liberty were expressed in burning, devastating, lofty words," wrote Liebknecht, "it is in *The Eighteenth Brumaire,* which combines the indignant severity of a Tacitus with the deadly satire of a Juvenal and the holy wrath of a Dante. Style here is the *stilus* that it was of old in the hand of the Romans, a sharp stiletto, used to write and to stab. Style is a dagger which strikes unerringly at the heart" (*Reminiscences of Marx and Engels*, Moscow, 1956, p. 57).

Marx and Engels used artistic imagery to express their thoughts more forcefully and vividly in their journalistic and polemical works, and even in their fundamental theoretical works such as *Capital* and *Anti-Dühring*. Marx's pamphlet *Herr Vogt*, directed against Karl Vogt who was slandering the proletarian party, is one of the most striking examples. The biting sarcasm of this pamphlet is particularly effective due to the author's skilful use of works by classical writers such as Virgil, Plautus, and Persius, by the medieval German poets Gottfried von Strassburg and Wolfram von Eschenbach, and also by such classics of world literature as Balzac, Dickens, Schiller and Heine.

Their superb knowledge of world art helped Marx and Engels to elaborate genuinely scientific aesthetic principles. The founders of scientific communism were thus not only able to answer the complex aesthetic questions of the previous age, but also to elaborate a fundamentally new system of aesthetic science. They did so only as a result of the great revolutionary upheaval they had brought about in philosophy by creating dialectical and historical materialism and laying down the foundations for the materialist conception of history. Though Marx and Engels have left no major writings on art, their views in this field, when collected together, form a harmonious whole which is a logical extension of their scientific and revolutionary *Weltanschauung*. They explained the nature of art and its paths of development, its tasks in society and social aims. Marxist aesthetics, like the whole teaching of Marx and Engels, are subordinated to the struggle for the communist reorganisation of society.

When developing their theory of aesthetics, Marx and Engels naturally based themselves on the achievements of their predecessors. But the main aesthetic problems—and above all the problem of the relationship between art and reality—were solved by them in a fundamentally new way, on the basis of materialist dialectics. Idealist aesthetics considered art as a reproduction of the ideal, standing over and above actual reality. The origin of any art form, its development, flowering, and decay, all remained incomprehensible to the art theoreticians and historians of the pre-Marxian period, inasmuch as they studied these in isolation from man's social existence.

Marx and Engels considered it absolutely impossible to understand art and literature proceeding only from their internal laws of development. In their opinion, the essence, origin, development, and social role of art could only be understood through analysis of the social system as a whole, within which the economic factor—the development of productive forces in complex interaction with production relations—plays the decisive role. Thus art, as defined by Marx and Engels, is one of the forms of social consciousness and it therefore follows that the reasons for its changes should be sought in the social existence of men.

Marx and Engels revealed the social nature of art and its development in the course of history and showed that in a society with class antagonisms it was influenced by class contradictions and by the politics and ideologies of particular classes.

Marx and Engels gave a materialist explanation of the origin of the aesthetic sense itself. They noted that man's artistic abilities, his capacity for perceiving the world aesthetically, for comprehending its beauty and for creating works of art appeared as a result of the long development of human society and were the product of man's labour. As early as in his *Economic and Philosophic Manuscripts of 1844*, Marx pointed to the role of labour in the development of man's capacity to perceive and reproduce the beautiful and to form objects also "in accordance with the laws of beauty" (Marx and Engels, *Collected Works*, Vol. 3, Moscow, 1975, p. 277).

This idea was later developed by Engels in his work *Dialectics of Nature*, in which he noted that efforts of toil "have given the human hand the high degree of perfection required to conjure into being the pictures of a Raphael, the statues of a Thorwaldsen, the music of a Paganini" (see pp. 128-29 of this book). Thus both Marx and Engels emphasise that man's aesthetic sense is not an inborn, but a socially-acquired quality.

The founders of Marxism extended their dialectical view of the nature of human thought to analysis of artistic creativity. In examining the development of art together with that of the material world and the history of society, they noted that the content and forms of art were not established firmly once and for all, but that they inevitably developed and changed according to definite laws along with the development of the material world and of human society. Each historical period has inherent aesthetic ideals and produces works of art corresponding to its particular character and unrepeatable under other conditions. Comparing, for example, the works of Raphael, Leonardo da Vinci and Titian, Marx and Engels emphasised that "Raphael's works of art depended on the flourishing of Rome at that time, which occurred under Florentine influence, while the works of Leonardo depended on the state of things in Florence, and the works of Titian, at a later period, depended on the totally different development of Venice" (p. 177).

The fact that the level of development of society and its social structure determine the content of artistic works and the prevalence of any particular literary or artistic genre was seen by Marx as the main reason that art in different periods never repeats itself and, in particular, that there was no possibility to create the mythology or epic poetry similar to those of the ancient Greeks under the conditions of the nineteenth century. "Is the conception of nature and of social relations which underlies Greek imagination and therefore Greek (art)," wrote Marx, "possible when there are self-acting mules, railways, locomotives and electric telegraphs?" (p. 83).

It goes without saying that Marxism has a far from open-and-shut understanding of the relations between the forms of social consciousness (and of art in particular) and their economic basis. For Marx and Engels, any social formation constituted a complex and dynamic system of interacting elements, each influencing the other—a system in which the economic factor is the determining one only in the final analysis. They were in no way inclined to qualify art as a passive product of the economic system. On the contrary, they emphasised that the various forms of social consciousness—including, of course, artistic creation—actively influence the social reality from which they emerge.

As if to forestall sociological vulgarisations of the problems of artistic creation, Marx and Engels drew attention to the fact that social life and the ideology of particular classes are reflected in art in a far from mechanistic manner. Artistic creativity is subordinate to the general laws of social development but, being a special form of consciousness, has its own distinctive features and specific patterns.

One of art's distinctive features is its relative independence as it develops. The fact that works of art are connected historically with particular social structures does not mean that they lose their significance when these social structures disappear. On this point Marx cites the art and epic poetry of the ancient Greeks which "still give us aesthetic pleasure and are in certain respects regarded as a standard and unattainable ideal." (p. 84). He also provides a profound explanation for this phenomenon: Greek art reflected the naive and at the same time healthy, normal perception of reality characteristic of mankind in those early stages of its development, the period of its childhood; it reflected the striving for "natural veracity", with its unique attractiveness and special charm for all (p. 84).

This example expresses an important Marxist aesthetic principle: in looking at works of art as basically reflections of particular social conditions and relationships, it is imperative also to see the features that make the lasting value of these works.

Marx and Engels considered as another particular feature of art the fact that its periods of upsurge do not automatically coincide with social progress in other fields, including that of material production. Thus Marx wrote in the Introduction to his *Economic Manuscripts of 1857-1858*: "As regards art, it is well known that some of its peaks by no means correspond to the general development of society; nor do they therefore to the material substructure" (p. 82 of this book). Marx and Engels saw the reason for this imbalance between the development of art and of society as a whole in the fact that the spiritual culture of any period is determined not only by the level of development of material production—the "material basis" of society—but also by the character of the social relations peculiar to that period. In other words, such factors as the specific character of social relations, the degree of development of class antagonisms and the existence in any period of specific conditions for the development of man's individuality, all have an important bearing on art, determining its nature and development.

As far as capitalist society is concerned, this imbalance, according to Marx and Engels, must be considered as an expression of capitalism's fundamental contradiction, the contradiction between the social nature of production and the private form of appropriation. From his analysis of the contradictions of capitalism, Marx draws a conclusion which is of extraordinary importance for aesthetics, namely that "capitalist production is hostile to certain branches of spiritual production, for example, art and poetry" (p. 141). This proposition in no way denies the development of literature and art under capitalism, but means that the very nature of the capitalist system of exploitation is in profound contradiction with the humanist ideals which inspire genuine artists. The more conscious artists are of the contradiction between their ideals and the capitalist reality, the louder and clearer do their works (often despite the class origin of the very author) protest against the inhumanity of capitalist relations. Bourgeois society's hostility towards art begets, even in bourgeois literature, criticism of capitalism in one form or another, with capitalist reality being depicted as one filled with tragic collisions. This, in Marx's and Engels' opinion, is a dialectical feature of the development of art under capitalism. It is for this very reason that bourgeois society has produced Shakespeare, Goethe, Balzac and other writers of genius who were capable of rising above their epoch and class environment and condemning with immense artistic power the vices of the capitalist system of exploitation.

In their works, Marx and Engels set forth a number of profound ideas on the class nature of art in a society of antagonisms. They showed that even great writers, who were able, often despite their own class positions, to give a true and vivid picture of real life, were, in a class society, pressured by the ideas and interests of the ruling classes and frequently made serious concessions to these in their works. Taking Goethe, Schiller, Balzac, and other writers as examples, Marx and Engels found that the contradictions peculiar to them were not the result of purely individual features of their psychological make-up, but an ideological reflection of real contradictions in the life of society.

The founders of Marxism emphasised that art was an important weapon in the ideological struggle between classes. It could reinforce just as it could undermine the power of the exploiters, could serve to defend class oppression or, on the contrary, contribute to the education and development of the consciousness of the toiling masses, bringing them closer to victory over their oppressors. Marx and Engels therefore called for a clear distinction to be made between progressive and reactionary phenomena in feudal and bourgeois culture and put forward the principle of the Party approach to art—that it be evaluated from the position of the revolutionary class.

While showing that a link existed between art and the class struggle, Marx and Engels always fought against attempts to schematise this problem. They pointed out that classes were not static and unchangeable but that class interrelationships changed in the course of history, the role of the classes in the life of society undergoing complex metamorphoses. Thus, in the period of struggle against feudalism, the bourgeoisie was able to create considerable spiritual values, but having come to power as a result of the anti-feudal revolutions, it gradually began to reject the very weapon it had itself forged in the struggle against feudalism. The bourgeoisie accomplishes this break with its revolutionary past when a new force appears on the historical arena—the proletariat. Under these conditions, attempts by individual members of the bourgeois intelligentsia, in particular cultural and artistic figures, to gain a deeper understanding of reality, to go beyond the framework of bourgeois relations and express their protest against these in some art form, inevitably lead them to conflicts with official bourgeois society and to their departure from bourgeois positions.

Marx and Engels apply their dialectical and materialist

theory of knowledge to analysis of art and literature. In their opinion, artistic creation is one of the ways of reflecting reality and, at the same time, of perceiving and apprehending it; it is also one of the strongest levers of influencing the spiritual development of humanity. This approach to art forms the basis of the materialist understanding of its social importance and prominent role in the progress of society.

Naturally enough, when examining literature and art, Marx and Engels concentrated their attention on the problem of realism—the most accurate depiction of reality in an artistic work.

They considered realism, as a trend in literature and a method of artistic creation, to be the supreme achievement of world art. Engels formulated what is generally recognised as the classical definition of realism. "Realism, to my mind," he wrote, "implies, besides truth of detail, the truthful reproduction of typical characters under typical circumstances" (p. 90). Realistic representation, Marx and Engels emphasised, is by no means a mere copy of reality, but a way of penetrating into the very essence of a phenomenon, a method of artistic generalisation that makes it possible to disclose the typical traits of a particular age. This is what they valued in the work of the great realist writers such as Shakespeare, Cervantes, Goethe, Balzac, Pushkin and others. Marx described the English realists of the 19th century—Dickens, Thackeray, the Brontës, and Gaskell—as a brilliant pleiad of novelists "whose graphic and eloquent pages have issued to the world more political and social truths than have been uttered by all the professional politicians, publicists and moralists put together" (p. 339). Engels developed a similar line of thought when analysing the works of the great French realist writer Balzac. Writing about the *Comédie humaine*, he noted that Balzac gave the reader "a most wonderfully realistic history of French society ... from which, even in economic details (for instance the re-arrangement of real and personal property after the Revolution) I have learned more than from all the professed historians, economists and statisticians of the period together" (p. 91).

Marx and Engels set out some very important ideas about realism in their letters to Lassalle in the spring of 1859, in which they sharply criticise his historical drama *Franz von Sickingen* dealing with the knights' rebellion of 1522-23, on the eve of the Peasant War in Germany. These two letters are of great significance because they contain a statement of the fundamental principles of Marxist aesthetics (pp. 98-107).

Marx's and Engels' demands on the artist include truthfulness of depiction, a concrete historical approach to the events described and personages with live and individual traits reflecting typical aspects of the character and psychology of the class milieu to which they belong. The author of genuinely realistic works communicates his ideas to the reader not by didactic philosophising, but by vivid images which affect the reader's consciousness and feelings by their artistic expressiveness. Marx and Engels considered that Lassalle had carried even further some of the weaknesses in the artistic method of the great German poet and playwright Schiller—in particular his *penchant* for abstract rhetoric, which resulted in his heroes becoming abstract and one-dimensional declaimers of certain ideas. In this regard they preferred Shakespeare's realism to Schiller's method. Both pointed out to Lassalle that, in imitating Schiller, he was forgetting the importance for the realist writer to combine depth of content and lofty ideals with efforts to achieve a Shakespearian ability to depict genuine passions and the multiple facets of the human character.

In their letters to Lassalle, Marx and Engels also touched upon the question of the links between literature and life, between literature and the present day. Marx by no means condemned Lassalle for his intention to draw an analogy between the events of the 16th century described in the play and the situation in the mid-19th century, and to bring out the truly tragic collision which "spelled the doom ... of the revolutionary party of 1848-1849" (p. 98). He saw the author's mistake in his incorrect, idealistic interpretation of this collision, in the reduction of the reasons for it to the allegedly age-old abstract "tragedy of revolution", which lacks any concrete historical or class content. Marx criticised Lassalle not for the political tendency of his drama, but for the fact that it was essentially mistaken from the point of view of the materialist conception of history and of the world outlook of the proletarian revolutionaries. Marx and Engels were highly critical of attempts to place literature above politics and of the theory of "art for art's sake". They insisted that the works of realist writers should reflect a progressive world outlook, be permeated with progressive ideas and deal with truly topical problems. It was in this sense that they welcomed tendentiousness in literature, interpreted as ideological and political partisanship. "I am by no means opposed to tendentious poetry as such," wrote Engels to the German writer Minna Kautsky on November 26, 1885. "Aeschylus, the father of tragedy, and Aristophanes, the father of comedy, were highly partisan poets, Dante and Cervantes were so no less, and the best thing that can be said about Schiller's *Kabale und Liebe* is that it represents the first German political problem drama. The modern Russians and Norwegians, who produce excellent novels, all write with a purpose" (p. 88). Marx and Engels were at the same time resolute opponents of stupid tendentiousness—bare-faced moralising, didacticism instead of artistic method, and abstract impersonations instead of live characters. They criticised the poets in the "Young Germany" literary movement for the artistic inferiority of their characters and attempts to make up for their lack of literary mastery with political arguments. Engels provides an apt definition of genuine tendentiousness in his letter to Minna Kautsky: "I think however that the purpose must become manifest from the situation and the action themselves without being expressly pointed out and that the author does not have to serve the reader on a platter the future historical resolution of the social conflicts which he describes" (p. 88).

Both Marx and Engels were deeply convinced that progressive literature had to reflect truthfully the deep-lying, vital processes of the day, to promulgate progressive ideas, and to defend the interests of the progressive forces in society. The modern term the Party spirit in literature expresses what they understood by this. They felt that the very quality that was lacking in Lassalle's play—the organic unity of idea and artistry—was the *sine qua non* of genuinely realistic art.

In setting out the principles of materialist aesthetics and the fundamental and most general laws governing the development of art, the founders of scientific communism laid the basis of Marxist literary and art criticism and proposed the primary tenets of the materialist interpretation of the history of art and literature. In their works and correspondence, they threw new light on the most important questions of the historical and literary process and revealed such aspects in the works of both classical and contemporary writers which were beyond the comprehension of bourgeois literary historians. In the present collection, the reader will find Marx's and Engels' views of the artistic works of the most important ages in mankind's history—their evaluation of art in ancient and medieval times, of Renaissance culture and literature, of literature in the period of the Enlightenment, and, finally, of the work of the romantic and realist writers of the 19th century. In addition, the reader will discover the attitude of the founders of Marxist aesthetics towards the main literary and artistic trends in general and their opinions on individual writers and other artists.

Marx's and Engels' view of ancient art has already been discussed briefly above. Let us now turn to their evaluation of the art of other ages.

Their genuinely scientific explanation of the specific features of the social system and culture of medieval times is of exceptional interest. Marx and Engels stripped away the romantic idealisation of the Middle Ages and, at the same time, demonstrated the inconsistency of the abstract view held by the Enlighteners that this was merely an age of social and cultural regression. They pointed out that the transition from slave-owning to feudal society was historically inevitable and showed that the establishment of the feudal mode of production was a step forward in the development of human society, compared to the reign of slavery which had preceded it. This enabled Marx and Engels to form a new approach to medieval culture and art and point out those features in them which reflected the progressive course of historical development. Engels wrote that "...as a result of the intermingling of nations in the early Middle Ages new nationalities gradually developed" (Marx/Engels, *Werke*, Bd. 21, S. 395), the appearance of which was a prerequisite for further social and cultural development of mankind. Analysing various epic poems of the early Middle Ages such as the *Elder Edda* and other Icelandic and Irish sagas, *Beowulf*, the *Lay of Hildebrand* and the *Chanson de Roland*, Marx and Engels showed that they reflected the gradual transition from the earliest stages of the tribal system to new levels of social consciousness connected with the early period of the formation of European nationalities. The epic and national-heroic poetry of the Middle Ages is notable, as Engels pointed out, for characteristics which show their new cultural-historical and aesthetic quality, as compared with the classical epic poetry of the ancient world. The same also applies to the later lyric poetry of the feudal Middle Ages—the medieval romance lyrics, best exemplified by the works of the Provençal troubadours. In his *The Origin of the Family, Private Property and the State* Engels wrote that "no such thing as individual sex love existed before the Middle Ages" (p. 215). For this reason, he said, the appearance and poetic glorification of individual love in the Middle Ages was a step forward compared to antiquity. Moreover, the medieval love poems influenced the following generations and prepared the ground for the flowering of poetry in the modern age.

Marx and Engels formulated and substantiated a new view of the Renaissance, one which differed radically from the views of earlier bourgeois cultural historians and also in many ways from those of contemporary and later bourgeois historiography. This new understanding of the basic historical meaning of the Renaissance in Western Europe was presented by Engels in its most developed form in 1875-76 in one of his versions for the Introduction to the *Dialectics of Nature* (pp. 251-53). Engels emphasised that, contrary to the traditional view of bourgeois science, the Renaissance must not be seen as merely an upheaval in the ideological and spiritual life of the times. The origins of this new age, he states, should be sought above all in the economic and political. changes that brought about the transition from the Middle Ages to modern times. Engels penetrated to the very essence of the phenomena which made possible the immense leap forward in the culture, literature and art of that period, some achievements of which remained unequalled even in the more mature bourgeois society. The art of the Renaissance, as Engels noted, developed not in a period of already settled bourgeois society but "in the midst of the general revolution" (Frederick Engels, *Dialectics of Nature*, Moscow, 1974, p. 21). Social relations were at that time in a state of constant flux and change and had not yet become, as they did in mature bourgeois society, a force which to a certain extent limited the development of personal initiative, talent and capabilities but, on the contrary, actively contributed to their development. Because of its revolutionary character this age, the one of "the greatest progressive revolution that mankind had so far experienced", stated Engels, "called for giants and produced giants ... in power of thought, passion and character, in universality and learning". This is why "the men who founded the modern rule of the bourgeoisie had anything but bourgeois limitations" (pp. 252-53). Engels also noted that "the heroes of that time were not yet in thrall to the division of labour, the restricting effects of which, with its production one-sidedness, we so often notice in their successors" (p. 253). To clarify his idea, Engels described Leonardo da Vinci who "was not only a great painter but also a great mathematician, mechanic and engineer, to whom the most diverse branches of physics are indebted for important discoveries" and reviewed the work of Albrecht Dürer, a "painter, engraver, sculptor, and architect" and inventor of a fortification system. Engels also pointed to the great diversity of interests and erudition of other Renaissance figures (p. 253).

Marx's and Engels' evaluation of the Renaissance as an age of "the general revolution", "the greatest progressive revolution", explains the warm sympathy they felt for the "giants" of that age. They saw the great men of the Renaissance not just as outstanding scholars, artists, or poets, but, at the same time, as great revolutionaries in world science and culture.

Engels considered the most important trait of the heroes of the Renaissance to be that "they almost all live and pursue their activities in the midst of the contemporary movements, in the practical struggle; they take sides and join in the fight, one by speaking and writing, another with the sword, many with both" (p. 253). It is not difficult to see that this was also what Engels expected of the artists of the future. Referring to the ability of the people of the Renaissance to live by the interests of their time, to "take sides", Engels emphasised those traits which lifted them above the level of the professionally narrow, armchair science of the bourgeoisie, and above the level of the 19th-century bourgeois writers and artists who preached "non-partisanship" and "pure art". These traits brought the great men of the Renaissance closer to the ideals of socialist culture and of the revolutionary movement of the working class.

Marx and Engels considered Dante one of the great writers whose works announced the transition from the

Middle Ages to the Renaissance. They saw him as a poet and thinker of genius and, at the same time, as an inflexible warrior whose poetic works were infused with Party spirit (Marx and Engels, *Collected Works*, Vol. 6, Moscow, 1976, p. 271) and were inseparable from his political ideals and aspirations. According to Wilhelm Liebknecht, Marx knew the *Divina Commedia* almost by heart and would often declaim whole sections of it aloud. Marx's "Introduction" to *Capital* in fact ends with the great Florentine's proud words: "Go your own way, and let people say what they will!" The author of *Capital* placed Dante among his most beloved poets—Goethe, Aeschylus, and Shakespeare. Engels called Dante a person of "unequalled classic perfection" (p. 247) and "a colossal figure" (p. 248). Marx and Engels held the great Spanish writer Cervantes in high esteem too. Paul Lafargue noted that Marx set the author of *Don Quixote*, together with Balzac, "above all other novelists" (p. 439). Finally, Marx's and Engels' admiration for Shakespeare, one of their most beloved writers, is known to all. Both considered his plays with their far-ranging depiction of the life of his time and their immortal characters to be classical examples of realist drama. Lafargue wrote that Marx "made a detailed study" of Shakespeare's works. "His whole family had a real cult for the great English dramatist" (p. 438). Engels shared his friend's views on Shakespeare. On December 10, 1873, he wrote to Marx: "There is more life and reality in the first act of the *Merry Wives* than in all German literature" (p. 260).

The most important comment by the founders of scientific communism about classicism, the literary movement of the 17th-18th centuries, was made by Marx in a letter to Lassalle on July 22, 1861 (p. 269). On the basis of a materialist understanding of the development of culture, Marx in his letter rejected the unhistorical idea that classicism was the result of a misunderstanding of the laws of classical drama and of classical aesthetics, with their famous principle of the three unities. He pointed out that, though the theoreticians of classicism had misunderstood classical Greek drama and Aristotle's *Poetics*, this was no accident or a misunderstanding of history, but a historical inevitability. Classicist playwrights "misunderstood" Aristotle because the "misunderstood" Aristotle corresponded exactly to their taste in art and their aesthetic requirements, formed by the specific social and cultural conditions of the time.

Unlike previous historians of culture who were unable to understand the class content of ideas, Marx and Engels uncovered the social, class-historical basis of the ideas of the 18th-century Enlightenment. They showed that the Enlightenment was not just a movement in social thought, but an ideological expression of the interests of the progressive bourgeoisie, which was rising up to struggle against feudal absolutism on the eve of the Great French Revolution.

Marx and Engels held in high esteem the heritage of the English and French 18th-century Enlighteners including their fiction and works on aesthetics. Their comprehensive analysis of the activity of the Enlighteners explains its close links with the life of society and the class struggle during the preparation for the French bourgeois revolution and draws a line between the moderately bourgeois and the democratic elements in their heritage.

Marx's and Engels' works and letters show that they had a superb knowledge of both English and French philosophical and economic literature and fiction of the age of the Enlightenment. They do not merely mention Defoe, Swift, Voltaire, Diderot, Rousseau, the Abbé Prévost, Beaumarchais, but give laconic and at the same time brilliantly profound and accurate evaluations of them, while also using their works to draw generalisations concerning the most important aspects of literary life in the age of the Enlightenment.

It should also be noted that Marx included Denis Diderot among his favourite writers. He delighted in Diderot's novels, especially *Le Neveu de Rameau*, which he called a "unique masterpiece" (p. 279). Engels shared his friend's opinion on Diderot and wrote in 1886: "If ever anybody dedicated his whole life to the 'enthusiasm for truth and justice'—using this phrase in the good sense—it was Diderot, for instance" (p. 279).

Marx and Engels also wrote about the leading men of the Enlightenment in Germany—Lessing, Goethe, Schiller, Herder, Wieland. Revealing the economic and socio-political conditions in Germany, whose feudal division and reactionary small-power absolutist system had been hardened as a result of the Thirty Years' War (1618-48), they showed that these conditions had made a definite mark on the ideas and feelings of the majority of the most prominent figures of the "great age of German literature" (p. 346). Together with the rebellious spirit and indignation at the social system of the time that were characteristic of German classical literature, it also reflected the feelings of the petty bourgeoisie (the predominating social stratum in Germany) whose inherent characteristic was admiration for and servility towards the powers that be. "Each of them was an Olympian Zeus in his own sphere," Engels wrote about Goethe and Hegel, "yet neither of them ever quite freed himself from German Philistinism" (p. 349). In spotlighting not only the strong, but also the weaker points in Goethe, Schiller, and other German writers and thinkers of that period, Marx and Engels in no way sought to belittle their immense, world-wide importance. This is confirmed by Marx's attitude towards Goethe, who, as already mentioned, was one of his most beloved poets. Contemporaries who knew Marx well stated that he was a constant reader of the great German poet's works. In their writings and conversations, both Marx and Engels frequently quoted from *Faust* and other works by Goethe. In 1837 the young Marx, while still a student at Berlin University, wrote an epigram defending Goethe against the Lutheran pastor Pustkuchen, who was one of the leaders in the struggle of German reactionaries of the 1830s against the poet. Engels devoted one of his essays in literary criticism to an analysis of Goethe's work. This was "German Socialism in Verse and Prose" (pp. 351-74) in which he attacked the aesthetics of German philistine "true socialism".

Marx's and Engels' analysis of West European romanticism is of great importance to the elaboration of a genuinely scientific history of literature. Considering romanticism a reflection of the age beginning after the Great French Revolution, of all its inherent social contradictions, they distinguished between revolutionary romanticism, which rejected capitalism and was striving towards the future, and romantic criticism of capitalism from the point of view of the past. They also differentiated between the romantic writers who idealised the pre-bourgeois social system: they valued those whose works concealed democratic and critical elements under a veneer of reactionary utopias and naive petty-bourgeois ideals, and criticised the reactionary romantics, whose sympathies for the past amounted to a defence of the interests of the nobility. Marx and Engels were especially fond of the works of such revolutionary romantics as Byron and Shelley.

Marx's and Engels' evaluation of the works of 19th-century realist writers has already been mentioned. Marx and Engels considered realist traditions to be the culmination of the whole of the previous literary process. Engels traced their development and enrichment in the works of Guy de Maupassant, of the creators of the Russian realist novel of the second half of the 19th century, and of Norway's contemporary dramatists. Marx and Engels had a lively interest in Russia and attached great importance to the Russian revolutionary movement. To be better able to follow the development of the economic and social life of Russia, they both learnt Russian. They were well acquainted not only with socio-economic and journalistic writings in Russia, but also with the country's fiction. They both read the works of Pushkin, Turgenev, Saltykov-Shchedrin, Chernyshevsky, and Dobrolyubov in Russian, while Marx also read Gogol, Nekrasov, and Lermontov in the original. Engels was also acquainted with English translations of the works of Lomonosov, Derzhavin, Khemnitser, Zhukovsky, Batyushkov, and Krylov. Marx and Engels thought Pushkin's *Eugene Onegin* to be an amazingly accurate depiction of Russian life in the first half of the 19th century. Both were especially fond of Chernyshevsky and Dobrolyubov. Engels considered these revolutionary writers "two socialist Lessings" (p. 414) and Marx called Chernyshevsky a "great Russian scholar and critic" (p. 415), while comparing Dobrolyubov "as a writer to Lessing and Diderot" (p. 415).

Characteristic of Marx and Engels was their profoundly internationalist approach to literature and art. They paid equal attention to the art of all nations, European and non-European, large and small, believing that every people makes its own unique contribution to the treasure-house of world art and literature. Their interests included the development of art and literature in England, France, Germany, Italy, Spain, and Russia as well as the artistic and cultural treasures of the East or of such small countries as Ireland, Iceland, and Norway. Judging by their notes, the ancient cultures of the indigenous inhabitants of the New World also came within their field of vision.

Marx and Engels had a special attitude towards the democratic and revolutionary poets and writers who were close to the proletariat. Throughout their lives, they strove to draw the best progressive writers of their time to the side of the socialist movement and to educate and temper them, while helping them to overcome the weaker aspects of their work. Marx and Engels actively contributed to the formation of a proletarian revolutionary trend in literature.

Marx's influence on the work of the great German revolutionary poet Heinrich Heine was immense. They met in Paris in 1843. The prime of Heine's political lyrics and satire comes in 1843-44, when he was in close and friendly contact with Marx. Marx's influence on Heine is clear in such remarkable works as his poems *The Silesian Loom Workers* and *Germany. A Winter Tale*. All his life Marx admired

Heine, who was one of the favourite poets in Marx's family. Engels was in complete agreement with his friend's sympathies and considered Heine to be "the most eminent of all living German poets" (p. 375). In their struggle against German reaction, Marx and Engels often quoted from Heine's bitingly satirical poems. Marx's and Engels' ideological influence played an exceptional role in Heine's development as an artist and helped him to realise that the communist revolution would inevitably be victorious.

Marx and Engels were close friends of the German poets Georg Weerth and Ferdinand Freiligrath, with whom they worked side by side on the *Neue Rheinische Zeitung* during the revolution of 1848-1849. Engels called Weerth "the German proletariat's first and most important poet" (p. 402). After Weerth's death, Marx and Engels carefully collected his literary works. In the 1880s Engels vigorously promoted these in the German Social-Democratic press.

It was only thanks to Marx's and Engels' influence that Freiligrath became, in 1848-49, one of the classics of German revolutionary poetry. His poems written at that time are closely linked to Marx's and Engels' ideas and are his best. The care and attention Marx and Engels showed for Freiligrath is a good example of their attitude towards revolutionary poets and of how they tried to help them in their noble cause. When Marx recommended Freiligrath to his comrade Joseph Weydemeyer, in 1852, for work on the journal *Revolution*, he specially asked Weydemeyer to write a friendly, praising letter to the poet to encourage him. It is no coincidence that Freiligrath's importance as a poet began to decline as soon as he moved away from Marx and Engels in the 1850s.

Marx and Engels had close links with many French and English revolutionary writers, in particular with the Chartist leader Ernest Jones. His best poems, written in the latter 1840s, show the influence of Marx's and Engels' ideas.

After Marx's death, Engels continued in the 1880s and

1890s to keep careful track of the revolutionary writings of those English authors who were ideologically close to the English socialist movement. This can be seen from Engels' letter to the writer Margaret Harkness (pp. 89-92) who had sent him her short story "A Poor Girl", his numerous comments about the plays of the English socialist Edward Aveling, and his notes on the ideological development of a number of other writers.

Important statements by Engels on the subject of proletarian art can also be found in his letters written toward the end of his life to German Social-Democratic leaders.

In this way, Marx and Engels strove to foster a new type of writer and artist who, assimmilating the finest traditions of classical literature, would take an active, creative part in the proletariat's struggle for emancipation, proceeding from a broad understanding of the experiences and the tasks of the revolutionary struggle.

This collection also contains valuable statements by Marx and Engels on the flowering of art in the future communist society. The founders of Marxism saw the contradictions in the development of art under capitalism as a manifestation of the antagonistic nature of bourgeois society as a whole and considered the solution of these problems to be possible only after the proletarian revolution and the social reorganisation of society.

Marx and Engels showed brilliant foresight in anticipating the basic traits of the new, communist society. Communism is above all true freedom for the all-round and harmonious development of the individual. "The realm of freedom," said Marx, "actually begins only where labour which is determined by necessity and mundane considerations ceases..." (p. 183).

Labour freed from exploitation becomes, under socialism, the source of all spiritual (and aesthetic) creativity. Marx and Engels point out that only given true economic, political, and spiritual freedom can man's creative powers develop to the full and that only proletarian revolution offers unbounded opportunities of endless progress in the development of literature. The great historical mission of the proletariat consists in the communist rebuilding of the world. It was in the proletariat that Marx and Engels saw the social force which could change the world and provide for further progress not only in economics and politics, but also in culture, the force which would bring about the conditions required for the full realisation of mankind's higher moral and aesthetic values.

B. Krylov

Materialist Conception
of the History of Culture

Social Being
and Social Consciousness

1

In the social production of their life, men enter into definite relations that are indispensable and independent of their will, relations of production which correspond to a definite stage of development of their material productive forces. The sum total of these relations of production constitutes the economic structure of society, the real foundation, on which rises a legal and political superstructure and to which correspond definite forms of social consciousness. The mode of production of material life conditions the social, political and intellectual life process in general. It is not the consciousness of men that determines their being, but, on the contrary, their social being that determines their consciousness. At a certain stage of their development, the material productive forces of society come in conflict with the existing relations of production, or—what is but a legal expression for the same thing—with the property relations within which they have been at work hitherto. From forms of development of the productive forces these relations turn into their fetters. Then begins an epoch of social revolution. With the change of the economic foundation the entire immense superstructure is more or less rapidly transformed. In considering such transformations a distinction should always be made between the material transformation of the economic conditions of production, which can be determined with the precision of natural science, and the legal, political, religious, aesthetic or philosophic—in short, ideological forms in which men become conscious of this conflict and fight it out. Just as our opinion of an individual is not based on what he thinks of himself, so can we not judge of such a period of transformation by its own consciousness; on the contrary, this consciousness must be explained rather from the contradictions of material life, from the existing conflict between the social productive forces and the relations of production. No social order ever perishes before all the productive forces for which there is room in it have developed; and new, higher relations of production never appear before the material conditions of their existence have matured in the womb of the old society itself. Therefore mankind always sets itself only such tasks as it can solve; since, looking at the matter more closely, it will always be found that the task itself arises only when the material conditions for its solution already exist or are at least in the process of formation. In broad outline Asiatic, ancient, feudal, and modern bourgeois modes of production can be designated as progressive epochs in the economic formation of society. The bourgeois relations of production are the last antagonistic form of the social process of production—antagonistic not in the sense of individual antagonism, but of one arising from the social conditions of life of the individuals; at the same time the productive forces developing in the womb of bourgeois society create the material conditions for the solution of that antagonism. This social formation brings, therefore, the prehistory of human society to a close.

> Karl Marx, "Preface to *A Contribution to the Critique of Political Economy*"
>
> Marx and Engels, *Selected Works*, Vol. 1, Moscow, 1973, pp. 503-04

2

The production of ideas, of conceptions, of consciousness, is at first directly interwoven with the material activity and the material intercourse of men—the language of real life. Conceiving, thinking, the mental intercourse of men at this stage still appear as the direct efflux of their material behaviour. The same applies to mental production as expressed in the language of the politics, laws, morality, religion, metaphysics, etc., of a people. Men are the producers of their conceptions, ideas, etc., that is, real, active men, as they are conditioned by a definite development of their productive forces and of the intercourse corresponding to these, up to its furthest forms.[a] Consciousness [*das Bewusstsein*] can never be anything else than conscious being [*das bewusste Sein*], and the being of men is their actual life-process. If in all ideology men and their relations appear upside-down as in a *camera obscura*, this phenomenon arises just as much from their historical life-process as the inversion of objects on the retina does from their physical life-process.

In direct contrast to German philosophy which descends from heaven to earth, here it is a matter of ascending from earth to heaven. That is to say, not of setting out from what men say, imagine, conceive, nor from men as narrated, thought of, imagined, conceived, in order to arrive at men in the flesh; but of setting out from real, active men, and on the basis of their real life-process demonstrating the development of the ideological reflexes and echoes of this life-process. The phantoms formed in the brains of men are also, necessarily, sublimates of their material life-process, which is empirically verifiable and bound to material premises. Morality, religion, metaphysics, and all the rest of ideology as well as the forms of consciousness corresponding to these, thus no longer retain the semblance of independence. They have no history, no development; but men, developing their material production and their material intercourse, alter, along with this their actual world, also their thinking and the products of their thinking. It is not consciousness that determines life, but life that determines consciousness. For the

---

[a] [The manuscript originally had:] Men are the producers of their conceptions, ideas, etc., and they are precisely men conditioned by the mode of production of their material life, by their material intercourse and its further development in the social and political structure.

first manner of approach the starting-point is consciousness taken as the living individual; for the second manner of approach, which conforms to real life, it is the real living individuals themselves, and consciousness is considered solely as *their* consciousness.

This manner of approach is not devoid of premises. It starts out from the real premises and does not abandon them for a moment. Its premises are men, not in any fantastic isolation and fixity, but in their actual, empirically perceptible process of development under definite conditions. As soon as this active life-process is described, history ceases to be a collection of dead facts, as it is with the empiricists (themselves still abstract), or an imagined activity of imagined subjects, as with the idealists.

Where speculation ends, where real life starts, there consequently begins real, positive science, the expounding of the practical activity, of the practical process of development of men. Empty phrases about consciousness end, and real knowledge has to take their place. When the reality is described, a self-sufficient philosophy [*die selbständige Philosophie*] loses its medium of existence. At the best its place can only be taken by a summing-up of the most general results, abstractions which are derived from the observation of the historical development of men. These abstractions in themselves, divorced from real history, have no value whatsoever. They can only serve to facilitate the arrangement of historical material, to indicate the sequence of its separate strata. But they by no means afford a recipe or schema, as does philosophy, for neatly trimming the epochs of history. On the contrary, the difficulties begin only when one sets about the examination and arrangement of the material—whether of a past epoch or of the present—and its actual presentation.

Karl Marx and Frederick Engels,
The German Ideology.

Marx and Engels, *Collected Works*,
Vol. 5, Moscow, 1976, pp. 36-37

Natural Conditions
and Development of Culture

Once having abstracted from the social mode of production, the productivity of labour depends on the natural conditions in which it is accomplished. These conditions can all be reduced to either the nature of man himself, his race, etc., or the nature which surrounds him. From an economic point of view, external natural conditions break down into two large classes: natural resources as means of subsistence, that is to say, the fertility of the soil, bodies of water containing fish, etc., and natural resources as means of labour, such as water-falls, navigable rivers, forests, metals, coal and so on. At the beginning of civilisation, it is the first class of natural resources which is of importance; later, in a more advanced society, it is the second. Compare, for example, Great Britain with India, or, in the Ancient World, Athens and Corinth with the countries situated on the Black Sea.

The fewer the natural requirements which must be satisfied and the more fertile the soil and favourable the climate, the less labour time is necessary for the maintenance and reproduction of the producer, and the more he can work for others rather than for himself. Diodorus of Sicily made this remark concerning the Ancient Egyptians:

> "It is unbelievable," he says, "how little effort and expense it costs them to bring up their children. They feed them on the simplest food, on the first thing that comes to hand; they also give them the edible part of the papyrus root that can be roasted, as well as the roots and stalks of marsh plants, raw, or boiled or roast. The air is so balmy that most children run barefoot and naked. So a child, right up to

maturity, costs its parents no more than twenty drachmas in all. This is the principal explanation of why the population in Egypt is so numerous and of how they could undertake such great structures."[a]

It is, however, less to the size of its population than to the possibility of employing a relatively large proportion of it in unproductive work that Ancient Egypt owes its great works of architecture. Just as the individual worker can supply the more surplus labour the less his necessary labour time, so the fewer working people required for the production of the necessary means of subsistence, the greater the number available for other work.

Once capitalist production is established, the amount of surplus labour will vary, all other things being equal, according to the natural conditions of labour and, above all, according to the fertility of the soil. It does not follow, however, that the most fertile soil is also the most suitable and favourable for the development of the capitalist mode of production, which presupposes the domination of man over nature. A too prodigious nature "holds man by the hand like a child on leading-reins"; it prevents him from developing without making his development a necessity of nature.[b] The homeland of capital is not in tropical climes, amid rich vegetation, but

---

[a] Diod., l.c., 1, ch. 80 [*Diodor's Sicilien Historische Bibliothek*, Bd. I, 1831].—*Ed*.

[b] "The first (natural wealth) as it is most noble and advantageous, so doth it make the people careless, proud, and given to all excesses; whereas the second enforceth vigilancy, literature, arts and policy." ("England's Treasure by Foreign Trade. Or the Balance of our Foreign Trade is the Rule of our Treasure. Written by Thomas Mun of London, merchant, and now published for the common good by his son John Mun." London, 1669, pp. 181, 182). "Nor can I conceive a greater curse upon a body of people, than to be thrown upon a spot of land, where the productions for subsistence and food were, in great measure, spontaneous, and the climate required or admitted little care for raiment and covering ... there may be an extreme on the other side. A soil incapable of produce by labour is quite as bad as a soil that produces plentifully without any labour." ("An Enquiry into the Causes of the Present High Price of Provisions." Lond. 1767, p. 10.)

in the temperate zone. It is not the absolute fertility of the soil, but rather the diversity of its chemical properties, of its geological composition, of its physical configuration, and the variety of its natural products which form the natural basis for the social division of labour and which urge man, as a result of the multifarious conditions in which he finds himself, to multiply his needs, his faculties, his means and methods of labour.

It is the necessity of establishing social control over a force of nature, of making use of it, in an economical way, and of appropriating it on a large scale through works of art, in a word of conquering it, that plays the decisive role in the history of industry. Such was the necessity of regulating and distributing the flow of water in Egypt,[a] Lombardy and Holland, etc. Such is it today in India, in Persia, etc., where irrigation by artificial canals supplies the soil not only with the water which it needs, but also with mineral fertilisers which it brings down from the mountains and deposits in the form of silt. Canalisation was the secret of the flourishing industries of Spain and Sicily under Arab dominion.[b]

Karl Marx, *Le Capital*, t. II, livre I, 1954, pp. 186-88

Translated from the French

---

[a] It was the necessity of calculating the periods when the Nile floods which created Egyptian astronomy and, at the same time, the domination of the caste of priests as directors of agriculture. "The solstice is the time of the year when the Nile begins to swell, and that which the Egyptians had to watch with the greatest attention.... It was this tropical year that they had to determine in order to direct their agricultural operations. So they had to search the heavens for a sign of its return." (Cuvier, *Discours sur les révolutions du globe*, éd. Hoefer, Paris, 1863, p. 141.)

[b] The distribution of water in India was one of the material foundations of central power over the small, unconnected, units of communal production. The Muslim conquerors of India understood this better than the English, their successors. It is sufficient to recall the famine of 1866, which cost the lives of a million Indians in the Orissa district of Bengal.

Landscapes

[*Telegraph für Deutschland* No. 122, July 1840]

Hellas had the good fortune of seeing the nature of her landscape brought to consciousness in the religion of her inhabitants. Hellas is a land of pantheism; all her landscapes are—or, at least, were—embraced in a harmonious framework. And yet every tree, every fountain, every mountain thrusts itself too much in the foreground, and her sky is far too blue, her sun far too radiant, her sea far too magnificent, for them to be content with the laconic spiritualisation of Shelley's spirit of nature,[a] of an all-embracing Pan. Each beautifully shaped individual feature lays claim to a particular god, each river will have its nymphs, each grove its dryads—and so arose the religion of the Hellenes. Other regions were not so fortunate; they did not serve any people as the basis of its faith and had to await a poetic mind to conjure into existence the religious genius that slumbered in them. If you stand on the Drachenfels or on the Rochusberg at Bingen, and gaze over the vine-fragrant valley of the Rhine, the distant blue mountains merging with the horizon, the green fields and vineyards flooded with golden sunlight, the blue sky reflected in the river—heaven with its brightness descends on to the earth and is mirrored in it, the spirit descends into matter, the word becomes flesh and dwells

---

[a] The words "spirit of nature" are in English in the original. In Shelley's works, in particular in *Queen Mab*, the pantheistic figurative symbol of Pan appears.—*Ed.*

among us—that is the embodiment of Christianity. The direct opposite of this is the North-German heath; here there is nothing but dry stalks and modest heather, which, conscious of its weakness, dare not raise itself above the ground; here and there is a once defiant tree now shattered by lightning; and the brighter the sky, the more sharply does its self-sufficient magnificence demarcate it from the poor, cursed earth lying below it in sackcloth and ashes, and the more does its eye, the sun, look down with burning anger on the bare barren sand—there you have a representation of the Jewish world outlook.

The heathland has been much reviled, all literature* has heaped curses on it and, as in Platen's *Oedipus*,[2] it has been used only as a background for satire, but people have scorned to seek out its rare charms, its hidden poetic connections. One must really have grown up in a beautiful region, on mountain heights or forest-crowned crags, to feel properly the frightening, depressing character of the North-German Sahara, but also to be able to detect with pleasure the beautiful features of this region, which, like the mirage in Libya, are not always visible to the eye. The really prosaic Germany is to be found only in the potato fields on the right[a] bank of the Elbe. But the homeland of the Saxons, the most active of the German races, is poetic even in its desolation. On a stormy night, when clouds stream ghost-like past the moon, when dogs bay to one another at a distance, gallop on snorting horses over the endless heath and leap with loose reins over the weathered granite blocks and the burial mounds of the Huns; in the distance the water of the moor glitters in the reflected moonlight, will-o'-the-wisps flit over it, and the howling of the storm sounds eerily over the wide expanse; the ground beneath you is unsafe, and you feel that you have entered the realm of German folk-lore. Only after I

* In the third volume of *Blasedow*[1] the old man is concerned for the heath.—*Note by Engels.*

[a] The *Telegraph für Deutschland* has "left", which is a misprint.—*Ed.*

became acquainted with the North-German heathland did I properly understand the Grimm brothers' *Kinder- und Haus-Märchen*. It is evident from almost all these tales that they had their origin here, where at nightfall the human element vanishes and the terrifying, shapeless creations of popular fantasy glide over a desolate land which is eerie even in the brightness of midday. They are a tangible embodiment of the feelings aroused in the solitary heath dweller when he wends his way in his native land on such a wild night, or when he looks out over the desolate expanse from some high tower. Then the impressions which he has retained from childhood of stormy nights on the heath come back to his mind and take shape in those fairy-tales. You will not overhear the secret of the origin of the popular fairy-tales on the Rhine or in Swabia, whereas here every lightning night—*bright* lightning night, says Laube—speaks of it with tongues of thunder.

The summer thread of my apologia for the heath, carried by the wind, would probably continue to be spun out, if it had not become entangled with an unfortunate signpost painted in the colours of the land of Hanover.[a] I have long pondered over the significance of these colours. It is true that the royal Prussian colours do not show what Thiersch tries to find in them in his bad song about Prussia[3]; nevertheless, by their prosiness they remind one of cold, heartless bureaucracy and of all that the Rhinelander still cannot find quite plausible about Prussianism. The sharp contrast between black and white can provide an analogy for the relation between king and subject in an absolute monarchy; and since, according to Newton, they are not colours at all, they can be an indication that the loyal frame of mind in an absolute monarchy is that which does not hold a brief for any colour. The gay red and white flags of the people of the Hanse towns were at least fitting in olden days; the French *esprit* displays its iridescence in the tricolour, the

---

[a] Yellow and white.—*Ed.*

colours of which have been appropriated by phlegmatic Holland too, probably in derision of itself; the most beautiful and significant, of course, is still the unhappy German tricolour. But the Hanoverian colours! Imagine a dandy in white trousers who has been chased for an hour at full speed through road-side ditches and newly ploughed fields, imagine Lot's pillar of salt[4]—an example of the Hanoverian *Nunquam retrorsum*[a] of former times as a warning for many—imagine this honourable memorial splashed with mud by ill-bred Bedouin youths, and you have a Hanoverian frontier post with its coat of arms. Or does the white signify the innocent basic law of the state and the yellow the filth with which it is being bespattered by certain mercenary pens?

To continue with the religious character of various regions, the *Dutch* landscapes are essentially Calvinist. The absolute prose of a distant view in Holland, the impossibility of its spiritualisation, the grey sky that is indeed the only one suited to it, all this produces the same impression on us as the infallible decisions of the Dordrecht Synod.[5] The windmills, the sole moving things in the landscape, remind one of the predestined elect, who allow themselves to be moved only by the breath of divine dispensation; everything else lies in "spiritual death". And in this barren orthodoxy, the Rhine, like the flowing, living spirit of Christianity, loses its fructifying power and becomes completely choked up with sand. Such, seen from the Rhine, is the appearance of its Dutch banks; other parts of the country may be more beautiful, I do not know them.—Rotterdam, with its shady quays, its canals and ships, is an oasis for people from small towns in the interior of Germany; one can understand here how the imagination of a Freiligrath could ply with the departing frigates to distant, more luxuriant shores. Then there are the cursed Zeeland islands, nothing but reeds and dykes, windmills and the tops of chiming church steeples, between which the steamboat winds its way for hours!

---

[a] Never turning back (inscription under the rampant steed of the Hanoverian coat of arms).—*Ed.*

But then, with what a blissful feeling we leave behind the philistine dykes and tight-laced Calvinist orthodoxy and enter the realm of the free-ranging spirit! Helvoetsluys vanishes, on the right and the left the banks of the Waal sink into the rising, jubilant waves, the sandy yellow of the water changes to green, and now what is behind is forgotten, and we go forward into the dark-green transparent sea!

> And now have done with grieving,
> And shed that bitter load.
> Time to be up and leaving
> To take the great highroad.
> The sky leans gently downwards
> To mingle with the sea —
> And you'd go travelling onwards
> In tired despondency?
>
> The sky bends downwards, holding
> The world with all its charms,
> Happy to be enfolding
> Such beauty in his arms.
> As if to kiss her lover
> The wave leaps up to the sky,
> And you'd wish life was over,
> In dark despondency?
>
> The God of Love, descending,
> Makes all this world his own;
> To dwell here without ending,
> He gives himself through Man.
> And does that God not really
> Abide within your breast?
> Then let him reign more freely
> And shine his worthiest.

Then climb on to the rigging of the bowsprit and gaze on the waves, how, cleft by the ship's keel, they throw the white spray high over your head, and look out, too, over the distant green surface of the sea, where the foaming crests of the waves spring up in eternal unrest, where the sun's rays are reflected into your eyes from thousands of dancing mirrors, where the green of the sea merges with the blue of the sky and the gold of the sun to produce a wonderful colour, and all your trivial cares, all remembrance of the enemies of light and their treacherous attacks disappear, and you stand upright, proudly conscious of the free, infinite mind! I have had only one impression that could compare with this; when for the first time the divine idea of the last of the philosophers,[a] this most colossal creation of the thought of the nineteenth century, dawned upon me, I experienced the same blissful thrill, it was like a breath of fresh sea air blowing down upon me from the purest sky; the depths of speculation lay before me like the unfathomable sea from which one cannot turn one's eyes straining to see the ground below; in God we live, move and have our being! We become conscious of that when we are on the sea; we feel that God breathes through all around us and through us ourselves; we feel such kinship with the whole of nature, the waves beckon to us so intimately, the sky stretches so lovingly over the earth, and the sun shines with such indescribable radiance that one feels one could grasp it with the hand.

The sun sinks in the north-west; on its left a shining streak rises from the sea—the Kentish coast and the southern bank of the Thames estuary. Already the twilight mist lies on the sea, only in the west is the purple of evening spread over the sky and over the water; the sky in the east is resplendent in deep blue, from which Venus already shines out brightly; in the south-west a long golden streak in the magical light along the horizon is Margate, from the windows of which the evening redness is reflected. So now wave your caps and greet free England with a joyful shout and a full glass. Good night, and a happy awakening in London!

[*Telegraph für Deutschland* No. 123, August 1840]

You who complain of the prosaic dullness of railways without ever having seen one should try travelling on the one from London to Liverpool. If ever a land was made to be traversed by railways it is England. No dazzlingly beau-

---

[a] Probably Hegel.—*Ed.*

tiful scenery, no colossal mountain masses, but a land of soft rolling hills which has a wonderful charm in the English sunlight, which is never quite clear. It is surprising how various are the groupings of the simple figures; out of a few low hills, a field, some trees and grazing cattle, nature composes a thousand pleasant landscapes. The trees, which occur singly or in groups in all the fields, have a singular beauty that makes the whole neighbourhood resemble a park. Then comes a tunnel, and for a few minutes the train is in darkness, emerging into a deep cutting from which one is suddenly transported again into the midst of smiling, sunny fields. At another time the railway track is laid on a viaduct crossing a long valley; far below it lie towns and villages, woods and meadows, between which a river takes its meandering course; to the right and left are mountains which fade into the background, and the valley is bathed in a magical light, half-mist and half-sunshine. But you have hardly had time to survey the wonderful scene before you are carried away into a bare cutting and have time to recreate the magical picture in your imagination. And so it goes on until night falls and your wearied eyes close in slumber. Oh, there is rich poetry in the counties of Britain! It often seems as if one were still in the golden days of merry England[a] and might see Shakespeare with his fowling-piece moving stealthily behind a hedge on a deer-poaching expedition, or you might wonder why not one of his divine comedies actually takes place on this green meadow. For wherever the scenes are supposed to occur, in Italy, France or Navarra, his baroque, uncouth rustics, his too-clever schoolmasters, and his deliciously bizarre women, all belong basically to merry England,[b] and it is remarkable that only an English sky is suited to everything that takes place. Only some of the comedies, such as the *Midsummer Night's Dream,* are as

---

[a] The words "golden days of merry England" are in English in the original.—*Ed.*

[b] The words "merry England" are in English in the original.—*Ed.*

completely adapted to a southern climate as *Romeo and Juliet,* even in the characters of the play.

And now back to our Fatherland! Picturesque and romantic Westphalia has become quite indignant at its son Freiligrath, who has entirely forgotten it on account of the admittedly far more picturesque and romantic Rhine. Let us console it with a few flattering words so that its patience does not give out before the second issue appears.[6] Westphalia is surrounded by mountain ranges separating it from the rest of Germany, and it lies open only to Holland, as if it had been cast out from Germany. And yet its children are true Saxons, good loyal Germans. And these mountains offer magnificent points of view; in the south the Ruhr and Lenne valleys, in the east the Weser valley, in the north a range of mountains from Minden to Osnabrück—everywhere there is a wealth of beautiful scenery, and only in the centre of the province is there a boring expanse of sand which always shows up through the grass and corn. And then there are the beautiful old towns, above all Münster with its Gothic churches, with its market arcades, and with Annette Elisabeth von Droste-Hülshoff and Levin Schücking. The last-named, whose acquaintance I had the pleasure of making there, was kind enough to draw my attention to the poems of that lady,[7] and I could not let this opportunity slip without bearing part of the blame which the German public has incurred in regard to these poems. In connection with them it has once again been proved that the much-vaunted German thoroughness treats the appreciation of poetry much too light-heartedly; people leaf through it, examine whether the rhymes are pure and the verses fluent, and whether the content is easy to understand and rich in striking, or at least dazzling, images, and the verdict is complete. But poems like these, which are marked by a sincerity of feeling, a tenderness and originality in the depiction of nature such as only Shelley can achieve, and a bold Byronic imagination—clothed, it is true, in a somewhat stiff form and in a language not altogether free from provincialism—such poems pass away without leaving a trace. Anyone, however, who is prepared to read them rather more slowly than usual—and, after all, one only takes up a book of poems in the hours of a siesta—could very well find that their beauty prevents him from going to sleep! Furthermore, the poetess is a fervent Catholic, and how can a Protestant take any interest in such? But whereas pietism[8] makes the man, the schoolmaster, the chief curate Albert Knapp, ridiculous, the childish faith of Fräulein von Droste becomes her very well. Religious independence of mind is an awkward matter for women. Persons like George Sand, Mistress Shelley,[a] are rare; it is only too easy for doubt to corrode the feminine mind and raise the intellect to a power which it ought not to have in any woman. If, however, the ideas by which we children of the new stand or fall are truth, then the time is not far off when the feminine heart will beat as warmly for the flowers of thought of the modern mind as it does now for the pious faith of its fathers—and the victory of the new will only be at hand when the young generation takes it in with its mother's milk.

Frederick Engels, "Landscapes"

Marx and Engels, *Collected Works*, Vol. 2, Moscow, 1975, pp. 95-101

---

[a] Mary Wollstonecraft-Shelley, *née* Godwin.—*Ed.*

Against Vulgarisation
of Historical Materialism

1

According to the materialist conception of history, the *ultimately* determining factor in history is the production and reproduction of real life. Neither Marx nor I have ever asserted more than this. Hence if somebody twists this into saying that the economic factor is the *only* determining one, he transforms that proposition into a meaningless, abstract, absurd phrase. The economic situation is the basis, but the various elements of the superstructure—political forms of the class struggle and its results, such as constitutions established by the victorious class after a successful battle, etc., juridical forms, and especially the reflections of all these real struggles in the brains of the participants, political, legal, philosophical theories, religious views and their further development into systems of dogmas—also exercise their influence upon the course of the historical struggles and in many cases determine their *form* in particular. There is an interaction of all these elements in which, amid all the endless host of accidents (that is, of things and events whose inner interconnection is so remote or so impossible of proof that we can regard it as non-existent and neglect it), the economic movement is finally bound to assert itself. Otherwise the application of the theory to any period of history would be easier than the solution of a simple equation of the first degree.

> Engels to Joseph Bloch,
> September 21-22, 1890
>
> Marx and Engels, *Selected Correspondence,* Moscow, 1975, pp. 394-95

2

Political, juridical, philosophical, religious, literary, artistic, etc., development is based on economic development. But all these react upon one another and also upon the economic basis. It is not that the economic situation is *cause, solely active*, while everything else is only passive effect. There is, rather, interaction on the basis of economic necessity, which *ultimately* always asserts itself. The state, for instance, exercises an influence by protective tariffs, free trade, good or bad fiscal system; and even the deadly inanition and impotence of the German philistine, arising from the miserable economic condition of Germany from 1648 to 1830 and expressing themselves at first in pietism, then in sentimentality and cringing servility to princes and nobles, were not without economic effect. That was one of the greatest hindrances to recovery and was not shaken until the revolutionary and Napoleonic wars made the chronic misery an acute one. So it is not, as people try here and there conveniently to imagine, that the economic situation produces an automatic effect. No. Men make their history themselves, only they do so in a given environment, which conditions them, and on the basis of actual relations already existing, among which the economic relations, however much they may be influenced by the other—the political and ideological relations—are still ultimately the decisive ones, forming the keynote which runs through everything and alone leads to understanding.

> Engels to W. Borgius,
> January 25, 1894
>
> Marx and Engels, *Selected Works*,
> Vol. 3, Moscow, 1973, pp. 502-03

3

As to the realms of ideology which soar still higher in the air—religion, philosophy, etc.—these have a prehistoric stock, found already in existence and taken over by the historical period, of what we should today call nonsense. These various false conceptions of nature, of man's own being, of spirits, magic forces, etc., have for the most part only a negative economic factor as their basis; the low economic development of the prehistoric period is supplemented and also partially conditioned and even caused by the false conceptions of nature. And even though economic necessity was the main driving force of the increasing knowledge of nature and has become ever more so, yet it would be pedantic to try and find economic causes for all this primitive nonsense. The history of science is the history of the gradual clearing away of this nonsense or rather of its replacement by fresh but less absurd nonsense. The people who attend to this belong in their turn to special spheres in the division of labour and they think that they are working in an independent field. And to the extent that they form an independent group within the social division of labour, their output, including their errors, exerts in its turn an effect upon the whole development of society, and even on its economic development. But all the same they themselves are in turn under the predominant influence of economic development. In philosophy, for instance, this can be most readily proved true for the bourgeois period. Hobbes was the first modern materialist (in the sense of the eighteenth century) but he was an absolutist at a time when absolute monarchy was in its heyday throughout Europe and began the battle against the people in England. Locke was in religion and in politics the child of the class compromise of 1688. The English deists and their more consistent followers, the French materialists, were the true philosophers of the bourgeoisie, the French even the philosophers of the bourgeois revolution. The German philistinism runs through German philosophy from Kant to Hegel, sometimes in a positive and sometimes a negative way. But the precondition of the philosophy of each epoch regarded as a distinct sphere in the division of labour, is a definite thought material which is handed down to it by its predecessors, and which is also its starting point. And that is why economically backward countries can still play first fiddle in philosophy: France in the eighteenth century as compared with England, on whose philosophy the French based themselves, and later Germany as compared with both. But both in France and in Germany philosophy and the general blossoming of literature at that time were also the result of an economic revival. The ultimate supremacy of economic development is for me an established fact in these spheres too, but it operates within the terms laid down by the particular sphere itself: in philosophy, for instance, by the action of economic influences (which in their turn generally operate only in their political, etc., make-up) upon the existing philosophic material which has been handed down by predecessors. Here economy creates nothing anew, but it determines the way in which the thought material found in existence is altered and further developed, and that too for the most part indirectly, for it is the political, legal and moral reflexes which exert the greatest direct influence on philosophy.

Engels to Conrad Schmidt,
October 27, 1890

Marx and Engels, *Selected Correspondence*, Moscow, 1975, pp. 400-01

4

Marx and I are ourselves partly to blame for the fact that the younger people sometimes lay more stress on the economic side than is due to it. We had to emphasise the main principle *vis-à-vis* our adversaries, who denied it, and we had not always the time, the place or the opportunity to give their due to the other factors involved in the interaction. But when it came to presenting a section of history, that is, to applying the theory in practice, it was a different matter and there no error was permissible. Unfortunately, however, it happens only too often that people think they have fully understood a new theory and can apply it without more ado as soon as they have assimilated its main principles, and even those not always correctly. And I cannot exempt many of the more recent "Marxists" from this reproach, for the most amazing stuff has been produced in that quarter, too.

> Engels to Joseph Bloch,
> September 21-22, 1890
>
> Marx and Engels, *Selected Correspondence*, Moscow, 1975, p. 396

5

In general, the word "materialist" serves many of the younger writers in Germany as a mere phrase with which anything and everything is labelled without further study, that is, they stick on this label and then consider the question disposed of. But our conception of history is above all a guide to study, not a lever for construction after the Hegelian manner. All history must be studied afresh, the conditions of existence of the different formations of society must be examined in detail before the attempt is made to deduce from them the political, civil-law, aesthetic, philosophic, religious, etc., views corresponding to them. Up to now very little has been done in this respect because only a few people have got down to it seriously. We need a great deal of help in this field, for it is immensely big, and anyone who will work seriously can achieve much and distinguish himself. But instead of this too many of the younger Germans simply make use of the phrase historical materialism (and *everything* can be turned into a phrase) only in order to get their own relatively scanty historical knowledge—for economic history is still in its swaddling clothes!—constructed into a neat system as quickly as possible, and they then fancy that they have achieved something tremendous. And after that a Barth can come along and attack the subject itself, which in his circle has indeed been degraded to a mere phrase.

>Engels to Conrad Schmidt,
>August 5, 1890
>
>Marx and Engels, *Selected Correspondence,* Moscow, 1975, pp. 393-94

Engels About Mehring's
The Lessing Legend

1

I am glad that *The Lessing Legend* has appeared as a separate book; works of this kind suffer greatly from being broken up. It was highly creditable on your part to have worked through the chaos of Prussian history and indicated the correct interconnections; current realities in Prussia make this absolutely necessary, no matter how unpleasant the work is in itself. I am not in complete agreement with your opinion on certain points, particularly in places concerning the causal links with the preceding period, but this does not prevent your book from being by far the best there is on this period of German history.

> Engels to Franz Mehring,
> April 11, 1893
>
> Marx/Engels, *Werke*,[a] Bd. 39, 1968, S. 64

2

Your Berlin correspondent is certainly highly subjective, but he knows how to write and has a very good grasp of the materialist conception of historical events; I would not

---

[a] Here and elsewhere the reference is to Marx/Engels, *Werke*, Dietz Verlag, Berlin.—*Ed.*

always say the same of his understanding of current events. *The Lessing Legend* was first-rate, although I place a different interpretation on certain points.

> Engels to Karl Kautsky,
> June 1, 1893
>
> Marx/Engels, *Werke*, Bd. 39, 1968,
> S. 77-78

3

Engels to Franz Mehring

London, July 14, 1893

Dear Mr. Mehring,

Today is my first opportunity to thank you for the *Lessing-Legende* you were kind enough to send me. I did not want to reply with a bare formal acknowledgement of receipt of the book but intended at the same time to say something about it, about its contents. Hence the delay.

I shall begin at the end—the appendix "Über den historischen Materialismus" ["On historical materialism"], in which you have summarised the main points excellently and for any unprejudiced person convincingly. If I find anything to object to, it is that you give me more credit than I deserve, even if I count everything which I might perhaps have found out for myself—in time—but which Marx with his more rapid *coup d'œil* and wider vision discovered much more quickly. When one had the good fortune to work for forty years with a man like Marx, one usually does not during his lifetime get the recognition one thinks one deserves. Then, when the greater man dies, the lesser easily gets overrated and this seems to me to be just my case at present; history will set all this right in the end, and by that time one will have managed to kick the bucket and will no longer know anything about anything.

Otherwise only one more point is lacking, which, however, Marx and I always failed to stress enough in our writings and in regard to which we are all equally guilty. That is to say, in the first instance we all laid, and *were bound to lay*, the main emphasis on the *derivation* of political, juridical and other ideological notions, and of actions arising through the medium of these notions, from basic economic facts. But at the same time we have on account of the content neglected the formal side—the manner in which these notions, etc., come about. This has given our adversaries a welcome opportunity for misunderstandings and distortions, of which Paul Barth is a striking example.

Ideology is a process which is indeed accomplished consciously by the so-called thinker, but it is the wrong kind of consciousness. The real motive forces impelling him remain unknown to the thinker; otherwise it simply would not be an ideological process. Hence he imagines false or illusory motive forces. Because it is a process of thinking he derives its form as well as its content from pure reasoning, either his own or that of his predecessors. He works exclusively with thought material, which he accepts without examination as something produced by reasoning, and does not investigate further for a more remote source independent of reason; indeed this is a matter of course to him, because, as all action is *mediated* by thought, it appears to him to be ultimately *based* upon thought.

The historical ideologist (historical is here simply a comprehensive term comprising political, juridical, philosophical, theological—in short, all the spheres belonging to *society* and not only to nature) thus possesses in every sphere of science material which has arisen independently out of the thought of previous generations and has gone through its own independent course of development in the brains of these successive generations. True, external facts belonging to one or another sphere may have exercised a co-determining influence on this development, but the tacit presupposition is that these facts themselves are also only the fruits of a process of thought, and so we still remain within that realm of mere thought, which apparently has successfully digested even the hardest facts.

It is above all this semblance of an independent history of state constitutions, of systems of law, of ideological conceptions in every separate domain that dazzles most people. If Luther and Calvin "overcome" the official Catholic religion, or Hegel "overcomes" Fichte and Kant, or Rousseau with his republican *Contrat social*[9] indirectly "overcomes" the constitutional Montesquieu, this is a process which remains within theology, philosophy or political science, represents a stage in the history of these particular spheres of thought and never passes beyond the sphere of thought. And since the bourgeois illusion of the eternity and finality of capitalist production has been added to this, even the "overcoming" of the mercantilists by the physiocrats[10] and Adam Smith is regarded as a sheer victory of thought; not as the reflection in thought of changed economic facts but as the finally achieved correct understanding of actual conditions subsisting always and everywhere—in fact, if Richard Coeur-de-Lion and Philip Augustus had introduced free trade instead of getting mixed up in the crusades we should have been spared five hundred years of misery and stupidity.

This aspect of the matter, which I can only indicate here, we have all, I think, neglected more than it deserves. It is the old story: form is always neglected at first for content. As I say, I have done that too and the mistake has always struck me only later. Hence I am not only far from reproaching you with this in any way—as the older of the guilty parties I certainly have no right to do so, on the contrary, but I would like all the same to draw your attention to this point for the future.

Connected with this is the fatuous notion of the ideologists that because we deny an independent historical development to the various ideological spheres which play a part in history we also deny them any *effect upon history*. The basis of this is the common undialectical conception of cause and effect as rigidly opposite poles, the total disregard of interaction. These gentlemen often almost deliberately forget that once an historic element has been brought into the world by other, ultimately economic causes, it reacts, and can react on its environment and even on the causes that have given rise to it. For instance, Barth when he speaks of the priesthood and religion, your page 475. I was very glad to see how you settled this fellow, whose banality exceeds all expectations; and such a man is made professor of history in Leipzig! Old Wachsmuth—also rather a bonehead but greatly appreciative of facts—was after all quite a different chap.

As for the rest, I can only repeat about the book what I repeatedly said about the articles when they appeared in the *Neue Zeit*;[11] it is by far the best presentation in existence of the genesis of the Prussian state. Indeed, I may well say that it is the only good presentation, correctly developing in most matters their interconnections down to the very details. One regrets only that you were unable to include the entire further development down to Bismarck and one cannot help hoping that you will do this another time and present a complete coherent picture, from the Elector Frederick William down to old William.[a] For you have already made the preliminary investigations and, in the main at least, they are as good as finished. The thing has to be done sometime anyhow before the shaky old shanty comes tumbling down. The dissipation of the monarchical-patriotic legends, although not really a necessary precondition for the abolition of the monarchy which screens class domination (for a *pure*, bourgeois republic in Germany has been made obsolete by events before it has come into existence) is nevertheless one of the most effective levers for that purpose.

---

[a] William I.—*Ed.*

Then you will also have more space and opportunity to depict the local history of Prussia as part of Germany's general misery. This is the point where I occasionally depart somewhat from your view, especially in the conception of the preliminary conditions for the dismemberment of Germany and of the failure of the bourgeois revolution in Germany during the sixteenth century. If I get down to reworking the historical introduction to my *Peasant War*,[12] which I hope I shall do next winter, I shall be able to develop there the points in question. Not that I consider those you indicated incorrect, but I put others alongside them and group them somewhat differently.

In studying German history—the story of a continuous state of wretchedness—I have always found that only a comparison with the corresponding French periods produces a correct idea of proportions, because what happens there is the direct opposite of what happens in our country. There, the establishment of a national state from the scattered parts of the feudal state, just when we pass through the period of our greatest decline. There, a rare objective logic during the whole course of the process; with us, increasingly dreary desultoriness. There, during the Middle Ages, the English conqueror, who intervenes in favour of the Provençal nationality against the Northern French nationality, represents foreign intervention, and the wars with England represent, in a way, the Thirty Years' War,[13] which there, however, ends in the ejection of the foreign invaders and the subjugation of the South by the North. Then comes the struggle between the central power and Burgundy, the vassal, which relies on its foreign possessions, and plays the part of Brandenburg-Prussia, a struggle which ends, however, in the victory of the central power and conclusively establishes the national state. And precisely at that moment the national state completely collapses in our country (in so far as the "German kingdom" within the Holy Roman Empire can be called a national state) and the plundering of German territory on a large scale sets in. This comparison is most humiliating for Germans but for that very reason the more instructive; and since our workers have put Germany back again in the forefront of the historical movement it has become somewhat easier for us to swallow the ignominy of the past.

Another especially significant feature of the development of Germany is the fact that not one of the two member states which in the end partitioned Germany between them was purely German—both were colonies on conquered Slav territory: Austria a Bavarian and Brandenburg a Saxon colony—and that they acquired power *within* Germany only by relying upon the support of foreign, non-German possessions: Austria upon that of Hungary (not to mention Bohemia) and Brandenburg upon that of Prussia. On the Western border, the one in greatest jeopardy, nothing of the kind took place; on the Northern border it was left to the Danes to protect Germany against the Danes; and in the South there was so little to protect that the frontier guard, the Swiss, even succeeded in tearing themselves loose from Germany!

But I am speaking of all kinds of extraneous matter, let this palaver at least serve you as proof of how stimulating an effect your work has upon me.

Once more cordial thanks and greetings from

Yours,

F. *Engels*

Marx and Engels, *Selected Correspondence*, Moscow, 1975, pp. 433-37

Class Relations and Class Ideology

1

The ideas of the ruling class are in every epoch the ruling ideas: i.e., the class which is the ruling *material* force of society is at the same time its ruling *intellectual* force. The class which has the means of material production at its disposal, consequently also controls the means of mental production, so that the ideas of those who lack the means of mental production are on the whole subject to it. The ruling ideas are nothing more than the ideal expression of the dominant material relations; the dominant material relations grasped as ideas; hence of the relations which make the one class the ruling one, therefore, the ideas of its dominance. The individuals composing the ruling class possess among other things consciousness, and therefore think. Insofar, therefore, as they rule as a class and determine the extent and compass of an historical epoch, it is self-evident that they do this in its whole range, hence among other things rule also as thinkers, as producers of ideas, and regulate the production and distribution of the ideas of their age: thus their ideas are the ruling ideas of the epoch. For instance, in an age and in a country where royal power, aristocracy and bourgeoisie are contending for domination and where, therefore, domination is shared, the doctrine of the separation of powers proves to be the dominant idea and is expressed as an "eternal law".

The division of labour, which we already saw above (pp. [15-18])[a] as one of the chief forces of history up till now, manifests itself also in the ruling class as the division of mental and [31] material labour, so that inside this class one part appears as the thinkers of the class (its active, conceptive ideologists, who make the formation of the illusions of the class about itself their chief source of livelihood), while the others' attitude to these ideas and illusions is more passive and receptive, because they are in reality the active members of this class and have less time to make up illusions and ideas about themselves. Within this class this cleavage can even develop into a certain opposition and hostility between the two parts, but whenever a practical collision occurs in which the class itself is endangered they automatically vanish, in which case there also vanishes the appearance of the ruling ideas being not the ideas of the ruling class and having a power distinct from the power of this class. The existence of revolutionary ideas in a particular period presupposes the existence of a revolutionary class; about the premises of the latter sufficient has already been said above (pp. [18-19, 22-23]).[b]

If now in considering the course of history we detach the ideas of the ruling class from the ruling class itself and attribute to them an independent existence, if we confine ourselves to saying that these or those ideas were dominant at a given time, without bothering ourselves about the conditions of production and the producers of these ideas, if we thus ignore the individuals and world conditions which are the source of the ideas, then we can say, for instance, *that during* the time that the aristocracy was dominant, the concepts honour, loyalty, etc., were dominant, during the dominance of the bourgeoisie the concepts freedom, equality, etc. The ruling class itself on the whole imagines this to be so. This conception of history, which is common to all

---

[a] See Marx and Engels, *Collected Works*, Vol. 5, pp. 44-48.—*Ed.*
[b] Ibid., pp. 48-49 and 52.—*Ed.*

historians, particularly since the eighteenth century, will necessarily come up against the phenomenon that ever more abstract ideas hold sway, i.e., ideas which increasingly take on the form of universality. For each new class which puts itself in the place of one ruling before it is compelled, merely in order to carry through its aim, to present its interest as the common interest of all the members of society, that is, expressed in ideal form: it has to give its ideas the form of universality, and present them as the only rational, universally valid ones. The class making a revolution comes forward from the very start, if only because it is opposed to a *class*, not as a class but as the representative of the whole of society, as the whole mass of society confronting the one ruling class.* It can do this because initially its interest really is as yet mostly connected with the common interest of all other non-ruling classes, because under the pressure of hitherto existing conditions its interest has not yet been able to develop as the particular interest of a particular class. Its victory, therefore, benefits also many individuals of other classes which are not winning a dominant position, but only insofar as it now enables these individuals to raise themselves into the ruling class. When the French bourgeoisie overthrew the rule of the aristocracy, it thereby made it possible for many proletarians to raise themselves above the proletariat, but only insofar as they became bourgeois. Every new class, therefore, achieves domination only on a broader basis than that of the class ruling previously; on the other hand the opposition of the non-ruling class to the new ruling class then develops all the more sharply and profoundly. Both these things determine the fact that the struggle to be waged against this new ruling class, in its turn, aims at a more decided and

* [Marginal note by Marx:] (Universality corresponds to 1) the class versus the estate, 2) the competition, world intercourse, etc., 3) the great numerical strength of the ruling class, 4) the illusion of the *common interests*; in the beginning this illusion is true, 5) the delusion of the ideologists and the division of labour.)

radical negation of the previous conditions of society than could all previous classes which sought to rule.

This whole appearance, that the rule of a certain class is only the rule of certain ideas, comes to a natural end, of course, as soon as class rule in general ceases to be the form in which society is organised, that is to say, as soon as it is no longer necessary to represent a particular interest as general or the "general interest" as ruling.

> Karl Marx and Frederick Engels,
> *The German Ideology*
>
> Marx and Engels, *Collected Works*, Vol. 5, Moscow, 1976, pp. 59-61

2

Does it require deep intuition to comprehend that man's ideas, views and conceptions, in one word, man's consciousness, changes with every change in the conditions of his material existence, in his social relations and in his social life?

What else does the history of ideas prove, than that intellectual production changes its character in proportion as material production is changed? The ruling ideas of each age have ever been the ideas of its ruling class.

When people speak of ideas that revolutionise society, they do but express the fact, that within the old society, the elements of a new one have been created, and that the dissolution of the old ideas keeps even pace with the dissolution of the old conditions of existence.

When the ancient world was in its last throes, the ancient religions were overcome by Christianity. When Christian ideas succumbed in the eighteenth century to rationalist ideas, feudal society fought its death battle with the then revolutionary bourgeoisie. The ideas of religious liberty and freedom of conscience merely gave expression to the sway of free competition within the domain of knowledge.

"Undoubtedly," it will be said, "religious, moral, philosophical and juridical ideas have been modified in the course of historical development. But religion, morality, philosophy, political science, and law, constantly survived this change."

"There are, besides, eternal truths, such as Freedom, Justice, etc., that are common to all states of society. But Communism abolishes eternal truths, it abolishes all religion, and all morality, instead of constituting them on a new basis; it therefore acts in contradiction to all past historical experience."

What does this accusation reduce itself to? The history of all past society has consisted in the development of class antagonisms, antagonisms that assumed different forms at different epochs.

But whatever form they may have taken, one fact is common to all past ages, *viz.*, the exploitation of one part of society by the other. No wonder, then, that the social consciousness of past ages, despite all the multiplicity and variety it displays, moves within certain common forms, or general ideas, which cannot completely vanish except with the total disappearance of class antagonisms.

The Communist revolution is the most radical rupture with traditional property relations; no wonder that its development involves the most radical rupture with traditional ideas.

Karl Marx and Frederick Engels,
Manifesto of the Communist Party

Marx and Engels, *Collected Works*,
Vol. 6, Moscow, 1976,
pp. 503-04

Scientific and Vulgar Conceptions of Class Ideology

Engels to Paul Ernst[14]

[Draft]

London, June 5, 1890

Dear Sir,

I am, unfortunately, unable to comply with your wish and write you a letter for use against Herr Bahr. That would involve me in an open polemic with him, which would take up too much of my time. I am writing, therefore, purely for your own private information.

In addition I have no knowledge at all of what you call the northern women's movement; I am acquainted with only a few Ibsen dramas and have absolutely no idea whether and to what extent Ibsen is to be held responsible for the more or less hysterical night vigils of bourgeois and petty-bourgeois careerist women.

The subject which has come to be known as the women's question is so expansive that it is impossible to say anything exhaustive or even satisfactory about it in one letter. Only one thing is certain: Marx could never have "behaved" as Bahr claims he did. He was not so idiotic.

As far as your attempt to treat the matter materialistically is concerned I must say in the first place that the materialist method turns into its opposite if it is not taken as one's guiding principle in historical investigation but as a ready-made pattern according to which one shapes the facts of history to suit oneself. And if Mr. Bahr thinks he caught you on this wrong tack he seems to me to be not altogether wrong.

You put all Norway and everything that happens there into one category: philistinism, and then you unhesitatingly attribute to this Norwegian philistinism the qualities which in your opinion distinguish *German* philistinism. But here two facts stand in the way.

First: when throughout Europe the victory over Napoleon became a victory of reaction over revolution and only in its cradle, France, did the revolution still inspire sufficient fear to wrest a liberal bourgeois constitution from the returning legitimist regime, at that time Norway found it possible to acquire a constitution that is far more democratic than any other of contemporary Europe.

Second: Norway has experienced in the last twenty years a literary upsurge unparalleled in any other country except Russia during this period. Whether they are philistines or not these people have achieved much more than others have and have left their imprint also on other literatures, and they have certainly exerted their influence on German literature.

These facts make it necessary, in my opinion, to investigate to some extent the specific features of Norwegian philistinism.

And here you will probably find that there is quite a substantial difference. In Germany philistinism is the outcome of a shipwrecked revolution, of an interrupted, repressed development. Cowardice, narrow-mindedness, helplessness and inability to take the initiative—the specific, abnormally developed traits of German philistinism are a result of the Thirty Years' War and the period following it, precisely the period of rapid rise of almost all other great peoples. It retained these characteristic features even when Germany was again swept into the historical movement. They were strong enough to more or less impress their mark as the general German type on all other classes of German society, until finally our working class broke through these narrow limits. The non-patriotism[15] of the German workers is expressed most strongly by the fact that they have cast off all German philistine narrow-mindedness.

German philistinism is therefore not a normal historical phase but an extreme caricature, a piece of degeneration, just as the Polish Jew is a caricature of Jewry. The English, French, etc., petty bourgeois are by no means on the same level as the German.

On the other hand in Norway the small peasantry and the petty bourgeoisie with a slight admixture of medium bourgeoisie—such as existed, say, in England and France in the seventeenth century—have constituted the normal state of society for several centuries. It was by no means an unsuccessful great movement or a Thirty Years' War which forcibly thrust the country back into antiquated conditions. The country was trailing behind on account of its isolation and natural conditions but the state of affairs in the country fully corresponded to its conditions of production and hence was normal. Only quite recently a modicum of modern industry has sporadically come into the land, but there is no room for the stock exchange, the most powerful lever of the concentration of capital, and it is precisely the enormous expansion of marine commerce that exerts a conservative influence. For, while everywhere else steam power is displacing sailing vessels, Norway is increasing its maritime fleet of sailing ships tremendously and has if not the biggest then surely the second biggest sailing fleet in the world, mostly the property of small and medium shipowners, a position similar to that in England say around 1720. Nevertheless this has brought movement into the old stagnant life and this movement is finding expression also in the literary resurgence.

The Norwegian peasant was *never a serf* and this provides an entirely different background for the whole development, which in a way is similar to that in Castile. The Norwegian petty bourgeois is the son of a free peasant and under these circumstances is a *man* in comparison with the debased German philistine. Likewise the Norwegian woman of the lower middle class stands sky-high above the spouse of the German philistine. And whatever the shortcomings of, for instance, Ibsen's plays may be, they mirror, it is true, a world of the small and medium bourgeoisie but there is an enormous difference between it and the position in Germany, they mirror a world in which people still have strength of character and initiative and act independently, even though according to the concepts prevalent in other countries their actions may often seem odd. I prefer to make a thorough study of such things before making a final judgment.

To return once more to the afore-mentioned subject, namely Herr Bahr, I am surprised that the people in Germany take one another so dreadfully seriously. Wit and humour seem to be more forbidden than ever and boredom appears to be a civic duty. Otherwise you would certainly have examined somewhat closely Herr Bahr's "woman" who is devoid of everything "historically developed". Her skin is historically developed, for it must be either white or black, yellow, brown or red—therefore she cannot have a human skin. Her hair is historically developed, whether frizzy and woolly, curly or straight, whether black, red or blond. Human hair is thus also forbidden her. So what is left, if you have taken away the historically developed with the skin and hair and "the woman herself appears"? What emerges? Simply the ape, anthropopithecus; and let Herr Bahr take this "quite palpable and transparent" woman to his bed together with her "natural instincts".

Marx/Engels, *Werke*, Bd. 37, 1967, S. 411-13

Historical Continuity and Its Contradictions

1

It depends purely on the extension of intercourse whether the productive forces evolved in a locality, especially inventions, are lost for later development or not. As long as there exists no intercourse transcending the immediate neighbourhood, every invention must be made separately in each locality, and mere chances such as irruptions of barbaric peoples, even ordinary wars, are sufficient to cause a country with advanced productive forces and needs to have to start right over again from the beginning. In primitive history every invention had to be made daily anew and in each locality independently. That even with a relatively very extensive commerce, highly developed productive forces are not safe from complete destruction, is proved by the Phoenicians, whose inventions were for the most part lost for a long time to come through the ousting of this nation from commerce, its conquest by Alexander and its consequent decline. Likewise, for instance, glass staining in the Middle Ages. Only when intercourse has become world intercourse and has as its basis large-scale industry, when all nations are drawn into the competitive struggle, is the permanence of the acquired productive forces assured.

Karl Marx and Frederick Engels, *The German Ideology*

Marx and Engels, *Collected Works*, Vol. 5, Moscow, 1976, p. 67

2

Men make their own history, but they do not make it just as they please; they do not make it under circumstances chosen by themselves, but under circumstances directly encountered, given and transmitted from the past. The tradition of all the dead generations weighs like a nightmare on the brain of the living. And just when they seem engaged in revolutionising themselves and things, in creating something that has never yet existed, precisely in such periods of revolutionary crisis they anxiously conjure up the spirits of the past to their service and borrow from them names, battle cries and costumes in order to present the new scene of world history in this time-honoured disguise and this borrowed language. Thus Luther donned the mask of the Apostle Paul, the Revolution of 1789 to 1814 draped itself alternately as the Roman republic and the Roman empire, and the Revolution of 1848 knew nothing better to do than to parody, now 1789, now the revolutionary tradition of 1793 to 1795. In like manner a beginner who has learnt a new language always translates it back into his mother tongue, but he has assimilated the spirit of the new language and can freely express himself in it only when he finds his way in it without recalling the old and forgets his native tongue in the use of the new.

Consideration of this conjuring up of the dead of world history reveals at once a salient difference. Camille Desmoulins, Danton, Robespierre, Saint-Just, Napoleon, the heroes as well as the parties and the masses of the old French Revolution, performed the task of their time in Roman costume and with Roman phrases, the task of unchaining and setting up modern *bourgeois* society. The first ones knocked the feudal basis to pieces and mowed off the feudal heads which had grown on it. The other created inside France the conditions under which alone free competition could be developed, parcelled landed property exploited and the unchained industrial productive power of the nation employed; and beyond the French borders he everywhere swept the feudal institutions away, so far as was necessary to furnish bourgeois society in France with a suitable up-to-date environment on the European Continent. The new social formation once established, the antediluvian Colossi disappeared and with them resurrected Romanity—the Brutuses, Gracchi, Publicolas,[16] the tribunes, the senators, and Caesar himself. Bourgeois society in its sober reality had begotten its true interpreters and mouthpieces in the Says, Cousins, Royer-Collards, Benjamin Constants and Guizots; its real military leaders sat behind the office desks, and the hogheaded Louis XVIII was its political chief. Wholly absorbed in the production of wealth and in peaceful competitive struggle, it no longer comprehended that ghosts from the days of Rome had watched over its cradle. But unheroic as bourgeois society is, it nevertheless took heroism, sacrifice, terror, civil war and battles of peoples to bring it into being. And in the classically austere traditions of the Roman republic its gladiators found the ideals and the art forms, the self-deceptions that they needed in order to conceal from themselves the bourgeois limitations of the content of their struggles and to keep their enthusiasm on the high plane of the great historical tragedy. Similarly, at another stage of development, a century earlier, Cromwell and the English people had borrowed speech, passions and illusions from the Old Testament for their bourgeois revolution. When the real aim had been achieved, when the bourgeois transformation of English society had been accomplished, Locke supplanted Habakkuk.

Thus the awakening of the dead in those revolutions served the purpose of glorifying the new struggles, not of parodying the old; of magnifying the given task in imagination, not of fleeing from its solution in reality; of finding once more the spirit of revolution, not of making its ghost walk about again.

Karl Marx, *The Eighteenth Brumaire of Louis Bonaparte*

Marx and Engels, *Selected Works*, Vol. 1, Moscow, 1973, pp. 398-99

Uneven Character
of Historical Development
and Questions of Art

6. *The unequal development of material production and, e.g., that of art.* The concept of progress is on the whole not to be understood in the usual abstract form. Modern art, etc. This disproportion is not as important and difficult to grasp as within concrete social relations, e.g., in education. Relations of the United States to Europe. However, the really difficult point to be discussed here is how the relations of production as legal relations take part in this uneven development. For example the relation of Roman civil law (this applies in smaller measure to criminal and constitutional law) to modern production.

7. *This conception appears to be an inevitable development.* But vindication of chance. How? (Freedom, etc., as well.) (Influence of the means of communication. World history did not always exist; history as world history is a result.)

8. *The starting point is of course the naturally determined factors*; both subjective and objective. Tribes, races, etc.

As regards art, it is well known that some of its peaks by no means correspond to the general development of society; nor do they therefore to the material substructure, the skeleton as it were of its organisation. For example the Greeks compared with modern [nations], or else Shakespeare. It is even acknowledged that certain branches of art, *e.g.*, the *epos,* can no longer be produced in their epoch-making classic form after artistic production as such has begun; in other words, that certain important creations within the compass of art are only possible at an early stage in the development of art. If this is the case with regard to different branches of art within the sphere of art itself, it is not so remarkable that this should also be the case with regard to the entire sphere of art and its relation to the general development of society. The difficulty lies only in the general formulation of these contradictions. As soon as they are reduced to specific questions they are already explained.

Let us take, for example, the relation of Greek art, and that of Shakespeare, to the present time. We know that Greek mythology is not only the arsenal of Greek art, but also its basis. Is the conception of nature and of social relations which underlies Greek imagination and therefore Greek [art] possible when there are self-acting mules, railways, locomotives and electric telegraphs? What is a Vulcan compared with Roberts and Co., Jupiter compared with the lightning conductor, and Hermes compared with the *Crédit mobilier*? All mythology subdues, controls and fashions the forces of nature in the imagination and through imagination; it disappears therefore when real control over these forces is established. What becomes of Fama side by side with Printing House Square?[17] Greek art presupposes Greek mythology, in other words that natural and social phenomena are already assimilated in an unintentionally artistic manner by the imagination of the people. This is the material of Greek art, not just any mythology, *i.e.*, not every unconsciously artistic assimilation of nature (here the term comprises all physical phenomena, including society); Egyptian mythology could never become the basis of or give rise to Greek art. But at any rate [it presupposes] a mythology; on no account however a social development which precludes a mythological attitude towards nature, *i.e.*, any attitude to nature which might give rise to myth; a society therefore demanding from the artist an imagination independent of mythology.

Regarded from another aspect: is Achilles possible when powder and shot have been invented? And is the *Iliad* possible at all when the printing press and even printing machines exist? Is it not inevitable that with the emergence of the press bar the singing and the telling and the muse cease, that is the conditions necessary for epic poetry disappear?

The difficulty we are confronted with is not, however, that of understanding how Greek art and epic poetry are associated with certain forms of social development. The difficulty is that they still give us aesthetic pleasure and are in certain respects regarded as a standard and unattainable ideal.

An adult cannot become a child again, or he becomes childish. But does the naïveté of the child not give him pleasure, and does not he himself endeavour to reproduce the child's veracity on a higher level? Does not the child in every epoch represent the character of the period in its natural veracity? Why should not the historical childhood of humanity, where it attained its most beautiful form, exert an eternal charm because it is a stage that will never recur? There are rude children and precocious children. Many of the ancient peoples belong to this category. The Greeks were normal children. The charm their art has for us does not conflict with the immature stage of the society in which it originated. On the contrary its charm is a consequence of this and is inseparably linked with the fact that the immature social conditions which gave rise, and which alone could give rise, to this art cannot recur.

Karl Marx, "Introduction" to *Economic Manuscripts of 1857-58*

Karl Marx, *A Contribution to the Critique of Political Economy*, Moscow, 1970, pp. 215-17

General Problems of Art

Ideological Content and Realism

1

Engels to Minna Kautsky

London, November 26, 1885

I have now also read *Die Alten und die Neuen* [*The Old Ones and the New*],[a] for which I sincerely thank you. The life of the salt-mine workers is described with as masterly a pen as were the portraits of the peasants in *Stefan*.[18] The descriptions of the life of Vienna society are for the most part likewise very fine. Vienna is indeed the only German city which has a society; Berlin possesses merely "certain circles", and still more uncertain ones, that is why its soil produces only novels about men of letters, officials or actors. You are in a better position to judge whether the plot in this part of your work develops sometimes too rapidly. Many things that may give us this impression, perhaps look quite natural in Vienna considering the city's peculiar international character and its intermixture with Southern and East-European elements. In both spheres the characters exhibit the sharp individualisation so customary in your work. Each of them is a type but at the same time also a definite individual, a "Dieser",[b] as old Hegel would say, and that is how it should be. And now, to be impartial, I have to find fault with something, which brings me to Arnold. He is really much too worthy a man and when he is finally killed in a landslide one can reconcile this with poetic justice only by assuming that he was too

---

[a] A novel by Minna Kautsky.—*Ed.*
[b] "This one."—*Ed.*

good for this world. But it is always bad if an author adores his own hero and this is the error which to some extent you seem to me to have fallen into here. In Elsa there is still a certain individualisation, though she is also idealised, but in Arnold the personality merges still more in the principle.

The novel itself reveals the origins of this shortcoming. You obviously felt a desire to take a public stand in your book, to testify to your convictions before the entire world. This has now been done; it is a stage you have passed through and need not repeat in this form. I am by no means opposed to partisan poetry as such. Both Aeschylus, the father of tragedy, and Aristophanes, the father of comedy, were highly partisan poets, Dante and Cervantes were so no less, and the best thing that can be said about Schiller's *Kabale und Liebe* is that it represents the first German political problem drama. The modern Russians and Norwegians, who produce excellent novels, all write with a purpose. I think however that the purpose must become manifest from the situation and the action themselves without being expressly pointed out and that the author does not have to serve the reader on a platter the future historical resolution of the social conflicts which he describes. To this must be added that under our conditions novels are mostly addressed to readers from bourgeois circles, i.e., circles which are not directly ours. Thus the socialist problem novel in my opinion fully carries out its mission if by a faithful portrayal of the real conditions it dispels the dominant conventional illusions concerning them, shakes the optimism of the bourgeois world, and inevitably instils doubt as to the eternal validity of that which exists, without itself offering a direct solution of the problem involved, even without at times ostensibly taking sides. Here your exact knowledge and admirably fresh and lifelike presentation of both the Austrian peasants and Vienna "society" find ample material, and in *Stefan* you have demonstrated that you are capable of treating your characters with the fine irony which attests to the author's dominion over the beings he has created.

But now I must finish, or I shall bore you to tears. Everything here is as before. Karl and his wife[a] are studying physiology in Aveling's evening classes, and are also working diligently; I am likewise engrossed in work; Lenchen, Pumps and her husband are going to the theatre this evening to see a sensational play, and meanwhile old Europe is preparing to set itself in motion again—and not before time, perhaps. I simply hope that it gives me time to finish the third volume of *Capital*, then it can begin!

In cordial friendship and with sincere respect I am
Yours,
F. Engels

Marx/Engels, *Werke*, Bd. 36, 1967, S. 393-94

2

Engels to Margaret Harkness in London

[Rough copy]

[London, beginning of April 1888]

Dear Miss Harkness,

I thank you very much for sending me your *City Girl*[b] through Messrs Vizetelly. I have read it with the greatest pleasure and avidity. It is indeed, as my friend Eichhoff your translator calls it, *ein kleines Kunstwerk*[c]; to which he adds, what will be satisfactory to you, that consequently

---

[a] Karl and Louise Kautsky.—*Ed.*
[b] A novel by Margaret Harkness.—*Ed.*
[c] A small work of art.—*Ed.*

his translation must be all but literal, as any omission or attempted manipulation could only destroy part of the original's value.

What strikes me most in your tale besides its realistic truth is that it exhibits the courage of the true artist. Not only in the way you treat the Salvation Army,[19] in the teeth of supercilious respectability, which respectability will perhaps learn from your tale, for the first time, *why* the Salvation Army has such a hold on the popular masses. But chiefly in the plain unvarnished manner in which you make the old, old story, the proletarian girl seduced by a middle-class man, the pivot of the whole book. Mediocrity would have felt bound to hide the, to it, commonplace character of the plot under heaps of artificial complications and adornments, and yet would not have got rid of the fate of being found out. You felt you could afford to tell an old story, because you could make it a new one by simply telling it truly.

Your Mr. Arthur Grant is a masterpiece.

If I have anything to criticise, it would be that perhaps, after all, the tale is not quite realistic enough. Realism, to my mind, implies, besides truth of detail, the truthful reproduction of typical characters under typical circumstances. Now your characters are typical enough, as far as they go; but the circumstances which surround them and make them act, are not perhaps equally so. In the *City Girl* the working class figures as a passive mass, unable to help itself and not even showing (making) any attempt at striving to help itself. All attempts to drag it out of its torpid misery come from without, from above. Now if this was a correct description about 1800 or 1810, in the days of Saint-Simon and Robert Owen, it cannot appear so in 1887 to a man who for nearly fifty years has had the honour of sharing in most of the fights of the militant proletariat. The rebellious reaction of the working class against the oppressive medium which surrounds them, their attempts—convulsive, half conscious or conscious—at recovering their status as human beings, belong to history and must therefore lay claim to a place in the domain of realism.

I am far from finding fault with your not having written a point-blank socialist novel, a "Tendenzroman",[a] as we Germans call it, to glorify the social and political views of the authors. That is not at all what I mean. The more the opinions of the author remain hidden, the better for the work of art. The realism I allude to may crop out even in spite of the author's opinions. Let me refer to an example. Balzac whom I consider a far greater master of realism than all the Zolas *passés, présents et à venir*,[b] in *La Comédie humaine* gives us a most wonderfully realistic history of French "Society", especially of *"le monde parisien"*, describing, chronicle-fashion, almost year by year from 1816 to 1848 the progressive inroads of the rising bourgeoisie upon the society of nobles, that reconstituted itself after 1815 and that set up again, as far as it could, the standard of *la vieille politesse française*.[c] He describes how the last remnants of this, to him, model society gradually succumbed before the intrusion of the vulgar moneyed upstart, or were corrupted by him; how the grande dame whose conjugal infidelities were but a mode of asserting herself in perfect accordance with the way she had been disposed of in marriage, gave way to the bourgeoisie, who horned her husband for cash or cashmere; and around this central picture he groups a complete history of French Society from which, even in economic details (for instance the re-arrangement of real and personal property after the Revolution) I have learned more than from all the professed historians, economists and statisticians of the period together. Well, Balzac was politically a Legitimist[20]; his great work is a constant elegy on the irretrievable decay of good society, his sympathies are all with the class doomed to ex-

---

[a] Problem novel.—*Ed.*
[b] Past, present, and yet to come.—*Ed.*
[c] Old French refinement.—*Ed.*

tinction. But for all that his satire is never keener, his irony never bitterer, than when he sets in motion the very men and women with whom he sympathises most deeply—the nobles. And the only men of whom he always speaks with undisguised admiration, are his bitterest political antagonists, the republican heroes of the Cloître Saint-Méry,[21] the men, who at that time (1830-36) were indeed the representatives of the popular masses. That Balzac thus was compelled to go against his own class sympathies and political prejudices, that he *saw* the necessity of the downfall of his favourite nobles, and described them as people deserving no better fate; and that he *saw* the real men of the future where, for the time being, they alone were to be found—that I consider one of the greatest triumphs of Realism, and one of the grandest features in old Balzac.

I must own, in your defence, that nowhere in the civilised world are the working people less actively resistant, more passively submitting to fate, more *hébétés*[a] than in the East End of London. And how do I know whether you have not had very good reasons for contenting yourself, for once, with a picture of the passive side of working class life, reserving the active side for another work?

Marx and Engels, *Selected Correspondence*, Moscow, 1975, pp. 379-81

3

Nothing is more to be desired than that the people who led the movement-party,[22] whether in the secret societies or the press before the Revolution, or later in official positions, should at long last be portrayed in the uncompromising manner of Rembrandt in the full flush of life. These

---

[a] Bewildered.—*Ed.*

personalities have never previously been depicted as they really were, but only in their official guise, with buskins on their feet and halos on their heads. All verisimilitude is lost in these idealised, Raphaelite pictures.

It is true that the two present publications[23] dispense with the buskins and halos, in which the "great men" of the February Revolution have hitherto appeared. They penetrate the private lives of these people, they show them to us in their shirt-sleeves, surrounded by all their various lackeys. But, for all that, they are just as far removed from being real, faithful representations of persons and events. Of their authors, the one is an exposed long-time *mouchard*[a] of Louis-Philippe, and the other a veteran conspirator by profession whose relations with the police are similarly extremely ambiguous and whose powers of observation can be judged if only from the fact that he claims to have seen "that splendid chain of the Alps, whose silver peaks dazzle the eye" between Rheinfelden and Basel, and the "Rhenish Alps, whose distant peaks are lost on the horizon" between Kehl and Karlsruhe. From such people, especially when in addition they are writing to justify themselves, we can of course only expect a more or less exaggerated *chronique scandaleuse*[b] of the February Revolution.

> Karl Marx and Frederick Engels,
> "Review of the books:
> A. Chenu, *Les Conspirateurs*
> and L. de la Hodde, *La
> naissance de la République*"
> en Février 1848
>
> Marx and Engels, *Werke*,
> Bd. 7, 1969, S. 266

---

[a] Police-spy.—*Ed.*
[b] Tale of gossip.—*Ed.*

The Tragic and the Comic in Real History

1

The struggle against the German political present is the struggle against the past of the modern nations, and they are still troubled by reminders of that past. It is instructive for them to see the *ancien régime,* which has been through its *tragedy* with them, playing its *comedy* as a German ghost. *Tragic* indeed was the history of the *ancien régime* so long as it was the pre-existing power of the world, and freedom, on the other hand, was a personal notion, i.e., as long as this regime believed and had to believe in its own justification. As long as the *ancien régime*, as an existing world order, struggled against a world that was only coming into being, there was on its side a historical error, not a personal one. That is why its downfall was tragic.

On the other hand, the present German regime, an anachronism, a flagrant contradiction of generally recognised axioms, the nothingness of the *ancien régime* exhibited to the world, only imagines that it believes in itself and demands that the world should imagine the same thing. If it believed in its own *essence*, would it try to hide that essence under the *semblance* of an alien essence and seek refuge in hypocrisy and sophism? The modern *ancien régime* is only the *comedian* of a world order whose *true heroes* are dead. History is thorough and goes through many phases when carrying an old form to the grave. The last phase of a world-historical form is its *comedy*. The gods of Greece, already tragically wounded to death in Aeshylus' *Prometheus Bound*, had to re-die a comic death in Lucian's *Dialogues*. Why this course of history? So that humanity should part with its past *cheerfully*. This *cheerful* historical destiny is what we vindicate for the political authorities of Germany.

> Karl Marx, "Contribution to the Critique of Hegel's Philosophy of Law. Introduction"
>
> Marx and Engels, *Collected Works*, Vol. 3, Moscow, 1975, pp. 178-79

2

Hegel remarks somewhere that all facts and personages of great importance in world history occur, as it were, twice. He forgot to add: the first time as tragedy, the second as farce. Caussidière for Danton, Louis Blanc for Robespierre, the *Montagne* of 1848 to 1851 for the *Montagne* of 1793 to 1795, the Nephew for the Uncle. And the same caricature occurs in the circumstances attending the second edition of the eighteenth Brumaire!

> Karl Marx, *The Eighteenth Brumaire of Louis Bonaparte*
>
> Marx and Engels, *Selected Works*, Vol. 1, Moscow, 1973, p. 398

3

Ignorance is a demon, we fear that it will yet be the cause of many a tragedy; the greatest Greek poets rightly depicted it as tragic fate in the soul-shattering dramas of the royal houses of Mycenae and Thebes.

> Karl Marx, "The Leading Article in No. 179 of the *Kölnische Zeitung*"
>
> Marx and Engels, *Collected Works*, Vol. 1, Moscow, 1975, p. 202

4

> Was schert mich Weib, was schert mich Kind,
> Ich trage höhres Verlangen;
> Lass sie betteln gehn, wenn sie hungrig sind —
> Mein Kaiser, Mein Kaiser gefangen![a]

World history is surely the greatest of poets, it has even succeeded in parodying Heine. My Emperor,[b] my Emperor a captive! And, what is more, of the "stinking Prussians". And poor William[c] stands by and assures everybody for the hundredth time that he is really quite innocent of the whole business and that it is purely the will of God. William behaves just like that schoolboy: "Who created the world?" "Please, teacher, I did—but I won't ever do it again!"

> Engels to Marx,
> September 4, 1870
>
> Marx and Engels, *Selected Correspondence*, Moscow, 1975, pp. 232-33

5

In short, the workers' party has declared itself[24] clearly and unmistakably, which means that next time both old parties will propose an alliance with it. The Tories will not enter into consideration as long as they are led by the present asses. The Liberals must, however, be taken into account and so must be the Irish. When Parnell was ostracised over the absurd adultery business he suddenly became friendly towards the workers, and when the Irish gentlemen in Parliament see that only the workers can ensure them home rule,[25] they will do the same. Then there will

---

[a] What care I for wife, what care I for child—I have higher yearnings; if hungry they are let them go and beg—my Emperor, my Emperor a captive! (From Heinrich Heine's "Die Grenadiere".)—*Ed.*

[b] Napoleon III.—*Ed.*

[c] William I.—*Ed.*

be compromises, and the Fabians,[26] who have shone in these elections by their absence, will also push forward, but this sort of thing cannot be avoided here. However, things are going ahead, as you see, and that is what matters.

A marvellous irony of world history: *both* old parties must appeal to the workers and make concessions to them if they are to remain at the helm or to reach it, and both feel that, in doing this, they are giving their own successors a leg up into the saddle. And yet they have no choice! What is our little joke by comparison with the enormous joke which is revealed in the course of historical development!

> Engels to August Bebel,
> July 7, 1892
>
> Marx/Engels, *Werke*, Bd. 38, 1968, S. 393-94

Problems of Revolutionary Tragedy

Marx and Engels to Ferdinand Lassalle on his Drama *Franz von Sickingen*

1

Marx to Ferdinand Lassalle

London, April 19, 1859

I am now coming to *Franz von Sickingen*.[a] First of all, I must praise the composition and action, and that is more than can be said of any other modern German drama. In the second instance, leaving aside the purely critical attitude to this work, it greatly excited me on first reading and it will therefore produce this effect in a still higher degree on readers who are governed more by their feelings. And this is a second and very important aspect.

Now the other side of the medal: *First*—this is a purely formal matter—since you have written it in verse, you might have polished up your iambs with a bit more artistry. But however much *professional poets* may be shocked by such carelessness I consider it on the whole as an advantage, since our brood of epigonous poets have nothing left but formal polish. *Second*: The intended conflict is not simply tragic but is really the tragic conflict that spelled the doom, and with reason, of the revolutionary party of 1848-49. I can therefore only most heartily welcome the idea of making it the pivotal point of a modern tragedy. But then I ask myself whether the theme you took is suitable for a presentation of this conflict. Balthasar may really imagine that if Sickingen had set up the banner of opposition to imperial power and open war against the princes

---

[a] A drama by Lassalle.—*Ed.*

instead of concealing his revolt behind a knightly feud, he would have been victorious. But can we subscribe to this illusion? Sickingen (and with him Hutten, more or less) did not go under because of his cunning. He went under because it was as a *knight* and a *representative of a moribund class* that he revolted against the existing order of things or rather against the new form of it. Strip Sickingen of his individual traits and his particular culture, natural ability, etc., and what is left is—Götz von Berlichingen. Götz, that *miserable* fellow, embodies in adequate form the tragic opposition of the knights to the Emperor and princes; and that is why Goethe has rightly made him the hero.[a] In so far as Sickingen—and even Hutten to a certain extent, although with regard to him and all ideologists of a class, statements of this kind ought to be considerably modified—fights against the princes (for the conflict with the Emperor arises only because the Emperor of the knights turns into an Emperor of the princes), he is indeed only a Don Quixote, although one historically justified. The fact that he began the revolt in the guise of a knightly feud means simply that he began it in a *knightly* fashion. Had he begun it otherwise he would have had to appeal directly and from the outset to the cities and peasants, i.e., precisely to the classes whose development was tantamount to the negation of the knights.

Hence, if you did not want to reduce the collision to that presented in *Götz von Berlichingen*—and that was not your plan—then Sickingen and Hutten had to succumb because they imagined they were revolutionaries (the latter cannot be said of Götz) and, just like the *educated* Polish nobility of 1830, on the one hand, made themselves exponents of modern ideas, while, on the other, they actually represented the interests of a reactionary class. The *aristocratic* representatives of the revolution—behind whose watchwords of unity and liberty there still lurked the dream of the old empire and of club-law—should, in that case, not have absorbed all

---

[a] Marx refers to Goethe's drama *Götz von Berlichingen*.—*Ed.*

interest, as they do in your play, but the representatives of the peasants (particularly these) and of the revolutionary elements in the cities ought to have formed a quite significant active background. In that case you could to a much greater extent have allowed them to voice the most modern ideas in their most naive form, whereas now, besides *religious* freedom, civil *unity* actually remains the main idea. You would then have been automatically compelled to write more in *Shakespeare*'s manner whereas I regard as your gravest shortcoming the fact that *à la Schiller* you transform individuals into mere mouthpieces of the spirit of the time. Did you not yourself to a certain extent fall into the diplomatic error, like your Franz von Sickingen, of placing the Lutheran-knightly opposition above the plebeian Münzer opposition?

Further. the characters are lacking in character. I exclude Charles V, Balthasar and Richard of Trier. Was there ever a time of more impressive characters than the 16th century? Hutten, I think, is too much just a representative of "inspiration" and this is boring. Was he not at the same time an ingenious person of devilish wit, and have you not therefore done him a great injustice?

The extent to which even your Sickingen, who incidentally is also much too abstractly depicted, is the victim of a collision independent of all his personal calculations is seen, on the one hand, in the way he must preach to his knights friendship with the cities, etc., and, on the other, in the pleasure with which he metes out fist-law justice to the cities.

As far as details are concerned, I must here and there censure the exaggerated introspections of the individuals—something which stems from your partiality for Schiller. E.g. p. 121. As Hutten tells Marie his life story, it would be absolutely natural to let Marie say:

> "The whole gamut of feelings"

etc., up to

> "And it is heavier than the weight of years".

The preceding verses from "It is said" up to "grown old", could then *follow*, but the reflection "The maid becomes a woman in one night" (although it shows that Marie knows more than the mere abstraction of love), was quite unnecessary; but least of all should Marie begin with the reflection on her own "age". After she had said all that she related in the "one" hour, she could give her feeling general expression in the sentence on her age. Further, in the following lines I was shocked by: "I considered it my *right*" (namely happiness). Why give the lie to the naive view of the world which Marie maintains to have had hitherto by converting it into a doctrine of right? Perhaps I shall set forth my view in greater detail for you another time.

I regard the scene between Sickingen and Charles V as particularly successful, although the dialogue becomes a little too defensive on both sides; further also the scenes in Trier. Hutten's sentences on the sword are very fine.

Enough for this time.

You have won a particular adherent for your drama in my wife. Marie is the only character with whom she is not satisfied.

Salut.

Yours, K. M.

Marx/Engels, *Werke*,
Bd. 29, 1967,
S. 590-93

2

Engels to Ferdinand Lassalle

Manchester, May 18, 1859

Dear Lassalle,

You will have thought it somewhat strange that I have not written for such a long time, especially as I was to give you my opinion on your *Sickingen*. But that is the very thing which has kept me from writing for so long. With the present ubiquitous dearth of good literature I seldom have the opportunity to read a work of this kind and it is years since I read one in *such a way* as to give an exhaustive judgment, a firmly established opinion at the end. Trash is not worth the trouble. Even the few better English novels which I come across from time to time, Thackeray, for example, have never been able to capture my interest in such a way, despite their indisputable literary, and cultural and historical significance. My judgment has, however, become very dulled after such a long period of inactivity, and it required some time before I could permit myself to voice an opinion. But your *Sickingen* deserves to be treated differently from that rubbish and so I took my time. The first and second readings of your work, which is in every sense, in terms of the subject-matter and treatment, a German national drama, excited me to such an extent that I had to put it aside for some time, especially, I am ashamed to say, as my taste has so dulled in these lean times that even things of inferior value have some effect on me on *first* reading. In order to be completely impartial, completely "critical", I put *Sickingen* aside, i.e., I lent it to some acquaintances (there are a few other Germans here who are more or less educated in the literary sense). *Habent sua fata libelli*[a]—if one lends them, one seldom sees them again, and so I had to win back my *Sickingen* by force. I can tell you that my impression on the third and fourth readings was the same, and convinced that your *Sickingen* can withstand criticism I shall give you my opinion on it.

I know that it will be no great compliment to you, if I say that none of the present official poets of Germany would be capable of writing such a drama. Nevertheless, this is a fact, and a fact too characteristic of our literature to be ignored. First, to deal with the form, I was very pleasantly surprised by the clever development of the plot and the intense dramatism of the piece. You have admittedly taken

---

[a] Books have their own fate.—*Ed.*

some liberties with the versification which, however, interfere more in the reading than on the stage. I should have liked to read the stage version; the piece certainly cannot be performed in its present form. I had a young German poet (Carl Siebel) here. He is a countryman and distant relative of mine and has had quite a lot to do with the stage; he may come to Berlin as a Prussian guards reservist, in which case I shall perhaps take the liberty of giving him a few lines to convey to you. He thinks a great deal of your drama, but considers it to be entirely unsuitable for the stage on account of the long monologues, during which one actor holds the stage and the others have to go through their entire mimicry two or three times so as not to stand like supernumeraries. The last two acts demonstrate clearly enough that you will have no difficulty in making the dialogue quick and lively and as, with the exception of a few scenes (which is the case with every drama), it seems to me that the same could be done in the first three, I do not doubt that you will have taken this into account in the stage version. The *idea content* must, of course, as a result suffer, but this is unavoidable. The full fusion of the greater depth of thought, of the conscious historical content, which you not unjustly attribute to German drama, with Shakespearian liveliness and fullness of treatment will probably be attained only in the future, perhaps not even by Germans. In any case I see in this the future of drama. Your *Sickingen* is on absolutely the right track; the main characters *are* representatives of definite classes and trends and therefore of definite ideas of their time. They find their motives not in petty individual lusts, but in the historical stream which is carrying them along. But the step forward which has still to be taken is that the action itself should bring these motives more vigorously, actively and, so to speak, elementally into the foreground, while the debates (in which, by the way, I recognised with pleasure your old oratorical gift which you displayed before the assizes and at the public meeting), on the contrary, become more and more superfluous. You seem to acknowledge this ideal yourself as the goal, since you make the distinction between stage drama and literary drama; I think *Sickingen* lends itself in this sense to conversion into a stage drama, although with some difficulty (for perfection is truly not easy to achieve). The characterisation of the *dramatis personae* is linked with this. You have every right to speak out against the prevalent *bad* individualisation which amounts simply to petty wise-cracking and is an essential sign of the impoverishing literature of epigones. It seems to me, however, that an individual is not merely characterised by *what* he does, but by *how* he does it, and, in this respect, I do not think the idea content of the drama would have suffered if individual characters had been somewhat more sharply differentiated and contrasted with each other. The characterisation of the *ancients* no longer suffices nowadays, and here, I think, it would have done no harm to have taken a little more account of the significance of Shakespeare in the development of drama. But these are side issues which I only mention so that you can see that I have also paid attention to the form of your drama.

Now as far as the historical content is concerned, the two sides of the movement of that time which were of greatest interest to you—the national movement of the nobility, represented by Sickingen, and the humanistic-theoretical movement with its further development in the theological and ecclesiastical sphere, the Reformation—have been depicted by you very vividly and with justified reference to subsequent developments. What I like most here is the scene between Sickingen and the Emperor and that between the legate and the archbishop of Treves. (Here you have succeeded in drawing fine individual portraits when you present the contrast between the well-bred, politically and theoretically far-seeing legate, who has an aesthetic and classical education, and the narrow-minded German ecclesiastical prince—a portrayal which nevertheless follows directly from the *representative* nature of the two characters.) The pen picture in the Sickingen-Karl scene is also very striking. In Hutten's autobiography, whose *content* you rightly described as essential, you have certainly chosen a desperate means of working this content into the drama. Of great importance is also the talk between Balthasar and Franz in Act V, in which the former explains to his master the *really revolutionary* policy he should have followed. It is here that the really tragic manifests itself; and it seems to me that just because it is so significant it should have been emphasised somewhat more strongly already in Act III, where there are several convenient places. But I am again lapsing into minor matters.

The position of the cities and the princes of that time is also set forth on several occasions with great clarity and thus the *official* elements, so to speak, of the contemporary movement are fairly well accounted for. I have the impression however that you have not laid due stress upon the non-official, the plebeian and peasant, elements and their concomitant representatives in the field of theory. The peasant movement was in its way just as national and just as much opposed to the princes as was that of the nobility, and the colossal dimensions of the struggle in which it succumbed contrast very strongly with the readiness with which the nobility, leaving Sickingen in the lurch, resigned itself to its historical calling, that of flunkeys. Even accepting your interpretation of the drama—which, as you will have seen, is somewhat too abstract, not realistic enough for me—I think the peasant movement deserves closer attention. Although the peasant scene with Fritz Jos is characteristic and the distinct personality of this "agitator" presented very correctly, it does not however depict with sufficient force the peasant unrest—which already at that time was a swelling torrent, in contrast to the movement of the nobility. In accordance with *my* view of drama, which consists in not forgetting the realistic for the idealistic, Shakespeare for Schiller, the inclusion of the sphere of the so wonderfully variegated plebeian society of that day would have supplied, in addition, entirely new material for enlivening the drama, an invaluable background for the national movement of the nobility in the foreground, and would have set this movement in the proper light. What peculiarly expressive types were produced during this period of the dissolution of the feudal ties is illustrated by the roaming beggar kings, unemployed *lansquenets* and adventurers of every description—a Falstaffian background which in an historical drama of *this* kind would have even greater effect than it did in Shakespeare! But apart from this, it seems to me that it is precisely by relegating the peasant movement to the rear that you have been induced, I believe, to misrepresent also one aspect of the national movement of the nobility and at the same time to allow the *really* tragic element in Sickingen's fate to escape you. As I see it, the majority of the nobility directly subject at that time to the emperor had no intention of concluding an alliance with the peasantry. Their dependence on incomes obtained by oppressing the peasants did not permit this. An alliance with the cities would have been more feasible. But no such alliance was effected, or was effected only to a very limited extent. But a national revolution of the nobility could have been accomplished only by means of an alliance with the towns and the peasants, particularly the latter. Precisely herein lies, in my opinion, the whole tragedy of the thing, that this fundamental condition, the alliance with the peasants, was impossible, that the policy of the nobility had therefore to be a petty one, that at the very moment when it wanted to take the lead of the national movement, the *mass* of the nation, the peasants, protested against its leadership and it thus necessarily had to collapse. I am unable to judge to what extent your assumption that Sickingen really did have some connection with the peasants has any basis in history, and it does not really matter. Incidentally, as far as I remember, wherever Hutten in his writings addresses the peasants, he just lightly touches on this ticklish question concerning the nobility and seeks to focus the wrath of the peasants on the priests. But I do not in the least dispute your right to depict Sickingen and Hutten as having intended to emancipate the peasants.

However, this put you at once up against the tragic contradiction that both of them were placed between the nobles, who were decidedly *against* this, and the peasants. Here, I dare say, lay the tragic collision between the historically necessary postulate and the practical impossibility of putting it into effect. By ignoring this aspect you reduce the tragic conflict to smaller dimensions, namely, that Sickingen, instead of at once tackling emperor and empire, tackled only a prince (although here too your correct intuition makes you bring in the peasants) and you simply let him perish as a result of the indifference and cowardice of the nobility. But the motivation of this would have been quite different if you had previously brought out more emphatically the rumbling peasant movement and the mood of the nobility, which became undoubtedly more conservative on account of the earlier peasant conspiracies of the Bundschuh and the Arme Konrad.[27] This is of course only *one* way in which the peasant and plebeian movement could have been incorporated in the drama. At least ten other ways of doing this just as well or better are conceivable.

You see that I make very high, that is to say, the very *highest* demands on your work both from the aesthetic and historical points of view, and the fact that I must do this to be able to make an objection here and there will be for you the best proof of my approval. *Among us*, criticism, in the interests of the Party itself, has for years been of necessity as open as possible; in general, however, I and all of us are always pleased when there is new proof that our Party, in whatever area it appears, always performs with superiority. And that you have done in this case too.

Marx/Engels, *Werke*, Bd. 29, 1967,
S. 600-05

Miscellaneous Items

Language and Literature

1

(Ideas are not transformed in language in such a way that they lose their peculiarity while their social character still exists alongside them in language, in the same way that prices exist alongside goods. Ideas do not exist separately from language. Ideas which must first be translated from their mother tongue into a foreign language in order to circulate and become exchangeable, already offer more of an analogy; the analogy, however, then lies not in the language but in its foreignness.)

> Karl Marx, *Outlines of Political Economy (Rough Draft)*
>
> Karl Marx, *Grundrisse der Kritik der politischen Ökonomie*, Berlin, 1953, S. 80

2

The clumsiness of the German language in everyday usage, combined with its enormous facility in dealing with the most difficult subjects is a cause—or symptom?—of the fact that the Germans have the greatest men in most fields, but that, at the same time, the mass productions are the most terrible trash. Literature: the numerous respectable second-rank poets in England and the brilliant mediocrity which makes up almost the whole of French literature are almost completely lacking in Germany. Our second-rank poets are scarcely readable after one generation. The same is true of philosophy: beside Kant and Hegel we find Herbart, Krug, Fries and finally Schopenhauer and Hartmann. The genius of the great is complemented by an absence of ideas among the educated masses and consequently no description is less apt than that of "a *nation* of thinkers". The same is true of millions of literati. Only in matters more or less independent of language is the position different and people of the second rank, too, are of significance in Germany; this applies to natural science and in particular to music. Our historical writings are unreadable.

Frederick Engels, "Materials on the History of France and Germany"

Published according to the photocopy

Improvisation and Poetry

Has one ever heard of great improvisators being also great poets? They are the same in politics as in poetry. Revolutions are never made to order. After the terrible experience of '48 and '49, it needs something more than paper summonses from distant leaders to evoke national revolutions.

Karl Marx, "The Milan Riot"

Written in English

New York Daily Tribune, No. 3, March 8, 1853

On Literary Style

1

Proudhon's earliest efforts I no longer remember. His school work about a *Universal Language* shows how little he hesitated to attack problems for the solution of which he lacked even the rudiments of knowledge.

His first work, *What Is Property?*, is by all means his best work. It is epoch-making, if not for the newness of its content, then at least for the new and audacious way in which old things are said. In the works of the French socialists and Communists whom he knew, "property" had, of course, been not only criticised in various ways but also *"abolished"* in the utopian manner. In this book Proudhon's relation to Saint-Simon and Fourier is about the same as that of Feuerbach to Hegel. Compared with Hegel, Feuerbach is exceedingly poor. All the same he was epoch-making *after* Hegel, because he laid stress on certain points which are disagreeable to the Christian consciousness while important for the progress of criticism, and which Hegel had left in mystic semi-obscurity.

In this book of Proudhon's there still prevails, if I may be allowed the expression, a strong muscular style. And its style is in my opinion its chief merit. One sees that even where he is only reproducing old stuff, Proudhon makes independent discoveries; that what he is saying was new to him himself and ranks as new. Provocative defiance, laying hands on the economic "holy of holies", superb paradox which makes a mock of bourgeois common sense, withering criticism, bitter irony, and, betrayed here and there, a deep and genuine feeling of indignation at the infamy of what exists, revolutionary earnestness—because of all this *What Is Property?* had an electrifying effect and produced a great impression upon its first appearance. In a strictly scientific history of political economy the book would hardly be worth mentioning. But sensational works of this kind play their part in the sciences just as much as in polite literature. Take, for instance, *Malthus' book On Population*. In its first edition it was nothing but a *"sensational pamphlet"* and *plagiarism* from beginning to end into the bargain. And yet what a stimulus was produced by this *libel on the human race*!

> Karl Marx, "On Proudhon"
> Marx and Engels, *Selected Works*,
> Vol. 2, Moscow, 1973, pp. 24-25

2

As for my work,[28] I want to tell you the unvarnished truth. Three chapters have still to be written to finish the theoretical part (the first three books). Then the fourth book,[29] the historical and literary part, remains to be written. This is, relatively speaking, the easiest part for me, as all the problems are solved in the first three books; consequently the last book is, rather, repetition in historical form. I cannot, however, make up my mind to send anything off before I have the whole thing in front of me. Whatever shortcomings they may have, my works have the advantage that they are an artistic whole, and this is attained only by my method of not having them printed before they are in front of me *in their entirety*. It is impossible using the Jacob Grimm method,[30] which in general is better suited to works not dialectically articulated.

> Marx to Engels,
> July 31, 1865
> Marx/Engels, *Werke*,
> Bd. 31, 1965, S. 132

3

The ass who wrote the article in the *Vossische*[31] (and *four* different people have sent me a copy) seems to have stirred up a good deal of sorrow about the sorrowful Marx in our good old Germany. When I'm in the mood for some fun perhaps I'll give him a good kick. If these oxen ever read the correspondence between the Moor and myself, they would be struck dumb. Heine's poetry is child's play compared to our impudent, laughing prose. The Moor might have raged, but mope—*jamais*! I rolled with laughter when I re-read the old things. This correspondence, remarkable also from the historical point of view, is going to fall into the proper hands as far as it depends on me. Unfortunately I have Marx's letters only from 1849 but these at least are complete.

Engels to Eduard Bernstein,
June 12-13, 1883

Marx/Engels, *Werke*, Bd. 36, 1967, S. 36

4

The purist who inveighs against our style and punctuation can't know either German or English, or he wouldn't find anglicisms where none exist. As for that German so beloved by him, which was crammed into our heads at school, with its wretched periods and verbs dangling at the tail end of the sentence, separated from the subject by ten miles of interpolations—I took thirty years to *un*learn it. This bureaucratic schoolmaster's German for which Lessing does not exist, is disappearing even in Germany today. What would the honourable gentleman say if he heard the members of the *Reichstag* speak; they have abandoned these awesome constructions, to avoid the terrible confusion they always caused, and speak like the Jews: "als der Bismarck ist gekommen vor die Zwangswahl, hat er lieber geküsst den Papst auf den Hintern als die Revolution auf den Mund" ["If Bismarck were forced to make a choice, he'd rather kiss the Pope's behind than the Revolution's mouth"], etc. Laskerchen is responsible for this progress, and it's the only good for which he is responsible. If Herr Purist comes to Germany with his schoolmaster's German, he will be told that he speaks "American". "You know how narrow-minded the learned German Philistine is", he seems so particularly in America. German sentence structure and punctuation, as taught in school forty or fifty years ago, are only worth being thrown in the rubbish-bin. This is what Germans are doing today.

> Engels to Friedrich Sorge,
> April 29, 1886
>
> Marx/Engels, *Werke*, Bd. 36, 1967, S. 477

On Literary Polemics

1

And that is supposed to "have a cheering effect"! It has, in fact, worked out that way, but not because Herr Brentano wished it. Marx and, later, his daughter and now I have all tried to give a lighter side to this polemic.[32] But whatever success we have had in this, great or small, has been at the expense of Herr Brentano. His articles are anything but "cheering". What is diverting in them is solely due to the blows Marx directs at the seamy side of his "still obscure personality", which the victim would now belatedly like to slide over as "pieces of insolence from his scurrilous polemic". Junkers, the gentlemen of the cloth, lawyers, and other able opponents of the sharp polemics of Voltaire, Beaumarchais and Paul-Louis Courier labelled them "pieces of insolence from scurrilous polemising", but this has not prevented these "pieces of insolence" from being regarded today as models and masterpieces. And we have derived too much pleasure from these and other models of "scurrilous polemic" for a hundred Brentanos to succeed in drawing us into the sphere of German university polemic, where nothing but the impotent malice of mere envy and the most desolate boredom prevail.

> Frederick Engels, *Concerning Brentano's Polemic Against Marx over Alleged Misquotation*
>
> Marx/Engels, *Werke*, Bd. 22, 1963, S. 115-16

2

But, says Herr Tkachov, I have used "every possible kind of abuse" against him. Now a certain kind of abuse, so-called invective, is one of the most effective forms of rhetoric which, when required, is employed by all great orators and of which William Cobbett, the most powerful English political writer, possessed such mastery that he is still admired and serves as a model that has yet to be matched.

> Engels, *Flüchtlingsliteratur*. IV
>
> Marx/Engels, *Werke*, Bd. 18, 1969, S. 549

3

You must read O'Connor's article in the last issue of the *Star*[33] directed against the six radical newspapers: it is a masterpiece of abuse, often better than Cobbett and reminiscent of Shakespeare.

> Engels to Marx,
> October 25-26, 1847
>
> Marx/Engels, *Werke*, Bd. 27, 1965, S. 99

4

Now the newspaper[34] can really encourage and cheer our people in Germany, which some of them very much need—the so-called leaders, at least. I have again received a number of letters full of lamentations, which I have answered in the appropriate way. Viereck was also very low-spirited initially, but a couple of days in the free London air have been sufficient to give him back his buoyancy. The newspaper must carry this free air to Germany, an end which will be served, primarily, by treating the enemy with contempt and derision. When people again learn simply to laugh at Bismarck and Co., much will have been gained. One must not forget, however, that this is the first time something like this has happened, at least to the great majority of people, and that, in particular, a great many agitators and editors have been rudely shaken from their rather comfortable positions. That is why encouragement is needed just as much as the constant reminder that Bismarck and Co. are still the same asses, the same *canailles*, the same pathetic manikins, powerless against the march of history, that they were before the attempted assasinations.[35] Therefore every joke at the expense of this rabble is valuable.

> Engels to Eduard Bernstein,
> March 12, 1881
>
> Marx/Engels, *Werke*, Bd. 35, 1967, S. 170-71

5

So you, too, are finally coming round to the view that one can, after all, deal with the "wise men" quite well. I sent for a few copies of *Neue Welt*[36] to get to know the gentlemen *chez eux*.[a] So far, I've only read the editorial post column. German schoolboy impudence, which assumes a very tame readership.

For the rest, don't allow yourself to be drawn by pinpricks, that is the first rule in battle. Remember that:

> There's nothing nicer in this world[37]
> Than all one's foes to answer back,
> Than about all those clumsy blokes
> One's feeble little jokes to crack.

Engels to Eduard Berstein,
June 29, 1884

Marx/Engels, *Werke*, Bd. 36, 1967,
S. 172

On Translation

1

Memorandum on translation of the first chapter
Ad generalia:
1. P[ieper] is evidently more used to free composition in English than to translation. He must, therefore, be all the more wary of resorting to that worst of all known aids, the *dictionary*, when at a loss for a word: in 99 cases out of 100 this will unevitably provide him with the least suitable word and invariably cause a fatal confusion of synonyms. Examples of this follow.
2. P[ieper] should study elementary English grammar. He makes many mistakes in it—particularly in the use of the article. There are also orthographical mistakes.

---

[a] On their own ground.—*Ed.*

3. Above all else, P[ieper] must beware of lapsing into the petty-bourgeois literary style of Cockney, of which there are several very disturbing examples.

4. P[ieper] uses too many words of French origin which, it is true, are sometimes convenient, inasmuch as their more abstract and less precise meaning is often a way of getting out of a dilemma. However, this waters down the best figures of speech and often makes them quite incomprehensible to the English. In practically all cases where live, concrete images occur in the original there is a no less concrete, live expression of *Saxon* origin, which will immediately clarify matters for the English reader.

5. When difficult passages occur, it would always be better to leave a space to be filled in than to write down, on the pretext of literal translation, things which P[ieper] himself well knows are completely meaningless.

6. The main objection to be levelled against the translation, summarising points 1-5, is the exceedingly flippant way in which it has been executed. There are enough passages to demonstrate that, when he really tries, P[ieper] is capable of achieving something, but his carelessness, first, makes work for him and, secondly, doubles my work. Occasional passages are quite excellent or could be, had he made a little more effort.

Engels to Marx,
September 23, 1852

Marx/Engels, *Werke*, Bd. 28, 1963, S. 138

2

Yesterday I read the chapter on factory legislation in the French translation of [*Capital*].[38] With all due respect for the skill with which it has been translated into elegant French, I am sorry for that beautiful chapter. All its power and life's blood have been sent to the devil. The mediocre writer castrates the language in order to express himself with a certain degree of elegance. It is becoming increasingly difficult to think in this modern constrained French. Already the sentence inversions, necessitated almost everywhere by pedantic formal logic, deprive the presentation of all its force and liveliness. I think it would be a grave mistake to use the French version as a basis for an English translation. The strength of expression in the original need not be diminished in English; whatever is inevitably lost from the truly dialectical passages will be balanced by the greater power and tenseness of the English language in many other passages.

Herr Kokosky, by the way, excuses his miserable translation by declaring that I write in the very difficult "Liebknechtian-*Marxian* style". What a compliment!

> Engels to Marx,
> November 29, 1873
>
> Marx/Engels, *Werke*, Bd. 33, 1966, S. 94

3

The critique of H. George, which Marx sent you, is so clearly a masterpiece in content, so stylistically monolithic, that it would be a shame to weaken it by adding the desultory English notes written in the margin of Marx's copy. These can always be used later. This letter to you is written, as was Marx's custom, with an eye to future publication *in toto*. You would therefore commit no indiscretion of you let it be printed. If it is to be published in English, I'll do the translation for you since, as the translation of the *Manifesto*[39] has shown once again, there seems to be no one over there who can convey *our* German into literary, grammatical English. For that one must have literary experience in both languages, and not only the experience of writing for the daily papers.

To translate the *Manifesto* is fearfully hard. The Russian translations are by far the best I've seen.

Engels to Friedrich Sorge,
June 29, 1883

Marx/Engels, *Werke*, Bd. 36, 1967, S. 45

4

Dear Bernstein,
One thing you can be sure of: I wish for no better translator than you.[40] In the first folio, in endeavouring to reproduce the sense correctly and accurately, you somewhat neglected the syntax—*voilà tout*. In addition, I wanted to render Marx's peculiar style, to which you are unaccustomed; hence the numerous alterations.

If, having once conveyed the sense in German, you read through the manuscript once more with a view to simplifying the syntax, and at the same time remember to avoid wherever possible clumsy, schoolmasterish syntax, which continually places the verb right at the end of the subordinate clause (and which we have all had crammed into us), then you will encounter little difficulty and will yourself put everything in order.

Engels to Eduard Bernstein,
February 5, 1884

Marx/Engels, *Werke*, Bd. 36, 1967, S. 97

5

To translate such a book,[a] a fair knowledge of literary German is not enough. Marx uses freely expressions of everyday life and idioms of provincial dialects; he coins new

---

[a] Karl Marx, *Capital.—Ed.*

words, he takes his illustrations from every branch of science, his allusions from the literatures of a dozen languages; to understand him, a man must be a master of German indeed, spoken as well as written, and must know something of German life too.

To use an illustration. When some Oxford Undergraduates rowed in a four-oar boat across the straits of Dover, it was stated in the Press reports that one of them "caught a crab". The London correspondent of the *Cologne Gazette* took this literally, and faithfully reported to his paper, that "a crab had got entangled in the oar of one of the rowers". If a man who has been living for years in the midst of London is capable of such a ludicrous blunder as soon as he comes across the technical terms of an art unknown to him, what must we expect from a man who with a passable knowledge of mere book-German, undertakes to translate the most untranslatable of German prose writers? And indeed we shall see that Mr. Broadhouse is an excellent hand at "catching crabs".

But there is something more required. Marx is one of the most vigorous and concise writers of the age. To render him adequately, a man must be a master, not only of German, but of English too. Mr. Broadhouse, however, though evidently a man of respectable journalistic accomplishments, commands but that limited range of English used by and for conventional literary respectability. Here he moves with ease; but this sort of English is not a language into which *Das Kapital* can ever be translated. Powerful German requires powerful English to render it; the best resources of the language have to be drawn upon; new-coined German terms require the coining of corresponding new terms in English. But as soon as Mr. Broadhouse is faced by such a difficulty, not only his resources fail him, but also his courage. The slightest extension of his limited stock-in-trade, the slightest innovation upon the conventional English of everyday literature frightens him, and rather than risk such a heresy, he renders the difficult German word by a more or less indefinite term which does not grate upon his ear but obscures the meaning of the author; or, worse still, he translates it, as it recurs, by a whole series of different terms, forgetting that a technical term has to be rendered always by one and the same equivalent.

Frederick Engels, "How Not To Translate Marx"

Written in English

The Commonweal, No. 10, November 1885

6

Anyhow you have done a marvellous thing in the *Senator*,[41] about the most difficult thing on earth to be put into English. Not only that you have done it with all the proper impropriety, but even with a near approach to the lightness of the original. And that while both subject and metre are rebellious to translation, the senator of Empire No. 1[42] being an unknown quantity over here. If you were a boy I should say: *Molodetz*, but I am not versed enough in Russian to know whether that epithet (equal about to the English: you're a brick!) can be feminised into: *Molodtza!*[a]

Engels to Laura Lafargue, November 16, 1889

Frederick Engels, Paul and Laura Lafargue, *Correspondence*, Vol. 2, Moscow, 1960, p. 342

---

[a] This word is in Russian in the original.—*Ed.*

7

My dear Laura,

Prosit Neujahr avant tout![a] *Et puis après,*[b] as I cannot bear the idea you should translate Walther von der Vogelweide from a modernisation, I send you a copy of the original.[43] You are quite right, the metre and rhyme of the original ought to be preserved in every translation of poetry, or else go the whole hog like the French and turn it at once into prose.

> Engels to Laura Lafargue,
> January 8, 1890
>
> Frederick Engels, Paul and
> Laura Lafargue, *Correspondence*,
> Vol. 2, Moscow, 1960, p. 355

---

[a] First of all, a happy New Year to you!—*Ed.*
[b] And then.—*Ed.*

Art in Class Society

The Origin of Art

Historical Development of the Artistic Sense

1

We see how the history of *industry* and the established *objective* existence of industry are the *open* book of *man's essential powers*, the perceptibly existing human *psychology*. Hitherto this was not conceived in its connection with man's *essential being*, but only in an external relation of utility, because, moving in the realm of estrangement, people could only think of man's general mode of being—religion or history in its abstract-general character as politics, art, literature, etc.—as the reality of man's essential powers and *man's species-activity*. We have before us the *objectified essential powers* of man in the form of *sensuous, alien, useful objects*, in the form of estrangement, displayed in *ordinary material industry* (which can be conceived either as a part of that general movement, or that movement can be conceived as a *particular* part of industry, since all human activity hitherto has been labour—that is, industry—activity estranged from itself).

A *psychology* for which this book, the part of history existing in the most perceptible and accessible form, remains a closed book, cannot become a genuine, comprehensive and *real* science.

Karl Marx, *Economic and Philosophic Manuscripts of 1844*

Marx and Engels, *Collected Works*, Vol. 3, Moscow, 1975, pp. 302-03

2

The extent to which the solution of theoretical riddles is the task of practice and effected through practice, the extent to which true practice is the condition of a real and positive theory, is shown, for example, in *fetishism*. The sensuous consciousness of the fetish-worshipper is different from that of the Greek, because his sensuous existence is different. The abstract enmity between sense and spirit is necessary so long as the human feeling for nature, the human sense of nature, and therefore also the *natural* sense of *man*, are not yet produced by man's own labour.

> Karl Marx, *Economic and Philosophic Manuscripts of 1844*
>
> Marx and Engels, *Collected Works*, Vol. 3, Moscow, 1975, p. 312

3

We have seen that man does not lose himself in his object only when the object becomes for him a *human* object or objective man. This is possible only when the object becomes for him a *social* object, he himself for himself a social being, just as society becomes a being for him in this object.

On the one hand, therefore, it is only when the objective world becomes everywhere for man in society the world of man's essential powers—human reality, and for that reason the reality of his *own* essential powers—that all *objects* become for him the *objectification* of himself, become objects which confirm and realise his individuality, become *his* objects: that is, *man himself* becomes the object. The *manner* in which they become *his* depends on the *nature of the objects* and on the nature of the *essential power* corresponding to *it*; for it is precisely the *determinate nature* of this relationship which shapes the particular, *real* mode of affirmation. To the *eye* an object comes to be other than it is to the *ear*, and the object of the eye *is* another object than the object of the *ear*. The specific character of each essential power is precisely its *specific essence*, and therefore also the specific mode of its objectification, of its *objectively actual*, living *being*. Thus man is affirmed in the objective world not only in the act of thinking, but with *all* his senses.

On the other hand, let us look at this in its subjective aspect. Just as only music awakens in man the sense of music, and just as the most beautiful music has *no* sense for the unmusical ear—is [no] object for it, because my object can only be the confirmation of one of my essential powers—it can therefore only exist for me insofar as my essential power exists for itself as a subjective capacity, because the meaning of an object for me goes only so far as *my* sense goes (has only a meaning for a sense corresponding to that object)—for this reason the *senses* of the social man *differ* from those of the non-social man. Only through the objectively unfolded richness of man's essential being is the richness of subjective *human* sensibility (a musical ear, an eye for beauty of form—in short, *senses* capable of human gratification, senses affirming themselves as essential powers of *man*) either cultivated or brought into being. For not only the five senses but also the so-called mental senses, the practical senses (will, love, etc.), in a word, *human* sense, the human nature of the senses, comes to be by virtue of *its* object, by virtue of *humanised* nature. The *forming* of the five senses is a labour of the entire history of the world down to the present. The *sense* caught up in crude practical need has only a *restricted* sense. For the starving man, it is not the human form of food that exists, but only its abstract existence as food. It could just as well be there in its crudest form, and it would be impossible to say wherein this feeding activity differs from that of *animals*. The care-burdened, poverty-stricken man has no *sense* for the finest play; the dealer in minerals sees only the commercial value but not the beauty and the specific character of the mineral: he has no mineralogical sense. Thus, the objectification of the human essence, both in its theoretical and practical aspects, is required to make man's *sense human*, as well as to create the *human sense* corresponding to the entire wealth of human and natural substance.

Karl Marx, *Economic and Philosophic Manuscripts of 1844*

Marx and Engels, *Collected Works*, Vol. 3, Moscow, 1975, pp. 301-02

The Role of Labour in the Origin of Art

The first operations for which our ancestors gradually learned to adapt their hands during the many thousands of years of transition from ape to man could have been only very simple ones. The lowest savages, even those in whom regression to a more animal-like condition with a simultaneous physical degeneration can be assumed, are nevertheless far superior to these transitional beings. Before the first flint could be fashioned into a knife by human hands, a period of time probably elapsed in comparison with which the historical period known to us appears insignificant. But the decisive step had been taken, *the hand had become free* and could henceforth attain ever greater dexterity; the greater flexibility thus acquired was inherited and increased from generation to generation.

Thus the hand is not only the organ of labour, *it is also the product of labour*. Labour, adaptation to ever new operations, the inheritance of muscles, ligaments, and, over longer periods of time, bones that had undergone special development and the ever-renewed employment of this inherited finesse in new, more and more complicated operations, have given the human hand the high degree of perfection required to conjure into being the pictures of a Raphael, the statues of a Thorvaldsen, the music of a Paganini.

> Frederick Engels, *Dialectics of Nature*, Moscow, 1974, pp. 171-72

Artistic Creation and Aesthetic Perception

Production not only provides the material to satisfy a need, but it also provides the need for the material. When consumption emerges from its original primitive crudeness and immediacy—and its remaining in that state would be due to the fact that production was still primitively crude—then it is itself as a desire brought about by the object. The need felt for the object is induced by the perception of the object. An *objet d'art* creates a public that has artistic taste and is able to enjoy beauty—and the same can be said of any other product. Production accordingly produces not only an object for the subject, but also a subject for the object.

> Karl Marx, "Introduction" to *Economic Manuscripts of 1857-58*
>
> Karl Marx, *A Contribution to the Critique of Political Economy*, Moscow, 1970, p. 197

Social Division of Labour

Division of Labour and Social Consciousness

Language is as old as consciousness, language *is* practical, real consciousness that exists for other men as well, and only therefore does it also exist for me; language, like consciousness, only arises from the need, the necessity, of intercourse with other men.* Where there exists a relationship, it exists for me: the animal does not *"relate"* itself to anything, it does not *"relate"* itself at all. For the animal its relation to others does not exist as a relation. Consciousness is, therefore, from the very beginning a social product, and remains so as long as men exist at all. Consciousness is at first, of course, merely consciousness concerning the *immediate* sensuous environment and consciousness of the limited connection with other persons and things outside the individual who is growing self-conscious. At the same time it is consciousness of nature, which first confronts men as a completely alien, all-powerful and unassailable force, with which men's relations are purely animal and by which they are overawed like beasts; it is thus a purely animal consciousness of nature (natural religion) precisely because nature is as yet hardly altered by history—on the other hand, it is man's consciousness of the

---

* [The following words are crossed out in the manuscript:] My relation to my surroundings is my consciousness.

necessity of associating with the individuals around him, the beginning of the consciousness that he is living in society at all. This beginning is as animal as social life itself at this stage. It is mere herd-consciousness, and at this point man is distinguished from sheep only by the fact that with him consciousness takes the place of instinct or that his instinct is a conscious one.* This sheep-like or tribal consciousness receives its further development and extension through increased productivity, the increase of needs, and, what is fundamental to both of these, the increase of population. With these there develops the division of labour, which was originally nothing but the division of labour in the sexual act, then the division of labour which develops spontaneously or "naturally" by virtue of natural predisposition (e.g., physical strength), needs, accidents, etc., etc.** Division of labour only becomes truly such from the moment when a division of material and mental labour appears.*** From this moment onwards consciousness *can* really flatter itself that it is something other than consciousness of existing practice, that it *really* represents something without representing something real; from now on consciousness is in a position to emancipate itself from the world and to proceed to the formation of "pure" theory, theology, philosophy, morality, etc. But even if this theory, theology, philosophy, morality, etc., come into contradiction with the existing relations, this can only occur because existing social

---

* [Marginal note by Marx:] We see here immediately: this natural religion or this particular attitude to nature is determined by the form of society and vice versa. Here, as everywhere, the identity of nature and man also appears in such a way that the restricted attitude of men to nature determines their restricted relation to one another, and their restricted attitude to one another determines men's restricted relation to nature.

** [Marginal note by Marx, which is crossed out in the manuscript:] Men's consciousness develops in the course of actual historical development.

*** [Marginal note by Marx:] The first form of ideologists, *priests*, is coincident.

relations have come into contradiction with existing productive forces; moreover, in a particular national sphere of relations this can also occur through the contradiction, arising not within the national orbit, but between this national consciousness and the practice of other nations,* i.e., between the national and the general consciousness of a nation (as is happening now in Germany).

> Karl Marx and Frederick Engels,
> *The German Ideology*
>
> Marx and Engels, *Collected Works*,
> Vol. 5, Moscow, 1976, pp. 44-45

**Estrangement of Labour
and the Condition
of the Working People
in Capitalist Society**

He [the economist] turns the worker into an insensible being lacking all needs, just as he changes his activity into a pure abstraction from all activity. To him, therefore, every *luxury* of the worker seems to be reprehensible, and everything that goes beyond the most abstract need—be it in the realm of passive enjoyment, or a manifestation of activity—seems to him a luxury. Political economy, this science of *wealth,* is therefore simultaneously the science of renunciation, of want, of *saving*—and it actually reaches the point where it *spares* man the *need* of either fresh *air* or physical *exercise*. This science of marvellous industry is simultaneously the science of *asceticism*, and its true ideal is the *ascetic* but *extortionate* miser and the *ascètic* but *productive* slave. Its moral ideal is the *worker* who takes part of his wages to the savings-bank, and it has even found ready-made a servile *art* which embodies this pet

---

* [Marginal note by Marx:] *Religions*. The Germans and *ideology* as such.

idea: it has been presented, bathed in sentimentality, on the stage. Thus political economy—despite its worldly and voluptuous appearance—is a true moral science, the most moral of all the sciences. Self-renunciation, the renunciation of life and of all human needs, is its principal thesis. The less you eat, drink and buy books; the less you go to the theatre, the dance hall, the public house; the less you think, love, theorise, sing, paint, fence, etc., the more you *save*—the *greater* becomes your treasure which neither moths nor rust will devour—your *capital*.

Karl Marx, *Economic and Philosophic Manuscripts of 1844*

Marx and Engels, *Collected Works*, Vol. 3 Moscow, 1975, pp. 308-09

Money and World Culture

The Distorting Power of Money

If man's *feelings,* passions, etc. are not merely anthropological phenomena in the [narrower][a] sense, but truly *ontological* affirmations of being (of nature), and if they are only really affirmed because their *object* exists for them as a *sensual* object, then it is clear that:

(1) They have by no means merely one mode of affirmation, but rather that the distinct character of their existence, of their life, is constituted by the distinct mode of their affirmation. In what manner the object exists for them, is the characteristic mode of their *gratification.*

(2) Whenever the sensuous affirmation is the direct annulment of the object in its independent form (as in eating, drinking, working up of the object, etc.), this is the affirmation of the object.

(3) Insofar as man, and hence also his feeling, etc., is *human,* the affirmation of the object by another is likewise his own gratification.

(4) Only through developed industry—i.e., through the medium of private property—does the ontological essence of human passion come into being, in its totality as well as in its humanity; the science of man is therefore itself a product of man's own practical activity.

(5) The meaning of private property—apart from its estrangement—is the *existence of essential objects* for man, both as objects of enjoyment and as objects of activity.

---

[a] This word cannot be clearly deciphered in the manuscript.—*Ed.*

By possessing the *property* of buying everything, by possessing the property of appropriating all objects, *money* is thus the *object* of eminent possession. The universality of its *property* is the omnipotence of its being. It is therefore regarded as omnipotent.... Money is the *procurer* between man's need and the object, between his life and his means of life. But *that which* mediates *my* life for me, also *mediates* the existence of other people for me. For me it is the *other* person.

> "What, man! confound it, hands and feet
> And head and backside, all are yours!
> And what we take while life is sweet,
> Is that to be declared not ours?
> > Six stallions, say, I can afford,
> > Is not their strength my property?
> > I tear along, a sporting lord,
> > As if their legs belonged to me."
> Goethe: *Faust* (Mephistopheles)[a]

Shakespeare in *Timon of Athens*:

> "Gold? Yellow, glittering, precious gold? No, Gods,
> I am no idle votarist!...
> Thus much of this will make black white, foul fair,
> Wrong right, base noble, old young, coward valiant.
> ... Why, this
> Will lug your priests and servants from your sides,
> Pluck stout men's pillows from below their heads:
> This yellow slave
> Will knit and break religions, bless the accursed;
> Make the hoar leprosy adored, place thieves
> And give them title, knee and approbation
> With senators on the bench: This is it
> That makes the wappen'd widow wed again;
> She, whom the spital-house and ulcerous sores
> Would cast the gorge at, this embalms and spices
> To the April day again. Come, damned earth,

---

[a] Goethe, *Faust*, Part 1, Faust's Study; (the English translation is taken from Goethe's *Faust*, Part 1, translated by Philip Wayne, Penguin, 1949, p. 91).—*Ed.*

Thou common whore of mankind, that put'st odds
Among the rout of nations."

And also later:

"O thou sweet king-killer, and dear divorce
'Twixt natural son and sire! thou bright defiler
Of Hymen's purest bed! thou valiant Mars!
Thou ever young, fresh, loved and delicate wooer,
Whose blush doth thaw the consecrated snow
That lies on Dian's lap! Thou *visible God*!
That solder'st *close impossibilities*,
And makest them kiss! That speak'st with every tongue,
To every purpose! O thou touch of hearts!
Think, thy slave man rebels, and by thy virtue
Set them into confounding odds, that beasts
May have the world in empire!"[a]

Shakespeare excellently depicts the real nature of *money*. To understand him, let us begin, first of all, by expounding the passage from Goethe.

That which is for me through the medium of *money*—that for which I can pay (i.e., which money can buy)—that am *I myself*, the possessor of the money. The extent of the power of money is the extent of my power. Money's properties are my—the possessor's—properties and essential powers. Thus, what I *am* and *am capable of* is by no means determined by my individuality. I *am ugly*, but I can buy for myself the *most beautiful* of women. Therefore I am not *ugly*, for the effect of *ugliness*—its deterrent power—is nullified by money. I, according to my individual characteristics, am *lame*, but money furnishes me with twenty-four feet. Therefore I am not lame. I am bad, dishonest, unscrupulous, stupid; but money is honoured, and hence its possessor. Money is the supreme good, therefore its possessor is good. Money, besides, saves me the trouble of being dishonest: I am therefore presumed honest. I am *brainless*, but money is the *real brain* of all things and how then

---

[a] Shakespeare, *Timon of Athens*, Act IV, Scene 3. (Marx quotes the Schlegel-Tieck translation.)—*Ed.*

should its possessor be brainless? Besides, he can buy clever people for himself, and is he who has[a] power over the clever not more clever than the clever? Do not I, who thanks to money am capable of *all* that the human heart longs for, possess all human capacities? Does not my money, therefore, transform all my incapacities into their contrary?

If *money* is the bond binding me to *human* life, binding society to me, connecting me with nature and man, is not money the bond of all *bonds*? Can it not dissolve and bind all ties? Is it not, therefore, also the universal *agent of separation*? It is the *coin* that really *separates* as well as the real *binding agent*—the [...][b] *chemical* power of society.

Shakespeare stresses especially two properties of money:

(1) It is the visible divinity—the transformation of all human and natural properties into their contraries, the universal confounding and distorting of things: impossibilities are soldered together by it.

(2) It is the common whore, the common procurer of people and nations.

The distorting and confounding of all human and natural qualities, the fraternisation of impossibilities—the *divine* power of money—lies in its *character* as men's estranged, alienating and self-disposing *species-nature*. Money is the alienated *ability of mankind.*

That which I am unable to do as a *man*, and of which therefore all my individual essential powers are incapable, I am able to do by means of *money*. Money thus turns each of these powers into something which in itself it is not— turns it, that is, into its *contrary.*

If I long for a particular dish or want to take the mailcoach because I am not strong enough to go by foot, money fetches me the dish and the mail-coach: that is, it converts my wishes from something in the realm of imagination,

---

[a] In the manuscript: "is".—*Ed.*

[b] In the manuscript one word cannot be deciphered.—*Ed.*

translates them from their meditated, imagined or desired existence into their *sensuous, actual* existence—from imagination to life, from imagined being into real being. In effecting this mediation, [money] is the *truly creative* power.

No doubt the *demand* also exists for him who has no money, but his demand is a mere thing of the imagination without effect or existence for me, for a third party, for the [others], and which therefore remains even for me *unreal* and *objectless*. The difference between effective demand based on money and ineffective demand based on my need, my passion, my wish, etc., is the difference between *being* and *thinking*, between the idea which merely *exists* within me and the idea which exists as a *real object* outside of me.

If I have no money for travel, I have no *need*—that is, no real and realisable need—to travel. If I have the *vocation* for study but no money for it, I have *no* vocation for study—that is, no *effective*, no *true* vocation. On the other hand, if I have really *no* vocation for study but have the will *and* the money for it, I have an *effective* vocation for it. *Money* as the external, universal *medium* and *faculty* (not springing from man as man or from human society as society) for turning an *image into reality* and *reality into a mere image*, transforms the *real essential powers of man and nature* into what are merely abstract notions and therefore *imperfections* and tormenting chimeras, just as it transforms *real imperfections and chimeras*—essential powers which are really impotent, which exist only in the imagination of the individual—into *real essential powers* and *faculties*. In the light of this characteristic alone, money is thus the general distorting of *individualities* which turns them into their opposite and confers contradictory attributes upon their attributes.

Money, then, appears as this *distorting* power both against the individual and against the bonds of society, etc., which claim to be *entities* in themselves. It transforms fidelity into infidelity, love into hate, hate into love, virtue into vice,

vice into virtue, servant into master, master into servant, idiocy into intelligence, and intelligence into idiocy.

Since money, as the existing and active concept of value, confounds and confuses all things, it is the general *confounding* and *confusing* of all things—the world upside-down—the confounding and confusing of all natural and human qualities.

He who can buy bravery is brave, though he be a coward. As money is not exchanged for any one specific quality, for any one specific thing, or for any particular human essential power, but for the entire objective world of man and nature, from the standpoint of its possessor it therefore serves to exchange every quality for every other, even contradictory, quality and object: it is the fraternisation of impossibilities. It makes contradictions embrace.

Assume *man* to be *man* and his relationship to the world to be a human one: then you can exchange love only for love, trust for trust, etc. If you want to enjoy art, you must be an artistically cultivated person; if you want to exercise influence over other people, you must be a person with a stimulating and encouraging effect on other people. Every one of your relations to man and to nature must be a *specific expression*, corresponding to the object of your will, of your *real individual* life. If you love without evoking love in return—that is, if your loving as loving does not produce reciprocal love; if through a *living expression* of yourself as a loving person you do not make yourself a *beloved one*, then your love is impotent—a misfortune.

Karl Marx, *Economic and Philosophic Manuscripts of 1844*

Marx and Engels, *Collected Works*, Vol. 3, Moscow, 1975, pp. 322-26

Capitalism and Spiritual Production

Relation of Art and Poetry to the Capitalist Mode of Production

With Storch himself the *theory of civilisation* does not get beyond trivial phrases, although some ingenious observations slip in here and there—for example, that the material division of labour is the pre-condition for the division of intellectual labour. How much it *was* inevitable that Storch could not get beyond trivial phrases, how little he had even *formulated* for himself the task, let alone its solution, is apparent from one *single* circumstance. In order to examine the connection between spiritual production and material production it is above all necessary to grasp the latter itself not as a general category but in *definite historical* form. Thus for example different kinds of spiritual production correspond to the capitalist mode of production and to the mode of production of the Middle Ages. If material production itself is not conceived in its *specific historical* form, it is impossible to understand what is specific in the spiritual production corresponding to it and the reciprocal influence of one on the other. Otherwise one cannot get beyond inanities. This because of the talk about "civilisation".

Further: from the specific form of material production arises in the first place a specific structure of society, in the second place a specific relation of men to nature. Their State and their spiritual outlook is determined by both. Therefore also the kind of their spiritual production.

Finally, by spiritual production Storch means also the professional activities of all the strata of the ruling class, who carry out social functions as a trade. The existence of these strata, like the function they perform, can only be understood from the specific historical structure of their production relations.

Because Storch does not conceive material production itself *historically*—because he conceives it as production of material goods in general, not as a definite historically developed and specific form of this production—he deprives himself of the basis on which alone can be understood partly the ideological component parts of the ruling class, partly the free spiritual production of this particular social formation. He cannot get beyond meaningless general phrases. Consequently, the relation is not so simple as he presupposes. For instance, capitalist production is hostile to certain branches of spiritual production, for example, art and poetry. If this is left out of account, it opens the way to the illusion of the French in the eighteenth century which has been so beautifully satirised by Lessing.[44] Because we are further ahead than the ancients in mechanics, etc., why shouldn't we be able to make an epic too? And the *Henriade*[45] in place of the *Iliad*!

Karl Marx, *Theories of Surplus-Value*,
Part I, Moscow, 1975, pp. 284-85

Bourgeois Taste and Its Evolution

Paul's examples of victorious German "*goût*" are mostly as old as the hills.[46] That German *gravures pour enfants* (Bilderbogen) are generally good, is simple enough. For more than 50 years they have been made chiefly at Düsseldorf, Munich, etc., and the designs are by young and often rising artists who do this work to earn a little money. 40 years ago, however, I recollect that French gravures of that sort came to Germany, a good many by Adam the horse-

and-soldier-painter, and they were immensely superior to the German ones in chic and life. If that has not been continued by French artists, they must have found no market.—As to *toys*, the German superiority is 1) cheapness, domestic industry at starvation level (described lately by Dr. Emanuel Sax, *die Hausindustrie in Thüringen*,[a] very good) and 2) in that they are invented by *peasants*; townspeople never will be fit to invent for children, least of all French townspeople who hate their own children.—For *furniture* Paul gives the reason himself: the stupid fiscal policy of the French Government.—*Flowers* similar: division of labour and low wages: who can compete against the East End of London and Germany in cheapness? Generally speaking, bourgeois taste is getting so much out of taste that even the Germans may hope to be able to satisfy it. And if any trade has become broken down enough to make "cheap and nasty" its market-rule, then you may be sure the Germans will step in and defeat all competition by starving their own work-people. And as this is the rule generally now for all trades, it explains the appearance of German goods in all trades and all markets.

> Engels to Laura Lafargue,
> January 14, 1884
>
> Frederick Engels, Paul and
> Laura Lafargue, *Correspondence*,
> Vol. 1, Moscow, 1959, pp. 166-67

The Work of the Artist in Capitalist Society

1

Productive labour is here defined from the standpoint of capitalist production, and Adam Smith here got to the very heart of the matter, hit the nail on the head. This

---

[a] Domestic industry in Thuringia.—*Ed.*

is one of his greatest scientific merits (as Malthus rightly observed, this critical differentiation between productive and unproductive labour remains the basis of all bourgeois political economy) that he defines productive labour as labour *which is directly exchanged with capital*; that is, he defines it by the exchange through which the conditions of production of labour, and value in general, whether money or commodity, are first transformed into capital (and labour into wage-labour in its scientific meaning).

This also establishes absolutely what *unproductive labour* is. It is labour which is not exchanged with capital, but *directly* with revenue, that is, with wages or profit (including of course the various categories of those who share as co-partners in the capitalist's profit, such as interest and rent). Where all labour in part still pays itself (like for example the agricultural labour of the serfs) and in part is directly exchanged for revenue (like the manufacturing labour in the cities of Asia), no capital and no wage-labour exist in the sense of bourgeois political economy. These definitions are therefore not derived from the material characteristics of labour (neither from the nature of its product nor from the particular character of the labour as concrete labour), but from the definite social form, the social relations of production, within which the labour is realised. An actor, for example, or even a clown, according to this definition, is a productive labourer if he works in the service of a capitalist (an entrepreneur) to whom he returns more labour than he receives from him in the form of wages; while a jobbing tailor who comes to the capitalist's house and patches his trousers for him, producing a mere use-value for him, is an unproductive labourer. The former's labour is exchanged with capital, the latter's with revenue. The former's labour produces a surplus-value; in the latter's, revenue is consumed.

Productive and unproductive labour is here throughout conceived from *the standpoint of the possessor of money, from the standpoint of the capitalist*, not from that of the *workman*; hence the nonsense written by Ganilh, etc., who have so little understanding of the matter that they raise the question whether the labour or service or function of the prostitute, flunkey, etc., brings in returns. A writer is a *productive labourer* not in so far as he produces ideas, but in so far as he enriches the publisher who publishes his works, or if he is a wage-labourer for a capitalist.

Karl Marx, *Theories of Surplus-Value*,
Part I, Moscow, 1975, pp. 157-58

2

The same kind of labour may be *productive* or *unproductive*.

For example Milton, who wrote *Paradise Lost* for five pounds, was an *unproductive labourer*. On the other hand, the writer who turns out stuff for his publisher in factory style, is a *productive labourer*. Milton produced *Paradise Lost* for the same reason that a silk worm produces silk. It was an activity of *his* nature. Later he sold the product for £5. But the literary proletarian of Leipzig, who fabricates books (for example, Compendia of Economics) under the direction of his publisher, is a *productive labourer*; for his product is from the outset subsumed under capital, and comes into being only for the purpose of increasing that capital. A singer who sells her song for her own account is an *unproductive labourer*. But the same singer commissioned by an entrepreneur to sing in order to make money for him is a *productive labourer*; for she produces capital.

Karl Marx, *Theories of Surplus-Value*,
Part I, Moscow, 1975, p. 401

3

Non-material production, even when it is carried on purely for exchange, that is, when it produces *commodities*, may be of two kinds:

1. It results in *commodities*, use-values, which have a form different from and independent of producers and consumers; these commodities may therefore exist during an interval between production and consumption and may in this interval circulate as *vendible commodities*, such as books, paintings, in a word, all artistic products which are distinct from the artistic performance of the artist performing them. Here capitalist production is applicable only to a very restricted extent: as for example when a writer of a joint work—say an encyclopaedia—exploits a number of others as hacks. In this sphere for the most part a *transitional form* to capitalist production remains in existence, in which the various scientific or artistic producers, handicraftsmen or experts work for the collective trading capital of the book-trade—a relation that has nothing to do with the capitalist mode of production proper and even formally has not yet been brought under its sway. The fact that the exploitation of labour is at its highest precisely in these transitional forms in no way alters the case.

2. The production cannot be separated from the act of producing, as is the case with all performing artists, orators, actors, teachers, physicians, priests, etc. Here too the capitalist mode of production is met with only to a small extent, and from the nature of the case can only be applied in a few spheres. For example, teachers in educational establishments may be mere wage-labourers for the entrepreneurs of the establishment; many such educational factories exist in England. Although in relation to the pupils these teachers are not *productive labourers*, they are productive labourers in relation to their employer. He exchanges his capital for their labour-power, and enriches himself through this process. It is the same with enterprises such as theatres, places of

entertainment, etc. In such cases the actor's relation to the public is that of an artist, but in relation to his employer he is a *productive labourer*. All these manifestations of capitalist production in this sphere are so insignificant compared with the totality of production that they can be left entirely out of account.

Karl Marx, Theories of Surplus-Value,
Part I, Moscow, 1975, pp. 410-11

Freedom of the Press and of Artistic Creation

1

The mover of the motion desires that *freedom of the press* should not be excluded from the *general freedom to carry on a trade*, a state of things that still prevails, and by which the inner contradiction appears as a classical example of inconsistency.

> "The work of arms and legs is free, but that of the brain is under tutelage. Of cleverer brains no doubt? God forbid, that does not come into question as far as the censors are concerned. To him whom God gives an official post, He gives also understanding!"

The first thing that strikes one is to see *freedom of the press* included under *freedom of trade*. However, we cannot simply reject the speaker's view. *Rembrandt* painted the Madonna as a Dutch peasant woman; why should our speaker not depict freedom in a form which is dear and familiar to him?

Karl Marx, "Debates on Freedom of the Press"

Marx and Engels, Collected Works,
Vol. 1, Moscow, 1975, pp. 171-72

2

However correct the conclusion that the existence of a higher form of right can be considered proved by the existence of a lower form, the *application* is wrong when it makes the lower sphere a *measure* of the higher and turns its laws, reasonable within their own limits, into caricatures by claiming that they are not laws of their own sphere, but of a higher one. It is as if I wanted to compel a giant to live in the house of a pigmy.

Freedom of trade, freedom of property, of conscience, of the press, of the courts, are all *species* of one and the same genus, of *freedom without any specific name*. But it is quite incorrect to forget the difference because of the unity and to go so far as to make a *particular species* the measure, the standard, the sphere of other species. This is an *intolerance* on the part of one species of freedom, which is only prepared to tolerate the existence of others if they renounce themselves and declare themselves to be its vassals.

Freedom of trade is precisely freedom of trade and no other freedom because within it the nature of the trade develops unhindered according to the inner rules of its life.

> Karl Marx, "Debates on Freedom of the Press"
>
> Marx and Engels, *Collected Works*, Vol. I, Moscow, 1975, p. 173

3

In order to defend, and even to understand, the freedom of a particular sphere, I must proceed from its essential character and not its external relations. But is the press true to its character, does it act in accordance with the nobility of its nature, *is the press free* which degrades itself to the level of a *trade*? The writer, of course, must earn in order to be able to live and write, but he must by no means live and write to earn.

When *Béranger* sings:

> Je ne vis, que pour faire des chansons,
> Si vous m'ôtez ma place Monseigneur,
> Je ferai des chansons pour vivre,[a]

this threat contains the ironic admission that the poet deserts his proper sphere when for him poetry becomes a means.

The writer does not at all look on his work as a *means*. It is an *end in itself*; it is so little a means for him himself and for others that, if need be, he sacrifices *his* existence to *its* existence. He is, in another way, like the preacher of religion who adopts the principle: "Obey God rather than man", including under man himself with his human needs and desires. On the other hand, what if a tailor from whom I had ordered a Parisian frock-coat were to come and bring me a Roman toga on the ground that it was more in keeping with the eternal law of beauty!

The primary freedom of the press lies in not being a trade. The writer who degrades the press into being a material means deserves as punishment for this internal unfreedom the external unfreedom of censorship, or rather his very existence is his punishment.

Karl Marx, "Debates on Freedom of the Press"

Marx and Engels, *Collected Works*, Vol. 1, Moscow, 1975, pp. 174-75

4

The press is the most general way by which individuals can communicate their intellectual being. It knows no respect for persons, but only respect for intelligence. Do you want ability for intellectual communication to be determined officially by special external signs? What I cannot be for

---

[a] I live only to compose songs.
If you dismiss me, Monseigneur,
I shall compose songs in order to live.—*Ed.*

others, I am not and cannot be for myself. If I am not allowed to be a spiritual force for others, then I have no right to be a spiritual force for myself; and do you want to give certain individuals the privilege of being spiritual forces? Just as everyone learns to read and write, so everyone must *have the right* to read and write.

For whom, then, is the division of writers into "authorised" and "unauthorised" intended? Obviously not for the truly authorised, for they can make their influence felt without that. It is therefore for the "unauthorised" who want to protect themselves and impress others by means of an external privilege?

Moreover, this palliative does not even make a *press law* unnecessary, for, as a speaker from the peasant estate remarks:

> "Cannot a privileged person, too, exceed his authority and be liable to punishment? Therefore, in any case, a press law would be necessary, with the result that one would encounter the same difficulties as with a *general law on the press.*"

If the German looks back on his history, he will find *one* of the main reasons for his slow political development, as also for the wretched state of literature prior to *Lessing*, in the existence of *"authorised writers"*. The learned men by profession, guild or privilege, the doctors and others, the colourless university writers of the seventeenth and eighteenth centuries, with their stiff pigtails and their distinguished pedantry and their petty hair-splitting dissertations, interposed themselves between the people and the mind, between life and science, between freedom and mankind. It was the *unauthorised* writers who created our literature. *Gottsched* and *Lessing*—there you have the choice between an "authorised" and "unauthorised" writer!

In general, we have no liking for "freedom" that *only* holds good in the plural. England is a proof on a big historical scale how dangerous for *"freedom"* is the restricted horizon of *"freedoms"*.

"Ce mot des *libertés*," says Voltaire, "des *privilèges*, suppose l'assujettissement. Des libertés sont des *exemptions* de la *servitude générale*."[a]

Karl Marx, "Debates on Freedom of the Press"

Marx and Engels, *Collected Works*, Vol. 1, Moscow, 1975, pp. 177-78

.5

The bill to lift stamp duty from newspapers was passed on its second reading in the House of Commons yesterday. The main provisions of this bill are as follows: 1. Compulsory stamp duty on newspapers is abolished; 2. Periodical publications printed on stamped paper continue to enjoy the privilege of being forwarded by post free of charge. A third clause concerns the size of printed material sent through the post and another states that stamped newspapers must deposit a bond against possible libel actions. Two facts are sufficient to characterise the old system of newspaper taxation: the publication of a daily newspaper in London requires a capital of at least £50,000-£60,000; and, with very few exceptions, the entire English press opposes the new bill shamelessly and with an utter lack of propriety. Is any further proof needed that the old system protects the existing press, and prohibits free spiritual production? In England press freedom has hitherto been the exclusive privilege of capital. The few weekly newspapers representing the interests of the working class—there could, of course, be no question of daily newspapers—survive on the basis of weekly contributions from workers, who in England make quite different sacrifices for the sake of common goals than do workers on the continent. The leviathan of the English press, *The Times*, filled with strident tragicomic emotion, battles

---

[a] "This word of the *liberties*, of the *privileges*, supposes subjection. Liberties are *exemptions* from the *general servitude*."—*Ed.*

pro aris et focis[a], i.e., for the newspaper monopoly, now modestly comparing itself with the Delphic oracle, now asserting that England possesses only one institution worthy of preservation, namely *The Times*, now claiming an autocratic position in world journalism and, without any Kuchuk-Kaïnardji agreement,[47] a protectorate over all Europe's journalists.

> Karl Marx, "Napoleon and Barbès. — Stamp Duty on Newspapers"
>
> Marx/Engels, *Werke*, Bd. 11, 1969, S. 158-59

Asceticism and Enjoyment

The *philosophy* which preaches enjoyment is as old in Europe as the Cyrenaic school. Just as in antiquity it was the *Greeks* who were the protagonists of this philosophy, so in modern times it is the *French*, and indeed for the same reasons, because their temperament and their society made them most capable of enjoyment. The philosophy of enjoyment was never anything but the clever language of certain social circles who had the privilege of enjoyment. Apart from the fact that the manner and content of their enjoyment was always determined by the whole structure of the rest of society and suffered from all its contradictions, this philosophy became a mere *phrase* as soon as it began to lay claim to a universal character and proclaimed itself the outlook on life of society as a whole. It sank then to the level of edifying moralising, to a sophistical palliation of existing society, or it was transformed into its opposite, by declaring compulsory asceticism to be enjoyment.

In modern times the philosophy of enjoyment arose with the decline of feudalism and with the transformation of the

---

[a] For hearth and home.—*Ed.*

feudal landed nobility into the pleasure-loving and extravagant nobles of the court under the absolute monarchy. Among these nobles this philosophy still has largely the form of a direct naive outlook on life which finds expression in memoirs, poems, novels, etc. It only becomes a real philosophy in the hands of a few writers of the revolutionary bourgeoisie, who, on the one hand, participated in the culture and mode of life of the court nobility and, on the other hand, shared the more general outlook of the bourgeoisie, based on the more general conditions of existence of this class. This philosophy was, therefore, accepted by both classes, although from totally different points of view. Whereas among the nobility this language was restricted exclusively to its estate and to the conditions of life of this estate, it was given a generalised character by the bourgeoisie and addressed to every individual without distinction. The conditions of life of these individuals were thus disregarded and the theory of enjoyment thereby transformed into an insipid and hypocritical moral doctrine. When, in the course of further development, the nobility was overthrown and the bourgeoisie brought into conflict with its opposite, the proletariat, the nobility became devoutly religious, and the bourgeoisie solemnly moral and strict in its theories, or else succumbed to the above-mentioned hypocrisy, although the nobility in practice by no means renounced enjoyment, while among the bourgeoisie enjoyment even assumed an official, economic form—that of *luxury*.

It was only possible to discover the connection between the kinds of enjoyment open to individuals at any particular time and the class relations in which they live, and the conditions of production and intercourse which give rise to these relations, the narrowness of the hitherto existing forms of enjoyment, which were outside the actual content of the life of people and in contradiction to it, the connection between every philosophy of enjoyment and the enjoyment actually present and the hypocrisy of such a philosophy which treated all individuals without distinction—it was, of course, only possible to discover all this when it became possible to criticise the conditions of production and intercourse in the hitherto existing world, i.e., when the contradiction between the bourgeoisie and the proletariat had given rise to communist and socialist views. That shattered the basis of all morality, whether the morality of asceticism or of enjoyment.

> Karl Marx and Frederick Engels,
> *The German Ideology*,
>
> Marx and Engels, *Collected Works*, Vol. 5, Moscow, 1976, pp. 417-19

Work and Play

Labour is, in the first place, a process in which both man and Nature participate, and in which man of his own accord starts, regulates, and controls the material re-actions between himself and Nature. He opposes himself to Nature as one of her own forces, setting in motion arms and legs, head and hands, the natural forces of his body, in order to appropriate Nature's productions in a form adapted to his own wants. By thus acting on the external world and changing it, he at the same time changes his own nature. He develops his slumbering powers and compels them to act in obedience to his sway. We are not now dealing with those primitive instinctive forms of labour that remind us of the mere animal. An immeasurable interval of time separates the state of things in which a man brings his labour-power to market for sale as a commodity, from that state in which human labour was still in its first instinctive stage. We pre-suppose labour in a form that stamps it as exclusively human. A spider conducts operations that resemble those of a weaver, and a bee puts to shame many an architect in the construction of her cells. But what distinguishes the worst architect from the best of bees is this, that the architect raises his structure in imagination before he erects it in reality. At the end of every labour-process, we get a result that already existed in the imagination of the labourer at its commencement. He not only effects a change of form in the material on which he works, but he also realises a purpose of his own that gives the law to his modus operandi, and to which he must subordinate his will. And this subordination is no mere momentary act. Besides the exertion of the bodily organs, the process demands that, during the whole operation, the workman's will be steadily in consonance with his purpose. This means close attention. The less he is attracted by the nature of the work, and the mode in which it is carried on, and the less, therefore, he enjoys it as something which gives play to his bodily and mental powers, the more close his attention is forced to be.

Karl Marx, *Capital*, Vol. I, 1974, pp. 173-74

Bourgeois Civilisation and Crime

A philosopher produces ideas, a poet poems, a clergyman sermons, a professor compendia and so on. A criminal produces crimes. If we look a little closer at the connection between this latter branch of production and society as a whole, we shall rid ourselves of many prejudices. The criminal produces not only crimes but also criminal law, and with this also the professor who gives lectures on criminal law and in addition to this the inevitable compendium in which this same professor throws his lectures onto the general market as "commodities". This brings with it augmentation of national wealth, quite apart from the personal enjoyment which—as a competent witness, Herr Professor Roscher, [tells] us—the manuscript of the compendium brings to its originator himself.

The criminal moreover produces the whole of the police and of criminal justice, constables, judges, hangmen, juries, etc.; and all these different lines of business, which form equally many categories of the social division of labour, develop different capacities of the human spirit, create new needs and new ways of satisfying them. Torture alone has given rise to the most ingenious mechanical inventions, and employed many honourable craftsmen in the production of its instruments.

The criminal produces an impression, partly moral and partly tragic, as the case may be, and in this way renders a "service" by arousing the moral and aesthetic feelings of the public. He produces not only compendia on Criminal Law, not only penal codes and along with them legislators in this field, but also art, *belles-lettres*, novels, and even tragedies, as not only Müllner's *Schuld* and Schiller's *Räuber* show, but also [Sophocles'] *Oedipus* and [Shakespeare's] *Richard the Third*. The criminal breaks the monotony and everyday security of bourgeois life. In this way he keeps it from stagnation, and gives rise to that uneasy tension and agility without which even the spur of competition would get blunted. Thus he gives a stimulus to the productive forces. While crime takes a part of the superfluous population off the labour market and thus reduces competition among the labourers—up to a certain point preventing wages from falling below the minimum—the struggle against crime absorbs another part of this population. Thus the criminal comes in as one of those natural "counterweights" which bring about a correct balance and open up a whole perspective of "useful" occupations.

The effect of the criminal on the development of productive power can be shown in detail. Would locks ever have reached their present degree of excellence had there been no thieves? Would the making of bank-notes have reached its present perfection had there been no forgers? Would the microscope have found its way into the sphere of ordinary commerce (see Babbedge) but for trading frauds? Doesn't practical chemistry owe just as much to adulteration of commodities and the efforts to show it up as to the honest zeal for production? Crime, through its constantly new methods of attack on property, constantly calls into being new methods of defence, and so is as productive as strikes for the invention of machines. And if one leaves the sphere of private crime: would the world-market ever have come into being but for national crime? Indeed, would even the nations have arisen? And hasn't the Tree of Sin been at the same time the Tree of Knowledge ever since the time of Adam?

In his *Fable of the Bees* (1705) Mandeville had already shown that every possible kind of occupation is productive, and had given expression to the line of this whole argument:

"That what we call Evil in this World, Moral as well as Natural, is the grand Principle that makes us Sociable Creatures, the solid Basis, the *Life and Support of all Trades and Employments* without exception [...] there we must look for the true origin of all Arts and Sciences; and [...] the moment Evil ceases, the Society must be spoil'd if not totally dissolve'd[a]" [2nd edition, London, 1723, p. 428].[48]

Only Mandeville was of course infinitely bolder and more honest than the philistine apologists of bourgeois society.

Karl Marx, *Theories of Surplus-Value*,
Part I, Moscow, 1975, pp. 387-88

---

[a] In the manuscript: "destroyed".—*Ed.*

Historical Mission of the Working Class

The Proletariat and Wealth

Proletariat and wealth are opposites; as such they form a single whole. They are both creations of the world of private property. The question is exactly what place each occupies in the antithesis. It is not sufficient to declare them two sides of a single whole.

Private property as private property, as wealth, is compelled to maintain *itself*, and thereby its opposite, the proletariat, in *existence*. That is the *positive* side of the antithesis, self-satisfied private property.

The proletariat, on the contrary, is compelled as proletariat to abolish itself and thereby its opposite, private property, which determines its existence, and which makes it proletariat. It is the *negative* side of the antithesis, its restlessness within its very self, dissolved and self-dissolving private property.

The propertied class and the class of the proletariat present the same human self-estrangement. But the former class feels at ease and strengthened in this self-estrangement, it recognises estrangement as *its own power* and has in it the *semblance* of a human existence. The latter feels annihilated in estrangement; it sees in it its own powerlessness and the reality of an inhuman existence. It is, to use an expression of Hegel, in its abasement the *indignation* at that abasement, an indignation to which it is necessarily driven by the contradiction between its human *nature* and its condition of life, which is the outright, resolute and comprehensive negation of that nature.

Within this antithesis the private property-owner is therefore the *conservative* side, the proletarian the *destructive* side. From the former arises the action of preserving the antithesis, from the latter the action of annihilating it.

Indeed private property drives itself in its economic movement towards its own dissolution, but only through a development which does not depend on it, which is unconscious and which takes place against the will of private property by the very nature of things, only inasmuch as it produces the proletariat *as* proletariat, poverty which is conscious of its spiritual and physical poverty, dehumanisation which is conscious of its dehumanisation, and therefore self-abolishing. The proletariat executes the sentence that private property pronounces on itself by producing the proletariat, just as it executes the sentence that wage-labour pronounces on itself by producing wealth for others and poverty for itself. When the proletariat is victorious, it by no means becomes the absolute side of society, for it is victorious only by abolishing itself and its opposite. Then the proletariat disappears as well as the opposite which determines it, private property.

When socialist writers ascribe this world-historic role to the proletariat, it is not at all, as Critical Criticism pretends to believe, because they regard the proletarians as *gods*. Rather the contrary. Since in the fully-formed proletariat the abstraction of all humanity, even of the *semblance* of humanity, is practically complete; since the conditions of life of the proletariat sum up all the conditions of life of society today in their most inhuman form; since man has lost himself in the proletariat, yet at the same time has not only gained theoretical consciousness of that loss, but through urgent, no longer removable, no longer disguisable, absolutely imperative *need*—the practical expression of *necessity*—is driven directly to revolt against this inhumanity, it follows that the proletariat can and must emancipate itself. But it cannot emancipate itself without abolishing the conditions of its own life. It cannot abolish the conditions of its own life without abolishing *all* the inhuman conditions of life of society today which are summed up in its own situation. Not in vain does it go through the stern but steeling school of *labour*. It is not a question of what this or that proletarian, or even the whole proletariat, at the moment *regards* as its aim. It is a question of *what* the proletariat *is*, and what, in accordance with this *being*, it will historically be compelled to do. Its aim and historical action is visibly and irrevocably foreshadowed in its own life situation as well as in the whole organisation of bourgeois society today.

Karl Marx and Frederick Engels,
The Holy Family

Marx and Engels, *Collected Works*,
Vol. 4, Moscow, 1975, pp. 35-37

The Working Class and the Progressive Development of Society

1

There is one great fact, characteristic of this our nineteenth century, a fact which no party dares deny. On the one hand, there have started into life industrial and scientific forces, which no epoch of the former human history had ever suspected. On the other hand, there exist symptoms of decay, far surpassing the horrors recorded of the latter times of the Roman empire. In our days everything seems pregnant with its contrary. Machinery, gifted with the wonderful power of shortening and fructifying human labour, we behold starving and overworking it. The new-fangled sources of wealth, by some strange weird spell, are turned into sources of want. The victories of art seem bought by the loss of character. At the same pace that mankind masters nature, man seems to become enslaved to other men or to his own infamy. Even the pure light of science seems unable to shine but on the dark background of ignorance. All our invention and progress seem to result in endowing material forces with intellectual life, and in stultifying human life into a material force. This antagonism between modern industry and science on the one hand, modern misery and dissolution on the other hand; this antagonism between the productive powers, and the social relations of our epoch is a fact, palpable, overwhelming, and not to be controverted.

Karl Marx, "Speech at the Anniversary of the *People's Paper*"

Marx and Engels, *Selected Works*, Vol. 1, Moscow, 1973, pp. 500-01

2

And it is precisely this industrial revolution which has raised the productive power of human labour to such a high level that—for the first time in the history of mankind—the possibility exists, given a rational division of labour among all, of producing not only enough for the plentiful consumption of all members of society and for an abundant reserve fund, but also of leaving each individual sufficient leisure so that what is really worth preserving in historically inherited culture—science, art, forms of intercourse—may not only be preserved but converted from a monopoly of the ruling class into the common property of the whole of society, and may be further developed. And here is the decisive point.

Frederick Engels, *The Housing Question*

Marx and Engels, *Selected Works*, Vol. 2, Moscow, 1973, p. 312

The Working Class and Culture

1

Thus, in England, the remarkable fact is seen that the lower the position of a class in society, the more "uneducated" it is in the usual sense of the word, the more closely is it connected with progress, and the greater is its future. In general, this is a feature of every revolutionary epoch, as was seen in particular in the religious revolution of which the outcome was Christianity: "blessed are the poor",[a] "the wisdom of this world is foolishness",[b] etc. But this portent of a great revolution has probably never been so clearly expressed and so sharply delineated as now in England. In Germany, the movement proceeds from the class which is not only educated but even learned; in England, for three hundred years the educated and all the learned people have been deaf and blind to the signs of the times. Well known throughout the world is the pitiful routine of the English universities, compared with which our German colleges are like gold; but on the Continent people cannot even imagine the kind of works produced by the foremost English theologians and even by some of the foremost English natural scientists, and what miserable reactionary publications form the bulk of the weekly "list of new books". England is the homeland of political economy, but what about the level of scholarship among professors and practical politicians? Adam Smith's free trade has been pushed to the insane conclusions of the Malthusian theory of population and has produced nothing but a new, more civilised form of the old monopoly system, a form which finds its representatives among the present-day Tories, and which successfully combated the Malthusian nonsense, but in the end arrived once more at Malthus' conclusions. Everywhere

---

[a] Matthew 5 : 3.—*Ed.*
[b] 1 Corinthians 1 : 20.—*Ed.*

there is inconsistency and hypocrisy, while the striking economic tracts of the Socialists and partly also of the Chartists are thrown aside with contempt and find readers only among the lower classes. Strauss' *Das Leben Jesu* was translated into English. Not a single "respectable" book publisher wanted to print it; finally it appeared in separate parts, 3d. per part, and that was done by the publishing house of a minor but energetic antiquarian. The same thing occurred with translations of Rousseau, Voltaire, Holbach, etc. Byron and Shelley are read almost exclusively by the lower classes; no "respectable" person could have the works of the latter on his desk without his coming into the most terrible disrepute. It remains true: blessed are the poor, for theirs is the kingdom of heaven and, however long it may take, the kingdom of this earth as well.

> Frederick Engels, "Letters from London"
>
> Marx and Engels, *Collected Works*, Vol. 3, Moscow, 1975, pp. 379-80

2

Thus the minds of the educated classes in England are closed to all progress and only kept to some degree in movement by the pressure of the working class. It cannot be expected that the literary diet of their decrepit culture should be different from these classes themselves. The whole of fashionable literature moves in never-ending circle and is just as boring and sterile as this blasé and effete fashionable society.

> Frederick Engels, *The Condition of England*
>
> Marx and Engels, *Collected Works*, Vol. 3, Moscow, 1975, p. 446

3

While the Church of England lived in luxury, the Socialists did an incredible amount to educate the working classes in England. At first one cannot get over one's surprise on hearing in the Hall of Science[a] the most ordinary workers speaking with a clear understanding on political, religious and social affairs; but when one comes across the remarkable popular pamphlets and hears the lecturers of the Socialists, for example Watts in Manchester, one ceases to be surprised. The workers now have good, cheap editions of translations of the French philosophical works of the last century, chiefly Rousseau's *Contrat social*, the *Système de la Nature*[49] and various works by Voltaire, and in addition the exposition of communist principles in penny and twopenny pamphlets and in the journals. The workers also have in their hands cheap editions of the writings of Thomas Paine and Shelley.

> Frederick Engels, "Letters from London"
> Marx and Engels, *Collected Works*,
> Vol. 3, Moscow, 1975, p. 387

4

Here Political Economy is preached, whose idol is free competition, and whose sum and substance for the working-man is this, that he cannot do anything more rational than resign himself to starvation. Here all education is tame, flabby, subservient to the ruling politics and religion, so that for the working-man it is merely a constant sermon upon quiet obedience, passivity, and resignation to his fate.

---

[a] This term is given in English in the original.—*Ed.*

The mass of working-men naturally have nothing to do with these institutes, and betake themselves to the proletarian reading-rooms and to the discussion of matters which directly concern their own interests, whereupon the self-sufficient bourgeoisie says its *Dixi et salvavi*,[a] and turns with contempt from a class which "prefers the angry ranting of ill-meaning demagogues to the advantages of solid education". That, however, the working-men appreciate solid education when they can get it unmixed with the interested cant of the bourgeoisie, the frequent lectures upon scientific, aesthetic, and economic subjects prove which are delivered especially in the Socialist institutes,[b] and very well attended. I have often heard working-men, whose fustian jackets scarcely held together, speak upon geological, astronomical, and other subjects, with more knowledge than most "cultivated" bourgeois in Germany possess. And in how great a measure the English proletariat has succeeded in attaining independent education is shown especially by the fact that the epoch-making products of modern philosophical, political, and poetical literature are read by working-men almost exclusively. The bourgeois, enslaved by social conditions and the prejudices involved in them, trembles, blesses, and crosses himself before everything which really paves the way for progress; the proletarian has open eyes for it, and studies it with pleasure and success. In this respect the Socialists, especially, have done wonders for the education of the proletariat. They have translated the French materialists, Helvétius, Holbach, Diderot, etc., and disseminated them, with the best English works, in cheap editions. Strauss' *Life of Jesus* and Proudhon's *Property*[50] also circulate among the working-men only. Shelley, the genius, the prophet, Shelley, and Byron, with his glowing sensuality and his bitter satire

---

[a] *Dixi et salvavi (animam meam)*: I have spoken and saved (my soul).—*Ed.*

[b] The German editions of 1845 and 1892 have here: "in all proletarian institutes, especially the socialist ones".—*Ed.*

upon our existing society, find most of their readers in the proletariat; the bourgeoisie owns only castrated editions, family editions, cut down in accordance with the hypocritical morality of today. The two great practical philosophers of latest date, Bentham and Godwin, are, especially the latter, almost exclusively the property of the proletariat; for though Bentham has a school within the Radical bourgeoisie, it is only the proletariat and the Socialists who have succeeded in developing his teachings a step forward. The proletariat has formed upon this basis a literature, which consists chiefly of journals and pamphlets, and is far in advance of the whole bourgeois literature in intrinsic worth.

> Frederick Engels, *The Condition of the Working-Class in England*
>
> Marx and Engels, *Collected Works*, Vol. 4, Moscow, 1975, pp. 527-28

5

As for the educational level or capacity for education of the German workers in general, I call to mind *Weitling*'s brilliant writings, which as regards theory are often superior even to those of *Proudhon*, however much they are inferior to the latter in their execution. Where among the bourgeoisie—including its philosophers and learned writers—is to be found a book about the emancipation of the bourgeoisie—*political* emancipation—similar to Weitling's work: *Garantien der Harmonie und Freiheit*? It is enough to compare the petty, faint-hearted mediocrity of German political literature with this *vehement* and brilliant literary debut of the German workers, it is enough to compare these gigantic *infant shoes* of the proletariat with the dwarfish, worn-out political shoes of the German bourgeoisie, and one is bound to prophesy that the *German Cinderella* will one day have the *figure of an athlete*.

> Karl Marx, "Critical Marginal Notes on the Article 'The King of Prussia and Social Reform. By a Prussian'"
>
> Marx and Engels, *Collected Works*, Vol. 3, Moscow, 1975, pp. 201-02

6

The author of this article is himself a *worker* in one of London's tailoring shops. We ask the German bourgeoisie how many authors it numbers who would be capable of grasping the real movement in a similar manner?

Before the proletariat fights out its victories on the barricades and in the lines of battle, it gives notice of its impending rule with a series of intellectual victories.

The reader will note how here, instead of the sentimental, moral and psychological criticism levelled at existing conditions by *Weitling* and other workers who engage in authorship, a purely materialist understanding and a freer one, unspoilt by sentimental whims, confronts bourgeois society and its movement. Whereas craftsmen resist the collapse of their semi-medieval position and would like to unite *as craftsmen*, particularly in Germany and to a great extent also in France, here the subjection of craft labour to large-scale industry is comprehended and celebrated as a step forward while, at the same time, in the results and productions of large-scale industry, the real preconditions of proletarian revolution, generated by history itself and daily generating themselves anew, are recognised and revealed.

> Karl Marx and Frederick Engels, "Editorial Note to Eccarius' Article 'Tailoring in London or the Struggle Between Big and Small Capital'"
>
> Marx/Engels, *Werke*, Bd. 7, 1969, S. 416

Proletarian Revolution and the Vandalism of the Bourgeoisie

1

The working men's Paris, in the act of its heroic self-holocaust, involved in its flames buildings and monuments. While tearing to pieces the living body of the proletariat, its rulers must no longer expect to return triumphantly into the intact architecture of their abodes. The Government of Versailles cries, "Incendiarism!" and whispers this cue to all its agents, down to the remotest hamlet, to hunt up its enemies everywhere as suspect of professional incendiarism. The bourgeoisie of the whole world, which looks complacently upon the wholesale massacre after the battle, is convulsed by horror at the desecration of brick and mortar!

When governments give state-licences to their navies to "kill, *burn* and destroy", is that a licence for incendiarism? When the British troops wantonly set fire to the Capitol at Washington and to the summer palace of the Chinese Emperor,[51] was that incendiarism? When the Prussians, not for military reasons, but out of the mere spite of revenge, burned down, by the help of petroleum, towns like Châteaudun and innumerable villages, was that incendiarism? When Thiers, during six weeks, bombarded Paris, under the pretext that he wanted to set fire to those houses only in which there were people, was that incendiarism?— In war, fire is an arm as legitimate as any. Buildings held by the enemy are shelled to set them on fire. If their defenders have to retire, they themselves light the flames to prevent the attack from making use of the buildings. To be burnt down has always been the inevitable fate of all buildings situated in the front of battle of all the regular armies of the world. But in the war of the enslaved against their enslavers the only justifiable war·in history, this is by no means to hold good! The Commune[52] used fire strictly as a means of defence. They used it to stop up to the Versailles troops those long, straight avenues which Haussmann had expressly opened to artillery fire; they used it to cover their retreat, in the same way as the Versaillese, in their advance, used their shells which destroyed at least as many buildings as the fire of the Commune. It is a matter of dispute, even now, which buildings were set fire to by the defence, and which by the attack. And the defence resorted to fire only when the Versaillese troops had already commenced their wholesale murdering of prisoners.—Besides, the Commune had, long before, given full public notice that, if driven to extremities, they would bury themselves under the ruins of Paris, and make Paris a second Moscow, as the Government of Defence, but only as cloak for its treason, had promised to do. For this purpose Trochu had found them the petroleum. The Commune knew that its opponents cared nothing for the lives of the Paris people, but cared much for their own Paris buildings. And Thiers, on the other hand, had given them notice that he would be implacable in his vengeance. No sooner had he got his army ready on one side, and the Prussians shutting up the trap on the other, than he proclaimed: "I shall be pitiless! The expiation will be complete, and justice will be stern!" If the acts of the Paris working men were vandalism, it was the vandalism of defence in despair, not the vandalism of triumph, like that which the Christians perpetrated upon the really priceless art treasures of heathen antiquity; and even that vandalism has been justified by the historian as an unavoidable and comparatively trifling concomitant to the titanic struggle between a new society arising and an old one breaking down. It was still less the vandalism of Haussmann, razing historic Paris to make place for the Paris of the sightseer!

Karl Marx, *The Civil War in France*
Marx and Engels, *Selected Works*, Vol. 2, Moscow, 1973, pp. 237-38

2

Situation, April 23 and 24

Reunion of the Paris artists under the chairmanship of citizen Courbet. Fellows do not want the Vendôme column[53] to be destroyed. (A completely free discussion.) (Public session.) The Commune has now in fact decided to pull down only Bonaparte and put Freedom in his place. (About 3,000 artists in Paris.)

"All big cities throughout the world envy ours; it is the genius of art which presides over the intelligent labour of our workers and has earned Paris its indisputable and unrivalled reputation" (says the lousy *Soir*[54] itself) [p. 2, c. 4]. It has been declared that women are to be equal to men, with the right both to vote and to be elected (the Artist Club) [p. 3, c. 1].

Leader: the sale of the column is on the order of the day; the Arc de Triomphe[55] is crumbling [p. 5, c. 4].

Karl Marx, "Notes from Newspapers"
Written in German and French
Published according
to the typewritten copy

Art and Communism

Criticism of Egalitarian Communism

1

For it the sole purpose of life and existence is direct, physical *possession*. The category of the *worker* is not done away with, but extended to all men. The relationship of private property persists as the relationship of the community to the world of things. Finally, this movement of opposing universal private property to private property finds expression in the brutish form of opposing to *marriage* (certainly a *form of exclusive private property*) the *community of women*, in which a woman becomes a piece of *communal* and *common* property. It may be said that this idea of the *community of women gives away the secret* of this as yet completely crude and thoughtless communism. Just as woman passes from marriage to general prostitution,* so the entire world of wealth (that is, of man's objective substance) passes from the relationship of exclusive marriage with the owner of private property to a state of universal prostitution with the community. This type of communism—since it negates the *personality* of man in every sphere—is but the logical expression of private property, which is this negation. General *envy* constituting itself as a power is the disguise in

---

* Prostitution is only a *specific* expression of the *general* prostitution of the *labourer*, and since it is a relationship in which falls not the prostitute alone, but also the one who prostitutes—and the latter's abomination is still greater—the capitalist, etc., also comes under this head.—*Note by Marx.*

which *greed* re-establishes itself and satisfies itself, only in *another* way. The thought of every piece of private property as such is *at least* turned against *wealthier* private property in the form of envy and the urge to reduce things to a common level, so that this envy and urge even constitute the essence of competition. Crude communism[a] is only the culmination of this envy and of this levelling-down proceeding from the *preconceived* minimum. It has a *definite, limited* standard. How little this annulment of private property is really an appropriation is in fact proved by the abstract negation of the entire world of culture and civilisation, the regression to the *unnatural* simplicity of the *poor* and crude man who has few needs and who has not only failed to go beyond private property, but has not yet even reached it.

The community is only a community of *labour*, and equality of *wages* paid out by communal capital—by the *community* as the universal capitalist. Both sides of the relationship are raised to an *imagined* universality—*labour* as the category in which every person is placed, and *capital* as the acknowledged universality and power of the community.

In the approach to *woman* as the *spoil* and handmaid of communal lust is expressed the infinite degradation in which man exists for himself, for the secret of this approach has its *unambiguous*, decisive, *plain* and undisguised expression in the relation of *man* to *woman* and in the manner in which the *direct* and *natural* species-relationship is conceived. The direct, natural, and necessary relation of person to person is the *relation of man to woman*. In this *natural* species-relationship man's relation to nature is immediately his relation to man, just as his relation to man is immediately his relation to nature—his own *natural* destination. In this relationship, therefore, is *sensuously manifested*, reduced to an observable *fact*, the extent to which the human essence has become nature to man, or to which nature to him has become the human essence of man. From this relationship one can

---

[a] The manuscript has "*Kommunist*".—*Ed.*

therefore judge man's whole level of development. From the character of this relationship follows how much *man* as a *species-being*, as *man*, has come to be himself and to comprehend himself; the relation of man to woman is the *most natural* relation of human being to human being. It therefore reveals the extent to which man's *natural* behaviour has become *human*, or the extent to which the *human* essence in him has become a *natural* essence—the extent to which his *human nature* has come to be *natural* to him. This relationship also reveals the extent to which man's *need* has become a *human* need; the extent to which, therefore, the *other* person as a person has become for him a need—the extent to which he in his individual existence is at the same time a social being.

The first positive annulment of private property—*crude* communism—is thus merely a *manifestation* of the vileness of private property, which wants to set itself up as the *positive community system*.

Karl Marx, *Economic and Philosophic Manuscripts of 1844*

Marx and Engels, *Collected Works*, Vol. 3, Moscow, 1975, pp. 294-96

2

Already among these precursors of the movement we find an asceticism typical of all medieval uprisings tinged with religion, and, in modern times, of the early stages of every proletarian movement. This ascetic austerity of morals, this demand to forsake all joys of life and all entertainments, opposes the ruling classes with the principle of Spartan equality, on the one hand, and is, on the other, a necessary transition stage, without which the lowest stratum of society can never set itself in motion. In order to develop their revolutionary energy, to become conscious of their own hostile attitude towards all other elements of society, to concentrate themselves as a class, the lower strata of society must begin by stripping themselves of everything that could reconcile them with the existing social system; they must renounce the few pleasures that make their grievous position in the least tolerable for the moment, and of which even the severest oppression could not deprive them. This *plebeian and proletarian asceticism* differs both in its wild fanatical form and in its essence from the bourgeois asceticism of the Lutheran burgher morality and of the English Puritans (as distinct from the Independents and the more radical sects), whose entire secret lay in *bourgeois thrift*. It stands to reason that this plebeian-proletarian asceticism gradually sheds its revolutionary nature when the development of modern productive forces infinitely multiplies the luxuries, thus rendering Spartan equality superfluous, and as the position of the proletariat in society, and thereby the proletariat itself, become ever more revolutionary. This asceticism disappears gradually from among the masses, and in the sects, which relied upon it, it degenerates either into bourgeois parsimony or into a high-sounding virtuousness which, in practice, also comes down to a Philistine, or guild-artisan, niggardliness. Besides, renunciation of pleasures need hardly be preached to the proletariat for the simple reason that it has almost nothing more to renounce.

> Frederick Engels, *The Peasant War in Germany*, Moscow, 1974, pp. 63-64

Individuality and Society

1

Here, as always Sancho is again unlucky with his practical examples. He thinks that "no one can compose your music for you, complete the sketches for your paintings. No one can do Raphael's works for him". Sancho could surely have known, however, that it was not Mozart himself, but someone else who composed the greater part of Mozart's *Requiem* and finished it, and that Raphael himself "completed" only an insignificant part of his own frescoes.

He imagines that the so-called organisers of labour[56] wanted to organise the entire activity of each individual, and yet it is precisely they who distinguish between directly productive labour, which has to be organised, and labour which is not directly productive. In regard to the latter, however, it was not their view, as Sancho imagines, that each should do the work of Raphael, but that anyone in whom there is a potential Raphael should be able to develop without hindrance. Sancho imagines that Raphael produced his pictures independently of the division of labour that existed in Rome at the time. If he were to compare Raphael with Leonardo da Vinci and Titian, he would see how greatly Raphael's works of art depended on the flourishing of Rome at that time, which occurred under Florentine influence, while the works of Leonardo depended on the state of things in Florence, and the works of Titian, at a later period, depended on the totally different development of Venice. Raphael as much as any other artist was determined by the technical advances in art made before him, by the organisation of society and the division of labour in his locality, and, finally, by the division of labour in all the countries with which his locality had intercourse. Whether an individual like Raphael succeeds in developing his talent depends wholly on demand, which in turn depends on the division of labour and the conditions of human culture resulting from it.

In proclaiming the uniqueness of work in science and art, Stirner adopts a position far inferior to that of the bourgeoisie. At the present time it has already been found necessary to organise this "unique" activity. Horace Vernet would not have had time to paint even a tenth of his pictures if he regarded them as works which "only this unique person is capable of producing". In Paris, the great demand for vaudevilles and novels brought about the organisation of work for their production; this organisation which at any rate yields something better than its "unique" competitors in Germany. In astronomy, people like Arago, Herschel, Encke and Bessel considered it necessary to organise joint observations and only after that obtained some moderately good results. In historical science, it is absolutely impossible for the "unique" to achieve anything at all, and in this field, too, the French long ago surpassed all other nations thanks to organisation of labour. Incidentally, it is self-evident that all these organisations based on modern division of labour still lead to extremely limited results, and they represent a step forward only compared with the previous narrow isolation.

Moreover, it must be specially emphasised that Sancho confuses the organisation of labour with communism and is even surprised that "communism" gives him no reply to his doubts about this organisation. Just like a Gascon village lad is surprised that Arago cannot tell him on which star God Almighty has built his throne.

The exclusive concentration of artistic talent in particular individuals, and its suppression in the broad mass which is bound up with this, is a consequence of division of labour.

Even if in certain social conditions, everyone were an excellent painter, that would by no means exclude the possibility of each of them being also an original painter, so that here too the difference between "human" and "unique" labour amounts to sheer nonsense. In any case, with a communist organisation of society, there disappears the subordination of the artist to local and national narrowness, which arises entirely from division of labour, and also the subordination of the individual to some definite art, making him exclusively a painter, sculptor, etc.; the very name amply expresses the narrowness of his professional development and his dependence on division of labour. In a communist society there are no painters but only people who engage in painting among other activities.

Karl Marx and Frederick Engels,
The German Ideology

Marx and Engels, *Collected Works*,
Vol. 5, Moscow, 1976, pp. 393-94

2

Within communist society, the only society in which the genuine and free development of individuals ceases to be a mere phrase, this development is determined precisely by the connection of individuals, a connection which consists partly in the economic prerequisites and partly in the necessary solidarity of the free development of all, and, finally, in the universal character of the activity of individuals on the basis of the existing productive forces. We are, therefore, here concerned with individuals at a definite historical stage of development and by no means merely with individuals chosen at random, even disregarding the indispensable communist revolution, which itself is a general condition for their free development. The individuals' consciousness of their mutual relations will, of course, likewise be completely changed, and, therefore, will no more be the "principle of love" or *dévoûment* than it will be egoism.

Karl Marx and Frederick Engels,
The German Ideology

Marx and Engels, *Collected Works*,
Vol. 5, Moscow, 1976, p. 439

3

This appropriation is further determined by the manner in which it must be effected. It can only be effected through a union, which by the character of the proletariat itself can again only be a universal one, and through a revolution, in which, on the one hand, the power of the earlier mode of production and intercourse and social organisation is overthrown, and, on the other hand, there develops the universal character and the energy of the proletariat, without which the appropriation cannot be accomplished, and the proletariat moreover rids itself of everything that still clings to it from its previous position in society.

Only at this stage does self-activity coincide with material life, which corresponds to the development of individuals into complete individuals and the casting-off of all natural limitations. The transformation of labour into self-activity corresponds to the transformation of the previously limited intercourse into the intercourse of individuals as such. With the appropriation of the total productive forces by the united individuals, private property comes to an end. Whilst previously in history a particular condition always appeared as accidental, now the isolation of individuals and each person's particular way of gaining his livelihood have themselves become accidental.

The individuals, who are no longer subject to the division of labour, have been conceived by the philosophers as an ideal, under the name "man", and the whole process which we have outlined has been regarded by them as the evolutionary process of "man", so that at every historical stage "man" was substituted for the individuals existing hitherto and shown as the motive force of history. The whole process was thus conceived as a process of the self-estrangement [*Selbstentfremdungsprozess*] of "man",* and this was essentially due to the fact that the average individual of the later stage was always foisted on to the earlier stage, and the consciousness of a later age on to the individuals of an earlier. Through this inversion, which from the first disregards the actual conditions, it was possible to transform the whole of history into an evolutionary process of consciousness.

Karl Marx and Frederick Engels,
The German Ideology

Marx and Engels, *Collected Works*, Vol. 5, Moscow, 1976, pp. 88-89

---

* [Marginal note by Marx:] Self-estrangement.

The Kingdom of Freedom
and Material Labour

1

The fact that, by the way, direct working time cannot itself remain in abstract contrast to free time—as it seems to do from the standpoint of bourgeois political economy—is self-evident. Work cannot become play, as desired by Fourier, whose great service is to have pronounced the elevation not of distribution, but of the mode of production itself into a higher form as the ultimate object. Free time—which is both leisure time and time for higher activity—has naturally transformed its owner into a different subject, and it is as this different subject that he then enters into the direct production process. This process is at the same time discipline in relation to the evolving man, and practice, experimental science, and materially creative and self-objectifying science in relation to the evolved man, in whose head the accumulated knowledge of society exists. For both, the production process is at the same time exercise, since work demands practical application of the hands and free movement, as in agriculture.

                        Karl Marx, *A Critique of Political Economy (Draft Manuscript of 1857-58)*

                        Karl Marx, *Grundrisse der Kritik der politischen Oekonomie*, Berlin, 1953, S. 600

2

In that case, it depends upon the labour productivity how much use-value shall be produced in a definite time, hence also in a definite surplus labour-time. The actual wealth of society, and the possibility of constantly expanding its reproduction process, therefore, do not depend upon the duration of surplus-labour, but upon its productivity and the more or less copious conditions of production under which it is performed. In fact, the realm of freedom actually begins only where labour which is determined by necessity and mundane considerations ceases; thus in the very nature of things it lies beyond the sphere of actual material production. Just as the savage must wrestle with Nature to satisfy his wants, to maintain and reproduce life, so must civilised man, and he must do so in all social formations and under all possible modes of production. With his development this realm of physical necessity expands as a result of his wants; but, at the same time, the forces of production which satisfy these wants also increase. Freedom in this field can only consist in socialised man, the associated producers, rationally regulating their interchange with Nature, bringing it under their common control, instead of being ruled by it as by the blind forces of Nature; and achieving this with the least expenditure of energy and under conditions most favourable to, and worthy of, their human nature. But it nonetheless still remains a realm of necessity. Beyond it begins that development of human energy which is an end in itself, the true realm of freedom, which, however, can blossom forth only with this realm of necessity as its basis. The shortening of the working-day is its basic prerequisite.

Karl Marx, *Capital*, Vol. III,
Moscow, 1971, pp. 819-20

History of Social Thought, Literature and Art

Antiquity, Middle Ages and Renaissance

Antiquity

The Dawn of Human Culture

After the second Ice Age, as the climate gradually grew warmer, man appeared all over Europe, North Africa, and the Anterior Asia all the way to India, accompanied by now extinct large pachyderms (the mammoth, the straight-tusked elephant, and the woolly rhinoceros) and predatory animals (the cave lion and cave bear), as well as by surviving species (the reindeer, horse, hyena, lion, bison, and aurochs). The implements belonging to this period indicate an extremely low level of culture; the crude stone knives, pear-shaped stone hoes or axes used without handles, scrapers used to clean animal hides, borers, all made of flint, are at about the level of those used by the present-day natives of Australia. Those bones that have been found permit no conclusions regarding the build of these men, but from their wide dissemination and the uniformity of their culture we may presume that the period lasted for a very long time.

We have no idea what became of this early Paleolithic man. None of the present-day races in any of the areas where he existed, even in India, can be considered as descending from him.

The implements of this extinct race have been discovered in the caves of England, France, Switzerland, Belgium, and Southern Germany, mostly in the undermost layers of soil deposit. Above this lowest level of culture, frequently separated from it by a thick or thin layer of stalactite, is a second layer containing implements. Belonging to a later period, these are far more skilfully crafted and made of various materials. True, the stone implements are not polished, but they are designed and executed so as to be more expedient. Next to these we discover spear- and arrow-heads of stone, reindeer antlers and bones, daggers and sewing needles made from bones or antlers, as well as necklaces made of bored animal's teeth, etc. Some implements bear vivid drawings of animals—reindeers, mammoths, aurochs, seals, whales—and hunting scenes with figures of naked men, even the beginnings of sculpture in horn.

Early Paleolithic man occurred together with animals of largely southern origin, while late Paleolithic man existed alongside animals of northern origin: two extant species of northern bears, the polar fox, the glutton, the snow owl. Late Paleolithic man probably moved down from the northeast together with these animals. The Eskimoes are probably his last surviving descendants. The implements of both cultures correspond fully not only in isolated instances, but as a totality. The same is true of the drawings. Both derived their sustenance from nearly the same animals, and the mode of life of the extinct race, insofar as we can ascertain it, was absolutely the same.

Frederick Engels, "A Contribution to Early German History"

Marx/Engels, *Werke*, Bd. 19, 1962, S. 425-26

The Beginnings of Mythology and Epos

I. and II. *Status of Savagery* and *Lower Status of Barbarism*, these *two ethnical periods* cover at least four-fifths of mankind's entire existence on Earth.

In the Lower Status, the higher attributes of mankind begin to develop: *personal dignity, eloquence, religious sensibility, rectitude, manliness* and *courage*, now *common traits of character*; but there was also *cruelty, treachery* and *fanaticism. Element worship in religion*, with a *dim conception of personal gods*, and of a *Great Spirit, rude verse-making, joint tenement houses*, and *bread from maize* belong to this period. It produced also *syndiasmian family* and *confederacy of tribes, organised into phratries and gentes*. The *imagination*, that great faculty so largely contributing to the elevation of mankind, was *now producing* an *unwritten literature of myths, legends and traditions*, already become a powerful stimulus upon the race.

Karl Marx, "Conspectus of Lewis Morgan's *Ancient Society*"

Written in German and English

Marx/Engels, *Über Kunst und Literatur*, Bd. I, Berlin, 1967, S. 624

Epic Tradition of the Semites

It seems that the Arabians, where they had settled down, in the South-West, were just as civilised a people as the Egyptians, Assyrians, etc., as is proved by the buildings they erected. This too explains much in the Mohammedan invasion. As far as the religious humbug is concerned, it seems to follow from the ancient inscriptions in the South, in which the old national-Arabian tradition of monotheism still predominates (as it does among the American Indians), the tradition of which the Hebrew tradition constitutes only a *small part*, that Mohammed's religious revolution, like *every* religious movement, was *formally a reaction*, an alleged return to the old, simple customs.

That Jewish so-called Holy Scripture is nothing more than a record of the old-Arabian religious and tribal tradition, modified by the early separation of the Jews from their consanguineous but nomadic neighbours—that is now perfectly clear to me. The circumstance that Palestine is surrounded on the Arabian side by nothing but deserts, Bedouin land, explains their distinct development. But the ancient Arabian inscriptions, traditions, and the Koran, and the ease with which all genealogies, etc., can now be unravelled prove that the main content was Arabic or rather Semitic in general, the position is rather similar here to what we see in the Edda and the German heroic saga.

> Engels to Marx,
> approx. May 26, 1853
>
> Marx and Engels, *Selected Correspondence*, Moscow, 1975 p. 74

Ancient Greek Society in Homer's Poems

1

In the poems of Homer, particularly the *Iliad*, we find the upper stage of barbarism at its zenith. Improved iron tools, the bellows, the handmill, the potter's wheel, the making of oil and wine, the working up of metals developing into an art, waggons and war chariots, shipbuilding with planks and beams, the beginning of architecture as an art, walled towns with towers and battlements, the Homeric epic and the entire mythology—these are the chief heritages carried over by the Greeks in their transition from barbarism to civilisation. If we compare with this Caesar's and even Tacitus' descriptions of the Germans, who were on the threshold of that stage of culture from which the Homeric Greeks were preparing to advance to a higher one, we will see how rich was the development of production in the upper stage of barbarism.

> Frederick Engels, *The Origin of the Family, Private Property and the State*
>
> Marx and Engels, *Selected Works*, Vol. 3, Moscow, 1973, p. 208

2

In the *Iliad* the ruler of men, Agamemnon, appears, not as the supreme king of the Greeks, but as supreme commander of a federal army before a besieged city. And when dissension broke out among the Greeks, it is to this quality of his that Odysseus points in the famous passage: the commanding of many is not a good thing; let us have one commander, etc. (to which the popular verse about the sceptre was added later).[57] "Odysseus is not here lecturing on the form of government, but is demanding obedience to the supreme commander of the army in the field. For the Greeks, who appear before Troy only as an army, the proceedings in the *agora* are sufficiently democratic. When speaking of gifts, that is, the division of the spoils, Achilles never makes Agamemnon or some other *basileus* the divider, but always the 'sons of the Achaeans',[58] that is to say, the people. The attributes 'begotten of Zeus', 'nourished by Zeus', do not prove anything, because *every* gens is descended from some god, and the gens of the tribal chief from a 'prominent' god, in this case Zeus. Even bondsmen, such as the swineherd Eumaeus and others, are 'divine'[59] (*dioi* or *theioi*), even in the *Odyssey*, and hence in a much later period than the *Iliad*. Likewise in the *Odyssey*, we find the name of *heros* given to the herald Mulios as well as to the blind bard Demodocus.[60] In short, the word *basileia*, which the Greek writers apply to Homer's so-called kingship (because military leadership is its chief distinguishing mark), with the council and popular assembly alongside of it, means merely—military democracy." (Marx.)

Frederick Engels, *The Origin of the Family, Private Property and the State*

Marx and Engels, *Selected Works*, Vol. 3, Moscow, 1973, p. 274

Greek Tragedy

1

Bachofen finds evidence in support of these propositions in countless passages of ancient classical literature, which he had assembled with extraordinary diligence. According to him, the evolution from "hetaerism" to monogamy, and from mother right to father right, takes place, particularly among the Greeks, as a consequence of the evolution of religious ideas, the intrusion of new deities, representatives of the new outlook, into the old traditional pantheon representing the old outlook, so that the latter is more and more driven into the background by the former. Thus, according to Bachofen, it is not the development of the actual conditions under which men live, but the religious reflection of these conditions of life in the minds of men that brought about the historical changes in the mutual social position of man and woman. Bachofen accordingly points to the *Oresteia* of Aeschylus as a dramatic depiction of the struggle between declining mother right and rising and victorious father right in the Heroic Age. Clytemnestra has slain her husband Agamemnon, just returned from the Trojan War, for the sake of her lover Aegisthus; but Orestes, her son by Agamemnon, avenges his father's murder by slaying his mother. For this he is pursued by the

Erinyes, the demonic defenders of mother right, according to which matricide is the most heinous and inexpiable of crimes. But Apollo, who through his oracle has incited Orestes to commit this deed, and Athena, who is called in as arbiter—the two deities which here represent the new order, based on father right—protect him. Athena hears both sides. The whole controversy is briefly summarised in the debate which now ensues between Orestes and the Erinyes. Orestes declares that Clytemnestra is guilty of a double outrage; for in killing *her* husband she also killed *his* father. Why then have the Erinyes persecuted him and not Clytemnestra, who is much the greater culprit? The reply is striking:

"*Unrelated by blood* was she to the man that she slew."[61]

The murder of a man not related by blood, even though he be the husband of the murderess, is expiable and does not concern the Erinyes. Their function is to avenge only murders among blood-relatives, and the most heinous of all these, according to mother right, is matricide. Apollo now intervenes in defence of Orestes. Athena calls upon the Areopagites—the Athenian jurors—to vote on the question. The votes for acquittal and for the conviction are equal. Then Athena, as President of the Court, casts her vote in favour of Orestes and acquits him. Father right has gained the day over mother right. The "gods of junior lineage", as they are described by the Erinyes themselves, are victorious over the Erinyes, and the latter allow themselves finally to be persuaded to assume a new office in the service of the new order.

This new but absolutely correct interpretation of the *Oresteia* is one of the best and most beautiful passages in the whole book, but it shows at the same time that Bachofen himself believes in the Erinyes, Apollo and Athena at least as much as Aeschylus did in his day; he, in fact, believes that in the Heroic Age of Greece they performed the miracle of overthrowing mother right and replacing it by father right. Clearly, such a conception—which regards religion as the decisive lever in world history—must finally end in sheer mysticism.

> Frederick Engels, *The Origin of the Family, Private Property and the State*
>
> Marx and Engels, *Selected Works*, Vol. 3, Moscow, 1973, pp. 194-96

2

The Turanian system of relations (Asia, Africa, Australia) corresponding to the *Ganovanian* in *America* must have also prevailed among *Greek and Latin tribes* in the same development period. One *characteristic of this*: the *children of brothers* are themselves *brothers and sisters*, and as such not intermarriable; the *children of sisters* are similarly related and come *under the same prohibition*. If Bachofen finds these punaluan marriages[62] *lawless*, then a man from that period would find *most present marriages* between near and distant cousins, be it on the father's side or the mother's side, *incestuous*, namely as marriages between *consanguineous* brothers and sisters. This explains the legend of the *Danaides* (on which *Æschylus* bases his *Supplices*).

Danaus and Ægyptus were brothers and descendants of the Argive *Io. Danaus* had *fifty daughters* by different wives and *Ægyptus fifty sons*; the latter sought the first in marriage; these, *according to the Turanian system*, were *brothers and sisters*, and so not intermarriable. If there had been *descent in male line*, they would also have belonged to *the same gens*, and this would have been another obstacle to marriage. The *fifty daughters of Danaus*—the Danaides —*fled from Egypt to Argos* to escape unlawful and incestuous wedlock. This event was foretold to Io by Prometheus *(Æschylus, 853)*.

In Æschylus' play *The Supplices* the Danaides declare to the *kindred Argives* (in Argos) that they had not been exiled from Egypt

> By *popular decree* on account of a *bloody deed* (murder)
> But [had fled] *out of fear of men*,
> Condemning *consanguineous and unholy marriage*
> *To the sons of Ægyptus*.

(The passage seems spoiled, *grammatically*; see Schütz, *"Æschylus"* (Vol. 2, p. 378).

Further: After they heard the case of the suppliants, the *Argives decided in council to grant them protection*, which implies the existence of a ban on such marriages and the validity of their objection. At the time this tragedy was performed, in Athens, *Athenian law itself facilitated and promoted marriage between children of brothers* in the case of *heiresses and orphans*, although this rule seems to have been confined to such exceptional cases.

Karl Marx, "Conspectus of Lewis Morgan's *Ancient Society"*

Written in German, English and Greek

Marx/Engels, *Über Kunst und Literatur*, Bd. I, Berlin, 1967, S. 630

Position of Women in Greece According to Ancient Writers

We are confronted with this new form of the family in all its severity among the Greeks. While, as Marx observes,[63] the position of the goddesses in mythology represents an earlier period, when women still occupied a freer and more respected place, in the Heroic Age we already find women degraded owing to the predominance of the man and the competition of female slaves. One may read in the *Odyssey* how Telemachus cuts his mother short[64] and enjoins silence upon her. In Homer the young female captives become the objects of the sensual lust of the victors; the military chiefs, one after the other, according to rank, choose the most beautiful ones for themselves. The whole of the *Iliad*, as we know, revolves around the quarrel between Achilles and Agamemnon over such a female slave. In connection with each Homeric hero of importance mention is made of a captive maiden with whom he shares tent and bed. These maidens are taken back home, to the conjugal house, as was Cassandra[65] by Agamemnon in Æschylus. Sons born of these slaves receive a small share of their father's estate and are regarded as freemen. Teukros was such an illegitimate son of Telamon and was permitted to adopt his father's name. The wedded wife is expected to tolerate all this, but to maintain strict chastity and conjugal fidelity herself. True, in the Heroic Age the Greek wife is more respected than in the period of civilisation; for the husband, however, she is, in reality, merely the mother of his legitimate heirs, his chief housekeeper, and the superintendent of the female slaves, whom he may make, and does make, his concubines at will. It is the existence of slavery side by side with monogamy, the existence of beautiful young slaves who belong to the *man* with all they have, that from the very beginning stamped on monogamy its specific character as monogamy *only for the woman*, but not for the man. And it retains this character to this day.

As regards the Greeks of later times, we must differentiate between the Dorians and the Ionians. The former, of whom Sparta was the classical example, had in many respects more ancient marriage relationships than even Homer indicates. In Sparta we find a form of pairing marriage—modified by the state in accordance with the conceptions there prevailing—which still retains many vestiges of group marriage. Childless marriages were dissolved: King Anaxandridas (about 560 B.C.) took another wife in addition to his first, childless one, and maintained two households; King Ariston of the same period added a third to two previous wives who were barren, one of whom he, however, let go. On the other hand, several brothers could have a wife in common. A person having a preference for his friend's wife could share her with him; and it was regarded as proper to place one's wife at the disposal of a lusty "stallion", as Bismarck would say, even when this person was not a citizen. A passage in Plutarch, where a Spartan woman sends a lover who is pursuing her with his attentions to interview her husband, would indicate, according to Schömann,[66] still greater sexual freedom. Real adultery, the infidelity of the wife behind the back of her husband, was thus unheard of. On the other hand, domestic slavery was unknown in Sparta, at least in its heyday; the Helot serfs lived segregated on the estates and thus there was less temptation for the Spartiates[67] to have intercourse with their women. That in all these circumstances the women of Sparta enjoyed a very much more respected position than all other Greek women was quite natural. The Spartan women and the *élite* of the Athenian *hetaerae* are the only Greek women of whom the ancients speak with respect, and whose remarks they consider as being worthy of record.

Among the Ionians—of whom Athens is characteristic—things were quite different. Girls learned only spinning, weaving and sewing, at best a little reading and writing. They were practically kept in seclusion and consorted only with other women. The women's quarter was a separate and distinct part of the house, on the upper floor, or in the rear building, not easily accessible to men, particularly strangers; to this the women retired when men visitors came. The women did not go out unless accompanied by a female slave; at home they were virtually kept under guard; Aristophanes speaks of Molossian hounds kept to frighten off adulterers,[68] while in Asiatic towns, at least, eunuchs were maintained to keep guard over the women; they were manufactured for the trade in Chios as early as Herodotus' day, and according to Wachsmuth,[69] not merely for the barbarians. In Euripides, the wife is described as *oikurema*,[70] a thing for housekeeping (the word is in the neuter gender), and apart from the business of bearing children, she was nothing more to the Athenian than the chief housemaid. The husband had his gymnastic exercises, his public affairs, from which the wife was excluded; in addition, he often had female slaves at his disposal and, in the heyday of Athens, extensive prostitution, which was viewed with favour by the state, to say the least. It was precisely on the basis of this prostitution that the sole outstanding Greek women developed, who by their *esprit* and artistic taste towered as much above the general level of ancient womanhood as the Spartiate women did by virtue of their character. That one had first to become a *hetaera* in order to become a woman is the strongest indictment of the Athenian family.

In the course of time, this Athenian family became the model upon which not only the rest of the Ionians, but also all the Greeks of the mainland and of the colonies increasingly moulded their domestic relationships. But despite all seclusion and surveillance the Greek women found opportunities often enough for deceiving their husbands. The latter, who would have been ashamed to evince any love for their own wives, amused themselves with *hetaerae* in all kinds of amours. But the degradation of the women recoiled on the men themselves and degraded them too, until they sank into the perversion of boy-love, degrading both themselves and their gods by the myth of Ganymede.

Frederick Engels, *The Origin of the Family, Private Property and the State*

Marx and Engels, *Selected Works*, Vol. 3, Moscow, 1973, pp. 237-39

Ancient Slavery and World Culture

1

Slavery had been invented. It soon became the dominant form of production among all peoples who were developing beyond the old community, but in the end was also one of the chief causes of their decay. It was slavery that first made possible the division of labour between agriculture and industry on a larger scale, and thereby also Hellenism, the flowering of the ancient world. Without slavery, no Greek state, no Greek art and science; without slavery, no Roman Empire. But without the basis laid by Grecian culture, and the Roman Empire, also no modern Europe. We should never forget that our whole economic, political and intellectual development presupposes a state of things in which slavery was as necessary as it was universally recognised. In this sense we are entitled to say: Without the slavery of antiquity no modern socialism.

It is very easy to inveigh against slavery and similar things in general terms, and to give vent to high moral indignation at such infamies. Unfortunately all that this conveys is only what everyone knows, namely, that these institutions of antiquity are no longer in accord with our present conditions and our sentiments, which these conditions determine. But it does not tell us one word as to how these institutions arose, why they existed, and what role they played in history. And when we examine these questions, we are compelled to say—however contradictory and heretical it may sound—that the introduction of slavery under the conditions prevailing at that time was a great step forward. For it is a fact that man sprang from the beasts, and had consequently to use barbaric and almost bestial means to extricate himself from barbarism. Where the ancient communities have continued to exist, they have for thousands of years formed the basis of the cruelest form of state, Oriental despotism, from India to Russia. It was only where these communities dissolved that the peoples made progress of themselves, and their next economic advance consisted in the increase and development of production by means of slave labour. It is clear that so long as human labour was still so little productive that it provided but a small surplus over and above the necessary means of subsistence, any increase of the productive forces, extension of trade, development of the state and of law, or foundation of art and science, was possible only by means of a greater division of labour. And the necessary basis for this was the great division of labour between the masses discharging simple manual labour and the few privileged persons directing labour, conducting trade and public affairs, and, at a later stage, occupying themselves with art and science. The simplest and most natural form of this division of labour was in fact slavery.

Frederick Engels, Anti-Dühring,
Moscow, 1975, pp. 207-09

2

The ancient poets of Sicily, Theocritus and Moschus, celebrated the idyllic life of the shepherd slaves, their contemporaries. This was, without doubt, poetic dreaming. But where is there a contemporary poet who would be so bold as to celebrate the idyllic life of the "free" worker of present-day Sicily? Would not the peasants of this island be happy if they could cultivate their plots even under the harsh conditions of the Roman system of *métayage*? This is the situation to which the capitalist system has led: free men mourn for the slavery of the past!

But they can take fresh heart. The dawn of a new and better society for the oppressed classes of all lands is breaking. Everywhere the oppressed are closing ranks; everywhere they are reaching out to each other over frontiers and over different languages. The army of the international proletariat is forming and the approaching new century will lead it to victory!

> Frederick Engels, "Message of Greetings to the Socialists of Sicily"
> Marx/Engels, *Werke*, Bd. 22, 1963, S. 476-77

The Plastic Element in Greek Arts

1

Thus, while the atom frees itself from its relative existence, the straight line, by abstracting from it, by swerving away from it; so the entire Epicurean philosophy swerves away from the restrictive mode of being wherever the concept of abstract individuality, self-sufficiency and negation of all relation to other things must be represented in its existence.

The purpose of action is to be found therefore in abstracting, swerving away from pain and confusion, in ataraxy. Hence the good is the flight from evil, pleasure the swerving away from suffering. Finally, where abstract individuality appears in its highest freedom and independence, in its totality, there it follows that the being which is swerved away from, is *all being, for this reason, the gods swerve away from the world*, do not bother with it and live outside it.

These gods of Epicurus have often been ridiculed, these gods who, like human beings, dwell in the intermundia[a] of the real world, have no body but a quasi-body, no blood but quasi-blood, and, content to abide in blissful peace, lend no ear to any supplication, are unconcerned with us and the world, are honoured because of their beauty,

---

[a] The spaces between the worlds (literally: inter-worlds).—*Ed.*

their majesty and their superior nature, and not for any gain.

And yet these gods are no fiction of Epicurus. They did exist. *They are the plastic gods of Greek art. Cicero*, the *Roman*, rightly scoffs at them,[71] but *Plutarch*, the *Greek*, has forgotten the whole Greek outlook when he claims that although this doctrine of the gods does away with fear[72] and superstition, it produces no joy or favour in the gods, but instead bestows on us that relation to them that we have to the Hyrcanian[73] fish, from which we expect neither harm nor advantage. Theoretical calm is one of the chief characteristics of the Greek gods. As *Aristotle* says:

"What is best has no need of action, for it is its own end."[74]

Karl Marx, "Doctoral Dissertation"
Marx and Engels, *Collected Works*, Vol. 1, Moscow, 1975, pp. 50-51

2

If the first Greek wise men are the real spirit, the embodied knowledge of substance, if their utterances preserve just as much genuine intensity as substance itself, if, as substance is increasingly idealised, the bearers of its progress assert an ideal life in their particular reality in opposition to the reality of manifested substance, of the real life of the people, then the ideality itself is only in the form of substance. There is no undermining of the living powers; the most ideal men of this period, the Pythagoreans and the Eleatics, extol state life as real reason; their principles are objective, a power which is superior to themselves, which they herald in a semi-mystical fashion, in poetic enthusiasm; that is, in a form which raises natural energy to ideality and does not consume it, but processes it and leaves it intact in the determination of the natural. This embodiment of the ideal substance occurs in the philosophers themselves who herald it; not only is its expression plastically poetic, its reality is this person, whose reality is its own appearance; they themselves are living images, living works of art which the people sees rising out of itself in plastic greatness; while their activity, as in the case of the first wise men, shapes the universal, their utterances are the really assertive substance, the laws.

Hence these wise men are just as little like ordinary people as the statues of the Olympic gods; their motion is rest in self, their relation to the people is the same objectivity as their relation to substance. The oracles of the Delphic Apollo were divine truth for the people, veiled in the chiaroscuro of an unknown power, only as long as the genuine evident power of the Greek spirit sounded from the Pythian tripod; the people had a theoretical attitude towards them only as long as they were the resounding theory of the people itself, they were of the people only as long as they were unlike them. The same with these wise men. But with the Sophists and Socrates, and by virtue of δύναμις [a] in Anaxagoras, the situation was reversed.

Karl Marx, "Notebooks on Epicurean Philosophy"
Marx and Engels, Collected Works, Vol. 1, Moscow, 1975, p. 436

Greek Enlightenment

1

The struggle of the ancients could only end by the visible heaven, the substantial nexus of life, the force of gravity of political and religious life being shattered, for nature must be split in two for the spirit to be one in itself. The Greeks broke it up with the Hephaestan hammer of art, broke it up in their statues; the Roman plunged his sword

---

[a] Potentialities.—*Ed.*

into its heart and the peoples died, but modern philosophy unseals the word, lets it pass away in smoke in the holy fire of the spirit, and as fighter of the spirit fighting the spirit, not as a solitary apostate fallen from the gravity of Nature, it is universally active and melts the forms which prevent the universal from breaking forth.

> Karl Marx, "Notebooks on Epicurean Philosophy"
>
> Marx and Engels, *Collected Works*, Vol. 1, Moscow, 1975, p. 431

2

Philosophy, as long as a drop of blood shall pulse in its world-subduing and absolutely free heart, will never grow tired of answering its adversaries with the cry of Epicurus:

'Ασεβὴς δέ, οὐχ ὁ τοὺς τῶν πολλῶν θεοὺς ἀναιρῶν, ἀλλ' ὁ τὰς τῶν πολλῶν δόξας θεοῖς προςάπτων.[a]

Philosophy makes no secret of it. The confession of Prometheus:

ἁπλῷ λόγῳ, τοὺς πάντας ἐχθαίρω θεούς[b]

is its own confession, its own aphorism against all heavenly and earthly gods who do not acknowledge human self-consciousness as the highest divinity. It will have none other beside.

But to those poor March hares who rejoice over the apparently worsened civil position of philosophy, it responds

---

[a] Not the man who denies the gods worshipped by the multitude, but he who affirms of the gods what the multitude believes about them, is truly impious.[75]—*Ed.*

[b] In simple words, I hate the pack of gods (*Prometheus Bound*)[76] —*Ed.*

again, as Prometheus replied to the servant of the gods, Hermes:

τῆς σῆς λατρείας τὴν ἐμὴν δυςπραξίαν,
σαφῶς ἐπίστασ', οὐκ ἂν ἀλλάξαιμ' ἐγώ.
κρεῖσσον γὰρ οἶμαι τῇδε λατρεύειν πέτρᾳ
ἢ πατρὶ φῦναι Ζηνὶ πιστὸν ἄγγελον.[a]

Prometheus is the most eminent saint and martyr in the philosophical calendar.

> Karl Marx, "Doctoral Dissertation"
>
> Marx and Engels, *Collected Works*, Vol. 1, Moscow, 1975, pp. 30-31

Religion and Culture in the Ancient World

"In those nations which attained higher historical significance, the flowering of their national life coincides with the highest development of their religious consciousness, and the decline of their greatness and their power coincides with the decline of their religious culture."

To arrive at the truth, the author's assertion[78] must be directly reversed; he has stood history on its head. Among the peoples of the ancient world, Greece and Rome are certainly countries of the highest "historical culture". Greece flourished at its best internally in the time of Pericles, externally in the time of Alexander. In the age of Pericles the Sophists, and Socrates, who could be called the embodiment of philosophy, art and rhetoric supplanted religion. The age of Alexander was the age of Aristotle, who rejected the eternity of the "individual" spirit and the God of positive religions. And as for Rome! Read Cicero! The Epicurean, Stoic or Sceptic philosophies were the religions

---

[a] Be sure of this, I would not change my state
Of evil fortune for your servitude.
Better to be the servant of this rock
Than to be faithful boy to Father Zeus.[77]

(Ibid.)—*Ed.*

of cultured Romans when Rome had reached the zenith of its development. That with the downfall of the ancient states their religions also disappeared requires no further explanation, for the "true religion" of the ancients was the cult of "their nationality", of their "state". It was not the downfall of the old religions that caused the downfall of the ancient states, but the downfall of the ancient states that caused the downfall of the old religions. And such ignorance as is found in this leading article proclaims itself the "legislator of scientific research" and writes "decrees" for philosophy.

> "The entire ancient world had to collapse because the progress achieved by the peoples in their scientific development was necessarily bound up with a revelation of the errors on which their religious views were based."

According to the leading article, therefore, the entire ancient world collapsed because scientific research revealed the errors of the old religions. Would the ancient world not have perished if scientific research had kept silent about the errors of religion, if the Roman authorities had been recommended by the author of the leading article to excise the writings of Lucretius and Lucian?

For the rest, we shall permit ourselves to enlarge Herr H.'s erudition in another communication.

At the very time when the downfall of the ancient world was approaching, there arose the *Alexandrine school*, which strove to prove by force the "eternal truth" of Greek mythology and its complete agreement "with the results of scientific research". The Emperor Julian, too, belonged to this trend, which believed that it could make the newly developing spirit of the times disappear by keeping its eyes closed so as not to see it.

Karl Marx, "The Leading Article in No. 179 of the *Kölnische Zeitung*"

Marx and Engels, *Collected Works*, Vol. 1, Moscow, 1975, pp. 189-90

Philosophical Trends in the Epoch of the Decline of the Ancient World

At such times half-hearted minds have opposite views to those of whole-minded generals. They believe that they can compensate losses by cutting the armed forces, by splitting them up, by a peace treaty with the real needs, whereas Themistocles, when Athens was threatened with destruction, tried to persuade the Athenians to abandon the city entirely and found a new Athens at sea, in another element.

Neither must we forget that the time following such catastrophes is an iron time, happy when characterised by titanic struggles, lamentable when it resembles centuries limping in the wake of great periods in art. These centuries set about moulding in wax, plaster and copper what sprang from Carrara marble like Pallas Athena out of the head of Zeus, the father of the gods. But titanic are the times which follow in the wake of a philosophy total in itself and of its subjective developmental forms, for gigantic is the discord that forms their unity. Thus Rome followed the Stoic, Sceptic and Epicurean philosophy. They are unhappy and iron epochs, for their gods have died and the new goddess still reveals the dark aspect of fate, of pure light or of pure darkness. She still lacks the colours of day.

The kernel of the misfortune, however, is that the spirit of the time, the spiritual monad, sated in itself, ideally formed in all aspects in itself, is not allowed to recognise any reality which has come to being without it. The fortunate thing in such misfortune is therefore the subjective form, the modality of the relation of philosophy, as subjective consciousness, towards reality.

Thus, for example, the Epicurean, [and the] Stoic philosophy was the boon of its time; thus, when the universal sun has gone down, the moth seeks the lamplight of the private individual.

> Karl Marx, "Notebooks on Epicurean Philosophy"
>
> Marx and Engels, *Collected Works*, Vol. 1, Moscow, 1975, p. 492

Lucretius Carus

1

As Zeus grew up to the tumultuous war dances of the Curetes,[79] so here the world takes shape to the ringing war games of the atoms.

Lucretius is the genuine Roman epic poet, for he sings the substance of the Roman spirit; in place of Homer's cheerful, strong, integral characters we have here solid, impenetrable armed heroes possessed of no other qualities, we have the war *omnium contra omnes*,[a] the rigid shape of the being-for-self, a nature without god and a god aloof from the world.

> Karl Marx, "Notebooks on Epicurean Philosophy"
>
> Marx and Engels, *Collected Works*, Vol. 1, Moscow, 1975, p. 475

2

As nature in spring lays herself bare and, as though conscious of victory, displays all her charm, whereas in winter she covers up her shame and nakedness with snow and ice, so Lucretius, fresh, keen, poetic master of the world, differs from Plutarch, who covers his paltry ego with the snow and ice of morality. When we see an indi-

---

[a] Of all against all.—*Ed.*

vidual anxiously buttoned-up and cringing into himself, we involuntarily clutch at coat and clasp, make sure that we are still there, as if afraid to lose ourselves. But at the sight of an intrepid acrobat we forget ourselves, feel ourselves raised out of our own skins like universal forces and breathe more fearlessly. Who is it that feels in the more moral and free state of mind—he who has just come out of Plutarch's classroom, reflecting on how unjust it is that the good should lose with life the fruit of their life, or he who sees eternity fulfilled, hears the bold thundering song of Lucretius:[80]

"... high hope of fame has struck my heart with its sharp goad and in so doing has implanted in my breast the sweet love of the Muses. That is the spur that lends my spirit strength to pioneer through pathless tracts of their Pierian realm where no foot has ever trod before. What joy it is to light upon virgin springs and drink their waters. What joy to pluck new flowers and gather for my brow a glorious garland from fields whose blossoms were never yet wreathed by the Muses round any head. This was my reward for teaching on these lofty topics, for struggling to loose men's minds from the tight knots of religion and shedding on dark corners the bright beams of my song that irradiate everything with the sparkle of the Muses."

II. 921 ff.

He who would not prefer to build the whole world out of his own resources, to be a creator of the world, rather than to be eternally bothering about himself, has already been anathematised by the spirit, he is under an interdict, but in the opposite sense; he is expelled from the temple and deprived of the eternal enjoyment of the spirit and left to sing lullabies about his own private bliss and to dream about himself at night.

"Blessedness is not the reward of virtue, but is virtue itself."[81]

Karl Marx, "Notebooks on Epicurean Philosophy"

Marx and Engels, *Collected Works*, Vol. 1, Moscow, 1975, pp. 468-69

Horace

Old Horace reminds me in places of Heine,[82] who learned so much from him and who was also *au fond*[a] quite as much a scoundrel *politice*.[b] Imagine this honest man, who challenges the *vultus instantis tyranni*[c] and grovels before Augustus. Apart from this, the foul-mouthed old so and so is still very lovable.

Engels to Marx,
December 21, 1866

Marx/Engels, *Werke*, Bd. 31, 1965, S. 270-71

Persius' Satire

The philosophers were either mere money-earning schoolmasters or buffoons in the pay of wealthy revellers. Some were even slaves. An example of what became of them under good conditions is supplied by Seneca. This stoic and preacher of virtue and abstinence was Nero's first court intriguer, which he could not have been without servility; he secured from him presents in money, properties, gardens and palaces and while he preached the poor man Lazarus of the Gospel he was in reality the rich man in the same parable. Not until Nero wanted to get at him did he request the emperor to take back all his presents, his philosophy being enough for him. Only completely isolated philosophers like Persius had the courage to brandish the lash of satire over their degenerated contemporaries. But as for the second type of ideologists, the jurists, they were enthusiastic over the new conditions because the abolition of all differences be-

---

[a] At bottom.—*Ed.*
[b] In the political respect.—*Ed.*
[c] The threatening face of a tyrant.—*Ed.*

tween estates allowed them broad scope in elaborating their favourite private law, in return for which they prepared for the emperor the vilest system of state law that ever existed.

> Frederick Engels, "Bruno Bauer and Early Christianity"
>
> Marx and Engels, *On Religion*, 1975, pp. 175-76

Lucian

One of our best sources on the first Christians is Lucian[83] of Samosata, the Voltaire of classic antiquity, who was equally sceptic towards every kind of religious superstition and therefore had neither pagan-religious nor political grounds to treat the Christians otherwise than some other kind of religious community. On the contrary, he mocked them all for their superstition, those who worshipped Jupiter no less than those who worshipped Christ; from his shallow rationalistic point of view one sort of superstition was as stupid as the other.

> Frederick Engels, "On the History of Early Christianity"
>
> Marx and Engels, *On Religion*, 1975, p. 277

Middle Ages

Germanic Culture

During the early sixties of this century, finds of outstanding importance were made in two Schleswig peat bogs; these were carefully studied by Engelhardt in Copenhagen and, after various wanderings, deposited in the Kiel Museum. They are distinguished from similar discoveries by the presence of coins, making it possible to determine their age with considerable certainty. Thirty-seven coins, from Nero to Septimius Severus, were found in Taschberg peat bog (Thorsbjerg in Danish) near Süderbrarup, and in Nydam bog, a sea inlet covered with silt and transformed into a peat bog, thirty-four coins from the reign of Tiberius to that of Macrinus (218) were unearthed. The finds undoubtedly therefore belong to the period between 220 and 250 A.D. The objects are not exclusively of Roman origin; many were made by the Germans in the area. Due to the almost total preservation of these finds in the iron-rich water of the bog, they reveal, in surprising ways, the state of the North-German metal, weaving, and shipbuilding industries, and, through the runic signs, the state of written culture in the first half of the third century.

We are even more astounded by the state of industry itself. The fine woven fabrics, delicate sandals, and well crafted saddler's goods indicate a far higher level of culture than that of the "Tacitean" Germans. Particularly amazing are the indigenous articles of metal.

Comparative philology proves that the Germans brought the knowledge of metals with them from their Asian homeland. Perhaps they also knew how to extract and work metal, but it is hardly likely that they still had this knowledge at the time when they clashed with the Romans. At least there is no indication in the writings of the first century that between the Rhine and the Elbe iron or bronze were being produced and worked; rather there is evidence to the contrary. Tacitus, it is true, mentions that the Goths (in Upper Silesia?) mined iron, and Ptolemy ascribes ironworks to the neighbouring Quades; in both cases, the knowledge of smelting could have been re-acquired from the shores of the Danube. Finds attested through coins as belonging to the first century include no indigenous metal products, only Roman. Why should all these Roman metal articles have been brought to Germany if there had been indigenous metalworking? One does find old casting moulds, unfinished castings, and scraps of bronze in Germany, but these are never accompanied by coins which could indicate their age; in all probability they are from pre-Germanic times, left by nomadic Etruscan bronze founders. Besides it is pointless to ask whether the immigrating Germans had *entirely* lost the art of metal-working; all facts indicate that in the first century metal-working was practically non-existent among them.

But here the Taschberg bog finds again reveal an unexpectedly high level of the indigenous metal industry. Here are buckles, decorative metal plates engraved with heads of men and animals, a silver helmet covering the whole face, except for eyes, nose and mouth, chain mail of woven wire, demanding an extraordinary amount of labour, for the wire had to be hammered out first (wire-drawing was invented only in 1306), a gold head band, not to mention other artifacts which might not be of local origin. These objects are similar to others found in the Nydam bog, in a bog on Fünen, and lastly to a find made in Bohemia (Horovice), also in the early sixties: magnificent bronze disks with human heads, buckles, clasps, etc., all similar to those found at Taschberg, and accordingly all from the same period.

From the third century on, the metal industry, steadily improving, must have spread over the whole territory of

Germany; by the time of the migration of peoples, say towards the end of the fifth century, it had reached a comparatively advanced stage. Not only iron and bronze, but gold and silver were regularly worked. Gold bracteates, modeled on Roman coins, were minted, and base metals gilded; one also comes across inlaid work, enamels, and filigree. An awkward form is often decorated with highly tasteful and artistic designs, only partially based on Roman work. This is mainly true of buckles, clasps and brooches which have certain characteristic forms in common. In the British Museum, clasps from Kerch, on the Sea of Azov, are exhibited together with similar clasps found in England, which could have come from the same metalworks. The style of such work, despite the often substantial local peculiarities, is essentially uniform from Sweden to the lower Danube, and from the Black Sea to France and England. This first period of German metal industry on the continent ceases with the cessation of the migration of peoples and with the general acceptance of Christianity. In England and Scandinavia, it continues for somewhat longer.

The wide extension of this industry among the Germans in the sixth and seventh centuries and its distinction as a special branch of industry is attested in various codes of law.[84] There are numerous references to blacksmiths, sword makers and gold- and silver-smiths even in the Alamannian statutes and even to publicly attested ones *(publice probati)*. Bavarian law punishes theft from a church, ducal palace, smithy, or mill more severely, "for these four buildings are public and remain open at all times". According to Frisian law, recompense for the murder of a goldsmith was 25 per cent higher than for others of the same social standing. Salic law values an ordinary serf at 12 solidi, but a blacksmith-serf *(faber)* at 35 solidi.

Engels, "A Contribution to Early German History"

Marx/Engels, *Werke*, Bd. 19, 1962, S. 456-59

Love in the Literature of Antiquity and the Middle Ages

No such thing as individual sex love existed before the Middle Ages. That personal beauty, intimate association, similarity in inclinations, etc., aroused desire for sexual intercourse among people of opposite sexes, that men as well as women were not totally indifferent to the question of with whom they entered into this most intimate relation is obvious. But this is still a far cry from the sex love of our day. Throughout antiquity marriages were arranged by the parents; the parties quietly acquiesced. The little conjugal love that was known to antiquity was not in any way a subjective inclination, but an objective duty; not a reason for but a correlate of marriage. In antiquity, love affairs in the modern sense occur only outside official society. The shepherds, whose joys and sorrows in love are sung by Theocritus and Moschus, or by Longus' *Daphnis and Chloë*, are mere slaves, who have no share in the state, the sphere of the free citizen. Except among the slaves, however, we find love affairs only as disintegration products of the declining ancient world; and with women who are also beyond the pale of official society, with *hetaerae*, that is, with alien or freed women: in Athens beginning with the eve of its decline, in Rome at the time of the emperors. If love affairs really occurred between free male and female citizens, it was only in the form of adultery. And sex love in our sense of the term was so immaterial to that classical love poet of antiquity, old Anacreon, that even the sex of the beloved one was a matter of complete indifference to him.

Our sex love differs materially from the simple sexual desire, the *eros*, of the ancients. First, it presupposes reciprocal love on the part of the loved one; in this respect, the woman stands on a par with the man; whereas in the ancient *eros*, the woman was by no means always consulted.

Secondly, sex love attains a degree of intensity and permanency where the two parties regard non-possession or separation as a great, if not the greatest, misfortune; in order to possess each other they take great hazards, even risking life itself—what in antiquity happened, at best, only in cases of adultery. And finally, a new moral standard arises for judging sexual intercourse. The question asked is not only whether such intercourse was legitimate or illicit, but also whether it arose from mutual love or not? It goes without saying that in feudal or bourgeois practice this new standard fares no better than all the other moral standards—it is simply ignored. But it fares no worse, either. It is recognised in theory, on paper, like all the rest. And more than this cannot be expected for the present.

Where antiquity broke off with its start towards sex love, the Middle Ages began, namely, with adultery. We have already described chivalrous love, which gave rise to the Songs of the Dawn. There is still a wide gulf between this kind of love, which aimed at breaking up matrimony, and the love destined to be its foundation, a gulf never completely bridged by the age of chivalry. Even when we pass from the frivolous Latins to the virtuous Germans, we find, in the *Nibelungenlied*,[85] that Kriemhild—although secretly in love with Siegfried every whit as much as he is with her—nevertheless, in reply to Gunther's intimation that he has plighted her to a knight whom he does not name, answers simply:

"You have no need to ask; as you command, so will I be for ever. He whom you, my lord, choose for my husband, to him will I gladly plight my troth."[86]

It never even occurs to her that her love could possibly be considered in this matter. Gunther seeks the hand of Brunhild without ever having seen her, and Etzel does the same with Kriemhild. The same occurs in the *Gudrun*,[87] where Sigebant of Ireland seeks the hand of Ute the Norwegian, Hettel of Hegelingen that of Hilde of Ireland; and lastly,

Siegfried of Morland, Hartmut of Ormany and Herwig of Seeland seek the hand of Gudrun; and here for the first time it happens that Gudrun, of her own free will, decides in favour of the last named. As a rule, the bride of a young prince is selected by his parents; if these are no longer alive, he chooses her himself with the counsel of his highest vassal chiefs, whose word carries great weight in all cases. Nor can it be otherwise. For the knight, or baron, just as for the prince himself, marriage is a political act, an opportunity for the accession of power through new alliances; the interest of the *House* and not individual inclination are the decisive factor. How can love here hope to have the last word regarding marriage?

>Frederick Engels, *The Origin of the Family, Private Property and the State*
>
>Marx and Engels, *Selected Works*, Vol. 3, Moscow, 1973, pp. 249-51

Wagner and Germanic Epos

Marx, in a letter written in the spring of 1882,[88] expresses himself in the strongest possible terms about the utter falsification of primeval times appearing in Wagner's *Nibelung* text.[89] "Whoever heard of a brother embracing his sister as his bride?" To these "lewd gods" of Wagner's, who in quite modern style spiced their love affairs with a little incest, Marx gave the answer: "In primeval times the sister *was* the wife, *and that was moral.*" [*Note by Engels to the 1884 edition.*]

A French friend [Bonnier] and admirer of Wagner does not agree with this note, and points out that already in the *Ögisdrecka*, the earlier *Edda*,[90] which Wagner took as his model, Loki reproaches Freya thus: "Thine own brother has thou embraced before the gods." Marriage between brother and sister, he claimed, was proscribed already at that time.

The *Ögisdrecka* is the expression of a time when belief in the ancient myths was completely shattered; it is a truly Lucianian satire on the gods. If Loki, as Mephistopheles, thus reproaches Freya, it argues rather against Wagner. A few verses later, Loki also says to Njord: "You begat [such] a son by our sister" [*vidh systur thinni gaztu slikan mög*]. Now, Njord is not an Asa but a Vana, and says, in the Ynglinga saga,[91] that marriages between brothers and sisters are customary in Vanaland, which is not the case amongst the Asas. This would seem to indicate that the Vanàs were older gods than the Asas. At any rate, Njord lived among the Asas as their equal, and the *Ögisdrecka* is thus rather a proof that intermarriage between brothers and sisters, at least among the gods, did not yet arouse any revulsion at the time the Norwegian Sagas of the gods originated. If one wants to excuse Wagner, one would do better to cite Goethe instead of the *Edda*, for Goethe, in his Ballad of God and the Bayadere, makes a similar mistake regarding the religious surrender of women, which he likens far too closely to modern prostitution.

Frederick Engels, *The Origin of the Family, Private Property and the State*

Marx and Engels, *Selected Works*, Vol. 3, Moscow, 1973, pp. 216-17

Legend of Siegfried and the German Revolutionary Movement

What is it about the legend of Siegfried that affects us so powerfully? Not the plot of the story itself, not the foul treason which brings about the death of the youthful hero; it is the deep significance which is expressed through his person. Siegfried is the representative of German youth. All of us, who still carry in our breast a heart unfettered by the restraints of life, know what that means. We all feel in ourselves the same zest for action, the same defiance of convention which drove Siegfried from his father's castle; we loathe with all our soul continual reflection and the philistine fear of vigorous action; we want to get out into the free world; we want to overrun the barriers of prudence and fight for the crown of life, action. The philistines have supplied giants and dragons too, particularly in the sphere of church and state. But that age is no more; we are put in prisons called schools, where instead of striking out around us we are made with cruel irony to conjugate the verb "to strike" in Greek in all moods and tenses, and when we are released from that discipline we fall into the hands of the goddess of the century, the police. Police for thinking, police for speaking, police for walking, riding and driving, passports, residence permits, and customs documents—the devil strike these giants and dragons dead! They have left us only the semblance of action, the rapier instead of the sword; but what use is all the art of fencing with the rapier if we may not apply it with the sword? And when the barriers are finally broken down, when philistinism and indifference are trodden underfoot, when the urge to action is no longer checked—do you see the tower of Wesel there across the Rhine? The citadel of that town, which is called a stronghold of German freedom, has become the grave of German youth, and has to lie right opposite the cradle of the greatest German youth! Who sat there in prison? Students who did not want to have learnt to fence to no purpose, *vulgo* duellists and demagogues.[92] Now, after the amnesty of Frederick William IV,[93] we may be permitted to say that this amnesty was an act not only of mercy but of justice. Granted all the premises, and in particular the need for the state to take measures against the student fraternities, nevertheless, everyone who sees that the good of the state does not lie in blind obedience and strict subordination will surely agree with me that the treatment of the participants demanded that they should be rehabilitated in honour and dignity. Under the Restoration[94] and after the July days[a] the demagogic fraternities were as understandable as they are now impossible. Who then suppressed every free movement, who placed the beating of the youthful heart under "provisional" guardianship? And how were the unfortunates treated? Can it be denied that this legal case is perfectly calculated to show in the clearest light all the disadvantages and errors of both public and secret judicature, to make manifest the contradiction that paid *servants of the state,* instead of independent jurors, try charges of offending against the state; can it be denied that all the sentencing was done summarily, "in bulk", as merchants say?

But I want to go down to the Rhine and listen to what the waves gleaming in the sunset tell Siegfried's mother earth about his grave in Worms and about the sunken hoard. Perhaps a friendly Morgan le Fay will make Siegfried's castle rise again for me or show my mind's eye what heroic deeds are reserved for his sons of the nineteenth century.

Frederick Engels, "Siegfried's Native Town"

Marx and Engels, *Collected Works,* Vol. 2, Moscow, 1975, pp. 135-36

Ancient Irish Literature

1

The writers of ancient Greece and Rome, and also the fathers of the Church, give very little information about Ireland.

Instead there still exists an abundant native literature, in spite of the many Irish manuscripts lost in the wars of the sixteenth and seventeenth centuries. It includes poems, grammars, glossaries, annals and other historical writings and

---

[a] The July 1830 revolution in France.—*Ed.*

law-books. With very few exceptions, however, this whole literature, which embraces the period at least from the eighth to the seventeenth century, exists only in *manuscript*. For the Irish language printing has existed only for a few years, only from the time when the language began to die out. Of this rich material, therefore, only a small part is available. Amongst the most important of these annals are those of Abbot *Tigernach* (died 1088), those of *Ulster*, and above all, those of the *Four Masters*. These last were collected in 1632-36 in a monastery in Donegal under the direction of Michael O'Clery, a Franciscan monk, who was helped by three other Seanchaidhes (antiquarians), from materials which now are almost all lost. They were published in 1856 from the original Donegal manuscript which still exists, having been edited and provided with an English translation by O'Donovan.[a] The earlier editions by Dr. Charles O'Connor[95] (the first part of the *Four Masters*, and the *Annals of Ulster*) are untrustworthy in text and translation.

The beginning of most of these annals presents the mythical prehistory of Ireland. Its base was formed by old folk-legends, which were spun out endlessly by poets in the 9th and 10th centuries and were then brought into suitable chronological order by the monk-chroniclers. *The Annals of the Four Masters* begins with the year of the world 2242, when Caesair, a granddaughter of Noah, landed in Ireland forty days before the Flood; other annals have the ancestors of the Scots, the last immigrants to Ireland, descend in direct line from Japheth and bring them into connection with Moses, the Egyptians and the Phoenicians, as the German chroniclers of the Middle Ages connected the ancestors of the Germans with Troy, Aeneas or Alexander the Great. The *Four Masters* devote only a few pages to this legend (in which the only valuable element, the original folk-legend, is

---

[a] *Annala Rioghachta Eireann. Annals of the Kingdom of Ireland by the Four Masters*. Edited, with an English Translation, by Dr. John O'Donovan. Second edition, Dublin, 1856, 7 volumes in 4°.

not distinguishable even now); the *Annals of Ulster* leave it out altogether; and Tigernach, with a critical boldness wonderful for his time, explains that all the written records of the Scots before King Cimbaoth (approximately 300 B.C.) are uncertain. But when new national life awoke in Ireland at the end of the last century, and with it new interest in Irish literature and history, just these monks' legends were counted to be their most valuable constituent. With true Celtic enthusiasm and specifically Irish naïveté, belief in these stories was declared an intrinsic part of national patriotism, and this offered the supercunning world of English scholarship—whose own efforts in the field of philological and historical criticism are gloriously enough well known to the rest of the world—the desired pretext for throwing everything Irish aside as arrant nonsense.[a]

> Frederick Engels, "History of Ireland"
> Marx and Engels, *Ireland and the Irish Question*, Moscow, 1974, pp. 191-92

2

The *Senchus Mor*[97] has until now been our main source for information about conditions in ancient Ireland. It is a collection of ancient legal decisions which, according to the

---

[a] One of the most naive products of that time is *The Chronicles of Eri, being the History of the Gaal Sciot Iber, or the Irish People, translated from the original manuscripts in the Phoenician dialect of the Scythian Language by O'Connor*, London, 1822, 2 volumes. The Phoenician dialect of the Scythian language is naturally Celtic Irish, and the original manuscript is a verse chronicle chosen at will. The publisher is Arthur O'Connor, exile of 1798,[96] uncle of Feargus O'Connor who was later leader of the English Chartists, an ostensible descendant of the ancient O'Connors, Kings of Connaught, and, after a fashion, the Irish Pretender to the throne. His portrait appears in front of the title, a man with a handsome, jovial Irish face, strikingly resembling his neph-

later composed introduction, was compiled on the orders of St. Patrick, and with his assistance brought into harmony with Christianity, rapidly spreading in Ireland. The High King of Ireland, Laeghaire (428-458, according to the *Annals of the Four Masters*), the Vice-Kings, Corc of Munster and Daire, probably a prince of Ulster, and also three bishops: St. Patrick, St. Benignus and St. Cairnech, and three lawyers: Dubthach, Fergus and Rossa, are supposed to have formed the "commission" which compiled the book—and there is no doubt that they did their work more cheaply than the present commission, who only had to publish it. The *Four Masters* give 438 as the year in which the book was written.

The text itself is evidently based on very ancient heathen materials. The oldest legal formulas in it are written in verse with a precise metre and the so-called consonance, a kind of alliteration or rather consonant-assonance, which is peculiar to Irish poetry and frequently goes over to full rhyme. As it is certain that old Irish law-books were translated in the fourteenth century from the so-called Fenian dialect (Bérla Feini), the language of the fifth century, into the then current Irish (Introduction (Vol. 1), p. xxxvi and following) it emerges that in the *Senchus Mor* too the metre has been more or less smoothed out in places; but it appears often enough along with occasional rhymes and marked consonance to give the text a definite rhythmical cadence. It is generally sufficient to read the translation in order to find out the verse forms. But then there are also throughout it, especially in the latter half, numerous pieces of undoubted prose; and, whereas the verse is certainly very ancient and has been handed down by tradition, these prose insertions seem to originate with the compilers of the book. At any rate, the

---

ew Feargus, grasping a crown with his right hand. Underneath is the caption: "O'Connor—cear-rige, head of his race, and O'Connor, chief of the prostrate people of his nation: 'Soumis, pas vaincus' [Subdued, not conquered]."

Senchus Mor is quoted frequently in the glossary composed in the ninth or tenth century, and attributed to the King and Bishop of Cashel, Cormac, and it was certainly written long before the English invasion.

All the manuscripts (the oldest of which appears to date from the beginning of the 14th century or earlier) contain a series of mostly concordant annotations and longer commenting notes on this text. The annotations are in the spirit of old glossaries; quibbles take the place of etymology and the explanation of words, and comments are of varying quality, being often badly distorted or largely incomprehensible, at least without knowledge of the rest of the law-books. The age of the annotations and comments is uncertain. Most of them, however, probably date from after the English invasion. As at the same time they show only a very few traces of developments in the law outside the text itself, and these are only a more precise establishment of details, the greater part, which is purely explanatory, can certainly also be used with some discretion as a source concerning earlier times.

The *Senchus Mor* contains:

1. The law of distraint [Pfändungsrecht], that is to say, almost the whole judicial procedure;

2. The law of hostages, which during disputes were put up by people of different territories;

3. The law of Saerrath and Daerrath[98] (see below); and

4. The law of the family.

From this we obtain much valuable information on the social life of that time, but, as long as many of the expressions are unexplained and the rest of the manuscripts is not published, much remains dark.

In addition to literature, the surviving architectural monuments, churches, round towers, fortifications and inscriptions also enlighten us about the condition of the people before the arrival of the English.

Frederick Engels, "History of Ireland"

Marx and Engels, *Ireland and the Irish Question*, Moscow, 1974, pp. 194-96

3

The manuscripts of still extant Irish poems believed to date from the early Milesian times,[99] are accompanied by interlinear glosses without which they would be incomprehensible; but the glosses themselves are in an extremely archaic language and very difficult to understand.

> Frederick Engels, *Manuscripts on the History of England and Ireland*
>
> Marx/Engels, *Über Kunst und Literatur*, Bd. I, Berlin, 1967, S. 325

4[100]

Some Irish folk-music is very ancient, some has arisen in the last three to four hundred years, and some only in the last century. Especially much was written at the time by one of the last Irish bards, Carolan. In the past these bards or harpists—poets, composers and singers in one person—were quite numerous. Every Irish chieftain had his own bard in his castle. Many travelled the country as wandering singers, persecuted by the English, who correctly saw in them the main bearers of the national, anti-English tradition. Ancient songs about the victories of Finn Mac Cumhal (whom Macpherson stole from the Irish and turned into a Scot under the name Fingal in his *Ossian*,[101] which is entirely based on Irish songs), about the magnificence of the ancient royal palace of Tara, the heroic deeds of King Brian Borumha, and later songs about the battles of Irish chieftains against the Sassenach (Englishmen) were all preserved in the living memory of the nation by the bards. And they also celebrated the exploits of contemporary Irish chieftains in their fight for independence. When in the 17th century, however, the Irish people were completely crushed by Elizabeth, James I,

Oliver Cromwell and William of Orange, their landholdings robbed and given to English invaders, the Irish people outlawed in their own land and transformed into a nation of outcasts, the wandering singers were hounded in the same way as the Catholic priests, and had gradually died out by the beginning of this century. Their names are lost, of their poetry only fragments have survived, the most beautiful legacy they have left their enslaved, but unconquered people is their music.

Irish poems are all written in four-line verses. For this reason a four-line rhythm always lies at the basis of most, especially the ancient, Irish melodies, though sometimes it may be a little hidden, and frequently a refrain or conclusion on the harp follows it. Some of these ancient songs are even now, when in the largest part of Ireland Irish is understood only by the old people or even not at all, known only by their Irish names or first words. But the greater, more recent part has English names or texts.

The melancholy dominating most of these songs is still the expression of the national disposition today. How could it be otherwise amongst a people whose conquerors are always inventing new, up-to-date methods of oppression? The latest method, which was introduced forty years ago and pushed to the extreme in the last twenty years, consists in the mass eviction of Irishmen from their homes and farms—which, in Ireland, is the same as eviction from the country. Since 1841 the population has dropped by two and a half million, and over three million Irishmen have emigrated. All this has been done for the profit of the big landowners of English descent, and on their instigation. If it goes on like this for another thirty years, there will be Irishmen only in America.

> Frederick Engels, "Notes for the Preface to a Collection of Irish Songs"
>
> Marx and Engels, *Ireland and the Irish Question*, Moscow, 1974, pp. 270-71

Ancient Scandinavian Epos

The quarrelling of the Irish princes amongst themselves greatly simplified pillage and settlement for the Norsemen, and even the temporary conquest of the whole island. The extent to which the Scandinavians considered Ireland as one of their regular pillage grounds is shown by the so-called death-song of Ragnar Lodbrôk, the *Krâkumâl*,[102] composed about the year 1000 in the snaketower of King Ella of Northumberland. In this song all the ancient pagan savagery is massed together, as if for the last time, and under the pretext of celebrating King Ragnar's heroic deeds in song, all the Nordic peoples' raids in their own lands, on coasts from Dünamünde to Flanders, Scotland (here already called Skotland, perhaps for the first time) and Ireland are briefly pictured. About Ireland it is said:

"We hew'd with our swords, heap'd high the slain,
Glad was the wolf's brother of the furious battle's feast;
Iron struck brass-shields; Ireland's ruler, Marsteinn,
Did not starve the murder-wolf or eagle;
In Vedhrafiördhr the raven was given a sacrifice.
We hew'd with our swords, started a game at dawn,
A merry battle against three kings at Lindiseyri;
Not many could boast that they fled unhurt from there.
Falcon fought wolf for flesh, the wolf's fury devoured many;
The blood of the Irish flow'd in streams on the beach in the battle."[a]

> Frederick Engels, "History of Ireland"
>
> Marx and Engels, *Ireland and the Irish Question*, Moscow, 1974, pp. 204-05

---

[a] "Hiuggu ver medh hiörvi, hverr lâ thverr of annan;
gladhr vardh gera brôdhir getu vidh sôknar laeti,
lêt ei örn nê ýlgi, sâ er Îrlandi stýrdhi,
(môt vardh mâlms ok rîtar) Marsteinn konungr fasta;
vardh î Vedhra firdhi valtafn gefit hrafni.

Hiuggu ver medh hiörvi, hâdhum sudhr at morni
leik fyrir Lindiseyri vidh lofdhûnga threnna;

Early Medieval Danish Poetry

By pure chance, the old Danish Kjämpe-Viser fell into my hands. Some very nice things here and there among a lot of rubbish. Here is one, translated by Uhland.

>Her Oluf hand rider saa vide,
>Alt til sit brøllup at byde,
>Men dandsen den gaar saa let gennem lunden.

>Der dandse fire, og der dandse fem:
>Elle kongens daater rekker haanden frem.

>"Velkommen, Her Oluf, lad fare din fig:
>Bi lidet, og træd her i dandsen med mig."

>"Ieg ikke tør, jeg ikke maa:
>I morgen skal mit brøllup staa."

>"Hør du, Her Oluf, træd dandsen med mig:
>To bukkeskinds støvle saa giver jeg dig.

>To bukkeskinds støvle, sider vel om been:
>Forgyldene spore derom spend.

>Hør du, Her Ole, træd dandsen med mig:
>En silke-skiørte giver jeg dig.

>En silke-skiorte saa hivid og fiin:
>Den blegte min moder veg maane skin."

>"Jeg ikke tør, jeg ikke maa etc."

>"Hør du, Her Oluf, træd dandsen med mig:
>Et hoved af guld saa giver jeg dig."

>"Et hoved af guld kand jeg vel faa:

---

fârr âtti thvî fagna (fêll margr î gyn ûlfi,
haukr sleit hold medh vargi), at hann heill thadhan kaemi;
Ŷra blödh î oegi aerit fêll um skaeru."

Vedhrafiördhr is, as we have said, Waterford; I do not know whether Lindiseyri has been discovered anywhere. On no account does it mean Leinster as Johnstone translates it; eyri (sandy neck of land, Danish öre) points to a quite distinct locality. Valtafn can also mean falcon feed and is generally translated as such here, but as the raven is Odin's holy bird, the word obviously has both meanings.

Men dandse med dig tør jeg ej saa."

"Og vil du ikke dandse med mig,
Sot og sygdom skal følge dig."

Hun slog hannem mellem sine hærde:
Aldrig var hand slagen verre.

Hun løfte, Her Oluf paa ganger rød:
"Og rid nu hiem til din festemø."

Der hand kom til borgeled:
Der staar hands moder og hviler ved.

"Hør du, Her Oluf, kier sønnen min:
Hvi bær du nu saa bleg en kind?"

Og jeg maa vel bære kinden bleg,
For jeg har været i Ellekonens leg."

"Hør du, Her Ole, min søn saa prud:
Hvad skal jeg svare din unge brud?"

"I skal sige, jeg er udi lunde,
At prøve min hest og saa mine hunde."

Aarle om morgen, dag det var:
Da kom den brud med brudeskar.

De skenkte miød, de skenkte viin:
"Hvor er, Her Ole, brudgom min?"

"Her Oluf hand reed sig hen i lunde:
Hand prøved sin hest og saa sine hunde."

Hun tog op det skarlagen rød:
Der laa Her Oluf og var død.[a]

---

[a] Herr Oluf fares both far and wide,
To fetch the wedding-guests he doth ride.

The elves dance on the green land,
The Elf King's daughter gives him her hand.

"Welcome, Herr Oluf, why wouldst thou flee?
Step into the ring and dance with me."

I like this much better than the very smooth Uhland version. Another, "Her Jon", is even nicer.

> Engels to Marx, June 20, 1860
> Written in German and Danish
> Marx/Engels, *Werke*, Bd. 30, 1964, S. 65-67

The Chanson de Roland

The oldest Provençal poems extant date from circa 1100, but there is no doubt that there were earlier experiments too. With the aid of a steadily growing number of documents, Paulin Paris has demonstrated that, contrary to Fau-

---

"But dance I neither will nor may,
Tomorrow dawns my wedding day."

"Oh list, Herr Oluf, come dance with me,
Two golden spurs I'll give to thee.

"A shirt all shining white so fine:
My mother shall bleach it with pale moonshine."

"But dance I neither will nor may,
Tomorrow dawns my wedding day."

"Oh list, Herr Oluf, come dance with me,
A pile of gold I'll give to thee."

"Gladly I'd take your gold away,
But dance I neither dare nor may."

"An thou, Herr Oluf, dance not with me,
Sickness and plague shall follow thee."

And then she touched him on the chest.
Never such pain had clutched his breast.

She helps him, half-swooning, his mount to bestride:
"Now get thee hence to thy fair bride."

As to his own door he drew near,
His mother was trembling there with fear.

riel, *epic poetry first originated in northern France* and spread from there to southern France (p. 342); *la date est certaine*,[a] since Taillefer sang the "Chanson de Roland" near Hastings; it has been established that its surviving, probably somewhat expanded text was in existence before the first Crusade. Edit. Francisque Michel, Paris 1837, and F. Génin, Paris 1850. The author is Théroulde (Turoldus). The unity of France, represented in the person of Charlemagne, an imaginary, ideal feudal monarchy, is celebrated in this *chanson*, while later poets of the Carolingian group of legends at the time of the monarchy's real resurgence celebrate local heroes and, particularly in "Fils Aymon", resistance to the central power, the feudal monarchy (pp. 345-46).

Frederick Engels, <i>Material on the
History of France and Germany</i>
Marx/Engels, <i>Über Kunst und Literatur,</i>
Bd. I, Berlin, 1967, S. 333

"Tell me quickly, oh quickly, my son,
Why are thy looks so pale and wan?"

"How should they not be pale and wan?
'Tis from the Elf King's realm I come."

"Oh list, dear son I love so well,
What to your bride am I to tell?"

"Say to the forest I am bound,
To exercise my horse and hound."

Next morning, when it was scarcely day,
There came the bride with her company.

They poured the mead, they poured the wine.
"Where is Herr Oluf, bridegroom of mine?"

"He's ridden hence, for the forest bound,
To exercise his horse and hound."

The bride uplifted the scarlet red.
There lay Herr Oluf, and he was dead.

(Translated by Alex Miller)

---

[a] The date is certain.—*Ed.*

Provençal Literature

1

"The people in southern France were in the Middle Ages not closer to the people in Northern France, than the Poles are now to the Russians. In the Middle Ages the southern French, commonly called Provençals, were not only "highly developed", they even led European development. They were the first of all modern nations to have a literary language. Their poetry was regarded by all Romance people, and even by the Germans and English, as a model that was unequalled at that time. They vied with the Castilians, the Northern Frenchmen and the English Normans in the perfection of feudal chivalry and were equal to the Italians in industry and commerce. They did not only "in a resplendent way" develop "one aspect of medieval life", they even produced a flash of the ancient Hellenic culture in the darkest Middle Ages."

> Karl Marx and Frederick Engels,
> "The Frankfurt Assembly Debates the Polish Question"
>
> Marx and Engels, *Collected Works*, Vol. 7, Moscow, 1976

2

In the 9th century—the new Franco-Romance language had developed to the extent that it became necessary to proceed to translation of the *Vulgate*[103]; this point came up for discussion, among others, at the Councils of *Tours* (813), *Mainz* (847) and *Arles* (851). Two of the oldest documents of the French language: *Translation of a poem on Boethius* (9th century) and a poem of the *Waldenses*,[104] treated as very important by *Reynouard* (historian of the troubadours). —The clergy in southern France engaged in biblical poetry and accurate translation of the sections of the holy scriptures told in poetic form. As early as the 11th century there were translations of the *Books of Samuel* and the *Books of Kings* or, as both are called in the *Vulgate*, the four books of Kings; these works indicate an attempt to combat the poetry of *secular (Provençal) poets* with *biblical* poetry.

> Karl Marx, "Chronological Extracts from Schlosser's *A World History for the German People*"
>
> Marx/Engels, *Über Kunst und Literatur*, Bd. I, Berlin, 1967, S. 331

Chivalrous Love Poetry

Although monogamy was the only known form of the family out of which modern sex love could develop, it does not follow that this love developed within it exclusively, or even predominantly, as the mutual love of man and wife. The whole nature of strict monogamian marriage under male domination ruled this out. Among all historically active classes, that is, among all ruling classes, matrimony remained what it had been since pairing marriage—a matter of convenience arranged by the parents. And the first form of sex love that historically emerges as a passion, and as a passion in which any person (at least of the ruling classes) has a right to indulge, as the highest form of the sexual impulse— which is precisely its specific feature—this, its first form, the chivalrous love of the Middle Ages, was by no means conjugal love. On the contrary, in its classical form, among the Provençals, it steers under full sail towards adultery, the praises of which are sung by their poets. The "*Albas*", in German *Tagelieder* [Songs of the Dawn], are the flower of Provençal love poetry. They describe in glowing colours how the knight lies with his love—the wife of another—while the watchman stands guard outside, calling him at the first faint streaks of dawn *(alba)* so that he may escape unobserved. The parting scene then constitutes the climax. The Northern French as well as the worthy Germans, likewise adopted this style of poetry, along with the manners of chivalrous love which corresponded to it; and on this same suggestive theme our own old Wolfram von Eschenbach has left us three exquisite Songs of the Dawn, which I prefer to his three long heroic poems.[105]

Frederick Engels, *The Origin of the Family, Private Property and the State*

Marx and Engels, *Selected Works*, Vol. 3, Moscow, 1973, pp. 243-44

Peasant Equalitarian Ideas in England. John Ball. William Langland's "Complaint of Piers the Ploughman"

Right after peace,[106] *"John Ball",* whom the courtly Froissart calls *"a mad priest of Kent",* finds for twenty years an audience for his sermons, despite interdict and imprisonment, in the *stout yeomen* gathered around him in the *churchyards of Kent.*

"Good People", cried *John Ball, "things will never be good in England so long as goods be not in common, and so long as there be villeins and gentlemen.* By what right are they whom we call lords greater folk than we? On what grounds have they deserved it? Why do they hold *us in serfage*? If we all came from the same father and mother, of Adam and Eve, how can they say or prove that they are better than we, if it be not *that they make us gain for them by our toil what they spend in their pride*? They are clothed in velvet and warm in their furs and their ermines, while we are covered with rags. They have wine and spices and fair bread; and we oat-cake and straw, and water to drink. They have leisure and fine houses; we have pain and labour, the rain and the wind in the fields. *And yet it is of us and our toil that these men hold* their state."

In popular rhyme is in fact condensed the levelling doctrine, says the green Green:

> "When Adam delved and Eve span,
> Who was then the gentleman?"

Contrast the contrast between: *William Langland's "Complaint of Piers the Ploughman"*, and the courtly Chaucer's *Canterbury Tales*. {Langland, nicknamed for his tall stature *"Long Bill"*, probably born in Shropshire where he had been to school and received minor orders as a cleric, found his way soon to London, etc.}

Karl Marx, "Chronological Extracts from Schlosser's *A World History for the German People*"

Written in English and German

Marx/Engels, *Über Kunst und Literatur*, Bd. I, Berlin, 1967, Anmerk. 196

German *Volksbücher*[a]

Is it not a great commendation for a book to be a popular book, a book for the German people? Yet this gives us the right to demand a great deal of such a book; it must satisfy all reasonable requirements and its value in every respect must be unquestionable. The popular book has the task of cheering, reviving and entertaining the peasant when he returns home in the evening tired from his hard day's work,

---

[a] German Volksbücher were similar to the English chap-books of the same period, that is, cheap popular books intended for the mass of the people and containing legends, tales, poetry, etc.—*Ed.*

making him forget his toil, transforming his stony field into a fragrant rose garden; it has the task of turning the craftsman's workshop and the wretched apprentice's miserable attic into a world of poetry, a golden palace, and showing him his sturdy sweetheart in the guise of a beautiful princess; but it also has the task, together with the Bible, of clarifying his moral sense, making him aware of his strength, his rights, his freedom, and arousing his courage and love for his country.

If, generally speaking, the qualities which can fairly be demanded of a popular book are rich poetic content, robust humour, moral purity, and, for a German popular book, a strong, trusty *German* spirit, qualities which remain the same at all times, we are also entitled to demand that it should be in keeping with its age, or cease to be a book for the people. If we take a look in particular at the present time, at the struggle for freedom which produces all its manifestations—the development of constitutionalism, the resistance to the pressure of the aristocracy, the fight of the intellect against pietism and of gaiety against the remnants of gloomy asceticism—I fail to see how it can be wrong to demand that the popular book should help the uneducated person and show him the truth and reasonableness of these trends, although, of course, not by direct deduction; but on no account should it encourage servility and toadying to the aristocracy of pietism. It goes without saying, however, that customs of earlier times, which it would be absurd or even wrong to practise today, must have no place in a popular book.

By these principles we should, and must, also judge those books which are now genuinely popular German books and are usually grouped together under this name. They are products in part of medieval German or Romance poetry, in part of popular superstition. Earlier despised and derided by the upper classes, they were, as we know, sought out by the romantics, adapted, even extolled. But romanticism looked at their poetic content alone, and how incapable it was of grasping their significance as popular books is shown by

Görres' work on them.[107] Görres, as he has shown but lately, actually *versifies* all his judgments. Nevertheless, the usual view of these books still rests on his work, and *Marbach* even refers to it in the announcement of his own publication. The three new revised adaptations of these books, by Marbach in prose, and *Simrock* in prose and poetry, two of which are again intended for the people, call for another precise examination of the material adapted here from the point of view of its popular value.

So long as opinions about the poetry of the Middle Ages vary so widely, the assessment of the poetic value of these books must be left to the individual reader; but naturally no one would deny that they really are genuinely poetic. Even if they cannot pass the test as popular books, their poetic content must be accorded full recognition; yes, in Schiller's words:

> What in immortal song shall live forever,
> Is doomed to die in life,[a]

many a poet may find yet one more reason to save for poetry by means of adaptation what proves impossible to preserve for the people.

There is a very significant difference between the tales of German and Romance origin. The German tales, genuine folk stories, place the man in action in the foreground; the Romance give prominence to the woman, either as one who suffers (Genovefa), or as one who loves, passive towards passion even in her love. There are only two exceptions, *Die Haimonskinder* and *Fortunat*, both Romance but also folk legends; while *Octavianus, Melusina*, etc., are products of court poetry which only reached the people later in prose adaptations.—Of the humorous tales only one, *Salomon und Morolf*, is not directly of Germanic origin, while *Eulenspiegel, Die Schildbürger*, etc., are indisputably ours.

If we view all these books in their entirety and judge them by the principles stated at the beginning, it is clear

---
[a] From Schiller's poem *Die Götter Griechenlands.—Ed.*

that they satisfy these requirements only in the one respect that they have poetry and humour in rich measure and in a form which is easily understood in general even by the least educated, but in other respects they are far from adequate, some of them a complete contradiction, others only partially acceptable. Since they are the products of the Middle Ages, they naturally fail entirely in the special purpose which the present age might require them to fulfil. Thus in spite of the outward richness of this branch of literature and in spite of the declamations of Tieck and Görres, they still leave much to be desired; whether this gap is ever to be filled is another question which I will not take it upon myself to answer.

To proceed now to individual cases, the most important one is undoubtedly the *Geschichte vom gehörnten Siegfried*.— I like this book; it is a tale which leaves little to be desired; it has the most exuberant poetry written sometimes with the greatest naivety and sometimes with the most beautiful humorous pathos; there is sparkling wit—who does not know the priceless episode of the fight between the two cowards? It has character, a bold, fresh, youthful spirit which every young wandering craftsman can take as an example, even though he no longer has to fight dragons and giants. And once the misprints are corrected, of which the (Cologne) edition[108] in front of me has more than a fair share, and the punctuation is put right, Schwab's and Marbach's adaptations will not be able to compare with this genuinely popular style. The people have also shown themselves grateful for it; I have not come across any other popular book as often as this one.

Herzog Heinrich der Löwe.—Unfortunately I have not been able to get hold of an old copy of this book; the new edition printed in Einbeck[109] seems to have replaced it entirely. It starts with the genealogy of the House of Brunswick going back to the year 1735; then follows a historical biography of Herzog Heinrich and the popular legend. It also contains a tale which tells the same story about Godfrey of Bouillon as the popular legend of Heinrich der Löwe, the story of the slave Andronicus ascribed to a Palestinian abbot called Gerasimi with the end substantially altered, and a poem of the new romantic school of which I cannot remember the author, in which the story of the lion is told once more. Thus the legend on which the popular book is based disappears entirely under the trappings with which the munificence of the clever publisher has furnished it. The legend itself is very beautiful, but the rest is of no interest; what do Swabians care about the history of Brunswick? And what room is there for the wordy modern romance after the simple style of the popular book? But that has also disappeared; the adapter, a man of genius, whom I see as a parson or schoolmaster at the end of the last century, writes as follows:

"Thus the goal of the journey was reached, the Holy Land lay before their eyes, they set foot on the soil with which the most significant memories of religious history are linked! The pious simplicity which had looked forward in longing to this moment changed into fervent devotion here, found complete satisfaction here and became the keenest joy in the Lord."

Restore the legend in its old language, add other genuine folk legends to make a complete book, send this out among the people, and it would keep the poetic sense alive; but in this form it does not deserve to circulate among the people.

Herzog Ernst.—The author of this book was no great poet, for he found all the poetical elements in oriental fairy-tales. The book is well written and very entertaining for the people; but that is all. Nobody will believe any longer in the reality of the fantasies which occur in it; it can therefore be left in the hands of the people without alteration.

I now come to two legends which the German people created and developed, the most profound that the folk poetry of any people has to show. I mean the legends of *Faust* and of *Der ewige Jude*. They are inexhaustible; any period can adopt them without altering their essence; and even if the adaptations of the Faust legend after Goethe belong with the Iliads *post Homerum*, they still always reveal to us new aspects, not to mention the importance of the Ahasuerus legend for the poetry of later times. But how do these legends appear in the popular books! Not as products of the free imagination are they conceived, no, as children of a slavish superstition. The book about the Wandering Jew even demands a religious belief in its contents which it seeks to justify by the Bible and a lot of stale legends; it contains only the most superficial part of the legend itself, but preaches a very lengthy and tedious Christian sermon on the Jew Ahasuerus. The Faust legend is reduced to a common witches' tale embellished with vulgar sorcerer's anecdotes; what little poetry is preserved in the popular comedy has almost completely disappeared. These two books are not only incapable of offering any poetical enjoyment, in their present shape they are bound to strengthen and renew old superstitions; or what else is to be expected of such devilish work? The awareness of the legend and its contents seems to be disappearing altogether among the people, too; Faust is thought to be no more than a common sorcerer and Ahasuerus the greatest villain since Judas Iscariot. But should it not be possible to rescue both these legends for the German *people*, to restore them to their original purity and to express their essence so clearly that the deep meaning does not remain entirely unintelligible even to the less educated? Marbach and Simrock have still to adapt these legends; may they exercise wise judgment in the process!

We have before us yet another series of popular books, namely, the humorous ones, *Eulenspiegel, Salomon und Morolf, Der Pfaff vom Kalenberge, Die sieben Schwaben*, and *Die Schildbürger*. This is a series such as few other nations have produced. The wit, the natural manner of both arrangement and workmanship, the good-natured humour which always accompanies the biting scorn so that it should not become too malicious, the strikingly comical situations could indeed put a great deal of our literature to shame. What author of the present day has sufficient inventiveness to create a book like *Die Schildbürger?* How prosaic Mundt's humour appears compared with that of *Die sieben Schwaben!* Of course, a quieter time was needed to produce such things than ours which, like a restless businessman, is always talking about the important questions it has to answer before it can think of anything else.—As regards the form of these books, little needs changing, except for removing the odd flat joke and distortions of style. Several editions of *Eulenspiegel*, marked with the stamp of Prussian censorship, are not quite complete; there is a coarse joke missing right at the beginning which Marbach illustrates in a very good woodcut.

In sharp contrast to these are the stories of *Genovefa, Griseldis* and *Hirlanda*, three books of Romance[a] origin, each of which has a woman for heroine, and a suffering woman at that; they illustrate the attitude of the Middle Ages to religion, and very poetically too; only *Genovefa* and *Hirlanda* are too conventionally drawn. But, for heaven's sake, what are the German people to do with them today? One can well imagine the German people as Griseldis, of course, and the princes as Markgraf Walther; but then the comedy would have to end quite differently from the way it does in the popular book; both sides would resent the comparison here and there on good grounds. If *Griseldis* is to remain a popular book I see it as a petition to the High German Federal Assembly for the emancipation of women. But one knows, here and there, how this kind of romantic petition was received four years ago,[110] which makes me wonder greatly that Marbach was not subsequently counted among the Young Germans.[111] The people have acted Griseldis and Genovefa long enough, let them now play Siegfried and Reinald for a change; but the right way to get them to do so is surely not to praise these old stories of humiliation.

---

[a] The *Telegraph für Deutschland* has "romantic", which is a misprint.—*Ed.*

The first half of the book *Kaiser Octavianus* belongs to the same class, while the second half is more like the love stories proper. The story of *Helena* is merely an imitation of *Octavianus*, or perhaps both are different versions of the same legend. The second half of *Octavianus* is an excellent popular book and one which can be ranked only with *Siegfried*; the characterisation of Florens and his fosterfather Clemens is excellent, and so is that of Claudius; Tieck had it very easy here.[112] But running right through is there not the idea that noble blood is better than common blood? And how often do we not find this idea among the people themselves! If this idea cannot be banished from *Octavianus* —and I think it is impossible—if I consider that it must first be eradicated where constitutional life is to arise, then let the book be as poetic as you like, *censeo Carthaginem esse delendam*[a].

In contrast to the tearful tales of suffering and endurance I have mentioned are three others which celebrate love. They are *Magelone, Melusina* and *Tristan*. I like *Magelone* best as a popular book; *Melusina* is again full of absurd monstrosities and fantastic exaggerations so that one could almost see it as a kind of Don Quixote tale, and I must ask again: what do the German people want with it? On top of that the story of Tristan and Isolde—I will not dispute its poetic value because I love the wonderful rendering by Gottfried von Strassburg,[113] even if one may find defects here and there in the narrative—but there is no book that it is less desirable to put into the hands of the people than this. Of course, here again there is a close connection with a modern theme, the emancipation of women; a skilful poet would today hardly be able to exclude it from an adaptation of *Tristan* without falling into a contrived and tedious form of moralising poetry. But in a popular book where this question is out of place the entire narrative is reduced to an apology for adultery and whether that should be left in the

---

[a] I am of the opinion that Carthage must be destroyed.—*Ed.*

hands of the people is highly questionable. In the meanwhile the book has almost disappeared and one only rarely comes across a copy.

Die Haimonskinder and *Fortunat*, where we again see the *man* in the centre of the action, are another couple of true popular books. Here the merriest humour with which the son of Fortunat fights all his adventures, there the bold defiance, the unrestrained 'relish in opposition which in youthful vigour stands up to the absolute, tyrannical power of Charlemagne and is not afraid, even before the eyes of the prince, to take revenge with its own hand for insults it suffered. Such a youthful spirit that allows us to overlook many weaknesses must prevail in the popular book; but where is it to be found in *Griseldis* and its like?

Last but not least, the *Hundertjährige Kalender*, a work of genius, the super-clever *Traumbuch*, the unfailing *Glücksrad*, and similar progeny of miserable superstition. Anyone who has even glanced at his book, knows with what wretched sophistries Görres made excuses for this rubbish. All these dreary books have been honoured with the Prussian censor's stamp. They are, of course, neither revolutionary, like Börne's letters,[114] nor immoral, as people claim *Wally*[115] is. We can see how wrong are the charges that the Prussian censorship is exceedingly strict. I hardly need waste any more words on whether such rubbish should remain among the people.

Nothing need be said of the rest of the popular books; the stories of *Pontus*, *Fierabras*, etc., have long been lost and so no longer deserve the name. But I believe I have shown, even in these few notes, how inadequate this literature appears, when judged according to the interest of the people and not the interest of poetry. What is necessary are adaptations of a strict selection which do not needlessly depart from the old style and are issued in attractive editions for the people. To eradicate forcibly any which cannot stand up to criticism would be neither easy nor advisable; only that which is pure superstition should be denied the stamp of the censor. The others are disappearing as it is; *Griseldis* is rare, *Tristan* almost unobtainable. In many areas, in Wuppertal, for example, it is not possible to find a single copy; in other places, Cologne, Bremen, etc., almost every shopkeeper has copies in his windows for the peasants who come into town.

But surely the German people and the best of these books deserve intelligent adaptations? Not everybody is capable of producing such adaptations, of course; I know only two people with sufficient critical acumen and taste to make the selection, and skill to handle the old style; they are the brothers *Grimm*. But would they have the time and inclination for this work? Marbach's adaptation is quite unsuitable for the people. What can one hope for when he starts straight away with *Griseldis*? Not only does he lack all critical sense, but he cannot resist making quite unnecessary omissions; he has also made the style quite flat and insipid—compare the popular version of the *Gehörnter Siegfried* and all the others with the adaptation. There is nothing but sentences torn apart, and changed word order for which the only justification was Herr Marbach's mania to appear original here since he lacked all other originality. What else could have driven him to alter the most beautiful passages of the popular book and furnish it with his unnecessary punctuation? For anyone who does not know the popular version, Marbach's tales are quite good; but as soon as one compares the two, one realises that Marbach's sole service has been to correct the misprints. His woodcuts vary greatly in value.—Simrock's adaptation is not yet far enough advanced for judgment to be passed on it; but I trust him more than his rival. His woodcuts are also consistently better than Marbach's.

These old popular books with their old-fashioned tone, their misprints and their poor woodcuts have for me an extraordinary, poetic charm; they transport me from our artificial modern "conditions, confusions and fine distinctions" into a world which is much closer to nature. But that is not what matters here; Tieck, of course, made this poetic charm his chief argument—but what weight has the authority of Tieck, Görres and all other romantics when reason contradicts it and when it is a question of the *German people*?

Frederick Engels, "German *Volksbücher*"

Marx and Engels, *Collected Works*, Vol. 2, Moscow, 1975, pp. 32-40

Renaissance

Difference Between the Situation at the End of the Ancient World, ca 300—and at the End of the Middle Ages—1453

1. Instead of a thin strip of civilisation along the coast of the Mediterranean, stretching its arms sporadically into the interior and as far as the Atlantic coast of Spain, France, and England, which could thus easily be broken through and rolled back by the Germans and Slavs from the North, and by the Arabs from the South-East, there was now a closed area of civilisation—the whole of West Europe with Scandinavia, Poland, and Hungary as outposts.

2. Instead of the contrast between the Greeks, or Romans, and the barbarians, there were now six civilised peoples with civilised languages, not counting the Scandinavian, etc., all of whom had developed to such an extent that they could participate in the mighty rise of literature in the fourteenth century, and guaranteed a far more diversified culture than that of the Greek and Latin languages, which were already in decay and dying out at the end of ancient times.

3. An infinitely higher development of industrial production and trade, created by the burghers of the Middle Ages; on the one hand production more perfected, more varied and on a larger scale, and, on the other hand, commerce much stronger, navigation being infinitely more enterprising since the time of the Saxons, Frisians, and Normans, and on the other hand also an amount of inventions and importation of oriental inventions, which not

only for the first time made possible the importation and diffusion of Greek literature, the maritime discoveries, and the bourgeois religious revolution, but also gave them a quite different and quicker range of action. In addition they produced a mass of scientific facts, although as yet unsystematised, such as antiquity never had: the magnetic needle, printing, type, flax paper (used by the Arabs and Spanish Jews since the twelfth century, cotton paper gradually making its appearance since the tenth century, and already more widespread in the thirteenth and fourteenth centuries, papyrus quite obsolete in Egypt since the Arabs), gunpowder, *spectacles, m e c h a n i c a l   c l o c k s*, great progress both of *chronology* and of *mechanics*.

(See No. 11 concerning inventions.)[116]

In addition material provided by travels (Marco Polo, *ca.* 1272, etc.).

General education, even though still bad, much more widespread owing to the universities.

With the rise of Constantinople and the fall of Rome, antiquity comes to an end. The end of the Middle Ages is indissolubly linked with the fall of Constantinople. The new age begins with the return to the Greeks—Negation of the negation!

Frederick Engels, *Dialectics of Nature*, Moscow, 1974, pp. 190-91

Italian Culture
from Dante to Garibaldi

1

Italy is the land of classicism. Ever since the great era when the dawn of modern times rose there, it has produced magnificent characters of unequalled classic perfection, from Dante to Garibaldi. But the period of its degradation and foreign domination also bequeathed it classic character-masks, among them two particularly clear-cut types, that of Sganarelle and Dulcamara. The classic unity of both is embodied in our *illustre* Loria.

Frederick Engels, "Preface" to
Marx's *Capital*, Vol. III
Karl Marx, *Capital*, Vol. III, 1974, p. 19

2

Türr, whom I know personally, is a brave soldier and an intelligent officer, but beyond the sphere of military activity he is a mere zero, below the average of common mortals, lacking not only training of mind and a cultivated intellect, but that natural shrewdness and instinct which may stand in place of education, learning, and experience. He is, in one word, an easy-going jolly good fellow, gifted with an extraordinary degree of credulity, but certainly not the man to politically control anybody, not to speak of Garibaldi, who, with a fire of soul still owns his grain of that subtle Italian genius you may trace in Dante no less than in Machiavelli.

Karl Marx, "Affairs in Prussia"
Written in English
New York Daily Tribune, October 15, 1860

Dante

The first capitalist nation was Italy. The close of the feudal Middle Ages, and the opening of the modern capitalist era are marked by a colossal figure: an Italian, Dante, both the last poet of the Middle Ages and the first poet of modern times. Today, as in 1300, a new historical era is approaching. Will Italy give us the new Dante, who will mark the hour of birth of this new, proletarian era?

> Frederick Engels, "To the Italian Reader" ("Preface to the Italian Edition of the *Manifesto of the Communist Party*")
>
> Marx and Engels, *Selected Works*, Vol. 1, 1973, p. 107

Petrarch

Tired from looking. I went into the wooden house which stands on the summit and ordered a drink. I received it, together with the visitors' book. We all know what is to be found in books of this kind: every philistine regards them as institutions for securing immortality, in which he can transmit his obscure name and one of his exceedingly trivial thoughts to posterity. The duller he is, the longer the commentaries with which he accompanies his name.

Merchants want to prove that besides coffee, train-oil or cotton, beautiful nature, which has created all this and even gold itself, still holds a tiny corner in their hearts; ladies give expression to their gushing sentiments, students to their high spirits and impertinence, and sage schoolmasters write out nature a bombastic certificate of maturity. "Magnificent Ütli, Rigi's dangerous rival!" a doctor of the illiberal arts began to apostrophise in Ciceronian style. In annoyance, I turned the page and left all the Germans, French, and English unread. Then I found a sonnet by Petrarch in Italian which in translation sounds roughly like this:

> I soared in spirit to the abode up there
> Of her I seek below but never find.
> Gentle the looks that once avoided mine —
> So stood she in the third celestial sphere.

> Taking my hand, she softly said, "No tear
> Can flow where we may never be disjoined.
> 'Tis I that long disturbed your peace of mind,
> Returning all too soon to my home here.
>
> "Oh, that man's mind my joy might understand!
> I seek but you, and the form that you loved
> And that I left down there so long ago."
>
> Why did she say no more, let go my hand?
> A little more of that sweet sound, I know,
> And then from Heaven had I never moved.[117]

The person who had copied this out was called Joachim Triboni from Genoa and by this entry at once became my friend. For the more hollow and nonsensical the other comments, the more sharply this sonnet stood out against such a background, and the more it moved me. Where nature displays all its magnificence, where the idea that is slumbering within it seems, if not to awaken, then to be dreaming a golden dream, the man who can feel and say nothing except "Nature, how beautiful you are!" has no right to think himself superior to the ordinary, shallow, confused mass. In a more profound mind, however, individual sorrows and sufferings rise, only to be merged in the splendour of nature and to dissolve in gentle reconciliation. This reconciliation could hardly be expressed more beautifully than in this sonnet. But there was yet another circumstance which made me a friend of that Genoese. So another before me had brought his lover's grief to this summit; so I did not stand there alone with a heart that only a month ago had been filled with infinite bliss and now was torn and desolate. And what pain has more right to speak out in face of the beauty of nature than the noblest and most profound of all personal sorrows, the sorrow of love?

Frederick Engels, "Wanderings in Lombardy. I. Over the Alps"

Marx and Engels, *Collected Works*, Vol. 2, Moscow, 1975, pp. 172-73

Boccaccio

The town heresies—and those are the actual official heresies of the Middle Ages—were turned primarily against the clergy, whose wealth and political importance they attacked. Just as the present-day bourgeoisie demands a *"gouvernement à bon marché"* (cheap government), the medieval burghers chiefly demanded an *"église à bon marché"* (cheap church). Reactionary in form, like any heresy that sees only degeneration in the further development of church and dogma, the burgher heresy demanded the revival of the simple early Christian Church constitution and abolition of exclusive priesthood. This cheap arrangement would eliminate monks, prelates, and the Roman court; in short, all the expensive element of the Church. The towns, which were republics by their own rights, albeit under the protection of monarchs, first enunciated in general terms through their attacks upon the Papacy that a republic was the normal form of bourgeois rule. Their hostility to some of the dogmas and church laws is explained partly by the foregoing, and partly by their living conditions. Their bitter opposition to celibacy, for instance, has never been better explained than by Boccaccio.

Frederick Engels, *The Peasant War in Germany*, Moscow, 1974, pp. 43-44

Great Renaissance

Modern research into nature, which alone has achieved a scientific, systematic, all-round development, in contrast to the brilliant natural-philosophical intuitions of antiquity and the extremely important but sporadic discoveries of the Arabs, which for the most part vanished without results, this modern research into nature dates, like all more recent history, from that mighty epoch which we Germans term the Reformation, from the national misfortune that overtook us at that time, and which the French term the Renaissance and the Italians the *Cinquecento*,[118] although it is not fully expressed by any of these names. It is the epoch which had its rise in the latter half of the fifteenth century. Royalty, with the support of the burghers of the towns, broke the power of the feudal nobility and established the great monarchies, based essentially on nationality, within which the modern European nations and modern bourgeois society came to development. And while the burghers and nobles were still fighting one another, the German Peasant War pointed prophetically to future class struggles, by bringing on to the stage not only the peasants in revolt—that was no longer anything new—but behind them the beginnings of the modern proletariat, with the red flag in their hands and the demand for common ownership of goods on their lips. In the manuscripts saved from the fall of Byzantium, in the antique statues dug out of the ruins of Rome, a new world was revealed to the astonished West, that of ancient Greece; the ghosts of the Middle Ages vanished before its shining forms; Italy rose to undreamt-of flowering of art, which was like a reflection of classical antiquity and was never attained again. In Italy, France, and Germany a new literature arose, the first modern literature; shortly afterwards came the classical epochs of English and Spanish literature. The bounds of the old *orbis terrarum*[119] were pierced, only now for the first time was the world really discovered and the basis laid for subsequent world trade and the transition from handicraft to manufacture, which in its turn formed the starting-point for modern large-scale industry. The dictatorship of the Church over men's minds was shattered; it was directly cast off by the majority of the Germanic peoples, who adopted Protestantism, while among the Latins a cheerful spirit of free thought, taken over from the Arabs and nourished by the newly-discovered Greek philosophy, took root more and more and prepared the way for the materialism of the eighteenth century.

It was the greatest progressive revolution that mankind had so far experienced, a time which called for giants and produced giants—giants in power of thought, passion and character, in universality and learning. The men who founded the modern rule of the bourgeoisie had anything but bourgeois limitations. On the contrary, the adventurous character of the time inspired them to a greater or lesser degree. There was hardly any man of importance then living who had not travelled extensively, who did not speak four or five languages, who did not shine in a number of fields. Leonardo da Vinci was not only a great painter but also a great mathematician, mechanician, and engineer, to whom the most diverse branches of physics are indebted for important discoveries. Albrecht Dürer was painter, engraver, sculptor, and architect, and in addition invented a system of fortification embodying many of the ideas that much later were again taken up by Montalembert and the modern German science of fortification. Machiavelli was statesman, historian, poet, and at the same time the first notable military author of modern times. Luther not only cleaned the Augean stable of the Church but also that of the German language; he created modern German prose and composed the text and melody of that triumphal hymn imbued with confidence in victory which became the Marseillaise of the sixteenth century.[120] The heroes of that time were not yet in thrall to the division of labour, the restricting effects of which, with its production of one-sidedness, we so often notice in their successors. But what is especially characteristic of them is that they almost all live and pursue their activities in the midst of the contemporary movements, in the practical struggle; they take sides and join in the fight, one by speaking and writing, another with the sword, many with both. Hence the fullness and force of character that makes them complete men. Men of the study are the exception—either persons of second or third rank or cautious philistines who do not want to burn their fingers.

Frederick Engels, *Dialectics of Nature*, Moscow, 1974, pp. 20-22

Titian

Everyone here [121] is now a friend of art and chatters about the paintings in the exhibition. The affair will be *plus ou moins*[a] a failure, financially at any rate. There are, by the way, some very fine pictures on show, however, most of those by the good and the best painters are only second-rate pieces. Among the finest exhibits is a splendid portrait of Ariosto by Titian. The modern German and French school is very bad and practically unrepresented. Three-quarters of the exhibition is English rubbish. The Spanish and Flemish painters are represented best of all, and after them the Italians. You must come over somehow this summer with your wife to have a look at the thing, *s'il y a moyen*.[b] It won't do to write anything about this business for the *Tribune*;[122] I wouldn't know where to begin in any case, and the *Tribune* can find the usual tittle-tattle in all the newspapers.

Engels to Marx,
May 20, 1857

Marx/Engels, *Werke*, Bd. 29,
1967, S. 135

Grobian Literature of the Reformation Period

Shortly before and during the period of the Reformation there developed amongst the Germans a type of literature whose very name is striking—*grobian* literature. In our own day we are approaching an era of revolution analogous to that of the sixteenth century. Small wonder that among the

---

a More or less.—*Ed.*
b If possible.—*Ed.*

Germans grobian literature is emerging once more. Interest in historical development easily overcomes the aesthetic revulsion which this kind of writing provokes even in a person of quite unrefined taste and which it provoked back in the fifteenth and sixteenth centuries.

Flat, bombastic, bragging, thrasonical,[123] putting on a great show of rude vigour in attack, yet hysterically sensitive to the same quality in others; brandishing the sword with enormous waste of energy, lifting it high in the air only to let it fall down flat; constantly preaching morality and constantly offending against it; sentiment and turpitude most absurdly conjoined; concerned only with the point at issue, yet always missing the point; using with equal arrogance petty-bourgeois scholarly semi-erudition against popular wisdom, and so-called "sound common sense" against science; discharging itself in ungovernable breadth with a certain complacent levity; clothing a philistine message in a plebeian form; wrestling with the literary language to give it, so to speak, a purely corporeal character; willingly pointing at the writer's body in the background, which is itching in every fibre to give a few exhibitions of its strength, to display its broad shoulders and publicly to stretch its limbs; proclaiming a healthy mind in a healthy body; unconsciously infected by the sixteenth century's most abstruse controversies and by its fever of the body; in thrall to dogmatic, narrow thinking and at the same time appealing to petty practice in the face of all real thought; raging agaist reaction, reacting against progress; incapable of making the opponent seem ridiculous, but ridiculously abusing him through the whole gamut of tones; Salomon and Marcolf,[124] Don Quixote and Sancho Panza, a visionary and a philistine in one person; a loutish form of indignation, a form of indignant loutishness; and suspended like an enveloping cloud over it all, the self-satisfied philistine's consciousness *of his own virtue*—such was the *grobian literature* of the sixteenth century. If our memory does not deceive us, the German folk anecdote has set up a lyrical monument to it in the song of *Heineke, der starke Knecht*. To Herr Heinzen belongs the credit of being one of the re-creators of grobian literature and in this field one of the German swallows heralding the coming springtime of the nations.

> Karl Marx, "Moralising Criticism and Critical Morality"
>
> Marx and Engels, *Collected Works*, Vol. 6, Moscow, 1976, pp. 312-13

Historical Significance of the Reformation

When Protestantism was finally crushed in France, it was no misfortune for France—*teste*[a] Bayle, Voltaire and Diderot, but its suppression in Germany would have been a calamity not for Germany, but indeed *for the world*. It would have forced the Catholic *form* of development of the Romance countries on Germany and, since the English form of development was also semi-Catholic and medieval (Universities, etc., colleges, public schools are all Protestant monasteries), all the free Protestant German forms of education (education at home or in private institutions, students living out of college and choosing their own courses) would have ceased to exist and Europe's spiritual development would have become infinitely monotonous. France and England have smashed prejudices *in essence*, while Germany has done away with prejudices as far as the *form* is concerned, has done away with the *set patterns*. From this stems in part the formlessness of everything German, which, up to the present day, has been connected with such great disadvantages as the plethora of small states, but which is an

---

[a] See.—*Ed.*

enormous advantage as regards the nation's capacity for development. This will bear its full fruit only in the future, when this stage, in itself one-sided, has been overcome.

> Frederick Engels, "Material on the History of France and Germany"
>
> Marx/Engels, *Über Kunst und Literatur*, Bd. 1, 1967, S. 352-53

Thomas More

1

In his "Utopia", Thomas More says, that in England "your shepe that were wont to be so meke and tame, and so smal eaters, now, as I heare saye, become so great devourers and so wylde that they eate up, and swallow downe, the very men themselfes," "Utopia", transl. by Robinson, ed., Arber, Lond., 1869, p. 41.

> Karl Marx, *Capital*, Vol. I, Moscow, 1974, p. 673

2

Thomas More says in his "Utopia": "Therfore that on covetous and unsatiable cormaraunte and very plage of his native contrey maye compasse aboute and inclose many thousand akers of grounde together within one pale or hedge, the husbandmen be thrust owte of their owne, or els either by coneyne and fraude, or by violent oppression they be put besydes it, or by wrongs and iniuries thei be so weried that they be compelled to sell all: by one meanes, therfore, or by other, either by hooke or crooke they must needes departe awaye, poore, selye, wretched soules, men, women husbands, wiues, fatherlesse children, widowes, wofull mothers with their yonge babes, and their whole householde smal in substance, and muche in numbre, as husbandrye requireth many handes. Awaye thei trudge, I say, owte of their knowen accustomed houses, fyndynge no place to reste in. All their housholde stuffe, which is very little woorthe, thoughe it might well abide the sale: yet beeynge sodainely thruste owte, they be constrayned to sell it for a thing of nought. And when they haue wandered abrode tyll that be spent, what cant they then els doe but steale, and then iustly pardy be hanged, or els go about beggyng. And yet then also they be caste in prison as vagaboundes, because they go aboute and worke not: whom no man wyl set a worke though thei neuer so willyngly profre themselues therto." Of these poor fugitives of whom Thomas More says that they were forced to thieve, "7,200 great and petty thieves were put to death", in the reign of Henry VIII. (Hollinshed, "Description of England", Vol. 1, p. 186.)

Karl Marx, *Capital*, Vol. I,
Moscow, 1974, pp. 687-88

3

Hitherto, force—from now on, sociality. A pure pious wish, the demand for "justice". But Th. More made this demand 350 years ago, and it has yet to be fulfilled.

Frederick Engels, "Preparatory
Writings for *Anti-Dühring*"
Marx/Engels, *Werke*, Bd. 20,
1968, S. 588

4

In his work on Thomas More, Karl Kautsky has demonstrated[125] how 15th- and 16th-century "humanism", the first form of the bourgeois Enlightenment, subsequently developed into Catholic Jesuitry. In precisely the same way, we see here its second, fully mature form in the 18th century develop into modern Jesuitry, Russian diplomacy. This sudden change into the opposite, this ultimate arrival at a point diametrically opposed to the starting point, is the natural and inevitable fate of all historical movements which lack a clear idea of their origins and the conditions of their existence and therefore set themselves totally illusory goals. They are unmercifully chastised by the "irony of history".

> Frederick Engels, "Foreign Policy of Russian Tsarism"
>
> Marx/Engels, *Werke*, Bd. 22, 1963, S. 21

Shakespeare

1

A singularity of English tragedy, so repulsive to French feelings that Voltaire used to call Shakespeare a drunken savage,[126] is its peculiar mixture of the sublime and the base, the terrible and the ridiculous, the heroic and the burlesque. But nowhere does Shakespeare devolve upon the clown the task of speaking the prologue of a heroic drama. This invention was reserved for the Coalition Ministry. Mylord Aberdeen has performed, if not the English Clown, at least the Italian Pantaloon.[127] All great historical movements appear, to the superficial observer, finally to subside into the farce, or at least the common-place. But to commence with this is a feature peculiar alone to the tragedy entitled, *War with Russia*,[128] the prologue of which was recited on Friday evening in both Houses of Parliament, where the Ministry's address in answer to the Ministry's message was simultaneously discussed and unanimously adopted, to be handed over to the Queen yesterday afternoon, sitting upon her throne in Buckingham Palace.

Karl Marx, "The War Debate in Parliament"

Written in English

New York Daily Tribune, March 17, 1854

2

That scamp Roderich Benedix has left a bad odour behind in the shape of a thick tome against "Shakespearomania".[129] He proved in it to a nicety that Shakespeare can't hold a candle to our great poets, not even to those of modern times. Shakespeare is presumably to be hurled down from his pedestal only in order that fatty Benedix is hoisted on to it. There is more life and reality in the first act of the *Merry Wives* alone than in all German literature, and Launce[130] with his dog Crab is alone worth more than all the German comedies put together. By way of contrast, Benedix with the weighty posterior will indulge in argumentations as serious as they are cheap over the unceremonious manner in which Shakespeare often makes short work of his dénouements and thereby cuts short the tedious twaddle, although in real life it is unavoidable. Let him have his way.

Engels to Marx, December 10, 1873

Marx and Engels, *Selected Correspondence*, Moscow, 1975, p. 269

3

How little connection there is between money, the most general form of property, and personal peculiarity, how much they are directly opposed to each other was already known to Shakespeare better than to our theorising petty bourgeois:

> Thus much of this will make black, white; foul, fair;
> Wrong, right; base, noble; old, young; coward, valiant.
> This yellow slave ...
> Will make the hoar leprosy adored ...
>   This it is
> That makes the wappened widow wed again;
> She, whom the spital-house and ulcerous sores
> Would cast the gorge at, this embalms and spices
> To th' April day again...
>   Thou visible god,
> That solder'st close impossibilities,
> And makest them kiss![131]

Karl Marx and Frederick Engels, *The German Ideology*

Marx and Engels, *Collected Works*, Vol. 5, Moscow, 1976, p. 230-31

4

As a relaxation in the evenings I have been reading Appian on the Roman Civil Wars in the original Greek. A very valuable book. The chap is an Egyptian by birth. Schlosser says he has "no soul", probably because in these civil wars he seeks to get to the root of the material foundation. Spartacus is revealed as the most splendid fellow in the whole of ancient history. Great general (no Garibaldi), noble character, real representative of the ancient proletariat. Pompey, an utter rotter; got his undeserved fame by snatching the credit, first for the successes of Lucullus (against Mithridates), then for the successes of Sertorius (Spain), etc., and as the "young man" of Sulla and others. As a general he was the Roman Odilon Barrot. As soon as he had to show his mettle against Caesar—he proved a lousy good-for-nothing. Caesar made the greatest possible military mistakes—deliberately idiotic—in order to bewilder the philistine who was opposing him. An ordinary Roman general—say Crassus—would have wiped him out six times over during the struggle in Epirus. But with Pompey everything was possible. Shakespeare, in his *Love's Labour's Lost*, seems to have had an inkling of what Pompey really was.[132]

Marx to Engels, February 27, 1861

Marx and Engels, *Selected Correspondence*, Moscow, 1975, pp. 115-16

Calderón

1

This power,[133] so clumsily composed, so nervelessly constituted, with such outlived reminiscences at its head, was called upon to accomplish a revolution and to beat Napoleon. If its proclamations were as vigorous as its deeds were weak, it was due to Don Manuel Quintana, a Spanish poet, whom the Junta had the taste to appoint as their secretary and to intrust with the writing of their manifestoes.

Like Calderón's pompous heroes who, confounding conventional distinction with genuine greatness, used to announce themselves by a tedious enumeration of all their titles, the Junta occupied itself in the first place with decreeing the honours and decorations due to its exalted position.

Karl Marx, "Revolutionary Spain"

Written in English

New York Daily Tribune, October 20, 1854

2

In my spare time I am now studying Spanish. Began with Calderón from whose *Mágico prodigioso*, the Catholic *Faust*, Goethe drew not only isolated passages but the conception of entire scenes for his own *Faust*. Then, *horribile dictu*,[a] I have read Spanish translations of things that would have been impossible to read in French: Chateaubriand's *Atala* and *René*, and some pieces by Bernardin de St. Pierre. Am now in the middle of *Don Quixote*. I find one has more need of a dictionary for Spanish at the beginning than for Italian.

Marx to Engels, May 3, 1854
Marx/Engels, *Werke*, Bd. 28, 1963, S. 356

3

In Spanish drama there are two jesters for every hero. Calderón provides holy Cyprian himself, the Spanish Faust, with a Moscón and a Clarin. In the same way, the reactionary General von Radowitz had two comic adjutants in the Frankfurt parliament, his harlequin Lichnowski and his clown Vincke.

Karl Marx, "Herr Vogt"
Marx/Engels, *Werke*, Bd. 14, 1969, S. 606

---

[a] Terrible to say.—*Ed*

Cervantes

1

Cervantes somewhere describes a worthy *alguacil*[a] and his clerk who, for the protection of public morality, kept two women of no ambiguous reputation.[134] These obliging nymphs appeared at big fairs or on other festive occasions in such attire that the bird could be recognised by its plumage from afar. If they managed to entrap some new arrival, they immediately contrived to inform their lovers of the inn to which they had gone. The *alguacil* and his clerk then broke into the room, to the immense horror of the women, enacted a scene of jealousy and allowed the stranger to escape only after lengthy pleading and payment of an appropriate monetary compensation. In this way they combined self-advantage with the interests of public morality, for the victim took care not to give way to his improper inclinations for some time afterwards.

Like these guardians of morality, the Prussian heroes of order have a simple procedure for ensuring normal tranquillity under martial law. The provocative despatch of some liquor-reeking pillars of justice, a few equally provocative sabre thrusts in among the people, and the rebellious desires thereby aroused in some remote town or village provide an opportunity for proclaiming martial law, for safeguarding the *whole province* against further improper disturbances and for cheating it out of the last remnants of its constitutional rights.

Karl Marx and Frederick Engels,
"The New Martial-Law Charter"
Marx/Engels, *Werke*, Bd. 6, 1968,
S. 495-96

---

[a] A Spanish police agent.—*Ed.*

2

This much, however, is clear, that the Middle Ages could not live on Catholicism, nor the ancient world on politics. On the contrary, it is the mode in which they gained a livelihood that explains why here politics, and there Catholicism, played the chief part. For the rest, it requires but a slight acquaintance with the history of the Roman republic, for example, to be aware that its secret history is the history of its landed property. On the other hand, Don Quixote long ago paid the penalty for wrongly imagining that knight errantry was compatible with all economic forms of society.

Karl Marx, *Capital*, Vol. I, Moscow, 1974, p. 86

History of Social Thought and Literature

The Modern Period

**Three Unities
of Classical Drama**

For example, it is certain that the theoretical construct of the three unities[135] by French playwrights under Louis XIV is based on a misunderstanding of Greek drama (and of Aristotle as its exponent). On the other hand, it is equally certain that they interpreted the Greeks in a way that corresponded to the needs of their own art and therefore clung tenaciously to this so-called "classical" drama for a long time, even after Dacier and others had correctly interpreted Aristotle to them.

> Marx to Ferdinand Lassalle,
> July 22, 1861
>
> Marx/Engels, *Werke*, Bd. 30, 1964,
> S. 614-15

La Rochefoucauld

When rearranging my bookshelves, I came across a small old edition of La Rochefoucauld's *Réflexions etc.*[136] Leafing through it I found this:

"Sobriety is a mystery of the body, invented to hide the defects of the spirit."

Thus *Stern* pinched it from La Rochefoucauld! Very nice, too:

"We are all strong enough to suffer the misfortunes of others."

"The old like to give good precepts as a consolation for no longer being able to give bad examples."

"Kings mint people like coins; they give them any value they wish; and one is forced to accept them according to their rate of exchange, and not according to their true price."

"When vices abandon us, we flatter ourselves with the belief that it is we who have abandoned them."

"Moderation is languor and indolence of the soul, just as ambition is its activity and ardour."

"We often pardon those who bore us, but we can never pardon those whom we bore."

"The reason that lovers never tire of each other's company, is that they always talk about themselves."

Marx to Engels, June 26, 1869

Written in German and French

Marx/Engels, *Werke*, Bd. 32, 1965, S. 326-27

Historic Significance of the Enlightenment

Modern socialism is, in its essence, the direct product of the recognition, on the one hand, of the class antagonisms existing in the society of today between proprietors and non-proprietors, between capitalists and wage-workers; on the other hand, of the anarchy existing in production. But, in its theoretical form, modern socialism originally appears ostensibly as a more logical extension of the principles laid down by the great French philosophers of the eighteenth century. Like every new theory, modern socialism had, at first, to connect itself with the intellectual stock-in-trade ready to its hand, however deeply its roots lay in [material][a] economic facts.

---

[a] The passages in square brackets are additions made subsequently by Engels to the text of three chapters from *Anti-Dühring* reworked for his *Socialism: Utopian and Scientific*. —*Ed.*

The great men, who in France prepared men's minds for the coming revolution, were themselves extreme revolutionists. They recognised no external authority of any kind whatever. Religion, natural science, society, political institutions—everything was subjected to the most unsparing criticism: everything must justify its existence before the judgment-seat of reason or give up existence. Reason became the sole measure of everything. It was the time, when, as Hegel says, the world stood upon its head;[137] first in the sense that the human head, and the principles arrived at by its thought, claimed to be the basis of all human action and association; but by and by, also, in the wider sense that the reality which was in contradiction to these principles had, in fact, to be turned upside down. Every form of society and government then existing, every old traditional notion was flung into the lumber-room as irrational; the world had hitherto allowed itself to be led solely by prejudices; everything in the past deserved only pity and contempt. Now, for the first time, appeared the light of day, [the kingdom of reason]; henceforth superstition, injustice, privilege, oppression, were to be superseded by eternal truth, eternal Right, equality based on nature and the inalienable rights of man.

We know today that this kingdom of reason was nothing more than the idealised kingdom of the bourgeoisie; that this eternal Right found its realisation in bourgeois justice; that this equality reduced itself to bourgeois equality before the law; that bourgeois property was proclaimed as one of the essential rights of man; and that the government of reason, the Contrat Social of Rousseau, came into being, and only could come into being, as a democratic bourgeois republic. The great thinkers of the eighteenth century could, no more than their predecessors, go beyond the limits imposed upon them by their epoch.

Frederick Engels, "Introduction"
to *Anti-Dühring*
Engels, *Anti-Dühring*, Moscow,
1975, pp. 24-25

The Materialism of the Encyclopedists

1

In the meantime materialism passed from England to France, where it met and coalesced with another materialistic school of philosophers, a branch of Cartesianism.[138] In France, too, it remained at first an exclusively aristocratic doctrine. But soon its revolutionary character asserted itself. The French materialists did not limit their criticism to matters of religious belief; they extended it to whatever scientific tradition or political institution they met with; and to prove the claim of their doctrine to universal application, they took the shortest cut, and boldly applied it to all subjects of knowledge in the giant work after which they were named—the *Encyclopédie*. Thus, in one or the other of its two forms—avowed materialism or deism—it became the creed of the whole cultured youth of France; so much so that, when the Great Revolution broke out, the doctrine hatched by English Royalists gave a theoretical flag to French Republicans and Terrorists, and furnished the text for the Declaration of the Rights of Man.[139]

> Frederick Engels, *Socialism: Utopian and Scientific*
>
> Marx and Engels, *Selected Works*, Vol. 3, Moscow, 1973, p. 107

2

Just as *Cartesian* materialism passes into *natural science proper*, the other trend of French materialism leads directly to *socialism* and *communism*.

There is no need for any great penetration to see from the teaching of materialism on the original goodness and equal intellectual endowment of men, the omnipotence of experience, habit and education, and the influence of environment on man, the great significance of industry, the justification of enjoyment, etc., how necessarily materialism is connected with communism and socialism. If man draws all his knowledge, sensation, etc., from the world of the senses and the experience gained in it, then what has to be done is to arrange the empirical world in such a way that man experiences and becomes accustomed to what is truly human in it and that he becomes aware of himself as man. If correctly understood interest is the principle of all morality, man's private interest must be made to coincide with the interest of humanity. If man is unfree in the materialistic sense, i.e., is free not through the negative power to avoid this or that, but through the positive power to assert his true individuality, crime must not be punished in the individual, but the anti-social sources of crime must be destroyed, and each man must be given social scope for the vital manifestation of his being. If man is shaped by environment, his environment must be made human. If man is social by nature, he will develop his true nature only in society, and the power of his nature must be measured not by the power of the separate individual but by the power of society.

These and similar propositions are to be found almost literally even in the oldest French materialists. This is not the place to assess them. The *Apologia of Vices* by *Mandeville,* one of Locke's early English followers, is typical of the socialist tendencies of materialism. He proves that in *modern* society vice is *indispensable* and *useful.*[a] This was by no means an apologia for modern society.

Fourier proceeds directly from the teaching of the French materialists. The *Babouvists* were crude, uncivilised materialists, but developed communism, too, derives *directly* from *French materialism.* The latter returned to its mother-country, *England,* in the form *Helvétius* gave it. *Bentham*

---

[a] Bernard de Mandeville, *The Fable of the Bees: or, Private Vices, Publick Benefits.—Ed.*

based his system of *correctly understood interest* on Helvétius' morality, and *Owen* proceeded from *Bentham*'s system to found English communism. Exiled to England, the Frenchman *Cabet* came under the influence of communist ideas there and on his return to France became the most popular, if the most superficial, representative of communism. Like Owen, the more scientific French Communists, *Dézamy, Gey* and others, developed the teaching of *materialism* as the teaching of *real humanism* and the *logical* basis of *communism*.

> Karl Marx and Frederick Engels,
> *The Holy Family*
>
> Marx and Engels, *Collected Works*,
> Vol. 4, Moscow, 1975, pp. 130-31

The Enlightenment and Dialectics

In the meantime, along with and after the French philosophy of the eighteenth century had arisen the new German philosophy, culminating in Hegel. Its greatest merit was the taking up again of dialectics as the highest form of reasoning. The old Greek philosophers were all born natural dialecticians, and Aristotle, the most encyclopaedic intellect of them, had already analysed the most essential forms of dialectic thought. The newer philosophy, on the other hand, although in it also dialectics had brilliant exponents (e.g., Descartes and Spinoza), had, especially through English influence, become more and more rigidly fixed in the so-called metaphysical mode of reasoning, by which also the French of the eighteenth century were almost wholly dominated, at all events in their special philosophical work. Outside philosophy in the restricted sense, the French nevertheless produced masterpieces of dialectic. We need only call to mind Diderot's *Le Neveu de Rameau* and Rousseau's *Discours sur l'origine et les fondements de l'inégalité parmi les hommes*.[a]

> Frederick Engels, "Introduction" to
> *Anti-Dühring*
> Engels, *Anti-Dühring*, Moscow, 1975,
> pp. 27-28

Utilitarian Philosophy of the Enlightenment

The apparent absurdity of merging all the manifold relationships of people in the *one* relation of usefulness, this apparently metaphysical abstraction arises from the fact that in modern bourgeois society all relations are subordinated in practice to the one abstract monetary-commercial relation. This theory came to the fore with Hobbes and Locke, at the same time as the first and second English revolutions, those first battles by which the bourgeoisie won political power. It is to be found even earlier, of course, among writers on political economy, as a tacit presupposition. Political economy is the real science of this theory of utility; it acquires its true content among the Physiocrats, since they were the first to treat political economy systematically. In Helvétius and Holbach one can already find an idealisation of this doctrine, which fully corresponds to the attitude of opposition adopted by the French bourgeoisie before the revolution. Holbach depicts the entire activity of individuals in their mutual intercourse, e.g., speech, love, etc., as a relation of utility and utilisation. Hence the actual relations

---

[a] *Discourse on the Origin and Foundations of Inequality among Men.—Ed.*

that are presupposed here are speech, love, definite manifestations of definite qualities of individuals. Now these relations are supposed not to have the meaning *peculiar* to them but to be the expression and manifestation of some third relation attributed to them, the *relation of utility or utilisation*. This *paraphrasing* ceases to be meaningless and arbitrary only when these relations have validity for the individual not on their own account, not as spontaneous activity, but rather as disguises, though by no means disguises of the category of utilisation, but of an actual third aim and relation which is called the relation of utility.

The verbal masquerade only has meaning when it is the unconscious or deliberate expression of an actual masquerade. In this case, the utility relation has a quite definite meaning, namely, that I derive benefit for myself by doing harm to someone else *(exploitation de l'homme par l'homme)*; in this case moreover the use that I derive from some relation is entirely extraneous to this relation, as we saw above in connection with ability [*Vermögen*] that from each ability a product alien to it was demanded, a relation determined by social relations—and this is precisely the relation of utility. All this is actually the case with the bourgeois. For him only *one* relation is valid on its own account—the relation of exploitation; all other relations have validity for him only insofar as he can include them under this one relation; and even where he encounters relations which cannot be directly subordinated to the relation of exploitation, he subordinates them to it at least in his imagination. The material expression of this use is money which represents the value of all things, people and social relations. Incidentally, one sees at a glance that the category of "utilisation" is first abstracted from the actual relations of intercourse which I have with other people (but by no means from reflection and mere will) and then these relations are made out to be the reality of the category that has been abstracted from them themselves, a wholly metaphysical method of procedure. In exactly the same way and with the same justification, Hegel depicts all relations as relations of the objective spirit. Hence Holbach's theory is the historically justified philosophical illusion about the bourgeoisie just then developing in France, whose thirst for exploitation could still be regarded as a thirst for the full development of individuals in conditions of intercourse freed from the old feudal fetters. Liberation from the standpoint of the bourgeoisie, i.e., competition, was, of course, for the eighteenth century the only possible way of offering the individuals a new career for freer development. The theoretical proclamation of the consciousness corresponding to this bourgeois practice, of the consciousness of mutual exploitation as the universal mutual relation of all individuals, was also a bold and open step forward. It was a kind of *enlightenment* which interpreted the political, patriarchal, religious and sentimental embellishment of exploitation under feudalism in a secular way; the embellishment corresponded to the form of exploitation existing at that time and it had been systematised especially by the theoretical writers of the absolute monarchy.

> Karl Marx and Frederick Engels,
> *The German Ideology*
>
> Marx and Engels, *Collected Works*, Vol. 5, pp. 409-10

Voltaire

1

Russian aristocrats are educated as youths at German universities and in Paris. They always snatch up the most extreme of what the West has to offer. This is pure *gourmandise*, and a part of the French aristocracy also carried on in this way during the eighteenth century. *"Ce n'est pas pour les tailleurs et les bottiers*",[a] said Voltaire at the time, speaking of his own Enlightenment philosophy. This does not prevent these Russians from becoming scoundrels as soon as they enter the civil service.

> Marx to Ludwig Kugelmann,
> October 12, 1868
>
> Marx/Engels, *Werke*, Bd. 32, 1965,
> S. 567

2

There was, at that time, already an enlightened "public opinion" in Europe. Although the *Times* newspaper had not yet begun to manufacture that article, there was that kind of public opinion which had been created by the immense influence of Diderot, Voltaire, Rousseau, and the other French writers of the eighteenth century. Russia always knew that it is important to have public opinion on one's side, if possible; and Russia took care to have it, too. The Court of Catherine II, was made the head-quarters of the enlightened men of the day, especially Frenchmen; the most enlightened principles were professed by the Empress and her Court, and so well did she succeed in deceiving them that Voltaire and many others sang the praise of the "Semiramis of the North", and proclaimed Russia the most progressive country in the world, the home of liberal principles, the champion of religious toleration.

> Frederick Engels, "What Have the Working Classes to Do with Poland"
> Written in English
> *The Commonwealth*, May 5, 1866

---

[a] This is not for tailors and shoemakers.—*Ed.*

Diderot

1

The conviction that humanity, at least at the present moment, moves on the whole in a progressive direction has absolutely nothing to do with the antagonism between materialism and idealism. The French materialists no less than the deists Voltaire and Rousseau held this conviction to an almost fanatical degree, and often enough made the greatest personal sacrifices for it. If ever anybody dedicated his whole life to the "enthusiasm for truth and justice"—using this phrase in the good sense—it was Diderot, for instance. If, therefore, Starcke declares all this to be idealism,[140] this merely proves that the word materialism, and the whole antagonism between the two trends, has lost all meaning for him here.

> Frederick Engels, *Ludwig Feuerbach and the End of Classical German Philosophy*
>
> Marx and Engels, *Selected Works*, Vol. 3, Moscow, 1973, pp. 352-53

2

Today I accidentally discovered two copies of *Neveu de Rameau* at our house, and so I am sending one to you. This unique masterpiece will once again afford you great pleasure. On this subject, old Hegel says:

"To be conscious of its own distraught and torn condition and to express itself accordingly,—this is to pour scornful laughter on its existence, on the confusion pervading the whole and on itself as well: it is at the same time this whole confusion dying away and yet apprehending itself to be doing so.

.... It is the condition in which the nature of all relationships is rent asunder, and it is the conscious rending of them all.... In respect of that return into self the vanity of all things is its own peculiar vanity, or it is itself vain. ... But only by self-consciousness being roused to revolt does it know its own peculiar torn and shattered condition; and in its knowing this it has *ipso facto* risen above this condition. Each part of this world comes to find there its spirit expressed, or gets to be spoken of with spirit and finds said of it what it is. The honest soul takes each moment as a permanent and essential fact, and is an uncultivated unreflective condition, which does not think and does not know that it is just doing the very inverse. The distraught and disintegrated soul is, however, aware of inversion; it is, in fact, a condition of absolute inversion: the conceptual principle predominates there, brings together into a single unity the thoughts that lie far apart in the case of the honest soul, and the language clothing its meaning is, therefore, full of *esprit* and wit (*geistreich*).

The content uttered by spirit and uttered about itself is, then, the inversion and perversion of all conceptions and realities, a universal deception of itself and of others. The shamelessness manifested in stating this deceit is just on that account the greatest truth. ... The placid soul that in simple honesty of heart takes the music of the good and true to consist in harmony of sound and uniformity of tone, i.e., in a melodious chord, etc." (a quote from Diderot follows).[141]

Even more amusing than Hegel's commentary is that of M. Jules Janin,[142] excerpted in the appendix to the volume. This *cardinal de la mer*[a] finds that Diderot's *Rameau* lacks any moral message and has rectified this by discovering that Rameau's pervertedness stems from his distress at not having been "born a gentleman". The Kotzebueian rubbish which he has heaped onto this cornerstone is being performed in melodramatic style in London. The path from Diderot to Jules Janin is exactly what physiologists call regressive metamorphosis: the mind of France *before* the French revolution, and *under* Louis Philippe!

Marx to Engels, April 15, 1869

Marx/Engels, *Werke*, Bd. 32, 1965, S. 303-04

---

[a] Cardinal of the sea.—*Ed.*

3

Many thanks for *Rameau,* which will give me a great deal of pleasure.

> Engels to Marx, April 16, 1869
> Marx/Engels, *Werke*, Bd. 32, 1965, S. 305

Rousseau

1

Finally: even the Rousseau doctrine of equality—of which Dühring's is only a feeble and distorted echo—could not have seen the light but for the midwife's services rendered by the Hegelian negation of the negation—though it was nearly twenty years before Hegel was born. And far from being ashamed of this, the doctrine in its first presentation[143] bears almost ostentatiously the imprint of its dialectical origin. In the state of nature and savagery men were equal; and as Rousseau regards even language as a perversion of the state of nature, he is fully justified in extending the equality of animals within the limits of a single species also to the animal-men recently classified by Haeckel hypothetically as *Alali:* speechless. But these equal animal-men had one quality which gave them an advantage over the other animals: perfectibility, the capacity to develop further; and this became the cause of inequality. So Rousseau regards the rise of inequality as progress. But this progress contained an antagonism: it was at the same time retrogression.

"All further progress [beyond the original state] meant so many steps seemingly towards the *perfection of the individual man,* but in reality towards the *decay of the race* . . . . Metallurgy and agriculture were the two arts the discovery of which produced this great revolution" (the transformation of the primeval forest into cultivated land, but along with this the introduction of poverty and slavery through property). "For the poet it is gold and silver, but for the philosopher iron and corn, which have civilised *men* and ruined the human *race*."

Each new advance of civilisation is at the same time a new advance of inequality. All institutions set up by the society which has arisen with civilisation change into the opposite of their original purpose.

"It is an incontestable fact, and the fundamental principle of all public law, that the peoples set up their chieftains to safeguard their liberty and not to enslave them."

And nevertheless the chiefs necessarily become the oppressors of the peoples, and intensify their oppression up to the point at which inequality, carried to the utmost extreme, again changes into its opposite, becomes the cause of equality: before the despot all are equal—equally ciphers.

"Here we have the extreme measure of inequality, *the final point which completes the circle and meets the point from which we set out*: here all private individuals become equal once more, just because they are ciphers, and the subjects have no other law but their master's will." But the despot is only master so long as he is able to use force and therefore "when he is driven out," he cannot "complain of the use of force.... Force alone maintained him in power, and force alone overthrows him; thus everything takes its natural course."

And so inequality once more changes into equality; not, however, into the former natural equality of speechless primitive men, but into the higher equality of the social contract. The oppressors are oppressed. It is the negation of the negation.

Already in Rousseau, therefore, we find not only a line of thought which corresponds exactly to the one developed in Marx's *Capital*, but also, in details, a whole series of the same dialectical turns of speech as Marx used: processes which in their nature are antagonistic, contain a contradiction; transformation of one extreme into its opposite; and finally, as the kernel of the whole thing, the negation of the negation.

Frederick Engels, *Anti-Dühring*,
Moscow, 1975, pp. 159-61

2

Like the historian *Raumer*, the petty bourgeois is composed of on-the-one-hand and on-the-other-hand. This is so in his economic interests and *therefore* in his politics, in his religious, scientific and artistic views. So in his morals, in everything. He is a living contradiction. If, like Proudhon, he is in addition a clever man, he will soon learn to play with his own contradictions and develop them according to circumstances into striking, spectacular, now scandalous, now brilliant paradoxes. Charlatanism in science and accommodation in politics are inseparable from such a point of view. There remains only one governing motive, the *vanity* of the subject, and the only question for him, as for all vain people, is the success of the moment, the sensation of the day. Thus the simple ethical tact, which always kept a Rousseau, for instance, far from even the semblance of compromise with the powers-that-be, necessarily fades out of existence.

Karl Marx, *On Proudhon*
Marx and Engels, *Selected Works*,
Vol. 2, Moscow, 1973, p. 30

Sentimentalism as a Reaction to the Revolutionary and Rationalist Trends of the Enlightenment

Any development, whatever its substance may be, can be represented as a series of different stages of development that are connected in such a way that one forms the *nega-*

tion of the other. If, for example, a people develops from absolute monarchy to constitutional monarchy, it *negates* its former political being. In no sphere can one undergo a development without negating one's previous mode of existence. *Negating* translated into the language of morality means: *denying.*

Denying! With this catchword the philistine as critic can condemn any development without understanding it; he can solemnly set up his undevelopable undevelopment beside it as moral immaculateness. Thus the religious phantasy of the nations has by and large stigmatised *history*, by transposing the age of innocence, the golden age, into *pre-history*, into the time when no historical development at all took place, and hence no negating and no denying. Thus in noisy eras of revolution, in times of strong, passionate negation and denial, as in the 18th century, there emerge honest, well-meaning men, well-bred, respectable satyrs like *Gessner*, who oppose the undevelopable state of the *idylls* to the corruption of history. It should nevertheless be observed to the credit of these idyll-poets, who were also critical moralists and moralising critics of a kind, that they conscientiously waver as to who should be accorded the palm of morality, the shepherd or the sheep.

> Karl Marx, "Moralising Criticism and Critical Morality"
>
> Marx and Engels, *Collected Works*, Vol. 6, Moscow, 1976, pp. 317-18

The Crisis of Enlightenment Ideals

We saw in the "Introduction"[144] how the French philosophers of the eighteenth century, the forerunners of the Revolution, appealed to reason as the sole judge of all that is.

A rational government, rational society, were to be founded; everything that ran counter to eternal reason was to be remorselessly done away with. We saw also that this eternal reason was in reality nothing but the idealised understanding of the eighteenth century citizen, just then evolving into the bourgeois. The French Revolution had realised this rational society and government.

But, the new order of things, rational enough as compared with earlier conditions, turned out to be by no means absolutely rational. The state based upon reason completely collapsed. Rousseau's Contrat Social had found its realisation in the Reign of Terror, from which the bourgeoisie, who had lost confidence in their own political capacity, had taken refuge first in the corruption of the Directorate, and, finally, under the wing of the Napoleonic despotism. The promised eternal peace was turned into an endless war of conquest. The society based upon reason had fared no better. The antagonism between rich and poor, instead of dissolving into general prosperity, has become intensified by the removal of the guild and other privileges, which had to some extent bridged it over, and by the removal of the charitable institutions of the Church. [The "freedom of property" from feudal fetters, now veritably accomplished, turned out to be, for the small capitalists and small proprietors, the freedom to sell their small property, crushed under the overmastering competition of the large capitalists and landlords, to these great lords, and thus, as far as the small capitalists and peasant proprietors were concerned, became "freedom *from property*".] The development of industry upon a capitalistic basis made poverty and misery of the working masses conditions of existence of society. [Cash payment became more and more, in Carlyle's phrase, the sole nexus between man and man.[145]] The number of crimes increased from year to year. Formerly, the feudal vices had openly stalked about in broad daylight; though not eradicated, they were, now at any rate, thrust into the background. In their stead, the bourgeois vices, hitherto practised in secret, began to blossom all the more luxuriantly. Trade became to a greater and greater extent cheating. The "fraternity" of the revolutionary motto was realised in the chicanery and rivalries of the battle of competition. Oppression by force was replaced by corruption; the sword, as the first social lever, by gold. The right of the first night was transferred from the feudal lords to the bourgeois manufacturers. Prostitution increased to an extent never heard of. Marriage itself remained, as before, the legally recognised form, the official cloak of prostitution, and, moreover, was supplemented by rich crops of adultery.

In a word, compared with the splendid promises of the philosophers, the social and political institutions born of the "triumph of reason" were bitterly disappointing caricatures.

Frederick Engels, *Anti-Dühring*, Moscow, 1975, pp. 291-92

Transition from the Enlightenment to Romanticism

The first reaction against the French Revolution and the Enlightenment which is connected with it was naturally to regard everything medieval as romantic; even people like Grimm are not free from this. The second reaction is to look beyond the Middle Ages into the primitive age of every nation, and that corresponds to the socialist trend, although those learned men have no idea that they have any connection with it. Then they are surprised to find what is newest in what is oldest—even equalitarians, to a degree which would have made Proudhon shudder.

Marx to Engels, March 25, 1868

Marx and Engels, *Selected Correspondence*, Moscow, 1975, p. 189

Criticism of Capitalist Progress from the Point of View of the Past. Feudal Socialism

Owing to their historical position, it became the vocation of the aristocracies of France and England to write pamphlets against modern bourgeois society. In the French revolution of July 1830, and in the English reform agitation, these aristocracies again succumbed to the hateful upstart. Thenceforth, a serious political contest was altogether out of question. A literary battle alone remained possible. But even in the domain of literature the old cries of the restoration period* had become impossible.

In order to arouse sympathy, the aristocracy were obliged to lose sight, apparently, of their own interests, and to formulate their indictment against the bourgeoisie in the interest of the exploited working class alone. Thus the aristocracy took their revenge by singing lampoons on their new master, and whispering in his ears sinister prophecies of coming catastrophe.

In this way arose Feudal Socialism: half lamentation, half lampoon; half echo of the past, half menace of the future; at times, by its bitter, witty and incisive criticism, striking the bourgeoisie to the very heart's core; but always ludicrous in its effect, through total incapacity to comprehend the march of modern history.

The aristocracy, in order to rally the people to them, waved the proletarian alms-bag in front for a banner. But the people, so often as it joined them, saw on their hindquarters the old feudal coats of arms, and deserted with loud and irreverent laughter.

---

* Not the English Restoration 1660 to 1689, but the French Restoration 1814 to 1830. [*Note by Engels to the English edition of 1888.*]

One section of the French Legitimists and "Young England"[146] exhibited this spectacle.

Karl Marx and Frederick Engels, *Manifesto of the Communist Party*

Marx and Engels, *Collected Works*, Vol. 6, Moscow, 1976, pp. 507-08

Petty-Bourgeois Criticism of Capitalism

The feudal aristocracy was not the only class that was ruined by the bourgeoisie, not the only class whose conditions of existence pined and perished in the atmosphere of modern bourgeois society. The medieval burgesses and the small peasant proprietors were the precursors of the modern bourgeoisie. In those countries which are but little developed, industrially and commercially, these two classes still vegetate side by side with the rising bourgeoisie.

In countries where modern civilisation has become fully developed, a new class of petty bourgeois has been formed, fluctuating between proletariat and bourgeoisie and ever renewing itself as a supplementary part of bourgeois society. The individual members of this class, however, are being constantly hurled down into the proletariat by the action of competition, and, as modern industry develops, they even see the moment approaching when they will completely disappear as an independent section of modern society, to be replaced, in manufactures, agriculture and commerce, by overlookers, bailiffs and shopmen.

In countries like France, where the peasants constitute far more than half of the population, it was natural that writers who sided with the proletariat against the bourgeoisie, should use, in their criticism of the bourgeois *régime*, the standard of the peasant and petty bourgeois, and from the standpoint of these intermediate classes should take up the cudgels for the working class. Thus arose petty-bourgeois Socialism. Sismondi was the head of this school, not only in France but also in England.

This school of Socialism dissected with great acuteness the contradictions in the conditions of modern production. It laid bare the hypocritical apologies of economists. It proved, incontrovertibly, the disastrous effects of machinery and division of labour; the concentration of capital and land in a few hands; over-production and crises; it pointed out the inevitable ruin of the petty bourgeois and peasant, the misery of the proletariat, the anarchy in production, the crying inequalities in the distribution of wealth, the industrial war of extermination between nations, the dissolution of old moral bonds, of the old family relations, of the old nationalities.

In its positive aims, however, this form of Socialism aspires either to restoring the old means of production and of exchange, and with them the old property relations, and the old society, or to cramping the modern means of production and of exchange, within the framework of the old property relations that have been, and were bound to be, exploded by those means. In either case, it is both reactionary and Utopian.

Its last words are: corporate guilds for manufacture; patriarchal relations in agriculture.

Ultimately, when stubborn historical facts had dispersed all intoxicating effects of self-deception, this form of Socialism ended in a miserable fit of the blues.

Karl Marx and Frederick Engels,
Manifesto of the Communist Party

Marx and Engels, *Collected Works*,
Vol. 6, Moscow, 1976, pp. 509-10

Restoration Writers

A very renowned reactionary writer loudly professed that the highest metaphysics of a de Maistre and of a de Bonald was in the end a question of money, and is not every question of money a directly social question? The men of the Restoration did not conceal the fact that to bring back good politics it was necessary to bring back good property rights, feudal property, moral property. Everybody knows that loyalty to monarchy cannot dispense with tithes and corvée labour.

Karl Marx and Frederick Engels,
"On the Polish Question"

Marx and Engels, *Collected Works*,
Vol. 6, Moscow, 1976, p. 546

French Literature

Abbé Prévost

> Tyndall's emotional need[147] proves nothing. The Chevalier des Grieux also had an emotional need to love and possess Manon Lescaut, who sold herself and him over and over again; for her sake he became a cardsharper and pimp, and if Tyndall wants to reproach him, he would reply with his "emotional need"!
>
> Frederick Engels, *Dialectics of Nature*, Moscow, 1974, p. 201

Chateaubriand

1

Dear Frederick!
In studying the Spanish rubbish I have also worked out the tricks of the worthy Chateaubriand, that fine writer who combines the aristocratic scepticism and Voltairianism of the 18th century with the aristocratic sentimentalism and romanticism of the 19th in the most repellent fashion. Naturally, this combination was bound, in terms of *style,* to be epoch-making in France, although even in the style the falsity often hits one in the eye, despite all the artistic tricks. As for his *political* views, this fellow has completely revealed himself in his *Congrès de Vérône*[148] and the only question is whether

he received hard cash from Alexander Pavlovich[a] or was bought simply with flatteries, to which this vain fop is more susceptible than anyone.

> Marx to Engels,
> October 26, 1854
> Marx/Engels, *Werke*, Bd. 28, 1963, S. 404

2

For the rest, I read Saint-Beuve's book on *Chateaubriand*,[149] a writer whom I have always found repugnant. The man is celebrated in France, because in every respect he is the most classical incarnation of French *vanité*, a *vanité* clothed not in light, frivolous eighteenth-century garb, but draped in romanticism and prancing about in newly coined phrases. Such false profundity, Byzantine exaggeration, flirtation with emotion, motley schillerism, word painting, theatrical *sublime*, or to put it concisely, such a hodge-podge of lies has never before been achieved, neither in form, nor in content.

> Marx to Engels, November 30, 1873
> Marx/Engels, *Werke*, Bd. 33, 1966, S. 96

Alexandre Dumas

As far as his [Louis Blanc's] historical works are concerned, he does them like A. Dumas does his feuilletons. He always studies just the material for the next chapter. This is how books like the *Histoire des dix ans* come out. On the

---

[a] Alexander I.—*Ed.*

one hand, this gives his accounts a certain freshness, since what he communicates is for him at least as new as for the reader; on the other hand, the whole is quite weak.

Marx to Engels, February 23, 1851

Marx/Engels, *Werke*, Bd. 27, 1965, S. 194

Lamartine

1

Lamartine sinks lower with every passing day.... The man addresses all his speeches to the bourgeois alone and tries to soothe them. The election proclamation of the Provisional Government is also intended entirely for the bourgeois so as to reassure them. It is no wonder that the fellows become insolent as a result.

Engels to Marx, March 18, 1848

Marx/Engels, *Werke*, Bd. 27, 1965, S. 123

2

Lamartine was the imaginary picture which the bourgeois republic had of itself, the exuberant, fantastic, visionary conception which it had formed for itself, the dream of its own splendour. It is quite remarkable what one can imagine! As Aeolus unleashed all the winds from his bag, so Lamartine set free all spirits of the air, all the phrases of the bourgeois republic and he blew them towards the east and the west, empty words of the fraternity of all nations, of the impending emancipation of all the nations by France and of France's sacrifice for all the nations.

He did *nothing*.

It was Cavaignac who undertook to supply the deeds corresponding to Lamartine's phrases and Bastide, his outward turned organ.

>Karl Marx and Frederick Engels,
>"English-French Mediation in Italy"
>
>Marx and Engels, *Collected Works*,
>Vol. 7, Moscow, 1976, p. 482

3

We have often enough pointed out that the romantic dreams which came into being after the revolutions of February and March,[150] such as ardent fantasies about the universal fraternal union of peoples, a European federative republic, and eternal world peace, were basically nothing but screens hiding the immeasurable perplexity and inactivity of the leading spokesmen of that time. People did not see, or did not want to see, what had to be done to safeguard the revolution; they were unable or unwilling to carry out any really revolutionary measures; the narrow-mindedness of some and the counter-revolutionary intrigues of others resulted in the people being given only revolutionary phrases instead of revolutionary deeds. The scoundrel Lamartine with his high-flown declarations was the classic *hero* of this epoch of betrayal of the people disguised by poetic flowery and rhetorical tinsel.

>Frederick Engels, "Democratic Panslavism"
>
>Marx and Engels, *Collected Works*,
>Vol. 8, Moscow, 1976

Victor Hugo

1

Of the writings dealing with the same subject[151] approximately *at the same time* as mine, only two deserve notice: Victor Hugo's *Napoleon the Little* and Proudhon's *Coup d'État*.

Victor Hugo confines himself to bitter and witty invective against the responsible publisher of the *coup d'état*. The event itself appears in his work like a bolt from the blue. He sees in it only the violent act of a single individual. He does not notice that he makes this individual great instead of little by ascribing to him a personal power of initiative such as would be without parallel in world history. Proudhon, for his part, seeks to represent the *coup d'état* as the result of an antecedent historical development. Unnoticeably, however, his historical construction of the *coup d'état* becomes a historical *apologia* for its hero. Thus he falls into the error of our so-called *objective* historians. I, on the contrary, demonstrate how the *class struggle* in France created circumstances and relationships that made it possible for a grotesque mediocrity to play a hero's part.

> Karl Marx, "Author's Preface to the Second Edition of *The Eighteenth Brumaire of Louis Bonaparte*"
>
> Marx and Engels, *Selected Works*, Vol. 1, Moscow, 1973, pp. 394-95

2

That "unfathomable" and extremely chaotic Germany which has never existed outside Victor Hugo's imagination. The Germany which was supposed to be interested only in music, dreams and clouds, and which left the care of matters here below to the French bourgeois and journalists.

> Engels to Paul
> Lafargue, December 5, 1892
>
> Frederick Engels, Paul and
> Laura Lafargue, *Correspondence*,
> Vol. 3, Moscow, 1963, p. 219

3

With the passing of time the war is assuming an unpleasant character.[152] The French have not yet been thrashed enough, and the German asses have won far too many victories. Victor Hugo writes nonsense in French, and fair William abuses the German language:[153]

"Nun lebe wohl mit bewegtem Herzen am Schluss eines solchen Briefes."[a]

This would be a king?! And of the most "cultured" nation in the world! And his wife has it printed!

> Engels to Marx,
> September 13, 1870
>
> Marx/Engels, *Werke*,
> Bd. 33, 1966, S. 63

4

The bombardment of a fortress, though still considered as a step permitted by the laws of war, yet is a measure implying such an amount of suffering to non-combatants that history will blame any one nowadays attempting it without reasonable chance of thereby extorting the surrender of the

---

[a] And now farewell, with trembling heart at the close of such a letter.—*Ed.*

place. We smile at the *chauvinisme* of a Victor Hugo, who considers Paris a holy city—very holy!—and every attempt to attack it a sacrilege. We look upon Paris as upon any other fortified town, which, if it chooses to defend itself, must run all the risks of fair attack, of open trenches, siege batteries, and stray shots hitting non-military buildings.

>Frederick Engels, "Notes on the War"
>
>Written in English
>
>*Pall Mall Gazette*, October 13, 1870

Eugène Sue

The well-known novel of Eugène Sue, *The Mysteries of Paris*, has made a deep impression upon the public mind, especially in Germany; the forcible manner in which this book depicts the misery and demoralisation falling to the share of the "lower orders" in great cities, could not fail to direct public attention to the state of the poor in general. The Germans begin to discover, as the *Allgemeine Zeitung*, the *Times* of Germany, says, that the style of novel writing has undergone a complete revolution during these last ten years; that instead of kings and princes, who formerly were the heroes of similar tales, it is now the poor, the despised class, whose fates and fortunes, joys and sufferings, are made the topic of romance; they are finding out at last that this new class of novel writers, such as G. Sand, E. Sue, and Boz,[a] is indeed a sign of the times.

>Frederick Engels, "Continental Movements"
>
>Marx and Engels, *Collected Works*, Vol. 3, Moscow, 1975, p. 415

---

[a] Charles Dickens.—*Ed.*

From Critical Analysis of Sue's *Mystères de Paris*

1

If Eugène Sue depicts the taverns, hide-outs and language of *criminals*, Herr Szeliga discloses the *"mystery"* that what the "author" wanted was not to depict that language or those hide-outs, but

> "to teach us the mystery of the mainsprings of evil, etc." "It is precisely in the most crowded places ... that criminals feel *at home*."

What would a natural scientist say if one were to prove to him that the bee's cell does not interest him as a bee's cell, that it has no mystery for one who has not studied it, because the bee "feels at home precisely" in the open air and on the flower? The hide-outs of the criminals and their language reflect the character of the criminal, they are part of his existence, their description is part of his description just as the description of the *petite maison* is part of the description of the *femme galante*.

For Parisians in general and even for the Paris police the hide-outs of criminals are such a "mystery" that at this very moment broad light streets are being laid out in the *Cité* to give the police access to them.

Finally, Eugène Sue himself states that in the descriptions mentioned above he was counting *"sur la curiosité craintive"*[a] of his readers. M. Eugène Sue has counted on the timid curiosity of his readers in all his novels. It is sufficient to recall *Atar Gull, Salamandre, Plick and Plock*, etc.

Karl Marx and Frederick Engels, *The Holy Family*

Marx and Engels, *Collected Works*, Vol. 4, Moscow, 1975, p. 57

---

[a] On the timid curiosity.—*Ed.*

2

Chourineur was a butcher by trade. Owing to a concourse of circumstances, this mighty son of nature becomes a murderer. Rudolph comes across him accidentally just when he is molesting Fleur de Marie. Rudolph gives the dexterous brawler a few impressive, masterly punches on the head, and thus wins his respect. Later, in the tavern frequented by criminals, Chourineur's kind-hearted disposition is revealed. "You still have heart and honour," Rudolph says to him. By these words he instils in Chourineur respect for himself. Chourineur is reformed or, as Herr Szeliga says, is transformed into a *"moral being"*. Rudolph takes him under his protection. Let us follow the course of Chourineur's education under the guidance of Rudolph.

1st Stage. The first lesson Chourineur receives is a lesson in hypocrisy, faithlessness, craft and *dissimulation*. Rudolph uses the reformed Chourineur in exactly the same way as *Vidocq* used the criminals he had reformed, i.e., he makes him a *mouchard*[a] and *agent provocateur*. He advises him to *"pretend"* to the *"maître d'école"*[b] that he has altered his "principle of not stealing" and to suggest a robbery so as to lure him into a trap set by Rudolph. Chourineur feels that he is being made a fool of. He protests against the suggestion of playing the role of *mouchard* and *agent provocateur*. Rudolph easily convinces the son of nature by the *"pure"* casuistry of Critical Criticism that a foul trick is not foul when it is done for *"good, moral"* reasons. Chourineur, as an *agent provocateur* and under the pretence of friendship and confidence, lures his former companion to destruction. For the *first time* in his life he commits an act of *infamy*.

2nd Stage. We next find Chourineur acting as *garde-malade*[c] to Rudolph, whom he has saved from mortal danger.

---

[a] Police spy.—*Ed.*

[b] The "maître d'école"—a nickname given by his fellow criminals. —*Ed.*

[c] Sick attendant.—*Ed.*

Chourineur has become such a *respectable moral* being that he rejects the Negro doctor David's suggestion to sit on the floor, for fear of dirtying the carpet. He is indeed too *shy* to sit on a chair. He first lays the chair on its back and then sits on the front legs. He never fails to apologise when he addresses Rudolph, whom he saved from a mortal danger, as "friend" or "*Monsieur*" instead of "*Monseigneur*".

What a wonderful training of the ruthless son of nature! Chourineur expresses the innermost secret of his Critical transformation when he admits to Rudolph that he has the same attachment for him as a *bulldog* for its master: "Je me sens pour vous, comme qui dirait *l'attachement* d'un *bouledogue* pour *son maître*." The former butcher is transformed into a dog. Henceforth all his virtues will be reduced to the virtue of a dog, pure "*dévouement*" to its master. His independence, his individuality will disappear completely. But just as bad painters have to label their pictures to say what they are supposed to represent, Eugène Sue has to put a label on "*bulldog*" Chourineur, who constantly affirms: "The two words, 'You still have heart and honour', made a *man* out of me." Until his very last breath, Chourineur will find the motive for his actions, not in his human individuality, but in that label. As proof of his moral reformation he will often reflect on his own excellence and the wickedness of other individuals. And every time he throws out moral sentences, Rudolph will say to him: "I like to hear you *speak* like that." Chourineur has not become an ordinary *bulldog* but a *moral one*.

3rd Stage. We have already admired the *petty-bourgeois respectability* which has taken the place of Chourineur's *coarse* but *daring* unceremoniousness. We now learn that, as befits a "*moral being*", he has also adopted the gait and demeanour of the *petty bourgeois*.

"A le voir marcher—on l'eût pris pour le *bourgeois* le plus inoffensif du monde."[a]

[a] "To see him walk you would have taken him for the most harmless *bourgeois* in the world."—*Ed.*

Still sadder than this form is the content that Rudolph gives his Critically reformed life. He sends him to Africa "to serve as a living and salutary example of repentance to the world of unbelievers". In future, he will have to represent, not his own human nature, but a Christian dogma.

4th Stage. The Critically moral transformation has made Chourineur a quiet, cautious man who behaves according to the rules of fear and worldly wisdom.

"Le Chourineur", reports Murph, who in his indiscreet simplicity continually tells tales out of school, "n'a pas dit un mot de l'exécution du maître d'école, de *peur* de *se* trouver compromis."[a]

So Chourineur knows that the punishment of the *maître d'école* was an illegal act. But he does not talk about it for fear of compromising himself. *Wise* Chourineur!

5th Stage. Chourineur has carried his moral education to such perfection that he gives his *dog-like* attitude to Rudolph a civilised form—he becomes conscious of it. After saving *Germain* from a mortal danger he says to him:

"I have a protector who is to me what *God* is to *priests* — he is such as to make one kneel before him."

And in imagination he kneels before his God.

"Monsieur Rudolph," he says to Germain, "protects you. I say '*Monsieur*' though I should say '*Monseigneur*'. But I am used to calling him '*Monsieur* Rudolph', and he allows me to."

"Magnificent awakening and flowering!" exclaims Szeliga in Critical delight.

6th Stage. Chourineur worthily ends his career of pure *dévouement*, or moral bulldoggishness, by finally letting himself be stabbed to death for his gracious lord. At the moment when Squelette threatens the prince with his knife, Chouri-

---

[a] "Chourineur said nothing of the punishment meted out to the *maître d'école* for *fear* of compromising *himself*."—*Ed.*

neur stays the murderer's arm. Squelette stabs him. But, dying, Chourineur says to Rudolph:

> "I was right when I said that a *lump of earth*" (a bulldog) "like me can sometimes be useful to a *great and gracious master* like you."

To this dog-like utterance, which sums up the whole of Chourineur's Critical life like *an* epigram, the label put in his mouth adds:

> "We are quits, Monsieur Rudolph. You told me that I had heart and honour."

Herr Szeliga cries as loud as he can:

> "What a merit it was for Rudolph to have restored the Schurimann[a] [?] to *mankind* [?]!"

Karl Marx and Frederick Engels,
The Holy Family

Marx and Engels, *Collected Works*,
Vol. 4, Moscow, 1975, pp. 163-65

3

We meet Marie surrounded by criminals, as a prostitute in bondage to the proprietress of the criminals' tavern. In this debasement she preserves a human nobleness of soul, a human unaffectedness and a human beauty that impress those around her, raise her to the level of a poetical flower of the criminal world and win for her the name of Fleur de Marie.

We must observe Fleur de Marie attentively from her first appearance in order to be able to compare her *original form* with her *Critical transformation*.

In spite of her frailty, Fleur de Marie at once gives proof of vitality, energy, cheerfulness, resilience of character—

---

[a] Schurimann is a Germanised form of Chourineur.—*Ed.*

qualities which alone explain her human development in her *inhuman* situation.

When Chourineur ill-treats her, she defends herself with her scissors. That is the situation in which we first find her. She does not appear as a defenceless lamb who surrenders without any resistance to overwhelming brutality; she is a girl who can vindicate her rights and put up a fight.

In the criminals' tavern in the Rue aux Fèves she tells Chourineur and Rudolph the story of her life. As she does so she *laughs* at Chourineur's wit. She blames herself because on being released from prison she spent the 300 francs she had earned there on amusements instead of looking for work. "But," she said, "I had no one to advise me." The memory of the catastrophe of her life—her selling herself to the proprietress of the criminals' tavern—puts her in a melancholy mood. It is the first time since her childhood that she has recalled these events.

"Le fait est, que ça me chagrine de regarder ainsi derrière moi... ça doit être bien bon d'être honnête."[a]

When Chourineur makes fun on her and tells her she must become honest, she exclaims:

"Honnête, mon dieu! et avec quoi donc veux-tu que je sois honnête?"[b]

She insists that she is not one "to have fits of tears": "*Je ne suis pas pleurnicheuse*"[c]; but her position in life is sad—"*Ça n'est pas gai.*"[d] Finally, contrary to Christian *repentance*, she pronounces on the past the human sentence at once *Stoic* and *Epicurean*, of a free and strong nature:

"*Enfin ce qui est fait, est fait.*"[e]

---

[a] "The fact is that it grieves me when I look back in this way ... it must be lovely to be honest."—*Ed.*

[b] "Honest! My God! What do you want me to be honest with?"—*Ed.*

[c] "I am no crybaby."—*Ed.*

[d] "It isn't a happy one."—*Ed.*

[e] "Well, what is done is done."—*Ed.*

Let us accompany Fleur de Marie on her first outing with Rudolph.

"The consciousness of your terrible situation has probably often distressed you," Rudolph says, itching to moralise.

> "Yes," she replies, "more than once I looked over the embankment of the Seine; but then I would gaze at the flowers and the sun and say to myself: the river will always be there and I am not yet seventeen years old. Who can say? Dans ces moments ——là il me semblait que mon sort n'était pas mérité, qu'il y avait en moi quelque chose de bon. Je me disais, on m'a bien tourmenté, mais au moins je n'ai jamais fait de mal à personne."[a]

Fleur de Marie considers her situation not as one she has freely created, not as the expression of her own personality, but as a fate she has not deserved. Her bad fortune can change. She is still young.

Good and *evil*, as Marie conceives them, are not the *moral abstractions* of good and evil. She is *good* because she has never caused *suffering* to anyone, she has always been *human* towards her inhuman surroundings. She is *good* because the sun and the flowers reveal to her her own sunny and blossoming nature. She is *good* because she is still *young*, full of hope and vitality. Her situation is *not good*, because it puts an unnatural constraint on her, because it is not the expression of her human impulses, not the fulfilment of her human desires; because it is full of torment and without joy. She measures her situation in life by her *own individuality*, her *essential nature*, not by the *ideal of what is good*.

In *natural* surroundings, where the chains of bourgeois life fall away and she can freely manifest her own nature, Fleur de Marie bubbles over with love of life, with a wealth of feeling, with human joy at the beauty of nature; these show

---

[a] "On such occasions it seemed to me that I had not deserved my fate, that I had something good in me. People have tormented me enough, I used to say to myself, but at least I have never done any harm to anyone."—*Ed.*

that her social position has only grazed the surface of her and is a mere misfortune, that she herself is neither good nor bad, but *human*.

> "Monsieur Rodolphe, quel bonheur... de l'herbe, des champs! Si voux vouliez me permettre de descendre, il fait si beau... j'aimerais tant à courir dans ces prairies!"[a]

Alighting from the carriage, she plucks flowers for Rudolph, "can hardly speak for joy", etc., etc.

Rudolph tells her that he is going to take her to *Madame George's farm*. There she can see dove-cotes, cow-stalls and so forth; there they have milk, butter, fruit, etc. Those are real *blessings* for this child. She will be *merry*, that is her main thought. "*C'est à n'y pas croire ... comme je veux m'amuser!*"[b] She explains to Rudolph in the most unaffected way her own *share* of responsibility for her misfortune. "*Tout mon sort est venu de ce que je n'ai pas économisé mon argent!*"[c] She therefore advises him to be thrifty and to put money in the savings bank. Her fancy runs wild in the castles in the air that Rudolph builds for her. She becomes sad only because she

> "has forgotten the *present*" and "the contrast of that present with the dream of a joyous and laughing existence reminds her of the cruelty of her situation".

So far we have seen Fleur de Marie in her original un-Critical form. Eugène Sue has risen above the horizon of his narrow world outlook. He has slapped bourgeois prejudice in the face. He will hand over Fleur de Marie to the hero Rudolph to atone for his temerity and to reap applause from all old men and women, from the whole of the Paris police, from the current religion and from "critical Criticism".

---

a "Monsieur Rudolph, what happiness! ... grass, fields! If you would allow me to get out, the weather is so fine ... I should love so much to run about in these meadows."—*Ed.*

b "You can't believe how I am longing for some fun!"—*Ed.*

c "My whole fate is due to the fact that I did not save up my money."—*Ed.*

Madame George, to whom Rudolph entrusts Fleur de Marie, is an unhappy, hypochondriacal religious woman. She immediately welcomes the child with the unctuous words: "*God* blesses those who love and fear him, who have been unhappy and who *repent*." Rudolph, the man of "pure Criticism", has the wretched priest *Laporte*, whose-hair has greyed in superstition, called in. He has the mission of accomplishing Fleur de Marie's Critical reform.

Joyfully and unaffectedly Marie approaches the old priest. In his Christian brutality, *Eugène Sue* makes a "marvellous instinct" at once whisper in her ear that "*shame* ends where *repentance* and *penance* begin", that is, in the church, which alone saves. He forgets the unconstrained merriness of the outing, a merriness which nature's grace and Rudolph's friendly sympathy had produced, and which was troubled only by the thought of having to go back to the criminals' landlady.

The priest Laporte immediately adopts a *supermundane* attitude. His first words are:

"*God*'s mercy is infinite, my dear child! He has proved it to you by not abandoning you in your severe trials.... The magnanimous man who saved you fulfilled the *word of the Scriptures*" (note — the word of the Scriptures, not a human purpose!): "Verily the Lord is nigh to those who invoke him; he will fulfil their desires... he will hear their voice and will save them... the Lord will accomplish *his* work."

Marie cannot yet understand the *evil* meaning of the priest's exhortations. She answers:

"I shall pray for those who pitied me and brought me back to God."

Her first thought is *not* for God, it is for her *human* saviour and she wants to pray for *him*, not for her *own* absolution. She attributes to her prayer some influence on the salvation of others. Indeed, she is still so naive that she supposes she has *already been brought back* to God. The priest feels it is his duty to destroy this unorthodox illusion.

"Soon," he says, interrupting her, "soon you will deserve absolution, absolution from your great errors... for, to quote the prophet once more, the Lord holdeth up those who are on the brink of falling."

One should not fail to see the inhuman expressions the priest uses. Soon you will deserve absolution. Your sins are *not yet forgiven.*

As Laporte, when he receives the girl, bestows on her the *consciousness of her sins,* so Rudolph, when he leaves her, presents her with a gold *cross,* the symbol of the *Christian crucifixion* awaiting her.

Marie has already been living for some time on Madame George's farm. Let us first listen to a dialogue between the old priest Laporte and Madame George.

He considers "marriage" out of the question for Marie "because no man, in spite of the priest's guarantee, will have the courage to face the past that has soiled her youth". He adds: "she has great errors to atone for, her moral sense ought to have kept her upright."

He proves, as the commonest of bourgeois would, that she could have remained good: "There are many virtuous people in Paris today." The hypocritical priest knows quite well that at any hour of the day, in the busiest streets, those virtuous people of Paris pass indifferently by little girls of seven or eight years who sell *allumettes*[a] and the like until about midnight as Marie herself used to do and who, almost without exception, will have the same fate as Marie.

The priest has made up his mind concerning Marie's *penance;* in his own mind he has already *condemned* her. Let us follow Marie when she is accompanying Laporte home in the evening.

"See, my child," he begins with unctuous eloquence, "the boundless horizon the limits of which are no longer visible" (for it is evening), "it seems to me that the calm and the vastness almost give us an idea of eternity.... I am telling you this, Marie, because you are sensitive to the beauties of creation.... I have often been moved by the religious admiration which they inspire in you—you who for so long were deprived of religious feeling."

The priest has already succeeded in changing Marie's immediate naive pleasure in the beauties of nature into a

---

[a] Matches.—*Ed.*

religious admiration. For her, *nature* has already become devout, *Christianised* nature, debased to *creation*. The transparent sea of space is desecrated and turned into the dark symbol of stagnant *eternity*. She has already learnt that all human manifestations of her being were "*profane*", devoid of religion, of real consecration, that they were impious and godless. The priest must soil her in her own eyes, he must trample underfoot her natural, spiritual resources and means of grace, in order to make her receptive to the supernatural means of grace he promises her, *baptism*.

When Marie wants to make a confession to him and asks him to be lenient he answers:

"The *Lord* has shown you that he is merciful."

In the clemency which she is shown Marie must not see a natural, self-evident attitude of a related human being to her, another human being. She must see in it an extravagant, supernatural, superhuman mercy and condescension; in *human leniency* she must see *divine mercy*. She must transcendentalise all human and natural relationships by making them *relationships to God*. The way Fleur de Marie in her answer accepts the priest's chatter about divine mercy shows how far she has already been spoilt by religious doctrine.

As soon as she entered upon her improved situation, she said, she had felt only her *new happiness*.

"Every instant I thought of Monsieur Rudolph. I often raised my eyes to heaven, to look there, not for God, but for Monsieur Rudolph, and to thank him. Yes, *I confess*, Father, *I thought more* of him than of God; for *he* did for me what God alone could have done.... I was *happy*, as happy as someone who has escaped a great danger for ever."

Fleur de Marie already finds it wrong that she took a new happy situation in life simply for what it *really* was, that she felt it as a new happiness, that her attitude to it was a natural, not a supernatural one. She accuses herself of seeing in the man who rescued her what he *really* was, her rescuer, instead of supposing some imaginary saviour, *God*, in his place. She is already caught in religious hypocrisy, which takes away from *another man* what he has deserved in respect of me in order to give it to God, and which in general regards everything human in man as alien to him and everything inhuman in him as *really* belonging to him.

Marie tells us that the *religious transformation* of her thoughts, her sentiments, her attitude to life was effected by Madame George and Laporte.

"When Rudolph took me away from the *Cité*, I already had a vague consciousness of my degradation. But the education, the advice and examples I got from you and Madame George made me understand... that I had been more guilty than unfortunate.... You and Madame George made me *realise the infinite depth of my damnation.*"

That is to say she owes to the priest Laporte and Madame George the replacement of the human and therefore bearable consciousness of her degradation by the Christian and hence unbearable consciousness of eternal damnation. The priest and the bigot have taught her to judge herself from the *Christian point of view.*

Marie feels the depth of the spiritual misfortune into which she has been cast. She says:

"Since the consciousness of good and evil had to be so frightful for me, why was I not left to my wretched lot?.... Had I not been snatched away from infamy, misery, and blows would soon have killed me. At least I should have died in ignorance of a purity that I shall, always wish for in vain."

The heartless priest replies:

"Even the most noble nature, were it to be plunged only for a day in the filth from which you have been saved, would be *indelibly branded.* That is the *immutability of divine justice!*"

Deeply wounded by this *priestly curse* uttered in such honeyed tones, Fleur de Marie exclaims:

"You see therefore, I must despair!"

The grey-headed slave of religion answers:

"You must renounce hope of effacing this desolate page from your life, but you must trust in the *infinite mercy of God*. Here *below,* my poor child, you will have tears, remorse and penance, but one day *up above,* forgiveness and *eternal bliss!"*

Marie is not yet stupid enough to be satisfied with eternal bliss and forgiveness up above.

"Pity, pity, my God!" she cries. "I am so young.... *Malheur à moi!"*a

Then the hypocritical sophistry of the priest reaches its peak:

"On the contrary, happiness for you, Marie; happiness for you to whom the Lord sends this bitter but saving remorse! It shows the *religious* susceptibility of your soul.... Each of your sufferings is counted up above. Believe me, God left you awhile on the path of evil only to reserve for you the *glory of repentance* and the eternal reward due to *atonement."*

From this moment Marie is *enslaved by the consciousness of sin.* In her former most unhappy situation in life she was able to develop a lovable, human individuality; in her outward debasement she was conscious that *her human* essence was *her true essence.* Now the filth of modern society, which has touched her externally, becomes her innermost being, and continual hypochondriacal self-torture because of that filth becomes her duty, the task of her life appointed by God himself, the self-purpose of her existence. Formerly she said of herself "*Je ne suis pas pleurnicheuse*" and knew that "*ce qui est fait, est fait*". Now self-torment will be her *good* and remorse will be her *glory.*

It turns out later that Fleur de Marie is Rudolph's daughter. We come across her again as Princess of Geroldstein. We overhear a conversation she has with her father:

"En vain je prie Dieu de me délivrer de ces obsessions, de remplir uniquement mon cœur de son pieux amour, de ses saintes espérances, de me prendre enfin toute entière, puisque je veux me donner toute

---

a "Woe unto me!"—*Ed.*

entière à lui ... il n'exauce par mes vœux — sans doute, parce que mes préoccupations *terrestres* me rendent indigne d'entrer en commun avec lui."[a]

When man has realised that his transgressions are *infinite* crimes against God he can be sure of *salvation* and *mercy* only if he gives himself *wholly* to God and becomes *wholly* dead to the world and worldly concerns. When Fleur de Marie realises that her delivery from her inhuman situation in life was a miracle of *God* she *herself* has to become a *saint* in order to be worthy of such a *miracle*. Her human love must be transformed into religious love, the striving for happiness into striving for eternal bliss, worldly satisfaction into holy hope, communion with people into communion with God. God must take her entirely. She herself reveals to us why he does not take her entirely. She has not yet *given* herself entirely to him, her heart is still preoccupied and engaged with earthly affairs. This is the last flickering of her strong nature. She gives herself entirely up to God by becoming wholly dead to the world and entering a *convent*.

> A monastery is no place for him
> Who has no stock of sins laid in,
> So numerous and great
> That be it early, be it late
> He may not miss the sweet delight
> Of penance for a heart contrite.
>
> (Goethe)[154]

In the convent Fleur de Marie is promoted to *abbess* through the intrigues of Rudolph. At first she refuses to accept this appointment because she feels unworthy. The old abbess persuades her:

"Je vous dirai plus, ma chère fille, avant d'entrer au bercail, votre existence aurait été aussi égarée, qu'elle a été au contraire pure et

---

[a] "In vain I pray to God to deliver me from these obsessions, to fill my heart solely with his pious love and his holy hopes; in a word, to take me entirely, because I wish to give myself entirely to him ... he does not grant my wishes, doubtless because my *earthly* preoccupations make me unworthy of communion with him."—*Ed.*

louable ... que les *vertus évangéliques,* dont vous avez donné l'exemple depuis votre séjour ici, expieraient et rachèteraient encore aux yeux du Seigneur un passé si coupable qu'il fût."[a]

From what the abbess says, we see that Fleur de Marie's earthly virtues have changed into evangelical virtues, or rather that her real virtues can no longer appear otherwise than as evangelical caricatures.

Marie answers the abbess:

"Sainte mère — je crois maintenant pouvoir accepter."[b]

Convent life does not suit Marie's individuality—she dies. Christianity consoles her only in imagination, or rather her Christian consolation is precisely the annihilation of her real life and essence—her death.

So Rudolph first changed Fleur de Marie into a repentant sinner, then the repentant sinner into a nun and finally the nun into a corpse. At her funeral not only the Catholic priest, but also the *Critical* priest Szeliga preaches a sermon over her grave.

Her *"innocent"* existence he calls her *"transient"* existence, opposing it to "eternal and unforgettable guilt". He praises the fact that her *"last breath"* was a "prayer for forgiveness and pardon". But just as the protestant minister, after expounding the necessity of the Lord's mercy, the participation of the deceased in universal original sin and the intensity of his consciousness of sin, must praise the virtues of the departed in *earthly* terms, so, too, Herr Szeliga uses the expression:

"And yet *personally,* she has nothing to ask forgiveness for."

---

[a] "I shall say more, my dear daughter: if before entering the fold your life had been as full of error as, on the contrary, it was pure and praiseworthy ... the *evangelical virtues* of which you have given an example since you have been here would have atoned for and redeemed your past in the eyes of the Lord, no matter how sinful it was."—*Ed.*

[b] "Holy Mother, I now believe that I can accept."—*Ed.*

Finally he throws on Marie's grave the most faded flower of pulpit eloquence:

"Inwardly pure as human beings seldom are, she has closed her eyes to this world."

Amen!

Karl Marx and Frederick Engels, *The Holy Family*

Marx and Engels, *Collected Works*, Vol. 4, Moscow, 1975, pp. 168-76

Balzac

1

Thus for instance, Balzac, who so thoroughly studied every shade of avarice, represents the old usurer Gobseck as in his second childhood when he begins to heap up a hoard of commodities.

Karl Marx, *Capital*, Vol. 1, Moscow, 1974, p. 552

2

Balzac, who is generally remarkable for his profound grasp of reality, aptly describes in his last novel, *Les paysans*, how a petty peasant performs many small tasks gratuitously for his usurer, whose good-will he is eager to retain, and how he fancies that he does not give the latter something for nothing because his own labour does not cost him any cash outlay. As for the usurer, he thus fells two dogs with one stone. He saves the cash outlay for wages and enmeshes the peasant, who is gradually ruined by depriving his own field of labour, deeper and deeper in the spider-web of usury.

Karl Marx, *Capital*, Vol. III, Moscow, 1974, p. 39

3

Paul's article in *Progress*[155] I read with much pleasure, it hits more than one nail on the head. Let us hope the *Blé*[156] will come out soon after the period of *étrennes*,[a] and be followed soon by that novel[157] which I am most anxious to see. Paul in Balzac's slippers, it will be good! By the by I have been reading scarcely anything but Balzac while laid up, and enjoyed the grand old fellow thoroughly. *There* is the history of France from 1815 to 1848, far more than in all the Vaulabelles, Capefigues, Louis Blancs et *tutti quanti*. And what boldness! What a revolutionary dialectic in his poetical justice!

Engels to Laura Lafargue,
December 13, 1883

Frederick Engels, Paul and Laura Lafargue, *Correspondence*, Vol. 1, Moscow, 1959, p. 160

4

What can one say about a little man[158] who, when he reads a novel by Balzac for the first time (and the *Cabinet des antiques* or *Père Goriot* at that), is infinitely superior and speaks of it with the greatest contempt as something commonplace that has been known for a long time.

Engels to Marx, October 4, 1852

Marx/Engels, *Werke*, Bd. 28, 1963, S. 152

5

I can write you but a few lines at this moment, as the landlord's agent is here and I must play opposite him in the role

---

[a] New Year gifts.—*Ed.*

of Mercadet in Balzac's comedy. Apropos of Balzac, I advise you to read his *Le Chef-d'Œuvre Inconnu* and *Melmoth réconcilié*. They are two little *chefs d'œuvres* full of delightful irony.

> Marx to Engels,
> February 25, 1867
> Marx/Engels, *Werke*, Bd. 31, 1965, S. 278

Pierre Dupont

In 1846, the town population in France was represented by 24.42, the agricultural by 75.58; in 1861, the town by 28.86, the agricultural by 71.14 per cent. During the last 5 years, the diminution of the agricultural percentage of the population has been yet more marked. As early as 1846, Pierre Dupont in his "Ouvriers" sang:

> Mal vêtus, logés dans des trous,
> Sous les combles, dans les décombres,
> Nous vivons avec les hiboux
> En les larrons, amis des ombres.

> Karl Marx, *Capital*, Vol. I, Moscow, 1974, p. 648

Arthur Ranc

Ranc's novel[159] is very nice.

> Engels to Marx, October 22, 1869
> Marx/Engels, *Werke*, Bd. 32, 1965, S. 376

Renan

1

Apropos of Lazarus[160] I am reminded of Renan's *The Life of Jesus*. In many regards this is a mere novel, full of pantheistic-mystical phantasies. However, the book is in some ways superior to its German predecessors, and since it isn't very long, you must read it. Naturally it is based on the German studies. Quite remarkable. Here in Holland, the German critical theological school is so much *à l'ordre du jour*[a] that clerics openly proclaim their allegiance to it from the pulpit.

> Marx to Engels,
> January 20, 1864
>
> Marx/Engels, *Werke*, Bd. 30, 1964, S. 386

2

I am studying early Christianity here, reading Renan[161] and the Bible. Renan is terribly shallow but, as a man of the world, has a wider view than the German University theologians. Otherwise, his book is a novel, to which his comment on Philostratus can equally be applied: one can use it as an historical source just as one would use, say, the novels of Alexandre Dumas père on the Fronde period. On individual points I have caught him out in dreadful mistakes. Moreover he cribs from the Germans with unbounded impudence.

> Engels to Victor Adler,
> August 19, 1892
>
> Marx/Engels, *Werke*, Bd. 38, 1968, S. 431

---

[a] The order of the day.—*Ed*.

Zola

I was obliged to give a card of introduction (to Paul)[a] to a young Dr. Conrad Schmidt of Königsberg, who dabbles in *question sociale*. He is about the greenest youth I ever saw, he was here about 3 months, seems a decent fellow, as decent fellows go nowadays, *frisst keine Schuhnägel und säuft keine Tinte*.[b] If Paul deposits him rue Richelieu, Bibliothéque nationale, he will not trouble him much. He admires Zola in whom he has discovered the *"materialistische Geschichtsanschauung."*[c]

Engels to Laura Lafargue,
June 15, 1887

Frederick Engels, Paul and
Laura Lafargue, *Correspondence*,
Vol. II, Moscow, 1960, p. 50

Maupassant

I had finished *Bel Ami* on Monday night[162] and was ruminating over the picture of Parisian journalism exhibited in it, thinking it must be exaggerated, when lo—on Tuesday morning your letter and Paul's unroll to me a scene—from life—of *Bel Ami*, and so I must take off my hat to Guy de Maupassant. Well, this will do. *Faut-il donc être canaille pour avoir un journal quotidien à Paris*[163]![d]

Engels to Laura Lafargue,
February 2, 1887

Written in English

Published according to
the photocopy

---

[a] Lafargue.—*Ed.*
[b] Eats no boot nails and drinks no ink.—*Ed.*
[c] The materialist conception of history.—*Ed.*
[d] Must one really be a villain to publish a daily newspaper in Paris!

English and Irish Literature

Daniel Defoe

1

Marx's Robinson is the *genuine*, original Robinson of Daniel Defoe, from which secondary features are also taken —the debris rescued from the shipwreck, etc. Later, he also had his own Friday, and was a shipwrecked merchant, who, if I am not mistaken, traded in slaves at one time. In a word, a true "bourgeois".

> Engels to Karl Kautsky,
> September 20, 1884
> Marx/Engels, *Werke*, Bd. 36, 1967, S. 210

2

Since Robinson Crusoe's experiences are a favourite theme with political economists,* let us take a look at him on his

---

* Even Ricardo has his stories *à la* Robinson. "He makes the primitive hunter and the primitive fisher straightway, as owners of commodities, exchange fish and game in the proportion in which labour-time is incorporated in these exchange-values. On this occasion he commits the anachronism of making these men apply to the calculation, so far as their implements have to be taken into account, the annuity tables in current use on the London Exchange in the year 1817. 'The parallelograms of Mr. Owen' appear to be the only form of society, besides the bourgeois form, with which he was acquainted." (Karl Marx: "Zur Kritik, &c.," pp. 38, 39.)

island. Moderate though he be, yet some few wants he has to satisfy, and must therefore do a little useful work of various sorts, such as making tools and furniture, taming goats, fishing and hunting. Of his prayers and the like we take no account, since they are a source of pleasure to him, and he looks upon them as so much recreation. In spite of the variety of his work, he knows that his labour, whatever its form, is but the activity of one and the same Robinson, and consequently, that it consists of nothing but different modes of human labour. Necessity itself compels him to apportion his time accurately between his different kinds of work. Whether one kind occupies a greater space in his general activity than another, depends on the difficulties, greater or less as the case may be, to be overcome in attaining the useful effect aimed at. This our friend Robinson soon learns by experience, and having rescued a watch, ledger, and pen and ink from the wreck, commences, like a true-born Briton, to keep a set of books. His stock-book contains a list of the objects of utility that belong to him, of the operations necessary for their production; and lastly, of the labour-time that definite quantities of those objects have, on an average, cost him. All the relations between Robinson and the objects that form this wealth of his own creation, are here so simple and clear as to be intelligible without exertion, even to Mr. Sedley Taylor. And yet those relations contain all that is essential to the determination of value.

> Karl Marx, *Capital*, Vol. I,
> Moscow, 1974, p. 81

Swift

Swift writes about grazing in *A Short View of the State of Ireland* in 1727: "As to the improvement of land, those few who attempt that or planting, thro' covetousness or want of skill generally leave things worse than they were, neither succeeding in trees nor hedges, and by running into the fancy of grazing, after the manner of the Scythians, are every day depopulating the country."

Frederick Engels, "Manuscripts on the History of England and Ireland"

Written in English

Marx/Engels, *Über Kunst und Literatur*, Bd. 1, 1967, S. 409

Pope

The *National-Zeitung*[164] has borne out Pope's words:

> Still her old empire to restore she tries,
> For born a goddess Dullness never dies.[165]

But Pope's realm of *dullness* differs from that of the *National-Zeitung* in that there "Dunce the second rules at present, as once did Dunce the first", while here the old Dunce, *Dunce the first*, still holds sway.

Karl Marx, "Herr Vogt"

Marx/Engels, *Werke*, Bd. 14, 1969, S. 593

Shelley and Byron[a]

Marx, who knew and understood poets just as well as philosophers and economists, used to say: "The true difference between Byron and Shelley consists in this, that those who understand and love them consider it fortunate that Byron died in his thirty-sixth year, for he would have become a reactionary bourgeois had he lived longer; conversely, they

---

[a] As an exception, this extract from the reminiscences of Marx's daughter Eleanor is included in the main part of the book.—*Ed.*

regret Shelley's death at the age of twenty-nine, because he was a revolutionary through and through and would consistently have stood with the vanguard of socialism."

Edward Aveling and Eleanor Marx-Aveling, "Shelley as Socialist"

Die Neue Zeit, VI. Jg., 1888, S. 541

Walter Scott

The downfall of the gentile order in Scotland dates from the suppression of the rebellion of 1745.[166] Precisely what link in this order the Scotch clan represents remains to be investigated; no doubt it is a link. Walter Scott's novels bring the clan in the Highlands of Scotland vividly before our eyes. It is, as Morgan says,

"an excellent type of the gens in organisation and in spirit, and an extraordinary illustration of the power of the gentile life over its members.... We find in their feuds and blood revenge, in their localisation by gentes, in their use of lands in common, in the fidelity of the clansman to his chief and of the members of the clan to each other, the usual and persistent features of gentile society.... Descent was in the male line, the children of the males remaining members of the clan, while the children of its female members belonged to the clans of their respective fathers."

Frederick Engels, *The Origin of the Family, Private Property and the State*

Marx and Engels, *Selected Works,* Vol. 3, Moscow, 1973, pp. 296-97

William Cobbett's Social Writings

Mr. Cobbett, who moved the bill,[a] is the son of the renowned William Cobbett, and represents the same borough his father did. His politics, like his seat, are the inheritance of his father,

---

[a] Bill on the ten-hour working day.—*Ed.*

and therefore independent indeed, but rather incoherent with the state of present parties. William Cobbett was the most able representative, or, rather, the creator of old English Radicalism. He was the first who revealed the mystery of the hereditary party warfare between Tories and Whigs, stripped the parasitic Whig Oligarchy of their sham liberalism, opposed landlordism in its every form, ridiculed the hypocritical rapacity of the Established Church, and attacked the moneyocracy in its two most eminent incarnations—the "Old Lady of Threadneedlest" (Bank of England) and Mr. Muckworm & Co. (the national creditors).[167] He proposed to cancel the national debt, to confiscate the Church estates, and to abolish all sorts of paper money. He watched step for step the encroachments of political centralisation on local self-government, and denounced it as an infringement on the privileges and liberties of the English subject. He did not understand its being the necessary result of industrial centralisation. He proclaimed all the political demands which have afterward been combined in the national charter; yet with him they were rather the political charter of the petty industrial middle-class than of the industrial proletarian. A plebeian by instinct and by sympathy, his intellect rarely broke through the boundaries of middle-class reform. It was not until 1834, shortly before his death, after the establishment of the new Poor Law,[168] that William Cobbett began to suspect the existence of a millocracy as hostile to the mass of the people, as landlords, banklords, public creditors, and the clergymen of the Established Church. If William Cobbett was thus, on one hand, an anticipated modern Chartist, he was, on the other hand, and much more, an inveterate John Bull. He was at once the most conservative and the most destructive man of Great Britain—the purest incarnation of Old England and the most audacious initiator of Young England. He dated the decline of England from the period of the Reformation, and the ulterior prostration of the English people from the so-called glorious Revolution of 1688. With him, therefore, revolution was not innovation, but restoration; not the creation of a new age, but the rehabilitation of the "good old times". What he did not see, was that the epoch of the pretended decline of the English people coincided exactly with the beginning ascendancy of the middle class, with the development of modern commerce and industry, and that, at the same pace as the latter grew up, the material situation of the people declined, and local self-government disappeared before political centralisation. The great changes attending the decomposition of the old English Society since the eighteenth century struck his eyes and made his heart bleed. But if he saw the effects, he did not understand the causes, the new social agencies at work. He did not see the modern *bourgeoisie*, but only that fraction of the aristocracy which held the hereditary monopoly of office, and which sanctioned by law all the changes necessitated by the new wants and pretensions of the middle-class. He saw the machine, but not the hidden motive power. In his eyes, therefore, the Whigs were responsible for all the changes supervening since 1688. They were the prime motors of the decline of England and the degradation of its people. Hence his fanatical hatred against, and his ever recurring denunciation of the Whig oligarchy. Hence the curious phenomenon, that William Cobbett, who represented by instinct the mass of the people against the encroachments of the middle-class, passed in the eyes of the world and in his own conviction for the representative of the industrial middle-class against the hereditary aristocracy. As a writer he has not been surpassed.

The present Mr. Cobbett, by continuing under altered circumstances the politics of his father, has necessarily sunk into the class of liberal Tories.

> Karl Marx, "Layard's Inquiry. Fight over the Ten-Hour Working Day"
>
> Written in English
>
> *New York Daily Tribune*, July 22, 1853

English Working-Class Poet Mead

The lord of the serf was a barbarian who regarded his villain as a head of cattle; the employer of operatives is civilised and regards his "hand" as a machine. In short, the position of the two is not far from equal, and if either is at a disadvantage, it is the free working-man. Slaves they both are, with the single difference that the slavery of the one is undissembled, open, honest; that of the other cunning, sly, disguised, deceitfully concealed from himself and every one else, a hypocritical[a] servitude worse than the old. The philanthropic Tories were right when they gave the operatives the name white slaves. But the hypocritical disguised slavery recognises the right to freedom, at least in outward form; bows before a freedom-loving public opinion, and herein lies the historic progress as compared with the old servitude, that the *principle* of freedom is affirmed, and the oppressed will one day see to it that this principle is carried out.[b]

At the close a few stanzas of a poem which voices the sentiments of the workers themselves about the factory system. Written by Edward P. Mead of Birmingham, it is a correct expression of the views prevailing among them.

> There is a King, and a ruthless King;
> Not a King of the poet's dream;
> But a tyrant fell, white slaves know well,
> And that ruthless King is Steam.
>
> He hath an arm, an iron arm,
> And tho' he hath but one,
> In that mighty arm there is a charm,
> That millions hath undone.

---

[a] The German editions of 1845 and 1892 have "theological" instead of "hypocritical". Lower "white slaves" is given in English, followed by the German equivalent.—*Ed.*

[b] The following paragraph and the poem were omitted from the 1887 American and 1892 English editions, which, however, included the Author's note to this passage.—*Ed.*

> Like the ancient Moloch grim, his sire
> In Himmon's vale that stood,
> His bowels are of living fire,
> And children are his food.
>
>> His priesthood are a hungry band,
>> Blood-thirsty, proud, and bold;
>> 'Tis they direct his giant hand,
>> In turning blood to gold.
>
> For filthy gain in their servile chain
> All nature's rights they bind;
> They mock at lovely woman's pain,
> And to manly tears are blind.
>
>> The sighs and groans of Labour's sons
>> Are music in their ear,
>> And the skeleton shades, of lads and maids,
>> In the Steam King's hell appear.
>
> Those hells upon earth, since the Steam King's birth,
> Have scatter'd around despair;
> For the human mind for Heav'n design'd
> With the body, is murdered there.

> Frederick Engels, *The Condition of the Working-Class in England*
>
> Marx and Engels, *Collected Works*, Vol. 4, Moscow, 1975, pp. 473-77

Thomas Carlyle

1

Of all the fat books and thin pamphlets which have appeared in England in the past year for the entertainment or edification of "educated society", the above work is the only one which is worth reading. All the multi-volume novels with their sad and amusing intricacies, all the edifying and meditative, scholarly and unscholarly Bible commentaries—and novels and books of edification are the two staples of

English literature—all these you may with an easy conscience leave unread. Perhaps you will find some books on geology, economics, history or mathematics which contain a small grain of novelty—however these are matters which one studies, but does not *read*, they represent dry, specialised branches of science, arid botanising, plants whose roots were long ago torn out of the general soil of humanity from which they derived their nourishment. Search as you will, Carlyle's book is the only one which strikes a human chord, presents human relations and shows traces of a human point of view.

Frederick Engels, "*The Condition of England. Past and Presend* by Thomas Carlyle"

Marx and Engels, *Collected Works*, Vol. 3, Moscow, 1975, p. 444

2

Thomas Carlyle is the only English writer on whom German literature has exercised a direct and very significant influence. Courtesy demands at the very least that a German should not let his writings pass without notice.

The latest publication by Guizot (issue No. II of the *Neue Rheinische Zeitung*),[169] has shown us the decline taking place in the intellectual powers of the bourgeoisie. In the present two pamphlets by Carlyle, we witness the decline of literary genius in the face of the current acute historical struggles, which it attempts to confront with its unrecognised, direct, prophetic inspirations.

To Thomas Carlyle belongs the credit of having come out in literature against the bourgeoisie at a time when its views, tastes and ideas held the whole of official English literature in thrall, and of doing so in a manner which is at times even revolutionary, as in his history of the French Revolution, in his apology for Cromwell, in the pamphlet on Chartism and in *Past and Present*. But in all these writings, the critique of the present is closely bound up with a strangely unhistorical apotheosis of the Middle Ages, which is a frequent characteristic of English revolutionaries too, for instance Cobbett and some of the Chartists. Whilst in the past he at least admires the classical period of a definite stage of society, the present drives him to despair and he dreads the future. Where he recognises the revolution, or indeed apotheosises it, to him it becomes concentrated in a single individual, a Cromwell or a Danton. His attitude to them is the same hero-worship that he preached in his *Lectures on Heroes and Hero-Worship* as the only refuge from a present pregnant with despair, as a new religion.

Carlyle's style corresponds to his ideas. It is a direct violent reaction against the modern bourgeois Pecksniff-style[170] in English, whose enervated affectedness, cautious circumlocutions and confused, sentimental moralising tediousness have spread from the original inventors, the educated Cockneys, to the whole of English literature. In contrast, Carlyle treated the English language as though it were completely raw material, which he had to cast absolutely anew. Ancient words and expressions were sought out again and new ones invented, in the German manner and especially in the manner of Jean Paul. The new style was often in bad taste and hugely pretentious, but frequently brilliant and always original. In this respect, too, the *Latter-Day Pamphlets* are a remarkable step backwards.

It is, incidentally, characteristic that, out of the whole of German literature, the mind that has had the greatest influence on Carlyle was not Hegel, but the literary apothecary Jean Paul.

In the cult of genius, which Carlyle shares with Strauss, the genius has got lost in the present pamphlets, while the cult remains.

The Present Time begins with the statement that the present is the child of the past and the parent of the future, but in any case, that is a *new era*.

The first manifestation of this new era is a *reforming* Pope. Gospel in hand, Pius IX wanted to preach *"the Law of Veracity"* to Christendom from the Vatican.

"More than three hundred years ago, the throne of St. Peter received peremptory judicial notice [... a] authentic order, registered in Heaven's chancery and since legible in the hearts of all brave men, to take itself away,— to begone, and let us have no more to do with *it*[b] and its delusions and impious deliriums;— and it has been sitting every day since [...] at its own peril [...] and will have to pay exact damages yet for every day it has so sat. Law of veracity? What this Popedom had to do by the law of veracity, was to give up its foul galvanic life, an offence to gods and men; honestly to die, and get itself buried!

"Far from this was the thing the poor Pope undertook [...];— and yet on the whole it was essentially this too. 'Reforming Pope?' [...] Turgot and Necker were nothing to this.

"God is great; and when a scandal is to end, brings some devoted man to take charge of it in hope, not in despair!"[c]

With his reform manifestoes, the Pope brought up questions,

"mothers of the whirlwinds, conflagrations, earthquakes [....] Questions which all official men wished, and almost[d] hoped, to postpone till Doomsday. Doomsday itself *had* come; that was the terrible truth".[e]

The law of veracity was proclaimed. The Sicilians

"were the first notable body[f] that set about applying this new [...] rule sanctioned by the general Father[g]; [...] We do not by the law of veracity belong to Naples and these Neapolitan Officials; we will, by favour of Heaven and the Pope, be free of these".

Hence the Sicilian revolution.

---

a Pluristops here and subsequently indicate omission by Engels.—*Ed.*
b The italics here and later are given according to Carlyle.—*Ed.*
c *Latter-Day Pamphlets.* Edited by Thomas Carlyle. London, 1850, p. 3.—*Ed.*
d Engels has "most".—*Ed.*
e Carlyle, op. cit., p. 4.—*Ed.*
f Engels has "the first people".—*Ed.*
g Engels has "holy Father".—*Ed.*

The French people, which considers itself as a "kind of Messiah people", as the "chosen soldiers of liberty", feared that the poor, despised Sicilians might take this trade out of their hands—February Revolution.

"As if by sympathetic subterranean electricities, all Europe exploded, boundless, uncontrollable; and we had the year 1848, one of the most singular, disastrous, amazing, and on the whole humiliating years the European world ever saw [....] Kings everywhere, and reigning persons, stared in sudden horror, the voice of the whole world bellowing in their ear, 'Begone, ye imbecile hypocrites, histrios not heroes! Off with you, off!'— and, what was peculiar and notable in this year for the first time,[a] the Kings all made haste to go, as if exclaiming, 'We *are* poor histrios, sure enough;—did you want[b] heroes? Don't kill us; we couldn't help it!' Not one of them turned round, and stood upon his Kingship, as upon a right he could afford to die for, or to risk his skin upon [....] That, I say,[c] is the alarming peculiarity at present. Democracy, on this new occasion, finds all Kings *conscious* that they are but Playactors [....] They fled precipitately, some of them with what we may call an exquisite ignominy,— in terror of the treadmill or worse. And everywhere the people, or the populace, take their own government upon themselves; and open 'kinglessness', what we call *anarchy*,— how happy if it be anarchy *plus* a street-constable!— is everywhere the order of the day. Such was the history, from Baltic to Mediterranean, in Italy, France, Prussia, Austria, from end to end of Europe, in those March days of 1848 [....]

"And so, then there remained no King in Europe; no King except the Public Haranguer, haranguing on barrelhead, in leading-article; or getting himself aggregated into a National Parliament to harangue.[d] And for about four months all France, and to a great degree all Europe, rough-ridden by every species of delirium [...] was a weltering mob, presided over by M. de Lamartine at the Hôtel-de-Ville [....] A sorrowful spectacle to men of reflection, during the time he lasted, that poor M. de Lamartine; with nothing in him but melodious wind and *soft sowder* [....] Sad enough: the eloquent[e] latest impersonation of Chaos-come-again; able to talk for itself, and declare persuasively that *it* is Cosmos! However, you have but to wait a little, in such cases;

---

[a] Engels has "heard of for the first time".—*Ed.*

[b] Engels has "need".—*Ed.*

[c] Engels has "repeat".—*Ed.*

[d] After these words Engels has "or assembling with his like in the National Parliament".—*Ed.*

[e] Engels has "most eloquent".—*Ed.*

all balloons [...] must give up their gas in the pressure of things, and are collapsed in a sufficiently wretched[a] manner before long".[b]

Who was it that kindled this universal revolution, the fuel for which was, of course, at hand?

"Students, young men of letters, advocates, editors[c]; hot inexperienced enthusiasts, or fierce and justly bankrupt desperadoes [....] Never till now did young men, and almost children, take such a command in human affairs. A changed time since the word *Senior* (Seigneur, or *Elder*) was first devised to signify 'lord' or superior;—as in all languages of men we find it [....] Looking more closely [...] you will find that [...] [the old man] has ceased to be venerable, and has begun to be contemptible; a foolish *boy* still, a boy without the graces, generosities and opulent strength of young boys [....] This mad state of matters will of course before long allay itself, as it has everywhere begun to do; the ordinary necessities of men's daily existence cannot comport with it, and these, whatever else is cast aside, will have their way. Some remounting [...] of the old machine, under new colours and altered forms, will probably ensue soon in most countries: the old histrionic Kings will be admitted back under conditions, under 'Constitutions', with national Parliaments, or the like fashionable adjuncts; and everywhere the old daily life will try to begin again. But there is now no hope that such arrangements can be permanent [....]

"In such baleful oscillation, afloat as amid raging bottomless eddies and conflicting sea-currents, not steadfast as on fixed foundations, must European Society continue swaying, now disastrously tumbling, then painfully readjusting itself, at ever shorter intervals,— till once the *new* rock-basis does come to light, and the weltering deluges of mutiny, and of need to mutiny, abate again."[d]

So much for history, which even in this form offers the old world little comfort. Now for the moral.

"For universal *Democracy*, whatever we may think of it, has declared itself as[e] an inevitable fact of the days in which we live."[f]

What is democracy? It must have some meaning or it would not exist. So, it is all a matter of finding the true

---

[a] Engels has "repulsively flabby".—*Ed.*
[b] Carlyle, op. cit., pp. 6-8.—*Ed.*
[c] Engels has "newspaper writers".—*Ed.*
[d] Carlyle, op. cit., pp. 8-10.—*Ed.*
[e] Engels has "is".—*Ed.*
[f] Carlyle, op. cit., p. 10.—*Ed.*

meaning of democracy. If we are successful in this, we can deal with it; if not, we are lost. The February Revolution was "a universal *Bankruptcy of Imposture*; that may be the brief definition of it".[a] *Semblances* and fakes, "shams", "delusions", "phantasms", instead of real relationships and things, names that have lost all meaning,—in a word, lies instead of truth have held sway in modern times. Individual and social divorce from these falsities and phantoms, that is the task of reform, and the necessity of putting an end to all sham and deceit cannot be denied.

"Yet strange to many a man it does[b] seem; and to many a solid Englishman, wholesomely digesting his pudding among what are called the cultivated classes, it seems strange exceedingly; a mad ignorant notion, quite heterodox, and big with mere ruin. He has been used to decent forms long since fallen empty of meaning, to plausible modes, solemnities grown ceremonial,— what you in your iconoclast humour call shams,—all his life long; never heard that there was any harm in them, that there was any getting on without them. Did not cotton spin itself, beef grow, and groceries and spiceries come in from the East and the West, quite comfortably by the side of shams?"[c]

Will democracy now accomplish this necessary reform, this liberation from shams?

"Democracy, once modelled into suffrages[d] [...] will itself accomplish the salutary universal change from Delusive to Real,[e] and make a new blessed world [...] by and by?"[f]

Carlyle denies this. Indeed, he sees democracy and universal suffrage only as a contagion of all nations by the superstitious English belief in the infallibility of parliamentary government. The crew of the ship that lost its course rounding

---

[a] Carlyle op. cit., p. 14.—*Ed.*
[b] Engels has "may".—*Ed.*
[c] Carlyle, op. cit., p. 15.—*Ed.*
[d] Engels has "when it is organised by means of universal suffrage". —*Ed.*
[e] Engels inserts "from false to true".—*Ed.*
[f] Carlyle, op. cit., p. 17.—*Ed.*

Cape Horn and, instead of keeping watch on wind and weather and using the sextant, voted on the course to be set, declaring the decision of the majority to be infallible—that is the universal suffrage that lays claim to steering the state. As for each individual, so for society it is just a matter of making out the true regulations of the universe, the everlasting laws of nature related to the given task, and acting accordingly. Whoever reveals these eternal laws to us, him shall we follow, "were it Russian Autocrat, Chartist Parliament, Grand Lama [...] [or] Archbishop of Canterbury[a]".[b] But how should we discover these eternal precepts of God? At all events universal suffrage, which gives each man a ballot paper and counts heads, is the worst method of doing so. The universe is of a very exclusive nature and has ever disclosed its secrets only to a select few, a small minority of noble-minded and wise alone. This is why no nation was ever able to exist on the basis of democracy. The Greeks and Romans? We all know today that theirs were no democracies, that slavery was the basis of their states. Nothing needs to be said about the various French Republics. And the model republic of North America? The Americans cannot yet even be said to form a nation or a state. The American population lives *without* government; what is constituted there is anarchy plus a street-constable. This condition is made possible by enormous expanses of yet untilled land and the respect brought over from England for the constable's truncheon. As the population grows, that too will end.

"What great human soul, what great thought, what great noble thing that one could worship or loyally admire, has yet been produced there[c]?"[d]

---

[a] Engels has "the Archbishop of Canterbury or the Dalai-Lama". —*Ed*.
[b] Carlyle, op. cit., p. 20.—*Ed*.
[c] Engels has "has America yet produced?" —*Ed*.
[d] Carlyle, op. cit., p. 25.—*Ed*.

It has doubled its population every twenty years—*voilà tout*.[a]

So on this and that side of the Atlantic, democracy is forever impossible. The universe itself is monarchy and hierarchy. No nation in which the divine everlasting duty of directing and controlling the ignorant is not entrusted to the *Noblest*, with his select ranks of *Nobler* ones, has the Kingdom of God, nor does it comply with the eternal laws of nature.

Now we also learn the secret, the origin and the necessity of modern democracy. This consists simply in the fact that the sham-noble has been raised up and consecrated by tradition or newly invented delusions.

And who is to discover the true gem with its whole setting of smaller human jewels and pearls? Certainly not universal suffrage, for only the noble can discern the noble. And so Carlyle declares that England still possesses many such nobles and "kings" and on p. 38 he summons them to him.

We see that the "noble" Carlyle starts out from a thoroughly pantheistic standpoint. The whole process of history is determined not by the development of the living masses themselves, which of course is dependent on certain changing conditions, themselves in turn the product of history; it is determined by an eternal law of nature, unalterable for all time, from which this process departs today and which it again approaches tomorrow, and on a correct understanding of which everything depends. This correct understanding of the eternal law of nature is the eternal truth, everything else is false. According to this view all real class conflicts, for all their variety in various periods, are finally resolved into the one great, eternal conflict, between those who have fathomed the eternal law of nature and act in keeping with it, the wise and the noble, and those who misunderstand it, distort it and act against it, the fools and the rogues. The historically produced distinction between classes thus becomes a natural

---

[a] That is all.—*Ed.*

distinction, which itself must be acknowledged and worshipped as a part of the eternal law of nature, by bowing to nature's noble and wise: the cult of genius. The whole conception of the development process of history is reduced to the shallow triteness of the lore of the Illuminati and the Freemasons[171] of the previous century, to the simple morality we find in the *Magic Flute*[172] and to an infinitely debased and trivialised Saint-Simonism. And there, of course, we come to the old question of who, in fact, should then rule, which is discussed at great length and with self-important shallowness and is finally answered to the effect that the noble, wise and knowledgeable should rule, which leads quite naturally to the conclusion that there has to be a great deal, a very great deal of governing, and there can never be too much governing, for after all, governing is the constant revelation and assertion of the law of nature *vis à vis* the masses. But how are the noble and the vise to be discovered? They will not be revealed by any celestial miracle; they will have to be sought out. And here the historical class distinctions which have been turned into mere natural distinctions once more rear their heads. The noble man is noble because he is wiser and more knowledgeable. He will therefore have to be sought among the classes which have the monopoly of education— among the privileged classes, and it will be the same classes who discern him in their midst, and are to judge his claims to the rank of a noble and wise man. The privileged classes thus automatically become if not precisely the noble and wise class, then at least the "articulate" class; the oppressed classes are of course the "silent, inarticulate" ones, and class rule is thus sanctioned anew. All this furiously indignant bluster turns out to be a thinly disguised recognition of existing class rule, of which the sole grumble and complaint is that the bourgeoisie does not accord its unrecognised geniuses a position at the top of society, and for highly practical reasons does not take up the starry-eyed drivellings of these gentlemen. Carlyle incidentally provides us with striking examples of how pompous cant becomes its opposite and the noble, knowledgeable and wise man is transformed in practice into a base, ignorant and foolish man.

Since for him everything depends on strong government, he turns upon the cry for liberation and emancipation with extreme indignation:

"Let us all be 'free' of one another [...] Free, without bond or connection except that of cash payment; fair day's wages for the fair day's work; bargained for[a] by voluntary contract, and the law of supply and demand: this is thought to be the true solution of all difficulties and injustices that have occurred between man and man. To rectify the relation that exists between two men, is there no method, then, but that of ending it?"[b]

This complete dissolution of all bonds and all relationships between men naturally reaches its climax in *anarchy*, the law of lawlessness, the condition in which the bond of bonds, the government, is completely cut to pieces. And this is what England and the Continent alike are striving towards, yes, even "solid Germany".

Carlyle blusters on like this for several pages, lumping together Red Republic, *fraternité*, Louis Blanc, etc., in a most disconcerting way with free trade, the abolition of the duty on corn, etc. Cf. pp. 29-42. The destruction of the remnants of feudalism which are still preserved by tradition, the reduction of the state to what is unavoidably necessary and absolutely the cheapest, the complete realisation of free competition by the bourgeoisie, are thus mixed up and identified by Carlyle with the elimination of these same bourgeois conditions, the abolition of the conflict between capital and wage-labour, and the overthrow of the bourgeoisie by the proletariat. Brilliant return to the "Night of the Absolute" in which all cats are grey! Deep knowledge of the "knowledgeable man" who does not know the first thing about what is happening around him! Strange perspicacity which believes that, with the abolition of feudalism or with free competition, all relations between men are abolished! Unfathomable fathoming of the "eternal law of nature", seriously believing that no

---
[a] Engels has "determined".—*Ed.*
[b] Carlyle, op. cit., p. 29.—*Ed.*

more children will be born from the moment the parents cease to go to the Mairies first to "bind" themselves in matrimony!

After this edifying example of a wisdom amounting to unmitigated ignorance, Carlyle goes on to demonstrate to us how high-principled nobility of character at once turns into undisguised meanness as soon as it descends from its heaven of sententious verbiage to the world of real relations.

"In all European countries, especially in England, one class of Captains and commanders of men, recognisable as the beginning of a new real and not imaginary 'Aristocracy', has already in some measure developed itself: the Captains of Industry;—happily the class who above all [...] are wanted in this time [...]. And surely, on the other hand, there is no lack of men needing to be commanded: the sad class of brother men whom we had to describe[a] as 'Hodge's emancipated horses' reduced to roving famine,—this too has in all countries developed itself; and, in fatal geometrical progression, is ever more developing itself, with a rapidity which alarms everyone. On this ground [...] it may be truly said, the 'Organisation of Labour' [...] is the universal vital Problem of the world".[b]

Thus after Carlyle has time and time again in the first forty pages vented all his virtuous fury against selfishness, free competition, the abolition of the feudal bonds between man and man, supply and demand, *laissez-faire*,[173] cotton-spinning, cash-payment, etc., etc., we now suddenly find that the main exponents of all these shams, the industrial bourgeoisie, are not merely counted among the celebrated heroes and geniuses, but even constitute a vitally indispensable part of these heroes, that the trump card in all his attacks on bourgeois relations and ideas is the apotheosis of the bourgeois individual. It appears yet odder that Carlyle, having discovered the commanders of labour and the commanded, in other words a certain organisation of labour, nevertheless declares this organisation to be a great problem requiring solution. But one should not be deceived. It is not a question of the organisation of those workers who have been regimented but of those who are unregimented and captainless,

---

[a] Engels has "have described".—*Ed.*
[b] Carlyle, op. cit., pp. 42-43.

and this Carlyle has reserved for himself. At the end of his pamphlet, we suddenly see him in the role of the British Prime Minister *in partibus*,[174] summoning together the three million Irish and other beggars, the able-bodied lackalls, nomadic or stationary, and the general national assembly of British paupers, outside and inside the workhouse, and "haranguing" them in a speech in which he first repeats everything to the lackalls that he has previously confided to the reader, and then addresses the select company as follows:

"Vagrant Lackalls,[a] foolish most of you, criminal many of you, miserable all; the sight of you fills me with astonishment and despair. [...] Here are some three millions of you [...]: so many of you fallen sheer over into the abysses of open Beggary; and, fearful to think, every new unit that falls is *loading* so much more the chain that drags the others over. On the edge of the precipice hang uncounted millions; increasing, I am told, at the rate of 1,200 a-day [...], falling, falling one after another; and the chain is getting *heavy*[b] [...]; and who at last will stand! What to do with you? [...] The others that still stand have their own difficulties, I can tell you!—But you, by imperfect energy and redundant appetite, by doing too little work and drinking too much beer, you [...] have proved that you cannot do it! [...].

"Know that, whoever may be 'sons of freedom', you for your part are not and cannot be such. Not 'free' you [....] You palpably are fallen captive [....] You are of the nature of *slaves*,—or if you prefer the word, of *nomadic* [...] *and vagabond servants that can find no master* [...]. Not as glorious unfortunate sons of freedom, but as recognised captives, as unfortunate fallen brothers requiring that I should command you, and if need were, control and compel you[c], can there henceforth be a relation between us [...]. Before Heaven and Earth, and God the Maker of us all, I declare it is a scandal to see *such* a life kept in you, by the sweat and heart's blood of your brothers; and that, if we cannot mend it, death were preferable! [...] Enlist in my Irish, my Scotch and English 'Regiments of the New Era' [...] ye poor wandering banditti; obey, work, suffer, abstain, as all of us have had to do [...] Industrial Colonels, Workmasters, Taskmasters, Lifecommanders, equitable as Rhadamanthus and inflexible as he: such [...] you do need; and such, you being once put under law as soldiers are, will be discoverable for you [...]. To each of you I will then say:

---

[a] Engels has "the have-nots and good-for-nothings".—*Ed.*
[b] Engels has "ever heavier".—*Ed.*
[c] Engels has "command ... control and compel them".—*Ed.*

Here is work for you; strike into it with manlike, soldierlike obedience and heartiness, according to the methods here prescribed,[a]—wages follow for you without difficulty [....] Refuse [...]; shirk the heavy labour, disobey the rules,— I will admonish and endeavour to incite you; if in vain, I will flog you; if still in vain, I will at last shoot you."[b]

The "New Era", in which genius reign, is thus distinguished from the old era primarily by the fact that the whip imagines it possesses genius. The genius Carlyle is distinguished from just any prison Cerberus or poor-law beadle by his virtuous indignation and the moral consciousness of flaying the paupers only in order to raise them to *his* level. We here observe the high-principled genius fantastically justifying and exaggerating the infamies of the bourgeoisie in his world-redeeming anger. If the English bourgeoisie equated paupers with criminals in order to create a deterrent to pauperism and brought into being the Poor Law of 1834, Carlyle accuses the paupers of *high treason* because pauperism generates pauperism. Just as previously the ruling class that had arisen in the course of history, the industrial bourgeoisie was privy to genius simply by virtue of ruling, so now any oppressed class, the more deeply it is oppressed, the more it is excluded from genius and the more exposed to the raging fury of our unrecognised reformer. So it is here with the paupers. But his morally noble wrath reaches its highest point with respect to those who are absolutely vile and ignoble, the "scoundrels", i.e., *criminals*. He treats these in the pamphlet on model prisons.

This pamphlet is distinguished from the first only by a fury much greater, yet all the cheaper for being directed against those officially expelled from the existing society, against people behind bars; a fury which sheds even that little shame which the ordinary bourgeoisie still displays for decency's sake. Just as in the first pamphlet Carlyle erects a complete hierarchy of Nobles and tracks the Noblest of the Noble, so

---

[a] Engels has "I here dictate".—*Ed.*
[b] Carlyle, op. cit., pp. 46-55.—*Ed.*

here he arranges an equally complete hierarchy of scoundrels and villains and seeks to hunt down the *worst of the bad*, the *Supreme Scoundrel* in England, for the exquisite pleasure of hanging him. Assuming he catches and hangs him, then another will be our Worst, and must be hanged in turn, and then another again, until the turn of the Noble and then the More Noble is reached and finally no one will be left but Carlyle, the Noblest, who as persecutor of scoundrels is at once the murderer of the Noble and has murdered what is noble in the scoundrels too, the Noblest of the Noble, who is suddenly transformed into the Vilest of Scoundrels and as such must *hang himself*. With that, all questions concerning government, state, the organisation of work, and the hierarchy of the Noble would be resolved and the eternal law of nature realised at last.

> Karl Marx and Frederick Engels,
> "*Latter-Day Pamphlets*, Edited by Thomas Carlyle"
>
> Marx/Engels, *Werke*, Bd. 7, 1969, S. 255-65

English Realists of the Mid-Nineteenth Century

The present splendid brotherhood of fiction-writers in England, whose graphic and eloquent pages have issued to the world more political and social truths than have been uttered by all the professional politicians, publicists and moralists put together, have described every section of the middle class from the "highly genteel" annuitant and fund-holder who looks upon all sorts of business as vulgar, to the little shopkeeper and lawyer's clerk. And how have Dickens and Thackeray, Miss Brontë and Mrs. Gaskell painted them? As full of presumption, affectation, petty tyranny and ignorance; and the civilised world have confirmed their verdict with the damning epigram that it has fixed to this class that "they are servile to those above, and tyrannical to those beneath them".

Karl Marx, "The English Middle Class"
Marx and Engels, *Articles on Britain*, Moscow, 1971, p. 218

Carleton

Since my arrival here I have not looked at any newspapers and have, in fact, read nothing apart from the first volume of Carleton's *Traits and Stories of the Irish Peasantry*. It was labour enough to get through the first volume and I shall put the second aside until a better time. The work consists of unconnected tales, in which Irish peasant life is illustrated now from this side and now from that; so the book is not the sort one can swallow at one gulp. For this very reason it is a book which one must buy and possess in order *au fur et à mesure*[a] to regale oneself now with this dish, now with another. Carleton is neither a good stylist nor a master of composition; his originality lies in the truth of his descriptions. As the son of an Irish peasant he knows his subject better than the Levers and Lovers.

Marx to Engels, August 14, 1879
Marx Engels, *Werke*, Bd. 34, 1966, S. 90-91

Bernard Shaw

The paradoxical man of letters Shaw—very talented and witty as a writer but absolutely useless as an economist and politician, although honest and not a careerist.

Engels to Karl Kautsky, September 4, 1892
Marx and Engels, *Selected Correspondence*, Moscow, 1975, p. 422

---

[a] According to need. —*Ed.*

Aveling

1

Aveling's play went off better than I had expected—it is a sketch, very well done, but ends—in Ibsen's manner—without a solution and the public here is not accustomed to that. This piece was followed by another—by Baby Rose and someone else—a very free English version of Echegaray's *Conflictos entre dos deberes*.[a] This one, being highly spiced with sensationalism, was very well received, although it is heavy and vulgar and to the English taste.

Engels to Paul Lafargue,
May 17, 1889

Frederick Engels, Paul and Laura Lafargue, *Correspondence*, Vol. 2, Moscow, 1960, pp. 254-55

2

Aveling seems to be making progress in his dramatic attempts; the latest play—a fortnight ago—was a great success.

Engels to Konrad Schmidt,
December 9, 1889

Marx/Engels, *Werke*, Bd. 37, 1967, S. 325

William Morris

Friday last[b] the S[ocial] D[emocratic] Federation[175] had a benefit. Tussy and Edward[c] played in a piece—I did not go, as I do not as yet see my way to sitting three hours consecu-

---

[a] Jose Echegaray's play *The Conflict of Two Duties*, written in 1882.—*Ed.*
[b] November 21.—*Ed.*
[c] Aveling.—*Ed.*

tively in a stiff chair. Nim says they played very well—the piece was more or less, she says, their own history. Mother Wright read—very well—Bax played the piano—rather long—Morris who was here the other night and quite delighted to find the Old Norse Edda on my table—he is an Icelandic enthusiast—Morris read a piece of his poetry (a *"refonte"* of the eddaic Helreid Brynhildar (the description of Brynhild burning herself with Sigurds corpse), etc., etc., it went off very well—their art seems to be rather better than their literature and their poetry better than their prose.

> Engels to Laura Lafargue,
> November 23, 1884
>
> Frederick Engels, Paul and
> Laura Lafargue, *Correspondence*,
> Vol. I, Moscow, 1959, pp. 245-46

German Literature

Situation of Germany and German Culture from the Mid-Seventeenth to the Early Nineteenth Century

1

1648-1789

a) Political situation. The German princes exploit the Westphalian peace, vying with one another to sell themselves to the foreign power, and these—France and the princes— exploit Germany's weakness in order gradually to appropriate all Germany's French possessions and to round off Alsace's boundaries. France's historical right and cries of "robbery" from the Teutons. Immutability of the linguistic frontier (see Menke) since c. A.D. 1000, with the exception of the left Vosges districts. This in general. In particular: the rise of Prussia in the north as a power competing with Austria and the empire. The division into north and south begins to be realised. Criticism of Prussian history. Frederick II.—The rise of Russia and Frederick II's subjection to Russian policy— because of Prussia, civil wars are now wars of competition between Austria and Prussia.

b) *Economic matters.* For all that, *slow recovery from the consequences of the Thirty Years' War*; the bourgeoisie scramble up again. In such a situation, this resurgence is possible only by dint of *infamous* virtues. Despite all this, economic progress is made possible only by political intervention, by the villainy of the princes and the money they receive from abroad. This demonstrates the depth of Germany's economic humiliation. This period is the source of the patriarchal regime. After 1648, the state is really called upon to carry out social functions and is forced to do this by financial necessity; where it neglected them—stagnation (the Westphalian bishoprics). What a state of humiliation! And how miserable state assistance is! Purely passive in relation to the world market; able to make some profit in large-scale world wars (the American and the revolutionary wars until 1801) as a *neutral* only. On the other hand, impotent against the robber states. (Thanks to the French Revolution, this shameful position in Europe is abolished.)

c) Literature and language in total decay; theology is petrified dogmatism; in other branches of learning, Germany is in full decline, but there are still glimmers of light: Jakob Böhme (a new portent of the coming philosophers), Kepler, Leibniz—again abstraction from the existing, from reality. *Bach.*

d) The situation of Germany in 1789. a) Agriculture—condition of the peasants, serfdom, floggings, payment of tax. b) Industry—unrelieved starvation, essentially manual labour, but in England large-scale industry is already beginning, while German industry is doomed even before it has fully developed. c) Trade—passive. d) Social position of the burghers in relation to the nobility and the government. e) Political impediment to development: fragmentation, description according to Menke. Customs duties, obstacle to river traffic; free trade confined to internal boundaries by disintegration, customs duties are for the most part municipal consumer taxes.

These princes, incapable of good, even when enlightened men—like the protectors of Schubart, and Karl August—all much preferred to enter the Rheinbund than to fight a war through. The proof was invasion of 1806 in which they found themselves with a knife pointed at their throats. Besides, each of these 1,000 princes is an absolute monarch—crude, uneducated blackguards, co-operation among whom is never to be expected, but always a multitude of whims (Schlözer). Trade in soldiers during the American war.—But their most shameful act was their *mere existence*. And alongside them, on the eastern frontier, Prussia to the north and Austria to the south, greedily reaching out their hands for new areas; the only two states which could still save the situation, had only one of the two existed. But their inevitable competition ruled out any solution. A genuine *cul-de-sac*; help could only come from outside—it was brought by the French Revolution. Only two signs of life: military ability and literature, philosophy, scrupulous, objective scientific research. Whereas in France political writings, even though of the first rank, predominated from as early as the 18th century, in Germany all this was a flight from reality into the sphere of the ideal. Man as such and the development of language; 1700 barbarism, 1750 Lessing and Kant, soon Goethe, Schiller, Wieland, Herder, Händel, Gluck, Mozart.

1789-1815

I. The German enclaves in Alsace-Lorraine, etc.—already half under French sovereignty—allied themselves with the French Revolution, thus giving a pretext for war. Prussia and Austria *are now suddenly at one.* Valmy. Defeat of linear tactics by the use of massed artillery. Fleurus and Jemmapes. Defeat of Austrian tactics, which are based on a chain of military posts? Conquest of the left bank of the Rhine. Jubilation of the peasants and the free-spirited towns, which is not dispelled even by individual instances of extortion or by Napoleon's blood tax. The peace of Amiens and the imperial deputies' main decision—dissolution of the German empire. The Rheinbund. The sweeping away of small states by Napoleon; unfortunately this is far from enough. He is always a revolutionary in relation to the princes and would have gone further had the petty princes not humbled themselves before him so abjectly. 1806—Napoleon's error was that he did not completely annihilate Prussia. Economic position of Germany during the Continental Blockade.—The period of greatest humiliation from abroad coincides with a period of great brilliance in literature and philosophy while music reaches its culmination in Beethoven.

Frederick Engels, "Notes on Germany"
Marx/Engels, *Werke*, Bd. 18, 1969,
S. 591-93

2

Such was the state of Germany towards the end of the last century. It was all over one living mass of putrefaction and repulsive decay. Nobody felt himself at ease. The trade, commerce, industry, and agriculture of the country were reduced to almost nothing; peasantry, tradesmen, and manufacturers felt the double pressure of a blood-sucking government and bad trade; the nobility and princes found that their incomes, in spite of the squeezing of their inferiors, could not be made to keep pace with their increasing expenditure; everything was wrong, and a general uneasiness prevailed throughout the country. No education, no means of operating upon the minds of the masses, no free press, no public spirit, not even an extended commerce with other countries—nothing but meanness and selfishness—a mean, sneaking, miserable shopkeeping spirit pervading the whole people. Everything worn out, crumbling down, going fast to ruin, and not even the slightest hope of a beneficial change, not even so much strength in the nation as might have sufficed for carrying away the putrid corpses of dead institutions.

The only hope for the better was seen in the country's literature. This shameful political and social age was at the same time the great age of German literature. About 1750 all the master-spirits of Germany were born, the poets Goethe and Schiller, the philosophers Kant and Fichte, and, hardly twenty years later, the last great German metaphysician,[176] Hegel. Every remarkable work of this time breathes a spirit of defiance, and rebellion against the whole of German society as it then existed. Goethe wrote *Goetz von Berlichingen*, a dramatic nomage to the memory of a rebel. Schiller, the *Robbers*, celebrating a generous young man, who declares open war against all society. But these were their juvenile productions; when they grew older they lost all hope; Goethe restrained himself to satire of the keenest order, and Schiller would have despaired if it had not been for the refuge which science, and particularly the great history of ancient Greece and Rome, afforded to him. These two may be taken as examples of the rest. Even the best and strongest minds of the nation gave up all hope as to the future of their country.

All at once, like a thunderbolt, the French revolution struck into this chaos, called Germany. The effect was tremendous. The people, too little instructed, too much absorbed in the ancient habit of being tyrannised over, remained unmoved. But all the middle classes, and the better part of the nobility, gave one shout of joyful assent to the national assembly and the people of France. Not one of all the hundreds of thousands of existing German poets failed to sing the glory of the French people. But this enthusiasm was of the German sort, it was merely metaphysical, it was only meant to apply to the theories of the French revolutionists. As soon as theories were shuffled into the background by the weight and bulk of facts; as soon as the French court and the French people could in practice no longer agree, notwithstanding their theoretical union, by the theoretical constitution of 1791; as soon as the people asserted their sovereignty *practically* by the "10th of August"[177]: and when, moreover, theory was entirely made silent on the 31st of May, 1793, by the putting down of the Girondists[178]—then this enthusiasm of Germany was converted into a fanatic hatred against the revolution. Of course this enthusiasm was meant to apply to such actions only as the night of the 4th of August, 1789, when the nobility resigned their privileges, but the good Germans never thought of such actions having consequences in practice widely differing from those inferences which benevolent theorists might draw. The Germans never meant to approve of these consequences, which were rather serious and unpleasant to many parties, as we all know well. So the whole mass, who in the beginning had been enthusiastic friends to the revolution, now became its greatest opponents, and getting, of course, the most distorted news from Paris by the servile German press, preferred their old quiet holy Roman dunghill[179] to the tremendous activity of a people who threw off vigorously the chains of slavery, and flung defiance to the faces of all despots, aristocrats and priests.

Frederick Engels, "The State of Germany"

Written in English

The Northern Star, October 25, 1845

Schiller. Shortcomings of his Poetry

No one has criticised more severely the impotent "categorical imperative" of Kant[180]—impotent because it demands the impossible, and therefore never attains to any reality—no one has more cruelly derided the Philistine sentimental enthusiasm for unrealisable ideals purveyed by Schiller than precisely the complete idealist Hegel. (See, for example, his *Phenomenology*.)

Frederick Engels, *Ludwig Feuerbach and the End of Classical German Philosophy*

Marx and Engels, *Selected Works*, Vol. 3, Moscow, 1973, p. 352

Goethe

1

The inner necessities of the system (of Hegel) are, therefore, of themselves sufficient to explain why a thoroughly revolutionary method of thinking produced an extremely tame political conclusion. As a matter of fact the specific form of this conclusion springs from this, that Hegel was a German, and like his contemporary Goethe had a bit of the Philistine's queue dangling behind. Each of them was an Olympian Zeus in his own sphere, yet neither of them ever quite freed himself from German Philistinism.

> Frederick Engels, *Ludwig Feuerbach and the End of Classical German Philosophy*
>
> Marx and Engels, *Selected Works*, Vol. 3, Moscow, 1973, p. 341

2

His (Dühring's) verbose lucubrations on themes worthy of philistines, such as the value of life and the best way to enjoy life, are themselves so steeped in philistinism that they explain his anger at Goethe's Faust. It was really unpardonable of Goethe to make the unmoral Faust and not the serious philosopher of reality, Wagner, his hero.

> Frederick Engels, *Anti-Dühring*, Moscow, 1975, p. 165

3

In accordance with all the rules of the Hegelian method of thought, the proposition of the rationality of everything which is real resolves itself into the other proposition: All that exists deserves to perish.[181]

> Frederick Engels, *Ludwig Feuerbach and the End of Classical German Philosophy*
>
> Marx and Engels, *Selected Works*, Vol. 3, Moscow, 1973, pp. 338-39

4

All of this may also be found in Goethe, the "prophet", and anyone who has his eyes open can read this between the lines. Goethe did not like to be concerned with "God"; the word made him uncomfortable, he felt at home only in human matters, and this humanity, this emancipation of art from the fetters of religion is precisely what constitutes Goethe's greatness. Neither the ancients nor Shakespeare can measure up to him in this respect. But this consummate humanity, this overcoming of the religious dualism can only be apprehended in its full historical significance by those who are not strangers to that other aspect of German national development, philosophy. What Goethe could only express spontaneously, and therefore, it is true, in a certain sense "prophetically", has been developed and substantiated in contemporary German philosophy.

> Frederick Engels, *"The Condition of England. Past and Present* by Thomas Carlyle"
>
> Marx and Engels, *Collected Works*, Vol. 3, Moscow, 1975, p. 465

5

Apropos of Grün—I shall revise the article on his Goethe, cut it down to 1/2-3/4 of a signature and prepare it for our publication, *if* you approve, about which you should write to me as soon as possible. The book is extremely characteristic.

Grün glorifies all Goethe's *philistinisms* as *human* and makes Goethe as an inhabitant of Frankfurt and an *official* into a "genuine man", while passing over or even abusing every manifestation of greatness and genius. The book thus provides the most brilliant proof that *man is equivalent to the German petty bourgeois*. I have only indicated this, but I could develop it and cut down the rest of the article considerably, as it is not suitable for our publication. What do you think?

Engels to Marx,
January 15, 1847

Marx/Engels, *Werke*, Bd. 27, 1965,
S. 75-76

6
Karl Grün,
Über Göthe vom Menschlichen Standpunkte
Darmstadt, 1846

Herr Grün relaxes after the exertions of his "*Soziale Bewegung* in Frankreich und Belgien" by glancing at the *lack* of social *movement*[a] in his native land. For the sake of variety, he decides to take a look at "the human aspect" of the elderly Goethe. He has exchanged his seven-league boots for carpet-slippers, donned his dressing-gown and stretches himself, full of self-satisfaction, in his arm-chair:

"We are not writing a commentary, we are only picking out what is there for all to see" (p. 244).

He has made things really snug for himself:

"I had put some roses and camellias in my room, and mignonette and violets by the open window" (p. III): "And above all, no commentaries!... But here, the complete works on the table and a faint scent of roses and

---

[a] In German there is a pun on the words *Bewegung*—movement and *Stillstand*—lack of movement.—*Ed.*

mignonette in the room! Let us just see where we get to.... Only a rogue offers more than he has!" (pp. IV, V). [...]

We are at last getting closer to Goethe. On p. 15 Herr Grün allows Goethe the right to exist. For Goethe and Schiller are the resolution of the contradiction between "pleasure without activity", i. e., Wieland, and "activity without pleasure", i. e., Klopstock. "Lessing first based man on himself." (One wonders whether Herr Grün can emulate him in this acrobatic feat.)—In this philosophic construction, we have all of Herr Grün's sources together. The form of the construction, the basis of the whole thing is Hegel's world-famous stratagem for the reconciliation of contradictions. "Man based on himself" is Hegelian terminology applied to Feuerbach. "Pleasure without activity" and "activity without pleasure", this contradiction on which Herr Grün sets Wieland and Klopstock to play the above variations, is borrowed from the Complete Works of M[oses] Hess. The only source which we miss is literary history itself, which has not the remotest inkling of the above hotch-potch and is therefore rightly ignored by Herr Grün.

Whilst we are on the subject of Schiller, the following observation of Herr Grün's should be apposite: "Schiller was everything one can be, insofar as one is not Goethe" (p. 311). Beg pardon, one can also be Herr Grün.—Incidentally, our author is here ploughing the same furrow as Ludwig of Bavaria:

> Rome, thou art lacking in Naples' gifts, she in those
> that thou layst claim to;
> Were but the two of you one, it had been too much for the earth.[a]

This historical construction prepares the way for Goethe's entry into German literature. "Man based on himself" by Lessing can continue his evolution only in Goethe's hands. For to Herr Grün belongs the credit of having discovered "man" in Goethe, not natural man, begotten by man and

---

[a] Ludwig I of Bavaria, "Florenz" (paraphrased).—*Ed.*

woman in the pleasures of the flesh, but man in the higher sense, dialectical man, the *caput mortuum*[a] in the crucible, in which God the Father, Son and Holy Ghost have been calcined, the *cousin germain* of Homunculus[182] in *Faust*— in short, not man as Goethe speaks of him, but man *as such*, as Herr Grün speaks of him. Who is "man as such", then, of whom Herr Grün speaks?

"There is nothing in Goethe that is not *human* content" (p. XVI).— On p. XXI we hear "that Goethe so portrayed and conceived of *man as such as we wish to realise him today*".—On p. XXII: "Goethe today, and that means his works, is a *true compendium of humanity*."—Goethe—"is *humanity fulfilled*" (Page XXV).—"Goethe's literary works are (!) *the ideal of human society*" (p. 12).—"Goethe could not become a national poet because he was destined to be the *poet of all that is human*" (p. 25).— Yet, according to p. 14, "*our nation*"— that is, the Germans — is nevertheless supposed to "discern its own essence transfigured" in Goethe.

This is the first revelation about "the essence of man", and we may trust Herr Grün all the more in this matter because he has no doubt "examined the concept of man" with the utmost thoroughness. Goethe portrays "man" as Herr Grün wishes to realise him, and at the same time he portrays the German nation transfigured—"man" is thus none other than "the German transfigured". We have confirmation of this throughout. Just as Goethe is not "a national poet" but "the poet of all that is human", so too the German nation is not a "national" nation, but the nation "of all that is human". For this reason we read on p. XVI again: "Goethe's literary works, emanating from life, ... neither had nor have anything to do with reality." Just like "man", just like "the Germans". And on p. 4: "At this very time *French* socialism aims to bring happiness to *France*, *German* writers have their eyes on *the human race*." (While "the human race" is for the most part accustomed to "having" them not before "their eyes" but before a somewhat opposite part of the anatomy.) On innumerable occa-

---

[a] Distillation product, distillate.—*Ed.*

sions Herr Grün therefore expresses his pleasure at the fact that Goethe wanted "to liberate man *from within*" (e. g., p. 225), which truly Germanic form of liberation has so far refused to emerge from *"within"*!

Let us duly note this first revelation then: "Man" is the *German "transfigured"*.

Let us now observe how Herr Grün pays homage to "the poet of all that is human", the "human content in Goethe". We shall thereby best discover who "man" is, of whom Herr Grün is speaking. We shall find that Herr Grün here reveals the most secret thoughts of true socialism,[183] which is typical of the way his general craving to outshout all his cronies leads him rashly to trumpet out to the world matters which the rest of the band prefer to keep to themselves. His transformation of Goethe into "the poet of all that is human" was incidentally facilitated for him by the fact that Goethe himself had a habit of using the words "man" and "human" with a special kind of emphasis. Goethe, it is true, used them only in the sense in which they were applied in his own day and later also by Hegel, for instance the attribute "human" was bestowed on the Greeks in particular as opposed to heathen and Christian barbarians, long before these expressions acquired their mystically philosophical meaning through Feuerbach. With Goethe especially they usually have a most unphilosophical and flesh-and-blood meaning. To Herr Grün belongs the credit of being the first to have turned Goethe into a disciple of Feuerbach and a true socialist.

We cannot of course speak of Goethe himself in any detail here. We would just draw attention to one point. In his works Goethe's attitude to contemporary German society is a dual one. Sometimes he is hostile towards it; he attempts to escape from what he finds repulsive in it, as in *Iphigenie* and above all throughout the Italian journey; he rebels against it as Götz, Prometheus and Faust, he lashes it with his bitterest satire as Mephistopheles. But then sometimes he is on friendly terms with it, "accommodates" himself to it, as in the majority of the *Zahme Xenien* and many prose writings; he celebrates it, as in the *Maskenzüge,* even defends it against the oncoming movement of history, as particularly in all the writings in which he comes to speak of the French Revolution. It is not just some aspects of German life which Goethe accepts in contrast to others which are repugnant to him. More frequently it is a question of the different moods he is in; there is a continuing battle within him between the poet of genius who feels revulsion at the wretchedness of his environment, and the cautious offspring of the Frankfurt patrician or the Weimar privy-councillor who finds himself compelled to come to terms with and accustom himself to it. Goethe is thus at one moment a towering figure, at the next petty; at one moment an obstinate, mocking genius full of contempt for the world, at the next a circumspect, unexacting, narrow philistine. Not even Goethe was able to conquer the wretchedness of Germany; on the contrary, it conquered him, and this victory of wretchedness over the greatest of Germans is the most conclusive proof that it cannot be surmounted at all "from within". Goethe was too universal, too active a nature, too much a man of flesh and blood to seek refuge from this wretchedness in a Schillerian flight to the Kantian ideal; he was too keen-sighted not to see how ultimately such a flight amounted to no more than the exchange of a prosaic form of wretchedness for a grandiloquent one. His temperament, his energies, his whole mental attitude disposed him to the practical life, and the practical life he found around him was wretched. This dilemma of having to exist in an environment which he could only despise, and yet being bound to this environment as the only one in which he could be active, this dilemma always faced Goethe, and the older he became, the more the mighty poet withdrew *de guerre lasse*[a] behind the insignificant Weimar minister. Unlike Börne and

---

[a] Tired of the struggle.—*Ed.*

Menzel, we do not criticise Goethe for not being liberal[a] but for being capable of occasional philistinism as well, not for being unsusceptible to any enthusiasm for German freedom but for sacrificing his spasmodically erupting and truer aesthetic instinct to a petty-bourgeois fear of all major contemporary historical movements, not for being a man of the court but for being capable of attending with such solemn gravity to the pettiest affairs and *menus plaisirs*[b] of one of the pettiest of the little German courts, at the time when a Napoleon was flushing out the great Augean stable that was Germany. We criticise him not from a moral or from a party point of view, but at the very most from the aesthetic and historical point of view; we measure Goethe neither by moral nor by political nor by "human" standards. We cannot here involve ourselves in a description of Goethe's relationship to his whole age, his literary precursors and contemporaries, his process of development and his station in life. We therefore restrict ourselves simply to noting the facts.

We shall see in respect of which of these aspects Goethe's works are a "true compendium of humanity", "humanity fulfilled" and the "ideal of human society".

Let us first of all take Goethe's critique of the existing society and then move on to the positive description of the "ideal of human society". In view of the wealthy content of Grün's book, it goes without saying that in either area we are only highlighting a few points of characteristic brilliance.

As a critic of society Goethe does indeed perform miracles. He "condemns civilisation" (pp. 34-36) by giving voice to a few romantic complaints that it blurs everything that is characteristic and distinctive about man. He "prophesies the world of the bourgeoisie" (p. 78) by depicting in *Prometheus tout bonnement*[c] the origin of private property. On p. 229 he

---

[a] L. Börne, *Pariser Briefe*; W. Menzel, *Die deutsche Literatur.—Ed.*
[b] Little entertainments (involving supplementary expenditure).—*Ed.*
[c] Quite simply.—*Ed.*

is "judge over the world..., the Minos of civilisation". But all these things are mere trifles.

On p. 253 Herr Grün quotes *Catechisation*:

> Reflect, my child! From whom have you these talents?
> You cannot have them from yourself, you know.—
> Why, father gave me everything.
> And who gave them to him?—My grandfather.—
> No, no! From whom could he, your grandfather, receive them?—
> Well, he just *took* them.

Hurrah! trumpets Herr Grün at the top of his voice, *la propriété, c'est le vol*[a]—Proudhon in person![b]

Leverrier can go back home with his planet and surrender his medal to Herr Grün—for this is something greater than Leverrier, this is something greater even than Jackson and his sulphuric ether fumes. For the man who condensed Proudhon's theft thesis, which is indeed disquieting for many peaceful members of the bourgeoisie, to the innocuous dimensions of the above epigram by Goethe—the only reward for him is the *grand cordon* of the Legion of Honour.

The *Bürgergeneral* presents more difficulties. Herr Grün gazes at it for a while from every side, makes a few doubtful grimaces, which is unusual for him, and begins to cogitate: "true enough ... somewhat wishy-washy ... this does not amount to a condemnation of the Revolution" (p. 150).... Wait! now he has it! What is the object at issue? *A jug of milk*[184] and so: "Let us not ... forget that here once again ... it is the *property question* that is being brought to the fore" (p. 151).

If two old women are quarrelling beneath Herr Grün's window over the head of a salted herring, may Herr Grün never find it too much trouble to descend from his room with its fragrance of "roses" and mignonette to inform them that for them too "it is the property question that is being

---

[a] Property is theft.—*Ed.*
[b] An allusion to P. J. Proudhon, *Qu'est-ce que la propriété?*—*Ed.*

brought to the fore". The gratitude of all right-thinking people will be the best reward for him.

Goethe performed one of the greatest feats of criticism when he wrote *Werther*. *Werther* is not by any means merely a sentimental love-story, as those who have hitherto read Goethe "from the human aspect" believed.

> In *Werther* "the human content has found so fitting a form that nothing can be found in any of the literatures of the world which might even remotely deserve to be set beside it" (p. 96). "Werther's love for Lotte is a mere instrument, a vehicle for the tragedy of the radical pantheism of emotion.... Werther is the man who has no vertebra, who has not yet become a subject" (pp. 93[94]). Werther shoots himself not from infatuation but "because he, that unhappy pantheistic spirit, could not come to terms with the world" (p. 94). "*Werther* depicts the whole rotten condition of society with artistic mastery, it seizes the wrongs of society by their deepest roots, by their philosophico-religious basis" (which "basis" everybody knows to be of more recent origin than the "wrongs"), "by the vague and nebulous understanding.... Pure, well-ventilated conceptions of true human nature" (and above all vertebra, Herr Grün, vertebra!) "would be the death of that state of wretchedness, those worm-eaten, crumbling conditions which we call bourgeois life!" [p. 95].

An example of how "*Werther* depicts the rotten condition of society with artistic mastery". Werther writes:

> "Adventures? Why do I use this silly word[185] ... our false bourgeois relationships, they are the real adventures, they are the real monstrosities!"[a]

This cry of lamentation from a lachrymose emotionalist at the discrepancy between bourgeois reality and his no less bourgeois illusions about this reality, this faint-hearted sigh which derives solely from a lack of the most ordinary experience, is given out by Herr Grün on p. 84 as incisive social criticism. Herr Grün even asserts that the "despairing agony of life" which the above words express, "this unhealthy urge to turn things on their heads so that they should

---

[a] J. W. Goethe, "Briefe aus der Schweiz" (written in the form of excerpts from letters supposedly found among the papers of the main character of *Die Leiden des jungen Werthers*).—*Ed.*

at least acquire a different appearance" (!) "ultimately dug for itself the burrow of the French Revolution". The Revolution, previously the realisation of Machiavellianism, here becomes merely the realisation of the sufferings of young Werther. The guillotine of the Place de la Révolution is only a pale imitation of Werther's pistol.

By the same token it is self-evident, according to p. 108, that in *Stella* too Goethe is dealing with "social material", although here only "the most disreputable circumstances" (p. 107) are depicted. True socialism is much more broad-minded than our Lord Jesus. For where two or three are forgathered—they need not even do so in its name—then it is in the midst of them and there is "social material". Like its disciple Herr Grün, it generally bears a striking resemblance to "that kind of dull-witted, self-satisfied nosey-parker who makes everything his business but gets to the bottom of nothing" (p. 47).

Our readers will perhaps remember a letter Wilhelm Meister writes to his brother-in-law[a] in the last volume of the *Lehrjahre*, in which, after a few rather trite comments on the advantages of growing up in well-to-do circumstances, the superiority of the aristocracy over the narrow-minded bourgeoisie is acknowledged and the subordinate position of the latter as well as of all other non-aristocratic classes is sanctioned on the grounds that it is not possible to change it for the present. It is said that only the individual is able in certain circumstances to attain a level of equality with the aristocracy.[b] Herr Grün remarks apropos of this:

"What Goethe says of the pre-eminence of the upper classes of society is *absolutely true* if one takes upper class as identical with educated class, and in Goethe's case this is so" (p.[p.] 264 [-65]).

And there let the matter rest.

Let us come to the much-discussed central point: Goethe's

---
a Werner.—*Ed.*
b J. W. Goethe, *Wilhelm Meisters Lehrjahre*, Buch 5, Kap. 3.—*Ed.*

attitude to politics and to the French Revolution. Here Herr Grün's book provides an object lesson in what it means to endure through thick and thin; here Herr Grün's devotion gives a good account of itself.

So that Goethe's attitude towards the Revolution may appear justified, Goethe must of course be *above* the Revolution and have transcended it even before it took place. As early as p. XXI we therefore learn:

> "Goethe had so far outstripped the *practical* development of his age that he felt he could only adopt towards it an attitude of rejection, a defensive attitude."

And on p. 84, apropos of *Werther*, who, as we saw already, embodies the whole Revolution *in nuce*[a]: "History shows 1789, Goethe shows 1889." Similarly on pp. 28 and 29 Goethe is obliged in a few brief words "radically to dispose of all the shouting about liberty" since back in the seventies he had an article[b] printed in the *Frankfurter Gelehrte Anzeigen*[186] which does not at all discuss the liberty which the "shouters" are demanding, but only engages in a few general and fairly sober reflections on liberty as such, the concept of liberty. Furthermore: because in his doctoral dissertation[c] Goethe propounded the thesis that it was actually the duty of every legislator to introduce a certain form of worship—a thesis which Goethe himself treats merely as an amusing paradox, inspired by all manner of small-town clerical bickering in Frankfurt (which Herr Grün *himself* quotes)—because of this "the student Goethe discarded the whole dualism of the Revolution and the present French state like an old pair of shoes" (pp. 26 and 27). It would appear as if Herr Grün has inherited "the student Goethe's worn-out shoes" and used them to sole the seven-league boots of his "social movement" with.

---

[a] In the germ.—*Ed.*

[b] J. W. Goethe, "Alexander von Joch über Belohnung und Strafen nach türkischen Gesetzen".—*Ed.*

[c] J. W. Goethe, "De Legislatoribus".—*Ed.*

This of course now sheds a new light for us on Goethe's statements about the Revolution. It is now clear that being high above it, having "disposed of it" as long as fifteen years previously, having "discarded it like an old pair of shoes" and being a hundred years in advance of it, he could have no sympathy with it and could take no interest in a nation of "shouters for liberty", with whom he had settled his accounts way back in the year seventy-three. Herr Grün now has an easy time of it. Goethe may turn as much trite inherited wisdom into elegant distiches, he may philosophise upon it with as much philistine narrow-mindedness, he may shrink with as much petty-bourgeois horror from the great ice-floes which threaten his peaceable poet's niche, he may behave with as much pettiness, cowardice and servility as he will, but he cannot carry things too far for his patient glosswriter. Herr Grün lifts him up on his tireless shoulders and carries him through the mire; indeed he transfers the whole mire to the account of true socialism, just to ensure that Goethe's boots stay clean. From the *Campagne in Frankreich* to the *Natürliche Tochter*, Herr Grün takes on responsibility (pp. 133-170) for everything, everything without exception, he shows a devotion which might move a Buchez to tears. And if all this does not help, if the mire is just too deep, then a higher social exegesis is harnessed to the task, then Herr Grün [p. 137] paraphrases the following:

> The sad destiny of France, let the mighty think on it,
> But verily the lowly should ponder it more.
> The mighty perished; but who defends the multitude
> From the multitude? The multitude was tyrant to itself.[187]

"Who defends", shouts Herr Grün for all he is worth, with italics, question marks and all the "vehicles of the tragedy of the radical pantheism of emotion", "who, in particular, defends the unpropertied multitude, the so-called rabble, against the propertied multitude, the legislating rabble?" (p. 137). "Who in particular defends" Goethe against Herr Grün?

In this way Herr Grün explains the whole series of worldly-wise bourgeois precepts contained in the Venetian *Epigramme*:

they "are like a slap in the face delivered by the hand of *Hercules* which only now" (after the danger is past for the philistine) "appear to us to smack home really tolerably now that we have a great and *bitter* experience" (bitter indeed for the philistine) "behind us" (p. 136).

From the *Belagerung von Mainz* Herr Grün

would not wish to pass over the following passage for anything in the world: "On Tuesday ... I hastened ... to *pay homage* to his *Highness* and had the *great good fortune* to *wait upon* the Prince ... *my ever gracious Lord*", etc. [p. 147].

The passage in which Goethe lays his humble devotion at the feet of Herr Rietz, the King of Prussia's[a] Gentleman, Cuckold and Pimp of the Bedchamber, Herr Grün does not think fit to quote.

Apropos of the *Bürgergeneral* and the *Ausgewanderte*[188] we read:

"Goethe's whole antipathy towards the Revolution, whenever it was expressed in literary form, was concerned with the eternal lament at seeing people driven out from circumstances of *well-deserved* and *well-accustomed* property, which intriguers and envious men, etc., then usurped ... this same *injustice of robbery*. ...His *peaceful, domesticated* nature became indignant at this violation of the right of property, which, being *arbitrarily* inflicted, made destitute refugees of whole masses of people" (p. 151).

Let us without more ado put this passage to the account of "man" whose "peaceful, domesticated nature" feels so much at ease in "well-deserved and well-accustomed", to put it bluntly, well-earned "circumstances of property" that

---

[a] Frederick William II.—*Ed.*

it declares the tempest of the Revolution which sweeps away these circumstances *sans façon* to be "arbitrary" and the work of "intriguers and envious men", etc.

In the light of this it does not surprise us that Herr Grün "finds the purest pleasure" (p. 165) in the bourgeois idyll *Hermann und Dorothea*, its timid, worldly-wise small-townsfolk and lamenting peasants who take to their heels in superstitious fear before the sansculotte army and the horrors of war. Herr Grün

> "even accepts with relief the pusillanimous role which is assigned at the end ... to the German people:
>
> It befits not a German to be at the head of a movement
> Fleeing in terror, nor to waver first this way, then that."[189]

Herr Grün is right to shed tears of sympathy for the victims of cruel times and to raise his eyes to heaven in patriotic despair at such strokes of fate. There are enough ruined and degenerate people anyway, who have no "human" heart in their bosoms, who prefer to join in singing the *Marseillaise* in the Republican camp and perhaps even make lewd jokes in Dorothea's deserted bedchamber. Herr Grün is a decent fellow who waxes indignant at the lack of feeling with which for instance a Hegel looks down on the "little, dumb flowers" which have been crushed underfoot by the onrush of history and mocks at the "litany of private virtues of modesty, humility, love of one's fellow-men and charity" which is held out "against the deeds of world history and those who perform them".[190] Herr Grün is right to do this. He will no doubt receive his reward in heaven.

Let us conclude these "human" remarks on the Revolution with the following: "A real humorist might well take the liberty of finding the *Convention itself infinitely ridiculous*", and until this "real humorist" is found, Herr Grün meanwhile provides the necessary instructions (pp. 151, 152).

Herr Grün similarly sheds some surprising light upon Goethe's attitude towards politics after the Revolution. Just one example. We already know of the profound resentment "man" feels in his heart towards the liberals. The "poet of all that is human" must of course not be allowed to go to his rest without having specifically had it out with them, without having pinned an explicit memorandum on Messrs Welcker, Itzstein and their cronies. This memorandum our "self-satisfied nosey-parker" unearths in the following of the *Zahme Xenien* (p. 319):

> All that is just the same old tripe,
> Do acquire some savvy!
> Don't be forever just marking time,
> But make some progress!

Goethe's verdict: "Nothing is more repulsive than the *majority*, for it consists of a few strong leaders, of rogues who accommodate themselves, of weaklings who adapt themselves, and the mass jogging along behind without having the faintest idea what it wants"[191]—this verdict so typical of the philistine, whose ignorance and short-sightedness are only possible within the narrow bounds of a petty German principality, appears to Herr Grün as "the critique of the later" (i.e. modern) "constitutional state".[a] How important it is one may discover "for instance in any Chamber of Deputies you care to choose" (p. 268). According to this, it is only out of ignorance that the "belly" of the French Chamber[192] looks after itself and its like in such an excellent manner. A few pages later, on p. 271, Herr Grün finds "the *Iuly Revolution*" "misbegotten", and as early as p. 34 the *Customs Union*[193] is sharply criticised because it "makes yet *more expensive* the rags the unclothed and the shivering need to cover their nakedness, in order to make the pillars of the throne (!!), the liberal-minded money-masters" (whom everyone knows to be opposed to

---

[a] The German original has: "Gesetzesstaat".—*Ed.*

"the throne" throughout the Customs Union) "somewhat more resistant to decay". Everyone knows how in Germany the philistines always bring out the "unclothed" and "shivering" whenever it is a question of combating protective tariffs or any other progressive bourgeois measure, and "man" joins their number.

What light does Goethe's critique of society and the state, as seen through Herr Grün's eyes, now shed on "the essence of man"?

Firstly, "man", according to p. 264, exhibits a most marked respect for "the educated estates" in general and a seemly deference towards a high aristocracy in particular. And then he is distinguished by a mighty terror of any great mass movement and any determined social action, at the approach of which he either scuttles timidly back into his fireside corner or takes to his heels with all his goods and chattels. As long as it lasts, such a movement is "a bitter experience" for him; scarcely is it over than he takes up a dominant position at the front of the stage and with the hand of Hercules delivers slaps in the face which only now appear to him to smack home really tolerably, and finds the whole business "infinitely ridiculous". And throughout he remains wholeheartedly attached to "circumstances of well-deserved and well-accustomed property"; apart from that he has a very "peaceful and domesticated nature", is undemanding and modest and does not wish to be disturbed in his quiet little pleasures by any storms. "Man is happy within a restricted sphere" (p. 191, as the *first sentence* of Part Two has it); he envies no one and gives thanks to his maker if he is left in peace. In short, "man", who, as we have already seen, is *German* by birth, is gradually beginning to turn into the spit image of a *German petty bourgeois*.

What actually does Goethe's critique of society as conveyed by Herr Grün amount to? What does "man" find in society to take exception to? Firstly that it does not correspond to his illusions. But these illusions are precisely the illusions of an ideologising philistine, especially a young one, and if philistine reality does not correspond to these illusions, this is only because they are illusions. For that very reason they correspond all the more fully to philistine reality. They differ from it only as the ideologising expression of a condition in general differs from that condition, and there can therefore be no further question of them being realised. A striking example of this is provided by Herr Grün's commentary on *Werther*.

Secondly "man's" polemic is directed against everything that threatens Germany's philistine régime. His whole polemic against the Revolution is that of a philistine. His hatred of the liberals, the July Revolution and protective tariffs is the absolutely unmistakable expression of the hatred an oppressed, inflexible petty bourgeois feels for the independent, progressive bourgeois. Let us give two further examples of this.

Every one knows that the guild system marked the period of efflorescence of the petty bourgeoisie. On p. 40 Herr Grün says, speaking on behalf of Goethe, in other words, of "man": "In the Middle Ages the corporation brought together *one strong man* in defensive alliance with other *strong men*." The guildsmen of those days are "strong men" in the eyes of "man".

But in Goethe's day the guild system was already in decay, competition was bursting in from all sides. As a true philistine, Goethe gives voice to a heart-rending wail at one point in his memoirs[a] which Herr Grün quotes on p. 88, about the rot setting among the petty bourgeoisie, the ruination of well-to-do families, the decay of family life associated with this, the loosening of domestic bonds and other petty-bourgeois lamentations which in civilised countries are treated with well-deserved contempt. Herr Grün, who scents a capital criticism of modern society in this passage,

---

[a] J. W. Goethe, *Aus meinem Leben*, Teil 2, Buch 7.—*Ed.*

can so little moderate his delight that he has its whole "human content" printed in italics.

Let us now turn to the positive "human content" in Goethe. We can proceed more quickly now that we are on the track of "man".

Before all else let us report the glad tidings that "Wilhelm Meister deserts his parental home" and that in *Egmont* "the citizens of Brussels are demanding privileges and liberties" for no other reason than to "become men" (p. XVII).

Herr Grün has detected affinities with Proudhon in the elderly Goethe once before. On p. 320 he has this pleasure once again:

"What he wanted, what we all want, to save our personalities, *anarchy* in the true sense of the word, on this topic Goethe has the following to say:
> Now why should anarchy have for me
> Such attraction in modern times?
> Each lives according to his lights
> And that is profit for me as well",[194] etc.

Herr Grün is beside himself with joy at finding in Goethe that truly "human" social anarchy which was first proclaimed by Proudhon and adopted by acclamation by the German true socialists. This time he is mistaken however. Goethe is speaking of the already existing "anarchy in modern times", which already "is" profit for him and by which each lives according to his lights, in other words of the independence in sociable intercourse which has been brought about by the dissolution of the feudal system and the guilds, by the rise of the bourgeoisie, and the exclusion of patriarchalism from the social life of the educated classes. Simply for *grammatical* reasons there can therefore be no question of the Herr Grün's beloved *future* anarchy in the higher sense. Goethe is here not talking at all about "what he wanted" but about what he found around him.

But such a little slip should not disturb us. For we do have the poem: *Eigentum*.

> I know that nothing is mine own
> Save the idea that peacefully
> Secretes itself from my spirit,
> And every instant of happiness
> Which destiny beneficent
> Gives me to savour fully.

If it is not clear that in this poem "property as it has existed up to now vanishes into smoke" (p. 320), Herr Grün's comprehension has come to a standstill.

But let us leave these entertaining little exegetical diversions of Herr Grün's to their fate. They are in any case legion and each invariably leads on to others still more surprising. Let us rather resume our search for "man".

"Man is happy within a restricted sphere," as we have read. So is the philistine.

> "Goethe's early works were of *purely social*" (i.e. human) "character.... Goethe clung to what was *most immediate, smallest, most domesticated*" (p. 88).

The first positive thing we discover about "man" is his delight in the "smallest, domesticated" still-life of the petty bourgeoisie.

> "If we can find a place in the world," says Goethe, as summarised by Herr Grün, "where to rest with our possessions, a field to provide us with food, a house to shelter us—is that not a Fatherland for us?"

And, exclaims Herr Grün,

> "How these words express our deepest thoughts today!" (p. 32).

Essentially "man" is dressed in a *redingote à la propriétaire* and by that too reveals himself as a thoroughbred *épicier*.[a]

The German bourgeois, as everyone knows, is a fanatic for freedom at most for a brief moment, in his youth. That is characteristic of "man" too. Herr Grün mentions with

---

[a] Grocer.—*Ed.*

approval how in his later years Goethe "damns" the "urge for freedom" which still haunts *Götz*, that "product of a free and ill-bred boy", and even quotes this cowardly recantation in extenso on p. 43. What Herr Grün understands by freedom can be deduced from the fact that in the same passage he identifies the freedom of the French Revolution with that of the free Switzers at the time of Goethe's Swiss journey, in other words, modern, constitutional and democratic freedom with the dominance of patricians and guilds in medieval Imperial Cities and especially with the early Germanic barbarism of cattle-rearing Alpine tribes. The montagnards[195] of the Bernese Oberland even have the same name as the Montagnards of the National Convention!

The respectable bourgeois is a sworn enemy of all frivolity and mockery of religion: "man" likewise. If Goethe on various occasions expressed himself in a truly bourgeois manner on this topic, Herr Grün takes this as another aspect of the "human content in Goethe". And to make the point quite credible, Herr Grün assembles not merely these grains of gold, but on p. 62 even adds a number of meritorious sentiments of his own, to the effect that "those who mock religion... are empty vessels and simpletons", etc. Which does much credit to his feelings as "man" and bourgeois.

The bourgeois cannot live without a "king he loves", a father to his country whom he holds dear. Nor can "man". That is why on p. 129 Karl August is for Goethe a "most excellent Prince". Stout old Herr Grün, still enthusing for "most excellent Princes" in the year 1846!

An event is of interest to the bourgeois insofar as it impinges directly on his private circumstances.

> "To Goethe even the events of the day become alien objects which either add to or detract from his *bourgeois comforts* and which may arouse in him an aesthetic or *human* but never a political interest" (p. 20).

Herr Grün "thus finds a human interest in a thing" if he notices that it "either adds to or detracts from his bourgeois comforts". Herr Grün here confesses as openly as possible that bourgeois comforts are the chief thing for "man".

Faust and *Wilhelm Meister* provide Herr Grün with an occasion for special chapters. Let us take *Faust* first.

On p. 116 we are told:

"Only the fact that Goethe came upon a clue to the mystery of the organisation of plants" enabled him "to complete his delineation of humanistic man" (for there is no way of escaping "human" man) "Faust. *For* Faust is brought to the peak of his own nature."(!) "just as much as by natural science."

We have already had examples of how that "humanistic man", Herr Grün, "is brought to the peak of his own nature by natural science". We observe that this is inherent in the race.

Then on p. 231 we hear that the "bones of brute and human skeletons" in the first scene signifies "the abstraction of our whole life"—and Herr Grün treats *Faust* in general exactly as though he had the Revelation of St. John the Theologian before him. The macrocosm signifies "Hegelian philosophy", which at the time when Goethe was writing this scene[196] (1806) happened to exist only in Hegel's mind or at most in the manuscript of the *Phänomenologie* which Hegel was then working on. What has chronology to do with "human content"?

The depiction of the moribund Holy Roman Empire in the Second Part of *Faust* Herr Grün (p. 240) imagines without more ado to be a depiction of the monarchy of Louis XIV, "in which," he adds, "we *automatically* have the Constitution and the Republic!" "Man" naturally "of himself has" everything that other people first have to provide for themselves by dint of toil and exertion.

On p. 246 Herr Grün confides to us that the Second Part of *Faust* has become, with regard to its scientific aspect, "the canon of modern times, just as Dante's *Divine Comedy* was the canon of the Middle Ages". We would commend this to natural scientists who have hitherto sought very little in the Second Part of *Faust*, and to historians, who have sought something quite other than a "canon of the Middle Ages" in the Florentine's pro-Ghibelline[197] poem! It seems as though Herr Grün is looking at history with the same eyes as Goethe, according to p. 49, looked at his own past: "In Italy Goethe surveyed his past *with the eyes* of the Belvedere Apollo", eyes which *pour comble de malheur*[a] do not even have eyeballs.

Wilhelm Meister is "a Communist", i.e., "in theory, on the basis of aesthetic outlook" (!!) (p. 254).

> On nothing does he set great store,
> And yet the whole wide world is his[198] (p. 257).

Of course, he has enough money, and the world belongs to him, as it belongs to every bourgeois, without his needing to go to the trouble of becoming "a communist on the basis of aesthetic outlook".—Under the auspices of this "nothing" on which Wilhelm Meister sets great store and which, as we see from p. 256, is indeed an extensive and most substantial "nothing", even hangovers are eliminated. Herr Grün "drains every cup to the lees, without ill effect, without a headache". So much the better for "man" who may now quietly worship Bacchus with impunity. For the day when all these things shall come to pass, Herr Grün has meanwhile already discovered the drinking song for "true man" in *On nothing do I set great store*—"this song will be sung when mankind has arranged its affairs in a manner worthy of itself"; but Herr Grün has reduced it to three verses and expunged those parts unsuitable for youth and "man".

In *W[ilhelm] M[eister]* Goethe sets up

> "the ideal of human society". "Man is not a teaching but a living, acting and creating being." "Wilhelm Meister is this man." "The essence of man is activity" (an essence he shares with any flea), pp. 257, 258, 261.

---

[a] As the final misfortune.—*Ed.*

Finally the *Wahlverwandtschaften*. This novel, moral enough in itself, is moralised even more by Herr Grün, so that it almost seems as though he were concerned to recommend the *Wahlverwandtschaften* as a suitable text-book for schools for young ladies. Herr Grün explains that Goethe

> "distinguished between love and marriage, so that for him love was *a search of marriage* and marriage was love *found* and fulfilled" (p. 286).

By this token, then, love is the *search* of "love that has been found". This is further elucidated to the effect that after "the freedom of youthful love", marriage must come about as "the final relationship of love" (p. 287). Exactly as in civilised countries a wise father first allows his son to sow his wild oats for a few years and then finds him a suitable wife as a "final relationship". However, whilst people in civilised countries have long passed the stage of regarding this "final relationship" as something morally binding, whilst on the contrary in those countries the husband keeps mistresses and his wife retaliates by cuckolding him, the philistine once again rescues Herr Grün:

> "If man has had a really free choice, ... if two people base their union on their mutual rational wishes" (there is no mention here of passion, flesh and blood) "it would require the outlook of a *libertine* to regard the upsetting of this relationship as a trifle, as not so fraught with suffering and unhappiness as Goethe did. But there can be no question of *libertinism* with Goethe" (p. 288).

This passage qualifies the timid polemic against morality which Herr Grün permits himself from time to time. The philistine has arrived at the realisation that there is all the more reason for having to turn a blind eye to the behaviour of the young since it is precisely the most dissolute young men who afterwards make the best husbands. But if they should misbehave themselves again after the wedding—then no mercy, no pity on them; for that "would require the outlook of a libertine".

"The outlook of a libertine!" "Libertinism!" One can just picture "man" as large as life before one, as he places his hand on his heart, and overflowing with pride exclaims: No! I am pure of all frivolity, of "fornication and licentiousness", I have never deliberately ruined the happiness of a contented marriage, I have always practised fidelity and honesty and have never lusted after my neighbour's wife—I am no "libertine"!

"Man" is right. He is not made for amorous affairs with beautiful women, he has never turned his mind to seduction and adultery, he is no "libertine", but a man of conscience, an honourable, virtuous, German philistine. He is

> ... l'épicier pacifique,
> Fumant sa pipe au fond de sa boutique;
> Il craint sa femme et son ton arrogant;
> De la maison il lui laisse l'empire,
> Au moindre signe obéit sans mot dire
> Et vit ainsi cocu, battu, content.[a]
> (Parny, *Goddam*, chant III.)

There remains just one observation for us to make. If above we have only considered one aspect of Goethe, that is the fault of Herr Grün alone. He does not present Goethe's towering stature at all. He either skims hurriedly over all works in which Goethe was really great and a genius, such as the *Römische Elegien* of Goethe the "libertine", or he inundates them with a great torrent of trivialities, which only proves that he can make nothing of them. On the other hand, with what is for him uncommon industry he seeks out every instance of philistinism, petty priggery and narrow-mindedness, collates them, exaggerates them in the manner of a true literary hack, and rejoices every time he

---

[a] ...the peaceful tradesman,
Smoking his pipe at the back of his shop;
He fears his wife and her domineering tone;
He leaves to her the government of the house,
Without a word he obeys her slightest signal;
Thus he lives, cuckolded, beaten and content.—*Ed.*

is able to find support for his own narrow-minded opinions on the authority of Goethe, whom he furthermore frequently distorts.

History's revenge on Goethe for ignoring her every time she confronted him face to face was not the yapping of Menzel nor the narrow polemic of Börne. No,

> Just as Titania in the land of fairy magic
> Found Nick Bottom in her arms,[199]

so one morning Goethe found Herr Grün in his arms. Herr Grün's apologia, the warm thanks he stammers out to Goethe for every philistine word, that is the bitterest revenge which offended history could pronounce upon the greatest German poet.

Herr Grün, however, "can close his eyes in the awareness that he has not disgraced his destiny of being a man" (p. 248).

Frederick Engels, *German Socialism in Verse and Prose*

Marx and Engels, *Collected Works*, Vol. 6, Moscow, 1976, pp. 249, 256-73

Heine

1

Just as in France in the eighteenth century, so in Germany in the nineteenth, a philosophical revolution ushered in the political collapse. But how different the two looked! The French were in open combat against all official science, against the church and often also against the state; their writings were printed across the frontier, in Holland or England, while they themselves were often in jeopardy of imprisonment in the Bastille. On the other hand, the Germans were professors, state-appointed instructors of youth;

their writings were recognised textbooks, and the terminating system of the whole development—the Hegelian system—was even raised, as it were, to the rank of a royal Prussian philosophy of state! Was it possible that a revolution could hide behind these professors, behind their obscure, pedantic phrases, their ponderous, wearisome sentences? Were not precisely those people who were then regarded as the representatives of the revolution, the liberals, the bitterest opponents of this brain-confusing philosophy? But what neither the government nor the liberals saw was seen at least by one man as early as 1833, and this man was indeed none other than Heinrich Heine.[200]

> Frederick Engels, *Ludwig Feuerbach and the End of Classical German Philosophy*
>
> Marx and Engels, *Selected Works*, Vol. 3, Moscow, 1973, p. 337

2

Besides those, Henry Heine, the most eminent of all living German poets, has joined our ranks, and published a volume of political poetry, which contains also some pieces preaching Socialism. He is the author of the celebrated *Song of the Silesian Weavers*, of which I give you a prosaic translation, but which, I am afraid, will be considered blasphemy in England. At any rate, I will give it you, and only remark, that it refers to the battle-cry of the Prussians in 1813:—"With God for King and fatherland!" which has been ever since a favourite saying of the loyal party. But for the song, here it is:[201]—

Without a tear in their grim eyes,
They sit at the loom, the rage of despair in their faces;
"We have suffered and hunger'd long enough;
Old Germany, we are weaving a shroud for thee
And weaving it with a triple curse.
    "We are weaving, weaving!

> "The first curse to the God, the blind and deaf god,
> Upon whom we relied, as children on their father;
> In whom we hoped and trusted withal,
> He has mocked us, he has cheated us nevertheless.
> "We are weaving, weaving!
> "The second curse for the King of the rich,
> Whom our distress could not soften nor touch;
> The King, who extorts the last penny from us,
> And sends his soldiers, to shoot us like dogs.
> "We are weaving, weaving!
> "A curse to the false fatherland,
> That has nothing for us but distress and shame,
> Where we suffered hunger and misery—
> We are weaving thy shroud, Old Germany!
> "We are weaving, weaving!"

With this song, which in its German original is one of the most powerful poems I know of, I take leave from you for this time, hoping soon to be able to report on our further progress and social literature.

> Frederick Engels, "Communism in Germany"
>
> Written in English
>
> *New Moral World*, December 13, 1844

3

Heine could not speak any more contemptuously of his philistine German public[202] than in the words: "The author finally gets used to his public as if it were a reasonable being."

> Frederick Engels, "Supplement to *Capital*, Volume Three"
>
> Karl Marx, *Capital*, Vol. III, Moscow, 1974, p. 894

4

Dear Friend,
I hope to have time to see you tomorrow. My departure is fixed for Monday.[203]

The publisher Leske has just been to see me. He publishes an uncensored quarterly[204] in Darmstadt. Engels, Hess, Herwegh, Jung, etc. and I contribute. He has requested me to talk to you about contributing, either poetry or prose. You will certainly not refuse, for we must use every opportunity of establishing ourselves in Germany.

Of all the people whom I must leave behind, it is most unpleasant to say farewell to Heine. I should very much like to take you with me. Kind regards from myself and my wife to your good lady.

Yours,
K. Marx

Marx to Heinrich Heine,
January 12, 1845

Marx/Engels, *Werke,* Bd. 27, 1965, S. 434

5

My dear Heine,
I am taking advantage of the fact that the bearer of these lines, Mr. Annenkov, an amiable and cultured Russian, is passing through to convey to you my best wishes.

A few days ago I chanced upon a little libel against you —Börne's letters published after his death. I would never have believed he was as tasteless, petty and insipid as the letters reveal, in black and white. And what miserable rubbish the postscript by Gutzkow, etc., is. I shall write a detailed review of your book on Börne[205] in a German periodical. One could hardly find in any literary period a more doltish treatment of a book than the one given yours by the Christian-German asses, and indeed, no German literary period is short of doltishness.

If you have anything "special" to tell me about your book, then do so posthaste.

Yours,
K. Marx

Marx to Heinrich Heine,
approx. April 5, 1846

Marx/Engels, *Werke*, Bd. 27,
1965, S. 441

6

Heine is fading fast. A fortnight ago I visited him, he was in bed with a nervous fit. Yesterday he got up but was in a very poor state. He can hardly make a few steps; leaning against the wall, he drags himself from armchair to bed and vice versa. Moreover, noise in his house, carpentry work, hammering, etc., is driving him mad. Mentally he is not as alert either. Heinzen wanted to see him but was not admitted.

Engels to Marx,
January 14, 1848

Marx/Engels, *Werke*, Bd. 27, 1965.
S. 110

"Young Germany"

German literature, too, laboured under the influence of the political excitement into which all Europe had been thrown by the events of 1830.[206] A crude constitutionalism, or a still cruder republicanism, were preached by almost all writers of the time. It became more and more the habit, particularly of the inferior sorts of *literati*, to make up for the want of cleverness in their productions by political allusions which were sure to attract attention. Poetry, novels, reviews, the drama, every literary production teemed with what was called "tendency", that is, with more or less timid exhibitions of an anti-governmental spirit. In order to complete the confusion of ideas, reigning after 1830 in Germany, with these elements of political opposition there were mixed up ill-digested university-recollections of German philosophy, and misunderstood gleanings from French socialism, particularly Saint-Simonism; and the clique of writers who expatiated upon this heterogeneous conglomerate of ideas, presumptuously called themselves "Young Germany", or "the Modern School". They have since repented their youthful sins, but not improved their style of writing.

Frederick Engels, *Revolution and Counter-Revolution in Germany*

Marx and Engels, *Selected Works*, Vol. 1, Moscow, 1973, p. 309

Alexander Jung

Finally, the author arrives at what he has been working up to from the outset—his precious Young Germany, which for him is the acme of the "modern". He begins with *Börne*. Actually, Börne's influence on Young Germany has not been so great; Mundt and Kühne said he was mad, Laube thought him too democratic, too categorical, and only on Gutzkow and Wienbarg did he exercise a more sustained influence. Gutzkow, in particular, owes a great deal to Börne. The latter's greatest effect lay in his quiet influence on the nation, which preserved his works as sacred objects and drew strength and support from them during the troubled times of 1832 to 1840, until the true sons of the author of the *Briefe aus*

Paris[207] appeared in the form of the new, philosophical liberals. Without the direct and indirect influence of Börne it would have been far more difficult for the free trend proceeding from Hegel to take shape. Then all that needed to be done was to clear out the silted-up paths of thought between Hegel and Börne, and that was not so difficult. These two men stood closer to each other than it seemed. Börne's directness and healthy outlook proved to be the practical side of what Hegel had in mind, theoretically at least. Naturally, Herr Jung does not see this either. True, for him Börne is to a certain extent a respectable person, even a man of character, which is obviously very valuable in the circumstances; he had undeniable merits, as perhaps Varnhagen and Pückler have also, and he wrote in particular good dramatic criticism, but he was a fanatic and terrorist, and from such may the good Lord deliver us! Shame on such a vapid, fainthearted conception of a man who by his mode of thought alone became a standard-bearer of his time! This Jung, who wishes to construct Young Germany and Gutzkow's personality out of the absolute concept, is not even capable of understanding such a simple character as Börne; he does not see how inevitably and logically the most extreme, the most radical pronouncements arise from Börne's innermost being, that *Börne was a republican by his very nature*, and that truly the *Briefe aus Paris* are not written in too strong terms for such a man. Or has Herr Jung never heard a Swiss or a North American talking about monarchical states? And who would reproach Börne for "considering life only from the political point of view"? Does not Hegel do the same? Is not for him, too, the state in its transition to world history, and therefore in the conditions of home and foreign policy, the concrete reality of the absolute spirit? And—ludicrously enough—confronted by this direct, naive outlook of Börne, which finds its completion in the wider Hegelian outlook and often coincides with it in the most surprising way, Herr Jung nevertheless concludes that Börne "outlined a system of politics and happiness of the peoples", a sort of abstract, cloudy conception which, in his view, must explain Börne's one-sidedness and obduracy! Herr Jung has not the slightest idea of Börne's importance, his iron, unyielding character, his imposing will-power, precisely because he himself is such an insignificant, soft-hearted, helpless, obsequious little man. He does not know that as a personality Börne is unique in German history; he does not know that Börne was the standard-bearer of German freedom, the only *real man* in the Germany of his day; he cannot imagine what it means to rise up against forty million Germans and proclaim the realm of the *idea*; he cannot understand that Börne is the John the Baptist of the new period, who preaches repentance to the self-satisfied Germans and tells them that already the axe is laid to the root of the tree and that one mightier will come, who will baptise with fire and mercilessly sweep away the chaff from the threshing-floor. Herr Jung should see himself as part of this chaff. Finally, Herr A. Jung arrives at his beloved Young Germany and begins with a tolerable, but much too detailed criticism of Heine. The others are then dealt with in turn; first Laube, Mundt, and Kühne, then Wienbarg, to whom homage is paid as he deserves, and finally *almost 50 pages* are devoted to Gutzkow. The first three receive the usual *juste-milieu* tribute, much approval and very modest censure; Wienbarg is given definite prominence, but only four pages are allotted to him; and finally, with shameless servility, Gutzkow is made the standard-bearer of the "modern", his image is constructed in accordance with the Hegelian scheme of concepts, and he is treated as a personage of the first rank.

If such judgments had been put forward by a young, budding author, one would let it pass; there are many who for a time set their hopes on the Young Literature, and with an eye to the expected future considered its works with more indulgence than they could otherwise have justified to themselves. In particular, anyone whose own mind has passed through the recent stages of the development of German thought will at some time have had a special liking for the works of Mundt, Laube, or Gutzkow. But since then progress beyond this trend has gone on much too vigorously, and the emptiness of most of the Young Germans has become horribly obvious.

Young Germany extricated itself from the unclearness of disturbed times, but itself remained tainted by this unclearness. Ideas which at that time were fermenting in people's minds in a still shapeless and undeveloped form and which only later were consciously perceived with the help of philosophy, were used by Young Germany to play a game of fantasy. Hence the vagueness, the confusion of concepts, which prevailed among the Young Germans themselves. Gutzkow and Wienbarg knew better than the others what they wanted, Laube least of all. Mundt pursued social whims; Kühne, in whom something of Hegel was visible, made schemes and classifications. But in view of the general unclearness of thought nothing of value could come of it. The idea of the justification of sensuality was conceived, following Heine's example, in a crude and shallow way; liberal political principles differed among various personalities and the position of women gave rise to the most sterile and confused discussions. No one knew where he stood in relation to another person. The measures adopted by the various governments against these people should also be ascribed to the universal confusion of the period. The fantastic form in which these views were propagated could only promote further confusion. Thanks to the outward brilliance of the Young Germans' works, to their witty, piquant and lively style, the enigmatic mysticism in which the main slogans were clothed, and thanks also to the revival of criticism and enlivening of the literary journals under their influence, the Young Germans soon attracted a mass of younger writers, and it was not long before each of them, with the exception of Wienbarg, had his own following. The old, flabby *belles-lettres* had to give way under pressure from the young forces, and the "Young Literature" took possession of the field it had conquered, divided it up—and disintegrated in the course of this division. Thus, the inadequacy of principle was disclosed. They had all been mistaken about one another. Principles vanished; it was now only a matter of personalities. Gutzkow or Mundt, that was the question. The periodicals began to be filled with the doings of the cliques, squabbles, and disputes about nothing at all.

> Frederick Engels, "Alexander Jung. 'Lectures on Modern German Literature' "
>
> Marx and Engels, *Collected Works*, Vol. 2, Moscow, 1975, pp. 288-91

German, or "True" Socialism

1

The Socialist and Communist literature of France, a literature that originated under the pressure of a bourgeoisie in power, and that was the expression of the struggle against this power, was introduced into Germany at a time when the bourgeoisie, in that country, had just begun its contest with feudal absolutism.

German philosophers, would-be philosophers, and *beaux esprits*, eagerly seized on this literature, only forgetting, that when these writings immigrated from France into Germany, French social conditions had not immigrated along with them. In contact with German social conditions, this French literature lost all its immediate practical significance, and assumed a purely literary aspect. Thus, to the German philosophers of the Eighteenth Century, the demands of the first French Revolution were nothing more than the demands of "Practical Reason" in general, and the utterance of the will of the revolutionary French bourgeoisie signified in their eyes the laws of pure Will, of Will as it was bound to be, of true human Will generally.

The work of the German *literati* consisted solely in bringing the new French ideas into harmony with their ancient philosophical conscience, or rather, in annexing the French ideas without deserting their own philosophic point of view.

This annexation took place in the same way in which a foreign language is appropriated, namely, by translation.

It is well known how the monks wrote silly lives of Catholic Saints *over* the manuscripts on which the classical works of ancient heathendom had been written. The German *literati* reversed this process with the profane French literature. They wrote their philosophical nonsense beneath the French original. For instance, beneath the French criticism of the economic functions of money, they wrote "Alienation of Humanity", and beneath the French criticism of the bourgeois State they wrote "Dethronement of the Category of the General", and so forth.

The introduction of these philosophical phrases at the back of the French historical criticisms they dubbed "Philosophy of Action", "True Socialism", "German Science of Socialism", "Philosophical Foundation of Socialism", and so on.

The French Socialist and Communist literature was thus completely emasculated. And, since it ceased in the hands of the German to express the struggle of one class with the other, he felt conscious of having overcome "French one-sidedness" and of representing, not true requirements, but the requirements of Truth; not the interests of the proletariat, but the interests of Human Nature, of Man in general, who belongs to no class, has no reality, who exists only in the misty realm of philosophical fantasy.

This German Socialism, which took its schoolboy task so seriously and solemnly, and extolled its poor stock-in-trade in such mountebank fashion, meanwhile gradually lost its pedantic innocence.

The fight of the German, and, especially, of the Prussian bourgeoisie, against feudal aristocracy and absolute monarchy, in other words, the liberal movement, became more earnest.

By this, the long wished-for opportunity was offered to "True" Socialism of confronting the political movement with the Socialist demands, of hurling the traditional anathemas against liberalism, against representative government, against bourgeois competition, bourgeois freedom of the press, bourgeois legislation, bourgeois liberty and equality, and of preaching to the masses that they had nothing to gain, and everything to lose, by this bourgeois movement. German Socialism forgot, in the nick of time, that the French criticism, whose silly echo it was, presupposed the existence of modern bourgeois society, with its corresponding economic conditions of existence, and the political constitution adapted thereto, the very things whose attainment was the object of the pending struggle in Germany.

To the absolute governments, with their following of parsons, professors, country squires and officials, it served as a welcome scarecrow against the threatening bourgeoisie.

It was a sweet finish after the bitter pills of floggings and bullets with which these same governments, just at that time, dosed the German working-class risings.

While this "True" Socialism thus served the governments as a weapon for fighting the German bourgeoisie, it, at the same time, directly represented a reactionary interest, the interest of the German Philistines. In Germany the *petty-bourgeois* class, a relic of the sixteenth century, and since then constantly cropping up again under various forms, is the real social basis of the existing state of things.

To preserve this class is to preserve the existing state of things in Germany. The industrial and political supremacy of the bourgeoisie threatens it with certain destruction; on the one hand, from the concentration of capital; on the other, from the rise of a revolutionary proletariat. "True" Socialism appeared to kill these two birds with one stone. It spread like an epidemic.

The robe of speculative cobwebs, embroidered with flowers of rhetoric, steeped in the dew of sickly sentiment, this transcendental robe in which the German Socialists wrapped their sorry "eternal truths", all skin and bone, served to wonderfully increase the sale of their goods amongst such a public.

And on its part, German Socialism recognised, more and more, its own calling as the bombastic representative of the petty-bourgeois Philistine.

It proclaimed the German nation to be the model nation, and the German petty Philistine to be the typical man. To every villainous meanness of this model man it gave a hidden, higher, Socialistic interpretation, the exact contrary of its real character. It went to the extreme length of directly opposing the "brutally destructive" tendency of Communism, and of proclaiming its supreme and impartial contempt of all class struggles. With very few exceptions, all the so-called Socialist and Communist publications that now (1847) circulate in Germany belong to the domain of this foul and enervating literature.*

Karl Marx and Frederick Engels,
Manifesto of the Communist Party

Marx and Engels, *Collected Works*,
Vol. 6, Moscow, 1976, pp. 510-13

2

True socialism has in fact enabled a host of Young-German literary men, quacks and other *literati* to exploit the social movement. Even the social movement was at first a *merely* literary one because of the lack of *real*, passionate, practical party struggles in Germany. True socialism is a perfect example of a social literary movement that has come into being without any real party interests and now, after the formation of the communist party, it intends to persist in spite of it. It is obvious that since the appearance of a real communist party in Germany, the public of the true so-

---

* The revolutionary storm of 1848 swept away this whole shabby tendency and cured its protagonists of the desire to dabble further in Socialism. The chief representative and classical type of this tendency is Herr Karl Grün. [*Note by Engels to the German edition of 1890*].

cialists will be more and more limited to the petty bourgeoisie and the sterile and broken-down *literati* who represent it.

> Karl Marx and Frederick Engels,
> *The German Ideology*
> Marx and Engels, *Collected Works*,
> Vol. 5, Moscow, 1976, p. 457

Karl Beck, *Lieder vom Armen Mann*, or the Poetry of True Socialism[a]

1

Right at the beginning he records his petty-bourgeois illusion that the "rule of gold" obeys Rothschild's "whims"; an illusion which gives rise to a whole series of fancies about the power of the house of Rothschild.

It is not the destruction of Rothschild's real power, of the social conditions on which it is based, which the poet threatens; he merely desires it to be humanely applied. He laments that bankers are not socialist philanthropists, not enthusiasts for an ideal, not benefactors of mankind, but just—bankers. Beck sings of the cowardly petty-bourgeois wretchedness, of the "poor man", the *pauvre honteux* with his poor, pious and contradictory wishes of the "little man" in all his manifestations, and not of the proud, threatening, and revolutionary proletarian. The threats and reproaches which Beck showers on the house of Rothschild, sound, for all his good intentions, even more farcical to the reader than a Capuchin's sermon. They are founded on the most infantile illusion about the power of the Rothschilds, on total ignorance of the connection between this power and existing conditions, and on a complete misapprehension about the means which the Roth-

---
[a] Karl Beck, *Lieder vom armen Mann*, Leipzig, 1846.—*Ed.*

schilds had to use to acquire power and to retain power. Pusillanimity and lack of understanding, womanish sentimentality and the wretched, prosaically sober attitudes of the petty bourgeoisie, these are the muses of this lyre, and in vain they do violence to themselves in an attempt to appear terrible. They only appear ridiculous. Their forced bass is constantly breaking into a comic falsetto, their dramatic rendering of the titanic struggle of an Enceladus only succeeds in producing the farcical, disjointed jerks of a puppet.

2

A regiment marches off with its band playing. The people call upon the soldiers to make common cause with them. The reader is glad that the poet is at last summoning up courage. But oh dear! We finally discover that the occasion is merely the Emperor's name-day and the people's words are only the improvised and unspoken reverie of a youth watching the parade. Probably a gymnasium boy:

Thus dreams a youth with burning heart [p. 76].

Whilst in the hands of Heine the same material, with the same point, would contain the most bitter satire on the German people, in Beck's case all that emerges is a satire on the poet himself, who identifies himself with the powerlessly rapturous youth. In Heine's case, the raptures of the bourgeoisie are deliberately high-pitched, so that they may equally deliberately then be brought down to earth with a bump; in Beck's case it is the poet himself who is associated with these fantasies and who naturally also suffers the consequences when he comes crashing down to earth. In the case of the one the bourgeoisie feels indignation at the poet's impertinence, in the case of the other reassurance at the attitudes of mind they have in common.

3

This complete inability to tell a story and create a situation, which is evident throughout the book, is characteristic of the poetry of true socialism. True socialism, in its vagueness, provides no opportunity to relate the individual facts of the narrative to general conditions and thus bring out what is striking or significant about them. That is why the true socialists shy away from history in their prose as well. Where they cannot avoid it, they content themselves either with philosophical constructions or with producing an arid and boring catalogue of isolated instances of misfortune and *social cases*. Furthermore, they all lack the necessary talent for narrative, both in prose and poetry, and this is connected with the vagueness of their whole outlook.

4

Beck has incontestably more talent and at the outset more energy too than most of the German scribbling fraternity. His great lament is the German misery, amongst whose theoretical manifestations also belong Beck's pompously sentimental socialism and Young German reminiscences. Until social conflicts in Germany are given a more acute form by a more distinct differentiation between classes and a momentary acquisition of political power by [the] bourgeoisie, there can be little hope for a German poet in Germany itself. On the one hand, it is impossible for him to adopt a revolutionary stand in German society because the revolutionary elements themselves are not yet sufficiently developed, and on the other, the chronic misery surrounding him on all sides has too debilitating an effect for him to be able to rise above it, to be free of it and to laugh at it, without succumbing to it again himself. For the present the only advice we can give to all German poets who still have a little talent is to emigrate to civilised countries.

Frederick Engels, *German Socialism in Verse and Prose*

Marx and Engels, *Collected Works*, Vol. 6, Moscow, 1976, pp. 235-36, 244, 244-45, 248-49

Gottfried Kinkel

"Sing, O immortal soul, the redemption of sinful mankind"[208]—through Gottfried Kinkel.

1

Gottfried Kinkel was born some 40 years ago. The story of his life has been made available to us in an autobiography. *Gottfried Kinkel. Truth without Poetry. A biographical sketch-book.* Published by Adolph Strodtmann. (Hamburg, Hoffmann & Campe, 1850, octavo.)

Gottfried is the hero of that democratic Siegwart epoch[209] that flooded Germany with endless torrents of patriotic melancholy and tearful lament. He made his debut as a simple lyrical Siegwart.

We are indebted to Strodtmann the Apostle, whose "narrative compilation" we follow here, both for the diary-like sketchiness in which his pilgrimage on this earth is presented to the reader, and for the glaring lack of discretion of these revelations....

2

With his capture, a new epoch opened in Kinkel's life and, at the same time, there began a new era in the history of German philistinism. The Maybug Club[210] had scarcely heard the news of his capture than they wrote to all the German papers that Kinkel, the great poet, was in danger of being court-martialled and shot and exhorted the German people, especially the educated among them, and above all the women and girls, to do all they could to save the life of the imprisoned poet. Kinkel himself composed a poem at about this time, as we are told, in which he compared himself to "Christ, his friend and teacher", adding: "My blood is shed for you." From this time the lyre became his emblem. In this way, Germany suddenly learned that Kinkel was a poet, a great poet moreover, and from this moment on the mass of German philistines and aestheticising drivellers joined in the farce of the Blue Flower put on by our Heinrich von Ofterdingen.

In the meantime, the Prussians brought him before a military tribunal. For the first time after a long interval he was offered the opportunity to try out one of those moving appeals to the tear ducts of his audience which—Mockel *teste*[a]—had brought him such success earlier, as an assistant preacher in Cologne. Cologne too was destined soon to witness his most glorious performance in this sphere. He made a speech in his own defence before the tribunal, which thanks to the indiscretion of a friend was unfortunately made available to the public by the Berlin *Abend-Post*. In this speech, Kinkel

"repudiates any connection between his activities and the filth and the dirt that, as I know, in the end unfortunately attached itself to this revolution".[211]

After this arch-revolutionary speech, Kinkel was sentenced to twenty years detention in a fortress. As an act of grace, this was commuted to hard labour and he was removed to Naugard, where he was allegedly employed in spinning wool, and so just as formerly he had appeared with the emblem first of the rucksack, then the musket and then the lyre, he now appears with that of the *spinning wheel*. We shall

---

[a] According to.—*Ed.*

see him later wandering over the ocean with the emblem of the purse.

In the meantime, a curious event took place in Germany. It is well known that the German philistine is endowed by nature with a beautiful soul. Now he found his most cherished illusions cruelly shattered by the hard blows of the year 1849. Not a single hope had become reality and even the noble hearts of young men began to despair over the fate of the Fatherland. Every heart yielded to a lachrymose torpor and the need began to be felt everywhere for a democratic Christ, for a real or imagined Sufferer who, in his torments, would bear the sins of the philistine world with the patience of a lamb and whose Passion would epitomise, in extreme form, the sloppy chronic self-pity of the whole mass of philistines. The Maybug Club, with Mockel at its head, set out to satisfy this universal need. And indeed, who was better fitted for enacting this great Passion farce than our captive passion flower, Kinkel at the spinning wheel, this sponge, capable of pouring out endless floods of sentimental tears, who was in addition preacher, professor of fine arts, deputy, political colporteur, musketeer, newly discovered poet and old impresario all rolled into one? Kinkel was the man of the moment and as such he was immediately accepted by the German philistines. Every paper abounded in anecdotes, vignettes, poems, reminiscences of the captive poet, his sufferings in prison were magnified a thousandfold and took on mythical stature; at least once a month his hair was reported to have gone grey; in every bourgeois meeting-place and at every tea party he was remembered with grief; the daughters of the educated classes sighed over his poems and old maids, who knew what yearning is, wept in various cities of the Fatherland at the thought of his shattered manhood. All other profane victims of the movement, all who had been shot, who had fallen in battle or who had been imprisoned, disappeared into naught beside this one sacrificial lamb, beside this one hero after the hearts of the philistines male and female. For him alone did the rivers of tears flow, and indeed, he alone was able to respond to them in kind. In short, it was the perfect image of the *democratic Siegwart epoch*, which yielded in nothing to the literary Siegwart epoch of the preceding century, and Siegwart-Kinkel never felt more at home in any role than in this one where he could seem great, not because of what he did, but because of what he did not do. He seemed great not by dint of strength and powers of resistance, but through his weakness and spineless behaviour in a situation where his only task was to endure with decorum and sentiment. Mockel, however, was able and experienced enough to take practical advantage of the public's soft heart and she immediately organised a highly efficient enterprise. She got all of Gottfried's published and unpublished works, which had suddenly become *en vogue* and were much in demand, to be printed and promoted. She also found a market for her own life-experiences from the insect world, e.g., her *Story of a Glowworm*; she employed the Maybug Strodtmann to assemble Gottfried's most secret diary-feelings and prostitute them to the public for a considerable sum of money; she organised collections of every kind and in general displayed undeniable business talent and great perseverance in converting the feelings of the educated public into hard cash. In addition, she had the satisfaction

"of seeing the greatest men of Germany, such as Adolf Stahr, meeting daily in her own little room".

The climax of this whole Siegwart mania, however, was to be reached at the Assizes in Cologne where Gottfried made a guest appearance early in 1850. This was the trial resulting from the attempted uprising in Siegburg and Kinkel was brought to Cologne for the occasion. As Gottfried's diaries play such a prominent part in this sketch, it will be appropriate if we insert here an excerpt from the diary of an eyewitness.

"Kinkel's wife visited him in gaol. She welcomed him from behind the grill with verses; he replied, I understand, in hexameters; whereupon they both sank to their knees before each other and the prison inspector, an old sergeant-major, who was standing by, wondered whether he was dealing with madmen or clowns. When asked later by the Chief Prosecutor about the content of their conversation he declared that the couple had indeed spoken German but that he had not been able to make head or tail of it. Whereupon Frau Kinkel is supposed to have retorted that a man who was so wholly innocent of art and literature should not be made an inspector."

Faced with the jury, Kinkel wriggled his way out by acting the pure tear-jerker, the poetaster of the Siegwart period of the vintage of *Werther's Sufferings*.

" 'Members of the Court, Gentlemen of the Jury—the blue eyes of my children—the green waters of the Rhine—it is no dishonour to shake the hand of the proletarian—the pallid lips of the prisoner—the peaceful air of one's home'—and similar muck, that was what the whole famous speech amounted to and the public, the jury, the prosecution and even the police shed their bitterest tears and the trial closed with a unanimous acquittal and a no less unanimous weeping and wailing. Kinkel is doubtless a dear, good man but he is also a repulsive mixture of religious, political and literary reminiscences."

It's enough to make you sick.

Fortunately this period of misery was soon terminated by the romantic liberation of Kinkel from Spandau gaol. His liberation was a re-enactment of the story of Richard Lionheart and Blondel,[212] with the difference that this time it was Blondel who was in prison while Lionheart played on the barrel-organ outside and that Blondel was an ordinary musichall minstrel and Lionheart basically little more than a rabbit. Lionheart was in fact the student Schurz from the Maybug Club, a little intriguer with great ambitions and limited achievements who was however intelligent enough to have seen through the "German Lamartine"! Not long after the escape student Schurz declared in Paris that he knew very well that Kinkel, of whom he was making use, was no *lumen mundi*, whereas he, Schurz, and none other was destined to be the future president of the German Republic. This manykin, one of those students "in brown jackets and pale-blue overcoats" whom Gottfried had once followed with his gloomily flashing eyes, succeeded in freeing Kinkel at the cost of sacrificing some poor devil of a warder, who is now doing time elevated by the feeling of being a martyr for freedom—the freedom of Gottfried Kinkel.

> Karl Marx and Frederick Engels,
> "Heroes of the Exile"
>
> Marx/Engels, *Werke*, Bd. 8, 1969,
> pp. 235, 261-64.

Freiligrath

1

[Editorial Statement Concerning the Re-appearance of the *Neue Rheinische Zeitung*][213]

Due to the interest shown, particularly in Cologne, *for the preservation of the* Neue Rheinische Zeitung, *we have been able to overcome the* financial *difficulties brought about by the state of siege and to let the paper re-appear. The editorial board remains the same.* Ferdinand Freiligrath *has newly joined it.*

Karl Marx
Editor-in-Chief of the Neue Rheinische Zeitung

> Marx and Engels, *Collected Works*,
> Vol. 7, Moscow, 1976, p. 458

2

Since we have just been talking of poems, we should like to say a few words about the six instigations to revolution which our Freiligrath issued under the title *Ça ira*, Herisau, 1846. The first of them is a German *Marseillaise* and sings of a "bold pirate", which "in Austria, just as in Prussia, is called revolution". The following request is addressed to this ship, which flies its own flag and represents an important reinforcement to the famous German fleet *in partibus infidelium*.[214]

> Gainst silver fleets of gains ill-gotten
> Bravely point the cannon's maw.
> On the ocean's rotting floor,
> May the fruits of greed go rotten. [p. 9.]

Incidentally, the whole song is written in such an easy-going mood that, in spite of the metre, it is best sung to the tune: "Get up, you sailors, the anchor to weigh."[a]

Most characteristic is the poem "Wie man's macht"[b], that is to say: how Freiligrath makes a revolution. Bad times have set in, people are hungry and go about in rags: "How can they obtain bread and clothes?" In this situation an "audacious fellow" comes forward who knows what to do. He leads the whole crowd to the stores of the militia and distributes the uniforms found there, which are at once put on. The crowd also takes hold of the rifles "as an experiment" and considers that "it would be fun" to take them as well. At that moment it occurs to our "audacious fellow" that this "joke with the clothes might perhaps even be called rebellion, house-breaking and robbery", and so one would have "to be ready to fight for one's clothes". And so helmets, sabres and cartridge belts are also taken and a beggar's sack hoisted as a flag. In this way they come into the streets. Then the "royal troops" make their appearance, the general gives the order to fire, but the soldiers joyously embrace the dressed-up militia. And since they have now got under way, they advance on the capital, also for "fun", find support there and thus as a result of a "joke over clothing": "Tumbling down comes throne and crown, the kingdom trembles on its base" and "triumphantly the people raise their long down-

---

[a] From Wilhelm Gerhard's poem "Matrose" ("Sailor")—*Ed.*
[b] "How It Is Done".—*Ed.*

trodden heads." Everything happens so rapidly and smoothly that during the whole procedure surely not a single member of the "proletarian battalion" finds that his pipe has gone out. One must admit that nowhere are revolutions accomplished more merrily and with greater ease than in the head of our Freiligrath. In truth it requires all the black-galled hypochondria of the *Allgemeine Preussische-Zeitung* to detect high treason in such an innocent, idyllic excursion.

Frederick Engels, "The True Socialists"

Marx and Engels, *Collected Works*,
Vol. 5, Moscow, 1975,
pp. 569-70

3

Moorish Prince,[215]

Enclosed is a letter from Ebner.

Today I also received another letter from Weydemeyer. Among other things he writes:

"A few days ago a delegate arrived from the London Agitation Union[216] to oppose the Kinkel loans. These people probably imagine that here in America, everybody is split into pro-Kinkel and anti-Kinkel factions, because a handful of fugitives have made much ado about nothing. The Kossuth sensation long ago made Kinkel a forgotten man and the few thousand dollars which he collects are not in fact worth all the fuss.

"I can in any case look after the sale of the *Revue* for you here. A few more of Freiligrath's new poems could also be accommodated here."

After W[eydemeyer] has given us another push he writes:

"But first and foremost a Freiligrath poem: that is the greatest attraction."

Take this to heart and concoct a New Year song to the New World. Under the present circumstances I believe it is really easier to write in verse than in prose, be it heavy or light-hearted. Incidentally, if you ever attempt to turn the humour that is peculiar to your African majesty in private life into artistic form, I am certain you would play a role in this genre too, for, as your wife has rightly noted, you are a sly one underneath.

Marx to Ferdinand Freiligrath,
December 27, 1851

Marx/Engels, *Werke*, Bd. 27, 1965, S. 597

4

On the other hand, I enclose a poem and a private letter from Freiligrath. I now reguest you to do the following: 1. Have the poem printed properly with reasonable spacing between the stanzas. Do not try to save space. Poems lose a great deal if they are printed in a cramped and conglomerate fashion. 2. Write Freiligrath a friendly letter. You do not have to be too sparing with compliments, for all poets, even the best ones, are *plus au moins*[a] *courtisanes* and *il faut les cajoler, pour les faire chanter*.[b] Our F[reiligrath] is the most amiable, unassuming man in private life, who beneath his real *bonhomie* conceals *un esprit très fin et très railleur*;[c] his emotion is "truthful" and does not make him "uncritical" and "superstitious". He is a genuine revolutionary and an honest man through and through—and this can be said of few men. Nevertheless, whatever kind of *homme* he is, the poet needs praise and admiration. I believe that the genre itself requires this. I am telling you all this simply to point out that in your correspondence with Frei-

---

[a] More or less.—*Ed.*
[b] One must cajole them to make them sing.—*Ed.*
[c] An extremely keen and scornful mind.—*Ed.*

ligrath, you should not forget the difference between the "poet" and the "critic".

Marx to Joseph Weydemeyer,
January 16, 1852
Marx/Engels, *Werke*, Bd. 28, 1963,
S. 475

5

I am downright annoyed by this whole Freiligrath business. It is always the same old story with this belletrist rabble: they for ever want to be lauded to the skies by the newspapers and have their names in the public eye. The most wretched verse they turn out is more important to them than the greatest event in history. As this cannot be brought about without a coterie organisation, it is natural that this becomes the principal requirement and, unfortunately, we unlucky Communists are quite unsuited to this. Even worse, we know this whole fraud, scorn this organisation *du succès*[a] and have an almost criminal aversion to becoming popular figures. If such a poet for this reason feels uneasy in such a party, it is indeed a sign of extreme narrow-mindedness, for he has absolutely none of the competition which he is sure to meet everywhere else; and he shows even greater narrow-mindedness, if he throws himself into the arms of a group where, right from the beginning, he has to face the competition of Kinkel. *Mais que voules-vous?*[b] For his very existence the poet needs incense, a great deal of incense....

It must be added that over the years the noble Ferdinand's flow of poetry has dried up and the little that he still manages to squeeze out of his cranium is ignominiously bad. Hence one has to resort to various dodges, with complete works, etc., which cannot be done every day. So, if one is not

---

[a] Of success.—*Ed.*
[b] But what can you do?—*Ed.*

to be forgotten, advertising becomes more necessary with every passing day. Who in fact spoke of Freiligrath from 1849 to 1858? No one. Only Bettziech has rediscovered this classic, who had been forgotten to such an extent that he was only used as a Christmas or birthday present, and who already figured in the history of literature, rather than in literature itself. The only one to blame for this was naturally Karl Marx with his "breathing". But once Freiligrath is warmed through again by the incense of *Gartenlaube*,[a] you will see what sort of poetry he will spout forth!

What a petty, wretched, miserable business with these poets! This is why I praise Siebel. He is a really bad poet, of course, but he knows that he is a humbug through and through and desires only that he be given access to the advertising trade as a necessary *procédé*[b] of the times, for without this he would be nothing.

> Engels to Jenny Marx,
> December 22, 1859
>
> Marx/Engels, *Werke*, Bd. 29, 1967, S. 637

6

The family poet Freiligrath amused me greatly with his "Räuber" and "Korsar"—Vienna man.

> Marx to Engels,
> July 17, 1869
>
> Marx/Engels, *Werke*, Bd. 32, 1965, S. 339

---

[a] Arbour.—*Ed.*
[b] Occupation.—*Ed.*

7

Freiligrath: "Hurrah! Germania!" Neither "god" nor the "Gaul" are missing from this laboriously long-winded song.

> I'd rather be a kitten and cry miaow
> Than such a rhyming-balled-monger![247]

Marx to Engels,
August 22, 1870

Marx/Engels, *Werke*, Bd. 33, 1966, S. 47

8

What have you to say about the family poet Freiligrath? Even historical catastrophes such as the present one[218] merely serve him for the glorification of his own brats. What is more, the volunteer "medical orderly" is thereby turned into a "surgeon" for the English.

Marx to Engels,
September 2, 1870

Marx/Engels, *Werke*, Bd. 33, 1966, S. 50

9

The noble poet Freiligrath is at the moment staying here at his daughters'. He does not dare to show himself to me. The 60,000 talers which the German Philistine gave him[219] must be worked off by composing Tyrtaian songs like: "Germania, You Proud Woman",[220] etc.

Marx to Sigfrid Meyer,
January 21, 1871

Marx/Engels, *Werke*, Bd. 33, 1966, S. 173

Weerth

"Song of the Apprentices" by Georg Weerth (1846)

> At the time when the cherries blossomed,
> In Frankfurt we did stay.
> At the time when the cherries blossomed,
> In that city we did stay.
>
> Up spake mine host, the landlord:
> "Your coats are frayed and worn."
> "Look here, you lousy landlord,
> That's none of your concern.
>
> "Now give us of your wine,
> And give us of your beer,
> And with the beer and wine,
> Bring us a roast in here."
>
> The cock crows in the cock-stop,
> Out comes a goodly flow,
> And in our mouths it tastes
> Like urinatio.
>
> And then he brought a hare
> In parsley leaves bedight,
> And at this poor dead hare
> We all of us took fright.
>
> And when we were in bed,
> Our nightly prayers reciting,
> Early and late in bed
> The bed-bugs kept on biting.
>
> It happened once in Frankfurt,
> That town so fine and fair,
> That knows who did once dwell
> And who did suffer there.[a]

I rediscovered this poem by our friend Weerth in Marx's effects. Weerth, the German proletariat's first and most important poet, the son of Rhineland parents, was born in Det-

---

[a] Translated into English by Alex Miller.—*Ed.*

mold, where his father was church superintendent. In 1843, when I was in Manchester, Weerth came to Bradford as an agent for his German firm, and we spent many a pleasant Sunday together. In 1845, when Marx and I lived in Brussels, Weerth took over the continental agency for his firm and arranged things so that he, too, could make Brussels his headquarters. After the revolution of March 1848, we all met up in Cologne to found the *Neue Rheinische Zeitung*. Weerth took on the feuilleton, and I don't think any other paper ever had one as hard-hitting and funny. "Leben und Thaten des berühmten Ritters Schnapphahnski", describing the adventures of Prince Lichnowski, whom Heine had given that name in "Atta Troll", was one of his most important contributions. The facts were all true; as to how we got hold of them, well about that another time, perhaps. The collected Schnapphahnski feuilletons were published in book form by Hoffmann and Campe in 1849, and they are still very amusing today. However, on September 18, 1848 Schnapphahnski-Lichnowski rode out with the Prussian General von Auerswald (also a member of parliament) to spy on peasant detachments on their way to join the fighters on the Frankfurt barricades. Both he and Auerswald were, deservedly, put to death by the peasants as spies, and so the German Imperial Administration charged Weerth with insulting the dead Lichnowski. Weerth, who had left for England long ago, was sentenced to three months imprisonment, long after reaction had put an end to the *Neue Rheinische Zeitung*. He later actually served those three months, because his business required him to visit Germany from time to time.

In 1850-51, he travelled to Spain for another Bradford firm, then to the West Indies, and across almost the whole of South America. After a short visit to Europe, he returned to his beloved West Indies, where he did not want to deny himself the pleasure of taking a look at the real original of Louis-Napoleon III, the negro king Soulouque in Haiti. However, as W. Wolff wrote to Marx on August 28, 1856, he had "difficulties with the quarantine authorities and had to give up the project. He had picked up (yellow) fever on the tour, which he carried with him to Havana. He lay down, a brain fever took hold too, and, on the 30th of July, our Weerth died in Havana."

I called him the German proletariat's first and *most important* poet. Indeed his socialist and political poems are far superior to Freiligrath's in originality and wit, and especially in fervent emotion. He often used the Heine forms, but only to invest them with an entirely original, independent content. Moreover, he differed from most other poets in that he was quite unconcerned about his poems once written. Having sent a copy to Marx or me, he let his verses lie and it was often hard to persuade him to get them printed. Only during the publication of the *Neue Rheinische Zeitung* was it different. The following extract from a letter of Weerth to Marx from Hamburg, April 28, 1851, shows why:

"Incidentally, I hope to see you again in London at the beginning of July, because I can't stand these grasshoppers in Hamburg any longer. Here, I am threatened by a truly splendid existence, and I am terrified of it. Everyone else would grab at it with both hands. However, I am too old to become a philistine, and across the sea lies the distant West. ...

"I have written all sorts of things lately, but have finished nothing, because I see no purpose, no goal in all this writing. When you write something on political economy, that has sense and reason. But I? Weak jokes and feeble sallies to coax an idiotic smile onto these ugly fatherland faces—honestly, I know of nothing more contemptible. My activities as a writer definitely ended with the *Neue Rheinische Zeitung*.

"I must admit that, just as I regret that I have lost the last three years for nothing, surely for nothing, it delights me when I remember our life in Cologne. We did *not* compromise ourselves! That is the most important thing. Not since Frederick the Great has anybody treated the German people so completely *en canaille*[a] as did the *Neue Rheinische Zeitung*.

"And though I do not say that this was my achievement, I was there....

"O Portugal, O Spain!" (Weerth had just come from there.) "Had we but your lovely skies, your wine, your oranges and myrtles! But no, not even that. Nothing but rain, long noses and smoked meat.

"With rain and a long nose, yours,
G. Weerth."

---

[a] Ungraciously.—*Ed.*

Where Weerth was master, where he surpassed Heine (because he was healthier and more genuine) and where he is second only to Goethe in German, is in his expression of natural robust sensuousness and physical lust. Many a reader of the *Sozialdemokrat*[221] would be appalled, were I to reprint some of the feuilletons from the *Neue Rheinische Zeitung*. I would not dream of doing this, but I cannot hold back the comment that the moment must also come for the German Socialists openly to cast aside this last German philistine prejudice. This hypocritical petty-bourgeois prudery is, in any case, no more than a cover for furtive whoring. Reading Freiligrath's poems, for instance, one might well believe that people simply have no sex organs. Yet no one got more pleasure from a dirty joke on the quiet than this same Freiligrath, who was so ultra-proper in his poetry. It is really time for the German workers, at least, to get used to speaking of things that they do daily or nightly, of natural, indispensable and exceptionally enjoyable things, as frankly as the Romance people do, as Homer did, and Plato, Horace and Juvenal, the Old Testament and the *Neue Rheinische Zeitung*.

Incidentally, Weerth also wrote less shocking pieces, and I shall take the liberty of sending some of these to the *Sozialdemokrat*'s feuilleton from time to time.

Frederick Engels, " 'Song of the Apprentices' by Georg Weerth"

Marx/Engels, *Werke*, Bd. 21, 1962, S. 5-8

Outstanding Personalities in the Working-Class Movement. Johann Philipp Becker

1

Dear Bebel,

I am writing this letter on account of my conversation with old Johann Philipp Becker, who stayed with me here for ten days and will now have returned to Geneva via Paris (where he unexpectedly found his daughter dead!). I was very pleased to see the old giant again; although he has aged physically, he is still cheerful and in good fighting spirit. He is a figure out of our Rhine-Frankish saga personified in the *Nibelungenlied*—Volker the Fiddler, his very self.

I asked him years ago to write down his reminiscences and experiences, and now he tells me that you and others also encouraged him in this, that he himself longed to do so and even began to write on several occasions, but met little real encouragement with fragmentary publication (such was the case with the *Neue Welt*,[222] to which he sent several quite splendid things some years ago; these, however, were found to be not sufficiently "novelistic", as Liebknecht informed him through Motteler).

Engels to August Bebel,
October 8, 1886

Marx/Engels, *Werke*, Bd. 36, 1967,
S. 541

2

Becker was a man of rare character. A single word gives a complete description of him; that word is *healthy*: he was healthy in both body and mind to the very last. A handsome man of powerful build and tremendous physical strength, thanks to his happy disposition and healthy activity he developed his unschooled but in no way uncultured mind just as harmoniously as his body. He was one of the few men who need only follow their own natural instincts to go the right way. This is why it was so easy for him to keep step with each development of the revolutionary movement and to stand just as keenly in the front ranks in his seventy-eighth year as in his eighteenth. The boy who in 1814 played with the Cossacks passing through his country and in 1820 saw the execution of Sand, Kotzebue's assassin, developed ever further from the indefinite oppositionist of the twenties and was still at the peak of the movement in 1886. Nor was he a gloomy, high-principled ignoramus like the majority of "serious" republicans of 1848, but a true son of the cheerful Pfalz, a man with a zest for life who loved wine, women and song like anyone. Having grown up in the country of the *Nibelungenlied* near Worms, he appeared even in his latter years like a character from our old epic poem: cheerfully and mockingly hailing the enemy between sword thrusts and composing folk songs when there was nothing to hit—thus and only thus must he have appeared, Volker the Fiddler!

> Frederick Engels, "Johann Philipp Becker"
>
> Marx/Engels, *Werke*, Bd. 21, 1962 S. 323-24

3

I was extraordinarily taken with your two short poems on Leibniz and "Alles Wurst"; it would be good if you enclosed them (should you agree to my proposal) in the first letter to Weydemeyer.

> Marx to Johann Philipp Becker, April 9, 1860
>
> Marx/Engels, *Werke*, Bd. 30, 1964, S. 527

Russian Literature

The Russian Language

1

I don't know whether I told you that at the beginning of 1870 I began to study Russian, which I now read fairly fluently. This came about because Flerovsky's very important work on *The Condition of the Working Class* (especially the peasants) *in Russia*, had been sent to me from Petersburg and because I also wanted to familiarise myself with the excellent economic works of Chernyshevsky (who was as a reward sentenced to the Siberian mines where he has been serving time for the past seven years). The result was worth the effort that a man of my age must make to master a language differing so greatly from the classical, Germanic, and Romance language groups. The intellectual movement now taking place in Russia testifies to the fact that fermentation is going on deep below the surface. Minds are always connected by invisible threads with the body of the people.

> Marx to Sigfrid Meyer,
> January 21, 1871
>
> Marx and Engels, *Selected Correspondence*, Moscow, 1975, p. 241

2

Many strange phenomena in the Russian movement are explained by the fact that for a long time every Russian work was for the West a book sealed with seven seals, and that it was therefore easy for Bakunin and Co. to conceal their activities, which had long been known to the Russians, from the West.... This has now stopped. Knowledge of the Russian language—a language whose study is richly rewarding both for its own sake, it being the most expressive and rich living language, and on account of the literature which it makes accessible—is no longer such a great rarity, at least among German Social-Democrats.

> Frederick Engels, "Flüchtlingsliteratur"
>
> Marx/Engels, *Werke*, Bd. 18, 1969, S. 544-45

3

I find your translation of my pamphlet excellent.[223] How beautiful the Russian language is! It has all the good points of the German without its horrible coarseness.

> Engels to Vera Zasulich, March 6, 1884
>
> Marx and Engels, *Selected Correspondence*, Moscow, 1975, p. 349

The Lay of Igor's Host

Eichhoff's *Histoire de la langue et de la littérature des Slaves* (Paris 1839) is a very miserable book. Apart from the grammatical part, about which I am unable to judge (I noticed, however, that the Lithuanians and the Letts are declared Slavs. Is this not nonsense?), the rest is for the most part plagiary from Šafařik. The fellow also gives samples from the national poetry of the Slavs in the original with a French translation alongside. Among them I found *The Lay of Igor's Host*. The essence of the poem is a call to the Russian princes to unite, just before the invasion of the Mongolian hordes. One passage is quite strange: *"Voici les jolies filles des Gothes entonnent leurs chants au bord de la Mer*

Noire."ᵃ According to this, the Geths, or Goths, were celebrating the Turkish Polovtsi's victory over the Russians. The entire lay is of a heroic-Christian nature, though the heathen elements are still strongly felt. The Bohemian hero epic *Zaboi* (Samo?) in the collection of heroic poems of the Bohemians,[224] published in German translation by *Hanka and Swoboda*, is on the other hand quite polemical and fanatically anti-German. It is apparently directed against a German captain of Dagobert whom the Bohemians had beaten. But it is just as much a call for vengeance against Christianity as against the Germans who, by the way, are reproached in a very naive poetical form with wanting to force the brave Bohemians to be satisfied with a single wife.

Marx to Engels, March 5, 1856

Marx/Engels, *Werke*, Bd. 29, 1967,
S. 23

Lomonosov
Slavic Languages and Philology[225]

Россійская антологія Specimens of the Russian Poets translated by J. Bowring. Second ed[ition]. London. 1821.

> Vam, vam pletut Charity
> Bezsmertnyje věncy!
> Ja vami zděs vkušaju
> Vostorgi Pierid,
> I v radosti vzyvaju
> O Muzy! ja Pilt!ᵇ
>
> Batjuskov

ᵃ See the pretty maidens of the Goths singing their songs on the shores of the Black Sea.—*Ed.*

ᵇ Heavenly choir! the graces twine
O'er you garlands all divine;
And with you the joys I drink,
Sparkling round Pierian brink,
While I sing in raptured glory,
"Ed io anche son pittore".

Mikhail Vasilyevich Lomonosov was born in Kholmogory in 1711. He was the son of a sailor. He studied in Zakonospasskaya School. In 1734[a] he entered the Imperial Academy, and in 1736 was sent to Germany as a student; then he became Professor of Chemistry in St. Petersburg; in 1751[b] he was made Member of the Academy, and in 1760 appointed Director of the Academical Gymnasium and of the University He died in 1765. Complete collection of works, published by the Petersburg Academy, third edition, 1804.

Kratkij Lětopisec (Short Russian Annals).
Drevněja Ross. Istorija—up to 1054 B.C.
Rossijskaja Grammatika.
Kratkoje Rukovodstvo k krasnorěčiju (Rhetoric).
Pis'mo ob pravilach Ross. Stichotvorstva.
Predislovie ob pol'zě knig cěrkovnych.
Slovo pochval'noje (éloge) Impě Jelisavetě I.
Do imperatoru Petru Velikomu.
Slovo o pol'zě chimiji (on the use of chemistry).
Do o javlenijech vozdušnych ot električeskoï sily proizchoděščich (on atmospheric phenomena caused by electric power).
Do o proizchoždenija světa, novuju teoriju o cvětach predstavlejuščeje (on the origin of light, a new theory of colours).
Do o roždeniju Metallov ot trěsenijá zemli (on changes produced in metals by earthquakes).
Rozuždenije o bolšej točnosti morskavo puta.
Javlenije Venery na Solnce.
Programma sočinennaja pri(?) načalě čtenije iz jasěnije Fiziki (programme, introductory to lectures in physics).
Opisanije v načalě 1744 g. jevivšejasja Komety.
Pervyje Oznovanie Metallurgiji.

---

[a] An inexactitude in Bowring: not in 1734 but in 1736.—*Ed.*
[b] Bowring made a mistake: it should be 1745.—*Ed.*

Šestnadzat Pisem k J. J. Šuvalovu.
Poems: Piotr Velikij, epic.
 Tamira i Selim, tragedy.
 Pis'mo o pol'zě stekla (poetical epistle on the merits of glass) (a French prose translation, Paris, 1800).
(Lomonosov)[a]
Oda na sčastije (ode to happiness).
Vančannaja nadežda Rossijskavo Imperii.
 Garlanded Hope, etc., translated into German by Prof. Junker.
Eleven spiritual hymns; encomiastic odes; 49 inscriptions; description of a firework; translations and imitations of Anacreon, etc., also translation of a dialogue of the dead by Lucian[b].

Frederick Engels, "Notes on Lomonosov"
Voprosy Filosofii, 1950, No. 3, p. 122

Derzhavin

About eighty years ago when the victorious armies of Catherine II were severing from Turkey province after province, prior to their transformation into what is now called South Russia, the poet Derzhavin, in one of the bursts of lyrical enthusiasm in which he was wont to celebrate the glories, if not the virtues of that Empress, and the destined grandeur of her empire, uttered a memorable couplet in which we may

---

[a] This concludes the first section on Lomonosov.—*Ed.*
[b] The reference is to the excerpts from Lucian's "Dialogues in the Realms of Death" translated by Lomonosov.—*Ed.*

still find condensed the scornful boldness and self-reliance of the Czarian policy:

> "And what to thee, O Russ, is any ally?
> Advance and the whole Universe is thine!"[226]

Frederick Engels, "The War on the Danube"

Written in English

New York Daily Tribune, July 25, 1854

Pushkin

Very interesting are your notes on the apparent contradiction that, with you, a good harvest does *not* necessarily mean a lowering of the price of corn. When we study the real economic relations in various countries and at various stages of civilisation, how singularly erroneous and deficient appear the rationalistic generalisations of the 18th century—good old Adam Smith who took the conditions of Edinburgh and the Lothians as the normal ones, of the universe! Well, Pushkin already knew that:

> ... и почему
> Не нужно золота ему,
> Когда простой продукт имеет.
> Отец понять его не мог
> И земли отдавал в залог. [a]

Engels to Nikolai Danielson, October 29-31, 1891

Marx and Engels, *Selected Correspondence*, Moscow, 1975, p. 413

---

[a] Of gold what has he
              any use
Whose wealth consists
              of nature's produce?
His son the father failed to understand
And mortgaged every acre of his land.[227]

Chernyshevsky and Dobrolyubov

1

A country that has produced two writers of the stature of Dobrolyubov and Chernyshevsky, two socialist Lessings, will not go down simply because it gives birth all at once to a humbug like Bakunin and a few green students who, with big words, puff themselves up like frogs and finally devour each other. Indeed, among the younger generation of Russians, too, we know people of excellent. theoretical and practical ability and great energy, who surpass the French and the English, by dint of their grasp of languages, in terms of intimate knowledge of the movement in different countries, and the Germans in worldly cleverness. Those Russians who understand the workers' movement and participate in it can only consider the fact that they have been absolved from responsibility for the Bakuninist villainous tricks as a service rendered to them.

Frederick Engels, "Flüchtlingsliteratur"
Marx/Engels, *Werke*, Bd. 18, 1969, S. 540

2

Are you not being somewhat unjust to your fellow-countrymen? The two of us, Marx and I, had no grounds for complaint against them. If certain schools were more notable for their revolutionary ardour than for their scientific study, if there was and still is a certain groping here and there, on the other hand a critical spirit has evinced itself there and a devotion to research even in pure theory worthy of the nation that produced a Dobrolyubov and a Chernyshevsky. I am not speaking only of active revolutionary Socialists but also of the historical and critical school in Russian literature, which is greatly surpassing anything produced in this line in Germany or France by official historical science.

> Engels to Eugenie Papritz,
> June 26, 1884
>
> Marx and Engels, *Selected Correspondence*, Moscow, 1975, p. 354

8

The writings of Ehrlieb I am partly acquainted with. I compare him as a writer to Lessing and Diderot.

> Marx to Nikolai Danielson,
> November 9, 1871
>
> Written in English
> Marx/Engels, *Werke*, Bd. 33, 1966, S. 311

Chernyshevsky as a Scholar and Critic

Men who still claimed some scientific standing and aspired to be something more than mere sophists and sycophants of the ruling-classes, tried to harmonise the Political Economy of capital with the claims, no longer to be ignored, of the proletariat. Hence a shallow syncretism, of which John Stuart Mill is the best representative. It is a declaration of bankruptcy by bourgeois economy, an event on which the great Russian scholar and critic, N. Tschernyschewsky, has thrown the light of a master mind in his "Outlines of Political Economy according to Mill".

> Karl Marx, *Capital*, Vol. 1,
> Moscow, 1974, p. 25

Chernyshevsky and the Russian Village Commune

1

In the Afterword to the second German edition of *Kapital* ... I speak of a "great Russian scholar and critic",[a] with the high consideration he deserves. In his remarkable articles this writer has dealt with the question whether, as her liberal economists maintain, Russia must begin by destroying the village commune in order to pass to the capitalist regime, or whether, on the contrary, she can, without experiencing the tortures of this regime, appropriate all its fruits by developing the historical conditions specifically her own. He pronounces in favour of this latter solution.

> Marx to the Editorial Board of the *Otechestvenniye Zapiski*
>
> Marx and Engels, *Selected Correspondence*, Moscow, 1975, p. 292

2

But the Russian village commune had caught the attention and won the recognition of men who were head and shoulders above the Herzens and the Tkachovs. Among them was Nikolai Chernyshevsky, that great thinker to whom Russia owes so much and whose slow destruction by long years of exile among the Yakuts in Siberia will forever remain an ignominious stain on the memory of Alexander II, the "Emancipator".

Because of the intellectual barrier separating Russia from Western Europe, Chernyshevsky had not read any of Marx's works, and by the time *Capital* made its appearance he had long been among the Yakuts in Sredne-Vilyuisk.[228] His spirit-

---

[a] N. G. Chernyshevsky.—*Ed.*

ual development had to proceed entirely in the conditions created by that intellectual barrier. What the tsarist censorship did not let through was virtually or altogether non-existent as far as Russia was concerned, so that if we do find a weak spot in his writings here and there, and some narrowness of horizon, the amazing thing is that there is not much more of it.

Chernyshevsky also saw the Russian village commune as a means of transition from the contemporary social form to a new stage of development, which is, on the one hand, higher than the Russian village commune, and on the other, higher than West-European capitalist society, with its class antagonisms. That Russia had such a means, while the West had none, was, in Chernyshevsky's view, Russia's advantage.

"The introduction of a better order of things is greatly hindered in Western Europe by the boundless extension of the rights of the individual ... it is not easy to renounce even a negligible portion of what one is used to enjoying, and in the West the individual is used to unlimited private rights. The usefulness and necessity of mutual concessions can be learned only by bitter experience and prolonged thought. In the West, a better system of economic relations is bound up with sacrifices, and that is why it is difficult to establish. It runs counter to the habits of the English and French peasants." But "what seems a utopia in one country exists as a fact in another ... habits which the Englishman and the Frenchman find immensely difficult to introduce into their national life exist in fact in the national life of the Russians.... The order of things for which the West is now striving by such a difficult and long road still exists in our country in the mighty national customs of our village life.... We see what deplorable consequences resulted in the West from the loss of communal land tenure and how difficult it is to give back to the Western peoples what they have lost. The example of the West must not be lost on us." (Chernyshevsky, *Works*, Geneva Edition, Vol. 5, pp. 16-19; quoted from Plekhanov, *Nashi raznoglasia*,[a] Geneva, 1885).

He says the following about the Urals Cossacks, who still had a system of cultivation of land in common, with a subsequent division of the product among the individual families:

---

[a] *Our Differences.* See Georgi Plekhanov, *Selected Philosophical Works*, Vol. I, Moscow, 1974, p. 135.—*Ed.*

"if the people of the Urals live under their present system to see machines introduced into corn-growing, they will be very glad of the retention among them of a system which allows the use of machines that require big-scale farming embracing hundreds of dessiatins" (Ibidem, p. 131a).

What should be borne in mind, though, is that these Urals Cossacks, with their communal cultivation of land, which is being safeguarded out of military considerations (after all, we too have barrack-room communism over here), stand quite apart in Russia, almost like our own household communities [*Gehöferschaften*] on the Moselle, with their periodic redistributions. And if the present order should remain intact until the introduction of machinery, it is not they but the Russian military fisc, whose servants they are, that will reap the benefits.

At any rate, the fact is this: whereas in Western Europe capitalist society is disintegrating and is threatened with destruction by the inescapable contradictions of its own development, in Russia almost one half of the cultivated land remains in the hands of the village communes as common property. If the resolution of antagonisms in the West through a new organisation of society implies, as a necessary condition, the transfer of all the means of production, and consequently of the land as well, into the ownership of society as a whole, what is the relation between this common property, which is still to be set up in the West, and the communal property, which already, or rather still, exists in Russia? Could it serve as a starting point for a popular movement which, leaping over the entire capitalist period, would instantly transform Russian peasant communism into a modern socialist communal property in all the means of production, enriching it with all the technical achievements of the capitalist era? Or as Marx formulated one of Chernyshevsky's ideas in a letter quoted below:[229] "Must Russia start, as her liberal economists wish, by destroying the commune so as to go over to the capitalist system, or can she, without undergoing the torments of

---

[a] G. Plekhanov, op. cit., p. 134.—*Ed.*

the system, secure all its fruits, while developing her own historical endowments?"

The bald statement of the question shows where the answer lies. The Russian community has been in existence for centuries without once producing within itself an impulse to transmute itself into a higher form of communal property, just as has been the case with the German mark, the Celtic clan, and the Indian and other communities with their primitive communistic order. In the course of time and under the influence of the production and exchange of commodities between families and individuals, which surrounded and developed inside them, and which gradually permeated them, they all came to shed more and more of their communistic character, falling apart into communities of landowners independent of each other. Consequently, if it is at all possible to ask whether or not a different or better future is in store for the Russian commune, the reason does not lie within itself, but solely in the fact that in one of the European countries it has retained a relative viability until a time when, in Western Europe, not only commodity production in general, but even its highest and final form—capitalist production—has run into contradiction with the productive forces it has itself created, when it has shown itself incapable of managing these forces, and when it is being ruined by these internal contradictions and the corresponding class conflicts. From this alone it follows that the initiative for such an eventual transformation of the Russian commune can never come from itself but only from the industrial proletariat of the West. A victory by the West-European proletariat over the bourgeoisie and the consequent substitution of a socially managed economy for the capitalist production—this is the necessary precondition for the raising of the Russian commune to the same stage of development.

> Frederick Engels, "Afterword to the Work 'On Social Relations in Russia'"
>
> Marx and Engels, *Selected Works*, Vol. 2, Moscow, 1973, pp. 399-402

Chernyshevsky as a Revolutionary

1

The second article[230] is entitled: "A Glance at the Former and Present Concept of the Cause". We have just seen Bakunin and Nechayev threatening the Russian organ of the International abroad.[231] In this article, we shall see them descend on Chernyshevsky, the man who, in Russia, had done most to draw into the socialist movement the student youth whom they claimed to represent.

Karl Marx and Frederick Engels,
The Alliance of Socialist Democracy and the International Workers' Association
The Hague Congress of the First International, Moscow, 1976, pp. 564-65

2

Chernyshevsky, I learnt from L[opatin], was sentenced in 1864 to eight years' *travaux forcés*[a] in the Siberian mines; so he has another two years to serve. The first court was decent enough to declare that there was absolutely *nothing* against him and that the alleged secret conspiratorial letters were obvious *forgeries* (which, indeed, they were). But, by order of the Tsar, the *Senate* overruled this judgment and sent the cunning man, who is "so skilful", as the sentence puts it, "that he keeps his works in a legally invulnerable form and yet openly pours out poison in them", to Siberia. *Voilà la justice russe.*[b]

Flerovsky is in a better position. He is simply in administrative exile in some miserable little place between Moscow and St. Petersburg.

Marx to Engels,
July 5, 1870
Marx/Engels, *Werke*, Bd. 32, 1965, S. 521.

---

[a] Hard labour.—*Ed.*
[b] That is Russian justice for you!—*Ed.*

3

I wish to print something about Chernyshevsky's life and personality[232] so as to arouse sympathy with him in the West. But for this I require some data.

Marx to Nikolai Danielson,
December 12, 1872
Marx/Engels, *Werke*, Bd. 33, 1966, S. 549

4

As far as Chernyshevsky is concerned, whether I touch on just the scientific, or also the other side of his activity, depends entirely on you.[233] In the second volume of my work[234] he will, of course, figure merely as an economist. I am acquainted with a major part of his works.

Marx to Nikolai Danielson,
January 18, 1873
Marx/Engels, *Werke*, Bd. 33, 1966, S. 559

5

We had heard here of the death of Н.Г.Ч.,[a] and with much sorrow and sympathy. But perhaps it is better so.

Engels to Nikolai Danielson,
June 10, 1890
Written in English
Published according to the photocopy

---

[a] N. G. Chernyshevsky.—*Ed.*

Shchedrin

I thank you very much for the Сказки[a] of Scedrin which I shall take in hand as soon as ever possible; a slight conjunctivitis of the left eye prevents me reading it at present, as the Russian type very much strains my eyesight.

Engels to Nikolai Danielson,
February 19, 1887
Written in English
Published according to the photocopy

Flerovsky

I have read the first 150 pages of *Flerovsky*'s book.[235] (They are taken up by Siberia, North Russia and Astrakhan.) This is the first work to tell the truth about Russian economic conditions. The man is a determined enemy of what he calls "Russian optimism". I never held very rosy views of this communistic Eldorado, Flerovsky however surpasses all expectations. It is indeed odd and certainly a sign of a sudden change that such a thing can be printed in Petersburg.

"We have few proletarians, but the mass of our working class consists of labouring people whose lot is worse than that of any proletarian."[b]

The method of presentation is quite original; at times it reminds one most of Monteil. One can see that the man has travelled around everywhere and seen things for himself. A glowing hatred of landlords, capitalists and officials. No socialist doctrine, no mysticism about the land (although in favour of the communal form of ownership), no nihilistic extravagance. Here and there a certain amount of well-mean-

---

[a] Tales.—*Ed.*

[b] In the letter the quotation is given in Russian.—*Ed.*

ing twaddle, which, however, is suited to the stage of development reached by the people for whom the book is intended. In any case this is the most important book which has appeared since your *Condition of the Working-Class*. The family life of the Russian peasant with the horrible beating to death of wives, vodka and concubines is also well portrayed. It will be very opportune, therefore, if you send me the fantastic fabrications of citizen Herzen.

Marx to Engels,
February 10, 1870

Marx/Engels, *Werke*, Bd. 32, 1965,
S. 437

Revolutionary
and Satirical Folk Poetry
of the Past

Herr Tidmann

I am sending the fellows[236] the little Danish folk song about Tidmann, who was killed by the old man at the Thing for imposing new taxes on the peasants. It is revolutionary, but not punishable nevertheless, and, above all, it is aimed at the feudal gentry, which the newspaper *absolutely must oppose*. I am supplying it with a few appropriate comments.

Engels to Marx,
January 27, 1865

Marx/Engels, *Werke*, Bd. 31, 1965, S. 45

Early one morning, when it was day,
Herr Tidmann dressed beside his bed,
And he put on his shirt so fine.
    That all the Süder people praise.

And he put on his shirt so fine,
His green silk coat did bravely shine,
Buckskin boots he laced on his legs.
    That all the Süder people praise.

Buckskin boots he laced on his legs,
Buckled on gilded spurs so neat,
And went to the Süder district Thing.
    That all the Süder people praise.

He went to the Süder district Thing,
Demanded the tax from each *edeling*,
Seven bushels of rye from each man's plough.
    That all the Süder people praise.

Seven bushels of rye from each man's plough,
One pig in four from the fattening woods —
But then up stood an aged man.
    That all the Süder people praise.

But then up stood an aged man:
"Pay such taxes none of us can.
Before so heavy a tax we pay —"
    That all the Süder people praise.

"Before so heavy a tax we pay,
None from this Thing shall go away.
You Süder peasants, stand in a ring."
    That all the Süder people praise.

"You Süder peasants, stand in a ring,
Herr Tidmann alive shan't leave the Thing."
The old man struck the very first blow.
    That all the Süder people praise.

The old man struck the very first blow,
Down to the ground did Herr Tidmann go.
There lies Herr Tidmann, he streams with blood.
    That all the Süder people praise.

There lies Herr Tidmann, he streams with blood,
But the plough goes free on the black soil,
The pigs go free in the fattening woods.
    That all the Süder people praise.[a]

Frederick Engels, "Herr Tidmann"
(old Danish folk song)

Marx/Engels, *Werke*, Bd. 16, 1968,
S. 33-34

Folk Songs on Stenka Razin

At that time Cossacks lived *on the banks of the Volga* in a separate community. They made their presence felt during the troubled period at the beginning of the 17th century and were involved in the war of the Poles with the Turks.

---

[a] Translated into English by Alex Miller.—*Ed.*

Wladislaw let them go and gave them presents. This *points to the mutual bonds that existed among the Cossacks*. As soon as the *Ukrainian Cossacks* came to the assistance of the Poles, so, too, did Cossacks from the *Volga plains* (20,000 came to the assistance of the Poles against the Turks). Apart from those settled along the Volga, Cossacks set off from the *Don*, the *Yaik* and all the regions of the Russian land for plunder. The *Volga*, the *main trading route*, offered a challenge to their daring. In *1621* they looted a convoy of ships, and this led to the founding of the town of *Chorny Yar*. In *1654*, the Cossacks attacked the Nizhny Yaik Uchug (an *uchug* is a fish weir, a barrier across the river forming a pen for catching fish), which belonged to a certain Guryev, destroyed it and won over his workers to their ranks. *Among the common people there was much sympathy for them*. The Volga over its whole immense expanse was the run of the "thieving Cossacks", whose deeds were sung and who were not regarded among the people as common robbers in the ordinary sense, for they operated on a grand scale. In their own songs they say of themselves: "We are not thieves, not bandits—we are good brave fellows". In the imagination of the people and in their songs (those of the Great Russians included) they are something like the heroes of the Greeks, the Western knights, the *yunaks* of Serbia.

Karl Marx, "Conspectus of Kostomarov's *Revolt of Stenka Razin*"

Published according to the typewritten copy

The Vicar of Bray

> In good King Charles's golden days
> When loyalty no harm meant,
> A zealous high-church man I was,
> And so I got preferment:

To teach my flock I never miss'd,
    Kings are by God appointed,
And damn'd are those that do resist.
    Or touch The Lord's Anointed.
And this is law I will maintain,
    Until my dying day, sir,
That whatsoever king shall reign,
    I'll be the vicar of Bray, sir.

When royal James obtain'd the crown,
    And popery came in fashion,
The penal laws I hooted down,
    And read the Declaration:
The church of Rome I found would fit
    Full well my constitution;
And had become a Jesuit,
    But for the Revolution
    And this is law, &c.

When William was our King declar'd,
    To ease the nation's grievance;
With this new wind about I steer'd,
    And swore to him allegiance:
Old principles I did revoke,
    Set conscience at a distance;
Passive obedience was a joke,
    A jest was non-resistance.
    And this is law, &c.

When gracious Ann became our queen,
    The church of England's glory,
Another face of things was seen,
    And I became a tory:
Occasional conformists base,
    I damn'd their moderation;
And thought the church in danger was,
    By such prevarication.
    And this is law, &c.

When George in pudding-time came o'er,
    And moderate men look'd big, sir,
I turn'd a cat-in-pan once more,
    And so became a whig, sir;

>And thus preferment I procur'd
>>From our new faith's-defender;
>And almost ev'ry day abjur'd
>>The Pope and the Pretender.
>And this is law &c.
>
>Th'illustrious house of Hanover,
>>And Protestant succession;
>To these I do allegiance swear —
>>While they can keep possession:
>For in my faith and loyalty,
>>I never more will falter,
>And George my lawful king shall be —
>>Until the times do alter.
>And this is law I will maintain,
>>Until my dying day, sir,
>That whatsoever king shall reign,
>>I'll be the vicar of Bray, sir![a]

The song given above is probably the only political folk song remaining popular in England for more than a hundred and sixty years. It owes this in great measure also to its wonderful tune, which is still sung widely today.

>Frederick Engels, "The Vicar of Bray"
>
>Marx/Engels, *Werke*, Bd. 19, 1962, pp. 309-11

German Revolutionary Songs

As regards the poems:

"Eine feste Burg ist unser Gott"[b][237] was the Marseillaise of the Peasant War. Triumphant as the words and tune are, one neither can nor should take them that way today. There are other songs of the time in folk-song collections,

---

[a] The English poem is cited from Joseph Ritson, *A Select Collection of English Songs*, in three volumes, 2nd ed., Vol. II, London, 1813, pp. 141-43.—*Ed.*

[b] "A safe stronghold our God is still".—*Ed.*

Des Knaben Wunderhorn,[238] etc., where a few more things may perhaps be found. However, the *Landsknecht* already had a firm grip on our folk poetry even in those times.

Of the foreign songs, I know only the lovely old Danish one about Herr Tidmann, which I translated in 1865 for the Berlin *Social-Demokrat*.

The Chartist songs, and there were many, are now no longer to be had. One of them started:

> Britannia's sons, though slaves you be,
> God your creator made you free;
> To all he life and freedom gave,
> But never, never made a slave.

I can't remember any more.

All that is dead and gone; anyway, the poetry wasn't worth much.

There were two songs around in 1848, both with the same tune.

1. Schleswig-Holstein.[239]
2. The Hecker Song.[240]

> All down along the German Rhine,
> Hecker, your name shall ring the higher.
> Your generous heart, ay, your very eyes
> With faith already us inspire.
> Hecker, man of Germany
> Who would die for Liberty.

I think that is enough. Then the variant:

> Hecker, Struve, Blenker, Zitz and Blum
> Knock off German nobledom!

Generally speaking, the poetry of past revolutions—always excepting the "Marseillaise"—will have little revolutionary effect in later times because, to influence the masses, it must also reflect the popular prejudices of the time—hence all that religious nonsense, even among the Chartists.

Engels to Hermann Schlüter,
May 15, 1885

Marx/Engels, *Werke*, Bd. 36, 1967,
S. 314-15

Weavers' Song[241]

In order to be able to compare the condition of the German workers with the condition of the French and English workers, the "Prussian"[242] would have had to compare the *first form*, the *start*, of the English and French workers' movement with the *German* movement that is *just beginning*. He failed to do so. Consequently, his arguments lead to trivialities, such as that *industry* in Germany is not yet so developed as in England, or that a movement at its start looks different from the movement in its subsequent progress. He wanted to speak about the *specific character* of the German workers' movement, but he has not a word to say on this subject of his.

On the other hand, suppose the "Prussian" were to adopt the correct standpoint. He will find that *not one* of the French and English workers' uprisings had such a *theoretical* and *conscious* character as the uprising of the Silesian weavers.

First of all, recall the *song of the weavers*, that bold *call* to struggle, in which there is not even a mention of hearth and home, factory or district, but in which the proletariat at once, in a striking, sharp, unrestrained and powerful manner, proclaims its opposition to the society of private property. The Silesian uprising *begins* precisely with what the French and English workers' uprisings *end*, with consciousness of the nature of the proletariat.

> Karl Marx, "Critical Marginal Notes on the Article 'The King of Prussia and Social Reform. By a Prussian'"
>
> Marx and Engels, *Collected Works*, Vol. 3, Moscow, 1975, p. 201

Songs of the German Revolution of 1848

1

In short, the German bourgeoisie had no illusions about Prussian kindness. If the idea of Prussian hegemony became popular with them since 1840, it was only because and insofar as the Prussian bourgeoisie, owing to its quicker economic development, assumed the economic and political leadership of the German bourgeoisie, only because and insofar as the Rottecks and Welckers of the old-constitutional South were placed in the shade by the Camphausens, Hansemanns and Mildes of the Prussian North, and the lawyers and professors were placed in the shade by the merchants and manufacturers. Indeed, in the years just preceding 1848, there developed among Prussian liberals, especially on the Rhine, a revolutionary trend that differed substantially from that of the cantonalist liberals of the South. Those days were marked by the appearance of the two best political folk songs since the 16th century, the song about Bürgermeister Tschech and the one about the Baroness von Droste-Fischering, whose wantonness appals the now aged people, who in 1846 gaily sang:

> Has ever man had such hard luck
> As our poor Bürgermeister Tschech,
> He shot at Fatty two paces away
> And yet his bullet went astray!

Frederick Engels, "The Role of Force in History"

Marx and Engels, *Selected Works*, Vol. 3, Moscow, 1973, pp. 390-91

2

Only if the thirty-six thrones fall,
Can the German republic prosper free.
Ruthlessly, brothers, overthrow them all,

> Risking blood, and lives, and property.
> To die for the republic
> Is a fate, lofty and great, is the aim of our courage.

Thus sang the volunteers on the railway when I was on my way to Neustadt to seek out Willich's temporary headquarters.

So from now on to die for the republic was the aim of my courage, or at least was supposed to be. It seemed strange to me to have this new aim. I looked at the volunteers, young, handsome, lively lads. They did not certainly look as if death for the republic was the aim of their courage at the moment.

> Frederick Engels, "German Campaign for the Imperial Constitution"
> Marx/Engels, *Werke*, Bd. 7, 1969, S. 162

Satirical Folk Song Against Louis Bonaparte

Recently, when Bonaparte and his wife were at the Odéon,[243] the students filling the stalls spent the whole evening singing "*Sire de France Boissy*" with special emphasis on certain significant passages. The workers in Paris sing a song that has the refrain:

> He is going away, he is going away,
> The little mustard-vendor.
> He is going away to his native land
> With all his goods and chattels.

The police banned the song so that all might know who this little mustard-vendor was.

> Engels to Marx, February 7, 1856
> Marx/Engels, *Werke*, Bd. 29, 1967, S. 9

Confessions of Marx and Engels

Karl Marx
Confessions[244]

Your favourite virtue	Simplicity
Your favourite virtue in man	Strength
Your favourite virtue in woman	Weakness
Your chief characteristic	Singleness of purpose
Your idea of happiness	To fight
Your idea of misery	Submission
The vice you excuse most	Gullibility
The vice you detest most	Servility
Your aversion	Martin Tupper
Favourite occupation	Book-worming
Poet	Shakespeare, Aeschylus, Goethe
Prose-writer	Diderot
Hero	Spartacus, Kepler
Heroine	Gretchen
Flower	Daphne
Colour	Red
Name	Laura, Jenny
Dish	Fish
Favourite maxim	*Nihil humani a me alienum puto.*
Favourite motto	*De omnibus dubitandum.*

Karl Marx

Written in English

Reminiscences of Marx and Engels, Moscow, 1956, p. 266

Frederick Engels
Confessions[245]

London, beginning of April 1868

Your favourite virtue	jollity
—quality in man	to mind his own business
— in woman	not to mislay things
Chief characteristic	knowing everything by halves
Idea of happiness	Château Margaux 1848.[a]
———misery	to go to a dentist
The vice you excuse	excess of any sort
———detest	cant
Your aversion	affected stuck up woman
The characters you most dislike	Spurgeon[b]
Favourite occupation	chaffing and being chaffed
—Hero	none
—Heroine	too many to name one
Poet	Reineke de Vos,[c] Shakespeare, Ariost, etc.
Prose writer	Goethe, Lessing, Dr. Samelson.[d]
Flower	Blue Bell
Colour	any one not Aniline
Dish	Cold: Salad, hot: Irish Stew
Maxim	not to have any
Motto	take it easy

F. Engels

Written in English
Published according to
the typewritten copy

---

[a] A sort of wine. The date is an allusion to the revolutionary events of 1848.—*Ed.*
[b] A popular Baptist preacher, fanatic.—*Ed.*
[c] Engels refers to Goethe's poem "Reineke Fuchs".—*Ed.*
[d] A German oculist in Manchester, who treated Engels at the time, member of a literary club.—*Ed.*

From Reminiscences of Marx and Engels

From Reminiscences of Marx

Paul Lafargue

1

He knew Heine and Goethe by heart and often quoted them in his conversations; he was an assiduous reader of poets in all European languages. Every year he read Aeschylus in the Greek original. He considered him and Shakespeare as the greatest dramatic geniuses humanity ever gave birth to. His respect for Shakespeare was boundless: he made a detailed study of his works and knew even the least important of his characters. His whole family had a real cult for the great English dramatist; his three· daughters knew many of his works by heart. When after 1848 he wanted to perfect his knowledge of English, which he could already read, he sought out and classified all Shakespeare's original expressions. He did the same with part of the polemical works of William Cobbett, of whom he had a high opinion. Dante and Robert Burns ranked among his favourite poets and he would listen with great pleasure to his daughters reciting or singing the Scottish poet's satires or ballads.

2

From time to time he would lie down on the sofa and read a novel; he sometimes read two or three at a time, alternating one with another. Like Darwin, he was a great reader of novels, his preference being for those of the eighteenth century, particularly Fielding's *Tom Jones*. The more modern novelists whom he found most interesting were Paul de Kock, Charles Lever, Alexander Dumas Senior and Walter Scott, whose *Old Mortality* he considered a masterpiece. He had a definite preference for stories of adventure and humour.

He ranked Cervantes and Balzac above all other novelists. In *Don Quixote* he saw the epic of dying-out chivalry whose virtues were ridiculed and scoffed at in the emerging bourgeois world. He admired Balzac so much that he wished to write a review of his great work *La Comédie humaine* as soon as he had finished his book on economics. He considered Balzac not only as the historian of his time, but as the prophetic creator of characters which were still in the embryo in the days of Louis Philippe and did not fully develop until after his death, under Napoleon III.

Marx could read all European languages and write in three: German, French and English, to the admiration of language experts. He liked to repeat the saying: "A foreign language is a weapon in the struggle of life."

He had a great talent for languages which his daughters inherited from him. He took up the study of Russian when he was already 50 years old, and although that language had no close affinity to any of the modern or ancient languages he knew, in six months he knew it well enough to derive pleasure from reading Russian poets and prose writers, his preference going to Pushkin, Gogol and Shchedrin. He studied Russian in order to be able to read the documents of official inquiries which were hushed over by the Russian Government because of the political revelations they made. Devoted friends got the documents for Marx and he was certainly the only economist in Western Europe who had knowledge of them.

3

On Sundays his daughters would not allow him to work, he belonged to them for the whole day. If the weather was fine, the whole family would go for a walk in the country.

On their way they would stop at a modest inn for bread and cheese and ginger beer. When his daughters were small he would make the long walk seem shorter to them by telling them endless fantastic tales which he made up as he went, developing and intensifying the complications according to the distance they had to go, so that the little ones forgot their weariness listening.

He had an incomparably fertile imagination: his first literary works were poems. Mrs. Marx carefully preserved the poetry her husband wrote in his youth but never showed it to anybody. His parents had dreamt of him being a man of letters or a professor and thought he was debasing himself by engaging in socialist agitation and political economy, which was then disdained in Germany.

Marx had promised his daughters to write a drama on the Gracchi for them. Unfortunately he was unable to keep his word. It would have been interesting to see how he, who was called "the knight of the class struggle", would have dealt with that terrible and magnificent episode in the class struggle of the ancient world.

> Paul Lafargue, "Reminiscences of Marx"
>
> *Marx and Engels Through the Eyes of Their Contemporaries*, Moscow, 1972, pp. 25, 26, 33

Eleanor Marx-Aveling

And so many and many a year later Marx told stories to his children. To my sisters—I was then too small—he told tales as they went for walks, and these tales were measured by miles not chapters. "Tell us another mile," was the cry of the two girls. For my own part, of the many wonderful tales Mohr told me, the most wonderful, the most delightful one, was "Hans Röckle". It went on for months and months;

it was a whole series of stories. The pity no one was there to write down these tales so full of poetry, of wit, of humour! Hans Röckle himself was a Hoffmann-like magician, who kept a toyshop, and who was always "hard up". His shop was full of the most wonderful things—of wooden men and women, giants and dwarfs, kings and queens, workmen and masters, animals and birds as numerous as Noah got into the Arc, tables and chairs, carriages, boxes of all sorts and sizes. And though he was a magician, Hans could never meet his obligations either to the devil or the butcher, and was therefore—much against the grain—constantly obliged to sell his toys to the devil. These then went through wonderful adventures—always ending in a return to Hans Röckle's shop. Some of these adventures were as grim, as terrible, as any of Hoffmann's; some were comic; all were told with inexhaustible verve, wit and humour.

And Mohr would also read to his children. Thus to me, as to my sisters before me, he read the whole of Homer, the whole *Nibelungen Lied, Gudrun, Don Quixote,* the *Arabian Nights,* etc. As to Shakespeare he was the Bible of our house, seldom out of our hands or mouths. By the time I was six I knew scene upon scene of Shakespeare by heart.

On my sixth birthday Mohr presented me with my first novel—the immortal *Peter Simple.*[a] This was followed by a whole course of Marryat and Cooper. And my father actually read every one of the tales as I read them, and gravely discussed them with his little girl. And when that little girl, fired by Marryat's tales of the sea, declared she would become a "Post-Captain" (whatever that may be) and consulted her father as to whether it would not be possible for her "to dress up as a boy" and "run away to join a man-of-war", he assured her he thought it might very well be done, only they must say nothing about it to anyone until all plans were well matured. Before these plans could be matured, however, the Scott mania had set in, and the little girl heard

---

[a] An adventure novel by the English writer Frederick Marryat.—*Ed.*

to her horror that she herself partly belonged to the detested clan of Campbell. Then came plots for rousing the Highlands, and for reviving "the forty-five".[a] I should add that Scott was an author to whom Marx again and again returned, whom he admired and knew as well as he did Balzac and Fielding. And while he talked about these and many other books he would, all unconscious though she was of it, show his little girl where to look for all that was finest and best in the works, teach her—though she never thought she was being taught, to that she would have objected—to try and think, to try and understand for herself.

> Eleanor Marx-Aveling, "Karl Marx"
> *Marx and Engels Through the Eyes of Their Contemporaries*, Moscow, 1972, pp. 155-56

Franzisca Kugelmann

Marx's taste was most refined in poetry as well as in science and the imitative arts. He was extraordinarily well-read and had a remarkable memory. He shared my father's enthusiasm for the great poets of classical Greece, Shakespeare and Goethe; Chamisso and Rückert were also among his favourites. He would quote Chamisso's touching poetry *The Beggar and His Dog*. He admired Rückert's art in writing and especially his masterly translation of Hariri's *Maqamas*, which are incomparable in their originality. Years later Marx presented it to my mother in remembrance of that time.

Marx was remarkably gifted for languages. Besides English, he knew French so well that he himself translated *Capital* into French,[b] and his knowledge of Greek, Latin, Span-

---

[a] The reference is to Walter Scott's novel *Waverley* which described the events of 1745 in Scotland—an uprising against the British rule.—*Ed.*

[b] Marx did not translate Book I of *Capital* into French, but carefully edited J. Roy's translation, with which he was not satisfied.—*Ed.*

ish and Russian was so good that he could translate from them at sight. He learned Russian by himself "as a diversion" when he was suffering from carbuncles.

He was of the opinion that Turgenev wonderfully renders the peculiarities of the Russian soul in its veiled Slavonic sensitivity. Lermontov's descriptions, he thought, were hardly to be excelled and seldom equalled.

His favourite among the Spaniards was Calderón. He had several of his works with him and often read us parts of them....

In our flat there was a large room with five windows which we called the hall and where we used to play music. Friends of the house called it Olympus because of the busts of Greek gods around the walls. Throned above them all was Zeus Otricolus.

My father thought Marx greatly resembled the last mentioned and many people agreed with him. Both had a powerful head with abundant hair, a magnificent thoughtful brow, an authoritative and yet kind expression. Marx's calm yet warm and lively nature, knowing no absent-mindedness or excitement, my father thought, also made him resemble his Olympian favourites. He liked to quote Marx's pertinent answer to the reproach that "the gods of the classics are eternal rest without any passions". On the contrary, Marx said, they were eternal passion without any unrest. My father could get very irritated when expressing his opinion of those who tried to drag Marx into the agitation of their political party undertakings. He wanted Marx, like the Olympian father of the gods and of men, only to flash his lightning into the world and occasionally hurl his thunder against it but not to waste his precious time in everyday agitation.

> Franzisca Kugelmann, "Small Traits of Marx's Great Character"
>
> *Marx and Engels Through the Eyes of Their Contemporaries*, Moscow, 1972, pp. 184-86

Anselmo Lorenzo

In a short time we stopped before a house. Framed in the doorway appeared an old man with a venerable patriarchal appearance.

I approached him with shy respect and introduced myself as a delegate of the Spanish Federation of the International. He took me in his arms, kissed me on the forehead and showed me into the house with words of affection in Spanish. He was Karl Marx.

The family had already retired and he himself served me an appetising refreshment with exquisite amiability. Then we had tea and spoke for a long time of revolutionary ideas, propaganda and organisation. Marx showed great satisfaction with what we had achieved in Spain....

Whether we had exhausted the subject or whether my honourable host desired to expand on some subject of his preference I do not know, but he spoke about Spanish literature, of which he had a detailed and profound knowledge. I was surprised at all he said about our ancient theatre, the history, vicissitudes and progress of which he was perfectly familiar with. Calderón, Lope de Vega, Tirso and other great masters, not only of the Spanish theatre, he said, but of European drama, were given a concise analysis and what seemed to me a very correct appraisal.

In the presence of that great man I could not help feeling very, very small. However, I made a tremendous effort not to give a deplorable impression of my ignorance and made the usual comparisons between Calderón and Shakespeare and also recalled Cervantes. Marx spoke of all that with great brilliance and expressed his admiration for the ingenious Hidalgo de la Mancha.

Anselmo Lorenzo, "Reminiscences of the First International"

Reminiscences of Marx and Engels, Moscow, 1956, pp. 289-90

From Reminiscences of Engels

N. S. Rusanov

Suddenly Engels quickly rose and exclaimed:
"By the way, I'll read you something out of Marx's old Russian library.... I gave most of his Russian books to other institutions and people who can make better use of them.... But I kept a few things for myself...."

In a friendly way he asked me to go with him into the next room. That was just as light and spacious—the library, judging by the long bookcases fixed to the walls. Engels went as quickly as before up to one of the shelves, looked at it for a moment and then, without any hesitation, took down a book in an old binding and showed it to me: it was one of the first editions of Pushkin's *Eugene Onegin*.

It was as if somebody had pressed a button in my memory, which was then good. I wanted to show Engels that we, victims of "political romanticism", had read a few things and knew something:

"Dear citizen, you apparently want to read me something out of that? Allow me to read you the very passage that you wanted to draw my attention to."

Engels looked askew at me in a friendly mocking way:
"Please do."

He gave me the book.

I held it shut and recited from memory:

> ... Читал Адама Смита
> И был глубокий эконом,

> То есть умел судить о том,
> Как государство богатеет,
>
> И отчего и почему
> Не нужно золота ему,
> Когда сырой продукт имеет...
> Его отец понять не мог
> И земли отдавал в залог. [a]

"*Donnerwetter!... Potztausend....*" Engels exlaimed several times. "Hell! you guessed right.... That's it, that's the very passage I wanted to read out to you. What put you on to it?"

"Association of ideas."

"Which?"

"You obviously wanted to quote something on the inevitable backwardness of Russian life. When I saw *Eugene Onegin* in your hands I immediately remembered that Marx quoted that very passage in his *A Contribution to the Critique of Political Economy* and in Russian at that:

> Его отец понять не мог
> И земли отдавал в залог, —

to prove that the ideas of bourgeois political economy cannot be applied to a society based on serf labour...."

N. S. Rusanov, "My Acquaintance with Engels"

Reminiscences of Marx and Engels, Moscow, 1956, pp. 322-23

---

[a] For having tackled Adam Smith,
And knowing all the means wherewith
A state may prosper, what it needed
To live, and how it might abide
The lack of gold if it provide
Itself with *simple product*; heeded
He wasn't by his father, who
Mortgaged his lands without ado.

Fanni Kravchinskaya

There were heated arguments among the guests, who got excited, shouted, and asked Engels for the answer to the question.

Suddenly Engels turned to me and, taking into account the fact that I knew no foreign languages, spoke Russian. He quoted from Pushkin:

V

>Since but a random education
>Is all they give us as a rule,
>With us, to miss a reputation
>For learning takes an utter fool.
>The strict and never doubting many
>Maintained the notion that Yevgeny
>Was "quite a learned lad", you see,
>But "with a turn for pedantry".
>Our hero had the lucky talent
>Of making witty repartees,
>Of speaking with unwonted ease,
>Of looking wise and keeping silent
>And of provoking ladies' smiles
>By unpremeditated guiles.

VI

>None really care for Latin lately:
>Our friend's sufficed him to translate,
>Although not very adequately,
>An epigraph, at any rate;
>To say a word on Juvenale,
>To wind a letter up with *Vale*
>And cite, with just a slip or two,
>A pair of Virgil's lines to you.
>He had no itch to dig for glories
>Deep in the dust that time has laid,
>He let the classic laurel fade.
>But all the most amusing stories
>Of every century and clime
>He could recall at any time.

VII

> Unable to divine the pleasure
> Of sacrificing life on rhyme,
> He couldn't tell a single measure
> However much we wasted time.
> He chid Theocritus and Homer,
> But might have won a Grand Diploma
> For having tackled Adam Smith,
> And knowing all the means wherewith
> A state may prosper, what it needed
> To live, and how it might abide
> The lack of gold if it provide
> Itself with *simple product*; heeded
> He wasn't by his father, who
> Mortgaged his lands without ado.

He recited the whole by heart in wonderful Russian. I clapped, but Engels said: "Alas, that's as far as my knowledge of Russian goes!"

The impression he produced on me was indelible, he was so hospitable and open-hearted.

Fanni Kravchinskaya, "Reminiscences"

Marx and Engels Through the Eyes of Their Contemporaries, Moscow, 1972, pp. 204-06

Critical Articles
by Jenny Marx[246]

1

**From London's
Theatre World**

London, November [1875]

John Bull is mightily proud of his glorious Constitution, his Milton, with whom he is not acquainted, his pork-pie, with which he is very well acquainted, and last but not least, his William Shakespeare. But it is all words and nothing more (he takes only his pork-pie seriously). All national conceit and hypocrisy! If the question arises of erecting a monument to the "Swan of Avon", the greatest of all poets, then it is only through the mites contributed by the lower strata of society that such an undertaking can be brought to fruition. Only actors, who love their Shakespeare, and workers, who have a thorough knowledge of him through shilling editions and who hold their "Will" deep in their hearts stood round the small oak that was planted eleven years ago on Primrose Hill to commemorate the three hundredth anniversary of Shakespeare's birth. More than twenty years ago the actor Phelps, working in a small theatre in the East End of London, succeeded for a number of years in keeping a taste for Shakespeare alive among the workers. At the same time, in the West End, the so-called educated classes were flooding to the "Shakespeare revivals" of Charles Kean. However, they were not thronging the theatre to hear the marvellous language of Shakespeare, but to see the splendid cloth-of-gold dresses of beautiful golden-locked Anne Boleyn. They wanted to feast their eyes on the banquet and ceremonial procession of Henry the Eighth, which Kean presented in historically faithful detail and even illuminated with electric light.

Many years ago a very talented Irish actor, Barry Sullivan, tried to rescue Shakespeare from oblivion. With him performed Mrs. Hermann Vezin, the best, indeed, one might say the only excellent Shakespearian actress. But it was all in vain. Othello and Desdemona, Hamlet and Ophelia, King Lear and Cordelia appeared before empty houses and after Sullivan had sacrificed the fortune he had earned in Australia from his Shakespearian productions, the enterprise had to be abandoned. Then Old Drury Lane stepped into the breach, an Old Drury still hallowed by memories of Kemble, Kean, Mrs. Siddons and Macready. The house remained empty, and after some weeks the manager was obliged to declare that "Shakespeare means bankruptcy". So Shakespeare was completely forgotten; only here and there a Hamlet or a Macbeth would appear in the workers' districts, quickly to disappear again. Then a year ago, a young actor named Henry Irving, who was known only in the provinces and whose London break-through had been made in melodramatic parts, ventured once again to bring Hamlet to the stage. He dared to defy the old, conventional tradition and create his own, faithful and original Shakespearian portrait, instead of the usual, all too familiar Hamlet. The critics grumbled, nagged and indulged in fault-finding; Irving had too little of the prince in him for one, while another did not like his walk, a third found him mannered and a fourth melodramatic. Nevertheless, he played to full houses. And then, suddenly, the wind changed, the critics ceased to cavil and began to praise—in fact to praise to the skies. The unheard-of happened: for two hundred nights attentive and enraptured audiences packed the theatre. It became fashionable to see Irving as Hamlet. It was *bon ton* to be enthusiastic about Shakespeare!

Greatly to the credit of the young artist, he did not allow himself to be taken in by the applause, but continued his efforts to perfect his part with the utmost conscientiousness and the greatest diligence, ever ready cheerfully to accept and make use of good advice and serious criticism. As a result, he succeeded, day by day, in increasingly overcoming the weaknesses and crudities from which his Hamlet was not yet free and in finally creating a complete, rich, rounded and harmonious portrait in which little fault could be found. On the two hundredth evening we bade farewell to an ideal Prince Hamlet.

For a month now he has been presenting *Macbeth* to us. The same grumbling, yelping and nagging from the press that greeted his production of *Hamlet* has been heard, but this time with an added bitterness and venom. Only the *Times* has treated this young, aspiring artist justly, acknowledging his achievement and encouraging him. The big daily papers have plunged into long and thoroughly contradictory critical reviews, one difficult to distinguish from the other; none of them examined Shakespeare deeply, but lost themselves in side issues and trivialities instead. "The small fry" gave themselves up to petty and purely personal attacks and observations, which bespoke only too clearly intrigues, envy and impotent spite. Nevertheless, there are full houses every day and tickets must be ordered weeks in advance. The audience sits in breathless silence, but there are only feeble signs of approval and no spontaneous enthusiasm to fire the young artist. Everyone sits mute and rigid, as if entranced. How is this rigidity of the public to be explained? Has the English middle class again grown tired of the chains of good taste binding it to Shakespeare? Does the *haute volée*[a] long to escape from true works of art to spectacular melodramas with burning ships, collapsing rocks and real carriages, horses, camels and goats? Perhaps fine ladies nourish a secret longing for a badly translated modern piece of Sardou, saccharine as a Jewish cherry brandy, for titillating phrases and equivocal situations? Or has the public allowed the critics to intimidate and frighten it? The English philistine seldom has the courage of his own con-

---
[a] High society.—*Ed.*

victions: he is a lion only in private. He has a lazy mind and every morning at breakfast his obligatory bacon and eggs are accompanied by his penny-a-liner, who thinks for him. How convenient it is to get into a bus, to drive to the City or the club or to sit in a box at the theatre in the evening with the rounded, ready-made phrases in one's pocket! That very morning the *Daily News*[247] has informed him that Irving's interpretation of Macbeth is wrong, that Macbeth is a frank, brave, daring general and that Irving presents him as a cruel, faint-hearted murderer, whom he allows to appear daring, mighty and brave only at the end of his life. What a contradiction in this interpretation! says the *Daily News*, and my newspaper-reading citizen believes his *Daily News*. Next to him sits a *Standard*[248] philistine or even someone who believes the *Saturday Review*,[249] each of them with ready-made opinions in his pocket. That is the great advantage of a working-class public: the working man does not allow the press to bewilder him; he goes to the theatre, relies on his own eyes and ears and applauds and hisses as his feelings and his own judgment and sense of what is proper impel him. For the good actor the pit and the gallery are, therefore, of decisive importance. That was why Edmund Kean was so delighted when the pit rose like one man during his performance of *Richard III* and he proudly cried: "The pit rose at me."

We hope that Irving will not be misled by the howling of the press and the apparent coldness of the public into abandoning his exploration of Shakespeare and returning to melodrama, for which he is considered qualified.

His Macbeth is not yet a finished work of art. During the first act his whole manner is uneven, unsure and therefore unsatisfactory; extreme anxiety often causes failures in intonation, and even his diction is faulty on occasion. In the second and third acts his performance rises to significant heights. His vision of the witches is presented in a masterly way and the banquet scene is powerfully gripping. During the whole of the last act, Irving's performance is peerless.

The audience is genuinely shocked by this broken man, his face twisted and aged by grief, wordless pain filling his expressive features at the news of the death of Lady Macbeth; the furious rage and heedless courage with which he throws himself into battle, the insane daring and despair of his fight with MacDuff and, finally, his death produce a powerful effect.

We are firmly convinced that Irving, with his conscientiousness and willingness to accept and make use of serious criticism will overcome the shortcomings, weaknesses and uneven parts of his Macbeth and that ultimately he will present consummate artistic creation, worthy of being placed beside his Hamlet. Of great assistance to the young artist in this serious and conscientious endeavour are his spiritual as well as his physical gifts: his beautiful, soft, resonant, albeit not very strong voice, his noble, expressive face and the remarkable mobility and fine play of his feature.

We hope that the artist will perform before German audiences: audiences that know and love Shakespeare and will greet this purposeful man with benevolent interest and encouragement. We also hope that in the future he receives better support from his fellow-actors and, finally, a critical response that is more fair, less contradictory and less misleading to the public.

2

The London Season

London, end of March [, 1876]

The London season has begun. Parliament is in session and "in" and "out"[250] quarrel with each other. In opposition the supple Gladstone attacks the sophistic Disraeli in government, as once the latter attacked him; the *Times* thunders against the Prime Minister's anti-Russian policies. The Queen has become Empress and is going to Germany,[251] and

John Bull huffs and puffs and is peeved because there is no one to rule him apart from the 12-year-old Prince of Wales. Bertchen Ulysses is returning home, heavily laden with the treasures of India, to his Penelope and the "youngsters", to recuperate from riding elephants and to the honours in the drawing rooms and at the *levées* of the Padisha-Mother.[252] The shops have put on their best spring and summer finery and the huge display windows are resplendent with the latest fashions. Light blue and dark blue, that is Cambridge and Oxford, will take each other's measure in the art of rowing on April 1 in the annual boat-race (there is no contest of minds). On this festive day the whole of London splits into two camps; elegant ladies sail forth in violet-blue silk, schoolchildren pin on Cambridge or Oxford bows and even the coachmen and horses are adorned with light- or dark-blue rosettes. It is a real holiday for the Cockneys.

The Italian Opera has opened the season with *Wilhelm Tell*. The Italian singers arrive with the swallows, most of them honest Germans, French, Hungarians and Russians, to whose names some kind of Italian final syllable is attached in order to lend them *cachet*. In their popular Monday concerts, Joachim and Clara Schumann are delighting, for the most part, musical philistines. Admirers of Shakespeare are, as before, making pilgrimages to see Irving's Othello at the Lyceum Theatre, where morning performances of *Othello, Hamlet* and *Macbeth* have been announced. High society, not excluding princes and princesses of the royal blood (conspicuous by its absence at Shakespeare performances), are streaming into the tiny Prince of Wales Theatre to see Marie Wilton as Peg Woffington in a mediocre drama by Tom Taylor. With her charm and naturalness, the originality of her acting and the unique personal magic with which she endows all her characters, Marie Wilton is reminiscent of Aimée Declée, too early departed from this life, and often, too, of the tiny and spirited Céline Chamont. Sardou's "*pattes de mouche*" are being presented at the Court Theatre in a limp and mutilated translation. A dramatised version of

Dickens *Bleak House* is on at the Globe Theatre, the little beggar-boy Jo being played with deeply affecting pathos by Jenny Lee.

The other thirty theatres are making great preparations to give a worthy reception to the foreigners who will be flocking here from all parts of the world, as well as to our own country cousins. Drawing rooms, *levées*, concerts, balls, gala performances, garden parties and flower, dog, cat and rabbit shows all come round every year with the spring. This season our good John Bull is the richer by two national institutions—the skating rink and the spelling bee. Your London correspondent has already described both of these and I will therefore limit myself to a few supplementary observations.

The largest possible arena is sought out for use as a skating rink. The floor is either of asphalt or polished wood. The skates, which are intended for this slippery terrain, are furnished with four small wheels. The English *petits crevés*[a] who tread on "thin ice" here appear in long ulsters like nightshirts, with a buttonhole of violets or a camellia; the young "bread and butter misses"[b] and more mature beauties, trembling with fright, parade in high-heeled boots, concealed springs in which lend an artificial aristocratic lift to flat English feet.

Spelling bees have sprung up in recent months like mushrooms and there are already more than three hundred. A committee, president, referees, examiners and prize-givers are chosen for these spelling tournaments and prizes of from £50 to five shillings are awarded. Last week a big spelling bee took place in St. James Hall. Well-known men of letters, lawyers and military gentlemen were on the committee; the examiner was a clergyman and the president a "nobleman valiant and bold, but his face and his family were wonderfully old". Two hundred ladies plunged into this

---

[a] Young men about town. —*Ed.*
[b] Teen-age girls. —*Ed.*

spelling battle, armed with heavy cannon in the shape of enormous dictionaries.

The prize was £50.

The competition began with easy Anglo-Saxon words and all went splendidly and in great good humour. Then followed difficult, outlandish, words of Greek origin and the heroines of the fray shrank to thirty-nine. By the time technical terms came up no more than nineteen champions of the ABC stood in the breach. Finally only two Richmonds[253] remained on the battlefield, one of whom won the prize. A discussion then developed over this, quarrels arose over formal details, the method of examination was attacked and people grew heated arguing "for" and "against". The tumult, shouting and noise grew, the nobleman was obliged to place the "hat" on his noble head and the gathering broke up amid violent argument and the greatest confusion.

Old merry England—"why skating rink and spelling bee, what on earth are they to thee?"

And we are asking—what next?

3

Shakespearian Studies in England

London, end of December [, 1876]

Three years ago a new Shakespeare society was founded here "to honour the great writer and stimulate and facilitate serious and intelligent study of his works among all classes of the population". Affiliated societies with corresponding members have been formed throughout England, Scotland and Ireland, in the colonies and in North America. Many German Shakespeare groups have joined and even those rare birds, French Shakespeare enthusiasts, have become members. Professor Delius of Bonn is one of the society's most loyal and active collaborators. In London, the society has many hundreds of members, each of whom pays an annual subscription of one guinea, and every four weeks, a meeting is held in the building of London University, at which contributions in the form of letters, essays, critical works and research papers are read and discussed. Apart from these transactions, the society, under the leadership of Frederick Furnivall, its active, able and enthusiastic president, is regularly reprinting the oldest Shakespeare editions in chronological sequence, as well as extremely rare and valuable works of that period and important modern criticism and research. In this way, a highly interesting and solidly-based literature on Shakespeare will gradually be built up.

This year every member has received splendidly-produced copies of the following works:

a) Tell-Trothes New-yeares gift, 1593, with the passionate Morrice; b) John Lane's Tom Tell-Troths message, and his Pen's Complaint, 1600; c) Thomas Powell's Tom of all Trades; or the Plaine Path-way to Preferment, 1631; d) the Glasse of Godley Love, 1569.

William Stafford's Compendious or brief Examination of certayne ordinary complaints of divers of our countrymen in these our Dayes, 1581 (presented by the Right Honourable the Earl of Derby).[254]

Philipp Stubbe's Anatomie of abuses, May 1, 1583, with extracts from his life and that of his wife, 1591.

Plays. The Two Noble Kinsmen by Shakespeare and Fletcher, reprinted from the 1634 quarto, and an edition of the play with corrections and notes by Harold Littledale of Trinity College, Dublin.

Miscellanea. The late Professor W. Spalding's letter on the authors of *The Two Noble Kinsmen*, the characteristic features of Shakespeare's style and the secret of his superiority, 1833.

The first publication for 1877 is now ready:

Shakespeare's England. William Harrison's Description of England, 1577, 1587, published by Furnivall, together with map of London by van den Keere, 1593, with notes by H. B. Wheatley.

The following publications are in the press:

1. The transactions;[255] 2. an article by Professor Delius on the epic element in Shakespeare, translated into English by two young ladies, one English and one German;[256] 3. a study of *Henry VI*, Part 2 and 3, and their original sources by Miss Jane Lee, daughter of the Archbishop of Dublin.

2. *The Two Noble Kinsmen* by Shakespeare and Fletcher, with an introduction and index by Harold Littledale of all words distinguishing Shakespeare from Fletcher.

3. *Cymbeline*, reprinted from the 1623 folio; a corrected edition with introduction and notes by W. J. Craig, Trinity College, Dublin.

4. *Henry V* with parallel texts from the quarto and the first folio, arranged to show the differences between them, and a revised edition of the play.

Mysteries. 15th Century Mysteries with a Morality from the Digby M. S. 133, published by Furnivall according to the only M. S. *Wills* of actors and writers under Elizabeth and James.

Edward III. Reprinted from the first quarto, 1596, and a revised edition with notes, the sources of the play by Froissart and Painter's *Palace of Pleasure*.

Robert Chester's *Love's Martyr*, from which Shakespeare's verses *Phoenix and Turtle* were taken.

Original sources and analogues. A. Shakespeare Holin'gshead, the chronicle and the historical plays, compared by W. Stone.

Some highly interesting works have been proposed for publication next year.

Meetings have hitherto been only sparsely attended; however, it is a true pleasure to spend some time among the small community of the faithful, all of whom (the ladies not excepted) treat the study of Shakespeare seriously and are enriching some branch of literature by their critical and often very original and detailed research.

In this Shakespearian lodge, a true spirit of brotherhood prevails; from downy-cheeked youngster to grizzled veteran, every newcomer receives a friendly welcome, and true Malvolio smiles and grins greet the youngest labourer in the lord's vineyard.

When the Englishman becomes enthusiastic about something (and there are, in fact, many enthusiasts in this matter-of-fact nation) and John Bull gets an idea into his head, it easily becomes an *idée fixe*, a mania, a fad, a declared hobby-horse. This is the spawning ground of humbugs and fanatics; this is how sects are formed. But among adherents of the sects one finds unimpeachably honest men and women in the greatest numbers—I would not like to say the only honest men and women—*whose principles are not for sale.* Honesty *toute pure* is rare and therefore often carries with it a slight touch of eccentricity, oddity and arrogance.

This is true of our worthy Shakespearians. It is also true of the tiny group of Comtists, some thirty strong who, fair-haired professors and grey-bearded doctors and lawyers alike, every Sunday make the pilgrimage to their "school", carrying their bibles under their arms, to burn incense to their humanitarian god, Auguste Comte, and the saints in his calendar. And it is true of the followers of Urquhart, who swear by Mohammed and his prophet "David" and who, in their journal the *Diplomatic Review*, demonstrate with excellently written, objective articles (in earlier years their most brilliant contributor was Urquhart, but at almost eighty, the old man's genius has now somewhat lost its edge) and reprints of highly interesting rare documents and diplomatic papers that they understand rather more about foreign policy and the "Eastern question" than the booming orators and the trumpeters of peace in St. James Hall,[a] the "Freemen" and the "Merrymen".

The beneficial effects of the Shakespeare society are al-

---

[a] December 8, 1876, a National Conference on the Oriental Question was held in London.—*Ed.*

ready becoming apparent in a variety of ways. Study of the great poet, for many years completely neglected, has revived among wide sections of the public; however, speaking of the growing interest among the people, one cannot help returning again and again to the great and undeniable service rendered by Henry Irving. It is he who has electrified the masses; and it is not only that his own theatre is filled every night—Shakespeare has begun to draw audiences in previously empty theatres.

Irving has been touring the provinces, Scotland and Ireland for six months, supported by the talented and charming sisters Kate, Isabel and Virginia Bateman. From beginning to end the tour has been a triumph, but reached its high point among the enthusiastic citizens of Dublin.

Irving was accorded the greatest honour that can be shown an artist when a "university festival" was organised for him. Only one other actress has ever received this distinction, and that twenty-five years ago, when Helen Faucit appeared as Antigone. This highly gifted and charming performer, who at that time shone in the company of Macready, is the wife of Theodor Martin, who recently published a life of Prince Albert, authorised by the Queen, and who is best known as an excellent translator of German and Danish works.

Some time ago Irving received an Address from the graduates and undergraduates of Dublin University. It was presented to him by a committee of twelve, including professors, scholars and well-known authorities on Shakespeare, among them Doctors Ingram and Dowden. Edward Gibson, Queen's Counsellor and a Member of Parliament, who headed the deputation, began with the following words: "It gives me particular pleasure to express to you on behalf of the graduates etc., etc., their great admiration and respect for so great a performer, so accomplished a gentleman and so charming a companion." He then read the Address, in which he especially stressed the rare pleasure given by Irving's performances, the new insights into the character of Hamlet he had afforded, even to those most intimately familiar with Shakespeare, and the fresh interest in the finest poetry he had awakened in the hearts of all. "Performances such as yours ennoble and elevate the stage and serve to lead it back to its true calling—as a powerful lever of intellectual and moral culture." Irving responded with a few words of thanks. The same day a "College Evening" was held, at which the foremost professors of the university and even Prince Arthur, the Duke of Connaught, were present (the royal princes are seldom or never seen at performances of Shakespeare). The hall was packed to suffocation and the enthusiasm was truly Irish. On Saturday, Irving returns to his London friends and admirers, who will be proud and pleased to welcome him as the Thane of Cawdor.

4

Shakespeare's *Richard III*
in London's Lyceum Theatre

London, February 1 [,1877]

Since the break-down of the conference,[257] a pause has ensued on the "Eastern question". There is no longer a rush to read the reports from Constantinople, Vienna and Berlin or greedily devour the yard-long despatches of special and non-special correspondents, from the Gallengas in Pera[258] and the Abels in Berlin. "The trumpet of war is silent" and the speculating philistines blathering about politics can lay their anxious heads quietly to rest and slumber peacefully, lulled by golden dreams of peace and prosperity.

It is thanks to this political lull that the great event of the week, the production of Shakespeare's *Richard III* at the Lyceum Theatre, has attracted general and undivided interest. To the German admirer of Shakespeare it will seem incredible and unheard-of that since the time of the great dramatist, who himself produced his *Richard III* at the Globe and Blackfriars theatres, the play had, until Monday evening's production, *never been presented* to an English audience in its *original version*. After Shakespeare's death, the play disappeared completely from the stage for half a century. In 1700 a totally mutilated and disjointed version of *Richard III* by Colley Cibber appeared, with passages of bombastic nonsense and melodramatic stage-effects added. A second still weaker version of the play appeared in 1821, but this, too, was unable to retain its place in the repertoire.

Many attempts have been made to present the drama in its original purity, but all have failed. Neither Garrick nor Cooke, Edmund Kean or Macready strayed from the beaten track. And so this bungled piece of work remained in unchallenged command of the stage for 177 years; indeed, Richard trod the boards of Old Drury in Cibber's customary garb only a few months ago. Every institution, every custom and practice, every idea in this country ossifies, petrifies, rusts and becomes an "historical" tradition, an article of faith—and woe betide anyone who dares to shake these dusty and weather-beaten traditions. Henry Irving had the bold idea, the courage and the energy to defy these deeply rooted prejudices and present Shakespeare to the public in his pure, undistorted and original form.

How successful this dangerous experiment has been was demonstrated on Monday by the enormous crowds which besieged the doors of the Lyceum. The pit and the gallery were virtually taken by storm, while in the boxes and stalls, the cream of society, and probably of the demi-monde as well, were enthroned in all their beauty, youth and elegance. Amid these brilliant blooms one picked out a young actress with a Dolly Warden (a kind of Black Forest peasant bonnet) perched high on her blond curls, seated beside a grey-haired duchess in a gold-embroidered mantle; next to a heavily powdered, hawk-nosed pure-blooded aristocrat sat the offshoot of a still older aristocracy, a beautiful, dark-skinned little daughter of Israel, and all were thrown together quite at random. In the front rows, close to the orchestra, sat the "Star Chamber", the gentlemen of the press, both great and small. How they looked, these knights of the mind or, rather, of pen and ink, as they sat there in formal black swallow-tail coats and small, muslin evening ties, preparing to pass sentence of life or death the following morning!

Time, space and staging considerations naturally demanded a certain amount of excision, compression and alteration of meaning. The intelligent, unconstrained and tactful way in which this has been done and the extent to which this old and unique drama has been brought into complete harmony with the demands of today's theatre were shown in the magical effect it produced on the packed audience. After Gloster's first monologue:

> "Now is the winter of our discontent
> Made glorious summer by this son of York"[259]

a breathless hush immediately descended on the audience and even the noisy "deities" on high listened entranced.

In his interpretation of Richard, Irving has cast all the old traditions aside. This is no "villain" with bushy brows and the stereotyped expression of a Mephistopheles who stamps about the stage. His deformity is not so striking as to make him grotesque: a raised left shoulder and a slight limp are the only indications. But Irving knows so well how to present the arch-hypocrite, and master of dissimulation, his criminal nature held in check by ambition and his baseness veiled by a fine tissue of deceit, hypocrisy and duplicity, through the subtlest traits, tiny, almost imperceptible movements of the features, faint twitches of his compressed lips and subtle, sarcastic, fleeting smiles, hand movements and tones of voice. Above all, Irving never exaggerates. Even during the most intense moments of passion he preserves a kind of fundamental dignity and never descends to the level of the vulgar, raging villain of melodrama. The narrow bounds of a single article make it impossible to cover every brilliant moment of his performance, from the tiny, delicate details of his characterisation to the spectacular energy of the final scene, the sword fight with Richmond, which concludes the play. We shall emphasise only a few especially successful scenes: for example, the scene with Lady Anne at the end of the first act, which is scarcely comprehensible on the printed page. But one understands her weakness when one sees the elegant, gallant, witty and repentant flatterer, with his smooth and supple tongue. Very characteristic, too, is his performance in the scene with the two young princes, whose parts are taken most intelligently by two young girls—his friendly, gentle, ingratiating manner. One actually sees the children cling to their good uncle Gloster, and involuntarily recalls the words of his mother, the aged Duchess of York:

> Tetchy and wayward was thy infancy.
> Thy school-days, frightful, desperate, wild and furious;
> Thy prime of manhood, daring, bold, and venturous;
> Thy age confirm'd, proud, subtle, sly, and bloody,
> *More mild*, but yet *more harmful, kind in hatred*.[260]

Also worthy of special note is the scene on the gallery with the two archbishops, in which this accomplished hypocrite casts his gaze, filled with "goodness, virtue and pious humility" from prayerbook to heaven.[261]

Seldom has so outstanding an artist found such support in his fellow players. We cannot praise the Margaret of Miss Bateman enough—this marvellously affecting, uncanny figure, eyes fixed, features distorted by grief, her wild, stormy outburst and the curse that breaks from her in mad despair!

Her younger sister Isabel presented Lady Anne with bewitching charm and captivating sweetness. She spoke her few words from the heart in Richard's tent with special feeling; the tent, like all the scenery, costumes, etc., was admirable in its picturesque accuracy of detail, which brought this ancient time vividly before the onlooker. All the small parts, including those of Elizabeth, the Duchess of York, Clarence, Richmond and Buckingham, were also very well performed, and this was true even of the tiniest roles, such as Catesby, Rivers, the murderers and, last but not least, the young princes, all of whom contributed much to the success of this great drama.

It is impossible to describe the excited scene in the theatre as Irving was greeted with stormy enthusiasm and frantic curtain-calls. For the English, the production came as a fresh revelation of the old master and they sat electrified, admiring the harmony of the whole, the clarity and distinctness of motivation, the gradual development of the plot, the completeness of characterisation and, above all, the inexhaustible and overflowing fount of poetry and passion. The scales fell from their eyes and they saw that their Shakespeare is greater than their Cibber. One German critic alone in our vicinity was heard to declare in broken English that "there was more 'stamina' in Cibber than in Shakespeare!" O thou, unique among thy nation!

5

From the London Theatre

London, May 22 [,1877]

There has been another first night at the Lyceum Theatre and the numerous and steadily growing theatre public were on the *qui vive* to see the new play at their favourite playhouse. For three years Mrs. Bateman has succeeded in keeping Shakespeare on the stage in an almost unbroken sequence of plays, thanks to the original and brilliant productions of Henry Irving. Incredible difficulties had to be overcome; there were struggles with a petty, malevolent and unjust clique of press critics, an indifferent and enervated public which, long unused to Shakespeare, had first to be drawn and educated, neglect by high society, which considers it good form to flock to the brazen charms, screened by English fig-leaves, of Sardou and Dumas fils, and finally lack of support from the royal family which, since the death of Prince Albert, has maintained an attitude of real awe towards

Shakespeare while bestowing its undivided favours on dubious productions of the type of *The Rose-Coloured Domino* at the Criterion Theatre.

In order both to give Irving an opportunity for rest and relaxation after his strenuous physical and mental exertions and to please that section of the public which pants, like the hart for cool water, after melodrama, the management of the Lyceum has decided to abandon its Shakespearian repertoire and make melodrama for a short time the *plat du jour*. The enthusiastic and delighted applause which greeted *The Lyons Mail*[262] on Saturday was proof of how fortunate Mrs. Bateman has been in her choice of a new drama.

The play, which was originally presented at the Gaité Theatre in Paris in 1850, is based on the famous trial which took place in France in 1794 under the Directory.[263] A physical similarity, striking enough to mislead judge and witnesses, was the cause of an innocent man being accused of a crime which had been committed by a villain.

In the village of Lieursaint, on the Paris-Lyons road, the Lyons mail-coach was attacked by a band of robbers. Dubosc, an escaped convict from the galleys and leader of the band, murdered the postilion and stole the sum of 75,000 francs. The crime took place close to the house of the old father of Joseph Lesurques, who was at that moment in the vicinity. The real criminal, Dubosc, got away, part of the gang with some of the money was arrested and, as the result of an unusual chain of circumstances, Joseph Lesurques was accused of the crime, condemned and, in fact, beheaded, while his double escaped. At the last moment, Lesurques was able to prove his alibi, but the court had passed sentence and its judgment was not rescinded. The descendants of the unfortunate victim of this judicial murder have expressed their gratitude to the author of the play and the management of the theatre where it was presented, with the explicit request that the real name of their grandfather, Joseph Lesurques, be used, so that posterity should thus be convinced of his innocence. Another interesting circumstance is that, during the Third Empire,[264] the descendants of the victim applied to the state for restitution of confiscated money and were represented by Jules Favre. Because of a formal error, the court decided against the family. In 1854 the drama, which had created a great sensation in Paris, due particularly to the excellent performance of Lacressonnière, was presented in a version by Charles Reade at the Princess Theatre under the direction of Charles Beau, who played the leading role.

The play is filled with simple, touching pathos and abounds in exciting scenes and interesting situations, which are arranged and brought into relief with the adroitness that is a familiar feature of French authors. Each act concludes with an effective tableau and the obligatory musical accompaniment of melodrama.

Henry Irving plays a double role—a gentle, lovable, tender paterfamilias, sure of his innocence, and a professional murderer and thief, a low brawler and drunkard. And how tactfully, with what consummate art he delineates with the utmost precision the two individual personalities in all their diversity through near-miraculous metamorphoses, going into the minutest details without ever losing the striking similarity which deceived all the witnesses and even the accused's own father. The whole is a splendid, finished work of art, which often produces an overwhelming and almost agonising effect. The role of Joseph Lesurques' father, as played by Read, was in the best of hands and was presented with an energy and dignity that essentially contributed to the success of the play's finest scenes.

The two sisters Isabel and Virginie Bateman merit special mention. Virginie has the small and unimportant role of Julia, Lesurques' daughter, and has extracted every last drop from it. The strange, peculiar costume of the period, with the strikingly short waist, narrow, close-fitting skirt and piled-up, curly hair-style, particularly suits her and highlights her youthful, blond beauty. In the scene in which she hears her father condemned and throws herself into his arms with a cry of horror, sobbing loudly and clinging to his neck, she produced a striking effect on the audience and many an eye filled with tears. Isabel Bateman's role is a more difficult one. She plays Jeannette, seduced and abandoned, by Dubosc, a girl wandering about in misery and despair. Her first appearance was truly touching and immediately engaged the sympathy of the audience. She brings an unsuspected energy and drive and a genuinely dramatic fire to the scene in which she accuses Dubosc. When, at the end of the play, she sinks, wounded by Dubosc, to the ground, then heaves herself up and staggers across the stage, she attains an artistic greatness of truly tragic dimensions.

Costumes, scenery and stage design are consistently excellent in this theatre and even the two white horses drawing the mail-coach played their part well and heightened the picturesque effect of the whole gripping scene.

Henry Irving has recently come before the English public in another double role, that of actor and author, and in this field, too, he cannot be denied recognition.

Irving has published two articles in two issues of the monthly journal, *The Nineteenth Century*, the contributors to which include some of England's leading literary and scientific figures. Entitled "Notes on Shakespeare by an actor",[265] the articles contain skilful and detailed studies of Shakespeare, one dealing with the third murderer in *Macbeth* and the other with the love relationship between Hamlet and Ophelia, and offer practical advice and suggestions for actors and theatre managements.

The same issue contains a poem by Tennyson, the poet laureate, and an article by Gladstone, both devoted to the heroic people of Montenegro. There is also an article by Archbishop Manning on "the true history of the Vatican", as well as a short contribution by Huxley to the present "symposium" on "the influence upon morality of a decline in religious belief". Earlier participants in this debate have included atheists, Comtists and pietists. It is greatly to Irving's credit that he has been able to hold his place among these literary giants.

Indeed, Irving stands out through his originality of form and the exquisite purity of his language. His quite unpretentious articles are totally free from the flavour of the penny-a-liner and other scribblers and this is what makes them so refreshing. Irving does not write for the sake of writing: he handles his subject, into which he puts his heart and soul, with complete seriousness and therefore treats it without the least affectation.

By contrast, his literary neighbour in the above-mentioned journal clearly belongs to the class of loud-mouthed literary charlatans. This is Mr. Ralston who, because he has spent some time in Russia and is capable of a little mangled Russian, has set himself up as a pundit on Russia, upon which he pontificates at meetings and in the press. He contributed an article to the last issue of *The Nineteenth Century* on current revolutionary literature in Russia and the latest revolutionary outbreaks,[a] in which he declared that he fully understands how someone could sacrifice himself for religion or personal allegiance, but not for other, immature ideas. It is, therefore, no surprise that he has nothing but derision, mockery and contempt for the unfortunate victims of the latest small revolutionary outbreak who were able to sacrifice themselves for the idea of freedom, even if they misunderstood it. Woe to the poor young girls who joined this movement and have already lost their health in the preliminary investigation and who are now serving fifteen years of penal servitude in Siberia, where they are being slowly murdered.

How is it that Mr. Ralston makes no mention in his article of *N. Chernyshevsky*, the greatest of today's revolutionary writers? Can it be that he does not know his principal work, on *Political Economy*, which has the form of a critique on

---

[a] The article appeared in May 1877 under the title "Russian Revolutionary Literature". Among other things it examined in detail the "Trial of the 50", which took place in St. Petersburg in February and March of 1877, when a group of revolutionary "Narodniks" were condemned (cf. Marx's letter to Engels, September 18, 1878, and Kovalevsky, *Recollections of Karl Marx*).—*Ed.*

the lines of John Stuart Mill's *Principles of Political Economy*?[266] Does Ralston not know that his collected works, which consist for the most part of critical writings in the fields of history, aesthetics, philosophy, literature and politics, now form twenty substantial volumes (not to mention a novel entitled *What Is to Be Done?*)? Is Ralston not acquainted with Chernyshevsky's journal, *The Contemporary*,[267] in which the latter spurred the Russian government to emancipate the serfs (in a different way, to be sure, from how the emancipation was in fact carried out) and scourged the sham liberalism of the Petersburg press of his time with such merciless harshness that its worthy representatives felt themselves relieved of a great burden when the government banished him to Siberia, because, for the first time, an ordinary critic and scholar had become a public force in Russia? Why does our gentleman of letters, who would not sacrifice himself for any idea, keep so silent about this man, while waxing so eloquent over nihilism and feigned marriages?

But after this digression into *The Nineteenth Century*, let us return to the point from which we began—the theatre. We hope soon to welcome Irving once again in his role of author and, before long, also in his native element—a new Shakespeare production.

Beiträge zur Geschichte der deutschen Arbeiterbewegung Nr. 6, 1966

Notes

[1] This refers to Karl Gutzkow's novel *Blasedow und seine Sohne* which appeared in Stuttgart in 1838. p. 49

[2] This refers to Platen's comedy in five scenes *Der romantische Oedipus*. p. 49

[3] This refers to the song "Ich bin ein Preuße" by I. B. Thiersch. p. 50

[4] An allusion to the account in Genesis according to which Lot's wife was turned into a pillar of salt because she looked back during their escape from Sodom (Genesis XIX). p. 51

[5] The Calvinist Synod, which met in Dordrecht (Holland) from November 13, 1618, to May 9, 1619, condemned the Arminian sect for its non-conformist views and reasserted strictly Calvinist dogmas. p. 51

[6] This refers to the second issue of the book by Ferdinand Freiligrath and Levin Schücking, *Das malerische und romantische Westphalen*, published in Barmen and Leipzig in 1840. p. 55

[7] In May 1840, when Engels was in Münster, Levin Schücking presented him with a copy of the above-mentioned book with a dedication: "In memory of Münster". Annette Elizabeth von Droste-Hülshoff's book of poems *Gedichte* was published in 1838 under the initials D. H. p. 55

[8] *Pietism* (from the Latin *pietas*—piety)—a trend in the Lutheran Church that emerged in Germany in the 17th century. p. 56

[9] According to Rousseau, people originally lived in a natural state where all were equal. The rise of private property and development of property inequality led to the transition from the natural to the civil state and to the formation of the state based on the *Contrat social*. Further development of political inequality, however, led to the violation of the *Contrat social* and the rise of a new natural state.

A rational state based upon a new *Contrat social* was to supersede it. (See pp. 281-83 of this book.) p. 66

¹⁰ *Mercantilism*—a system of economic views and economic policies of a number of European states during the 15th-18th centuries. The theoreticians of mercantilism looked for the source of wealth not in the production process but in the circulation process, and identified wealth with money. Countries that adhered to the Mercantile System attempted to regulate foreign trade in order to secure an excess of exports over imports.

The *physiocrats*—a trend in bourgeois political economy in the 18th century, the chief exponents of which were, in France, François Quesnay and A. R. F. Turgot. The physiocrats laid the foundation for scientific analysis of capitalist production having transferred the question of the origin of surplus value from the sphere of circulation to that of production. However, they considered agricultural labour to be the only type of productive labour and regarded industrialists and industrial workers as an "unproductive class".

p. 66

¹¹ *Die Neue Zeit*—a political and theoretical journal of the German Social-Democratic Party which appeared in Stuttgart from 1883 to 1923. It was edited by Karl Kautsky till 1917. During the period 1885-94 Engels published a number of articles in this journal; he always gave advice to its editors and not infrequently criticised them for departures from Marxism. p. 67

¹² This refers to the first chapter of Engels' work. In the 1880s Engels planned and started re-writing *The Peasant War in Germany* but he never finished this work. p. 68

¹³ The *Thirty Years' War* (1618-48)—the first all-European war which was caused by an aggravation of contradictions between different groupings of European states and which took the form of a struggle between Protestants and Catholics. Germany became the main battlefield, the object of plunder and territorial claims by the participants in this war. The Treaty of Westphalia, which legalised the political fragmentation of Germany, ended the war. p. 68

¹⁴ Engels wrote this letter in reply to Paul Ernst's request in his letter to Engels of May 31, 1890, to express his opinion on the stand taken by Ernst in the polemic with the Austrian impressionist writer Hermann Bahr. The subject of the polemic was the position of women and the women's movement in the Scandinavian countries. p. 75

¹⁵ Quoted from the *Manifesto of the Communist Party* (Marx and Engels, *Collected Works*, Vol. 6, p. 502). p. 76

¹⁶ These heroes of ancient republican virtue were popular at the time

NOTES

of the Great French Revolution and were frequently referred to by speakers and poets. Caesarism was an official prototype of the Napoleonic Consulate and Empire. p. 81

[17] *Roberts and Co.*—an iron and steel works; *Crédit mobilier*—a well-known French bank; Printing House—a printshop of *The Times* in London. p. 83

[18] *Stefan von Grillenhof* was the first novel written by Minna Kautsky. p. 87

[19] The *Salvation Army*—a bourgeois philanthropic organisation founded in 1865 in England by the clergyman W. Booth (the name was assumed in 1880 after its reorganisation in a military fashion). p. 90

[20] The *Legitimists*—adherents of the Bourbons overthrown in France in 1792, who represented the interests of the landed aristocracy. p. 91

[21] Engels refers to the barricade fighting between the insurgents who belonged to the Society of the Rights of Man and the Citizen, the Left wing of the Republican Party, and the Louis Philippe troops which took place in Paris, June 5 and 6, near the Cloître Saint-Méry. Balzac portrays the Republican Michel Crétien, who fell near its walls, in his novels *Illusions perdues* and *Les Secrets de la Princesse de Cadignan*. p. 92

[22] This refers to the petty-bourgeois democratic leaders of the revolution of 1848-49. p. 92

[23] A. Chenu, *Les conspirateurs*. L. de la Hodde, *La naissance de la République*. p. 93

[24] During the parliamentary elections of 1892 in England, the worker deputies won a majority in a number of election wards. p. 96

[25] *Home rule*—a moderate liberal-bourgeois programme of self-government for Ireland within the framework of the British Empire. p. 96

[26] The *Fabians*—members of the Fabian Society, a British reformist organisation founded in 1884. The members of the Fabian Society were mostly bourgeois intellectuals—scientists, writers and politicians (among them Sidney and Beatrice Webb, George Bernard Shaw, Ramsay MacDonald). They denied the necessity of the proletarian class struggle and of socialist revolution and maintained that the transition from capitalism to socialism can be achieved only by way of reforms. p. 97

[27] These were secret peasant associations, the actions of which paved the way for the Peasant War of 1524-25 in Germany. p. 107

[28] This refers to Marx's work on *Capital*. p. 111

[29] This refers to *Theories of Surplus-Value*. p. 111

[30] Jacob Grimm published his works by instalments. p. 111

[31] *Vossische Zeitung*—a Berlin bourgeois newspaper founded in 1785. Engels refers to the article entitled "Zur Beurteilung von Karl Marx" published in it on May 24, 1883, under the signature H. V. T. The author of the article gave an entirely distorted picture of Marx.
p. 112

[32] In 1872 Lujo Brentano, a German economist, published an unsigned article entitled "The Way Karl Marx Quotes" in *Concordia*, the periodical of German industrialists. Brentano blamed Marx for incorrectly quoting the speech delivered by Gladstone, British Liberal Minister, in the House of Commons (in 1863), first in the "Inaugural Address of the First International" and later in the first volume of *Capital*. Brentano's article was a foul attempt to discredit Marx as a scientist.

Brentano's sally started a prolonged controversy. Marx and, after his death, Eleanor Marx and Frederick Engels wrote in reply to Brentano. Marx's and Engels' articles provided irrefutable evidence of the absolute identity of Marx's quotation to the original. p. 113

[33] *The Northern Star*—an English weekly, central organ of the Chartists, appeared from 1837 to 1852. p. 114

[34] This refers to the weekly *Sozialdemokrat*, the central organ of the German Socialist Workers' Party at the time of the Anti-Socialist Law; appeared from 1879 to 1890. p. 115

[35] This refers to the assassination attempts on William II in 1878. They served as a pretext for Bismarck to intensify persecution of Social-Democrats and demand that the Reichstag adopt the Anti-Socialist Law. p. 115

[36] *Neue Welt*—a journal, the mouthpiece of the opportunist wing of German Social-Democracy. p. 116

[37] The initial line in Georg Weerth's poem. p. 116

[38] This refers to the French version of the first volume of *Capital* translated by Roi and edited by Marx (1872). p. 117

[39] This refers to the American edition of the *Manifesto of the Communist Party*. p. 118

[40] This refers to Bernstein's translation of Marx's *Poverty of Philosophy* from French into German in 1884. p. 119

[41] This refers to the translation of Béranger's song. At the end of the 1880s, Laura Lafargue was engaged in translating German and French poets into English. Engels guided her in this work, discussing

her poetical translations in his letters to her and giving advice.
p. 121

[42] An ironical name given by Engels to the Empire of Napoleon I (to distinguish it from the Second Empire). p. 121

[43] Engels enclosed in his letter a copy of the well-known song by Walther von der Vogelweide "Unter den Linden" (see *Werke*, Bd. 37, S. 334-37). p. 122

[44] Marx refers to Lessing's polemic against Voltaire in his *Hamburgische Dramaturgie* (1767-68). p. 141

[45] A poem by Voltaire on the French King Henry IV; it was first published in 1723. p. 141

[46] In his letter of January 7, 1884, Paul Lafargue cited several examples to show that the imported articles listed by Engels, particularly German ones, successfully competed with the home-made articles of the French industries. p. 141

[47] The *Treaty of Kuchuk Kaïnarji* was signed between Russia and Turkey on July 21 (10), 1774, when the Russo-Turkish war that lasted from 1768 to 1774 ended in Russia's victory. The Treaty gave Russia part of the northern coast of the Black Sea, Azov, Kerch and Yenikale and recognition of the independence of the Crimea. The Russian marine fleet received the right of free passage through the Straits of the Bosphorus and the Dardanelles. Under the Treaty, the Sultan was to grant a number of privileges to the Orthodox Church. p. 151

[48] Mandeville, B. *The Fable of the Bees, or Private Vices, Public Benefits*, London, 1728, p. 428. The first edition of the book came out in 1705. p. 156

[49] An allusion to Holbach's *Le Système de la nature*. p. 163

[50] This refers to his pamphlet *Qu'est-ce que la propriété?* (1840). p. 164

[51] In August 1814, during the war between Britain and the USA, the British troops, having captured Washington, set the Capitol, the White House and some other public buildings on fire.

In October 1860, during the colonial war of conquest waged by Britain and France against China, British and French troops plundered and then burnt down the summer palace near Peking, an exquisite collection of Chinese architecture and arts. p. 167

[52] This refers to the Paris Commune, the revolutionary workers' government set up during the proletarian revolution in Paris. It was the first historical experience of the dictatorship of the proletariat and lasted for 72 days (from March 18 to May 28, 1871). p. 167

⁵³ The *column on the Place Vendôme*, supporting the statue of Napoleon I, was erected in Paris in 1806-10 to commemorate his victories. By decree of the Commune it was demolished on May 16, 1871, as a symbol of militarism, but was restored in 1875 by the victorious reactionaries. p. 169

⁵⁴ *Soir*—a French Republican bourgeois daily, published in Paris from 1867 onwards. p. 169

⁵⁵ The *Arc de Triomphe* was erected in 1806 on the Place de l'Étoile in the Tuileries Gardens to commemorate the victories of Napoleon I. p. 169

⁵⁶ This refers to utopian socialists (in particular Fourier and his followers) who advocated a utopian plan for reorganising society through reform, by means of so-called "organisation of labour" which they counterposed to the anarchy of production under capitalism. p. 177

⁵⁷ Homer, *Iliad*, Ode II. p. 191

⁵⁸ *Iliad*, Ode I, verses 127-28, 161-62, etc. p. 191

⁵⁹ Homer, *Odyssey*, Ode XIV, verses 3, 48, etc. p. 191

⁶⁰ Homer, *Odyssey*, Ode VIII, verse 472; Ode XVIII, verse 424. p. 191

⁶¹ Aeschylus, *Oresteia. Eumenides*, verse 608. p. 193

⁶² A form of group marriage discovered by Morgan. Engels gives his analysis of this form of marriage in *The Origin of the Family, Private Property and the State* (Chapter II). p. 194

⁶³ See Karl Marx, "Conspectus of Lewis Morgan's *Ancient Society*" (Marx/Engels, *Über Kunst und Literatur*, Bd. I, Berlin, 1967, S. 630). p. 195

⁶⁴ Homer, *Odyssey*, Ode I, verses 352-56. p. 196

⁶⁵ Aeschylus, *Oresteia. Agamemnon*. p. 196

⁶⁶ The reference is to Plutarch, *Apophthegmata Laconica*, 242 B, ch. V; see also G. F. Schoemann, *Griechische Alterthümer*, Bd. I, Berlin, 1855, S. 268. p. 197

⁶⁷ *Spartiates*—citizens of ancient Sparta enjoying full civil rights.

Helots—citizens of ancient Sparta deprived of all rights; they were attached to the land and were duty bound to fulfil specific services for the Spartiates who owned that land. Their position in fact did not differ from that of the slaves. p. 197

⁶⁸ Aristophanes, *Thesmophoriazusae*, verses 417-18. p. 197

⁶⁹ Herodotus, *Historiae*, book VIII, ch. 105; see also W. Wachsmuth, *Hellenische Alterthumskunde aus dem Gesichtspunkte des Staates*, Th. II, Abt. II, Halle, 1830, S. 77. p. 198

NOTES

[70] Euripides, *Orestes*, verse 920.   p. 198

[71] Cicero, *Pro Caelio*, I, 38-39.   p. 202

[72] Plutarch, *Commentarius ne suaviter quidem vivi posse secundum Epicuri decreta, docens.*   p. 202

[73] The ancient name of the Caspian Sea.   p. 202

[74] Aristotle, *De caelo*, II, 12.   p. 202

[75] Marx quotes from a letter by Epicurus to Menoeceus; see *Diogenes Laertii de clarorum philosophorum vitis, dogmatibus et apophthegmatibus libri decem* (X, 123).   p. 204

[76] Aeschylus, *Prometheus Bound*.   p. 204

[77] Aeschylus, *Prometheus Bound*.   p. 205

[78] The article quoted by Marx was written for the *Kölnische Zeitung* by Carl Hermes, a reactionary journalist and one of its editors. p. 205

[79] *Curetes*, priests of Rhea, the mother of Zeus. According to Greek mythology the Curetes clashed their weapons to drown the cries of the infant Zeus and thus saved him from his father, Cronus, who devoured his own children for fear that they might deprive him of power.   p. 208

[80] Lucretius, *De rerum natura*, Book I.   p. 209

[81] Spinoza, *Ethics*, Part V, Prop. 42.   p. 209

[82] Engels recalls such facts from Heine's biography as the receipt of a pension from Louis Philippe and Heine's proposal to the Prussian Government in the 1830s to publish in Paris a newspaper in "the Prussian spirit".   p. 210

[83] See Lucian's *On the Death of Peregrinus* and pseudo-Lucian's *Philopatris*.   p. 211

[84] Codes of law and court decisions of the early Middle Ages.   p. 214

[85] *Nibelungenlied*—the major German heroic epic based on old German myths and lays of the period of the Exodus (III-V centuries). The extant text of this epic dates from about 1200.   p. 216

[86] *Nibelungenlied*, Song X.   p. 216

[87] A German epic of the 13th century.   p. 216

[88] This letter written by Marx is not extant. Engels mentions it in his letter to Kautsky of April 11, 1884.   p. 217

[89] This refers to the text of the operatic tetralogy *Ring of the Nibelungs* written by Richard Wagner on the basis of the Scandinavian epic

478 NOTES

Edda and the German epic *Nibelungenlied*. See R. Wagner, *Der Ring des Nibelungen, erster Tag, die Walküre*, Act. 2. p. 217

⁹⁰ *Edda*—a collection of Scandinavian myths, heroic lays and folk songs; is extant as a manuscript, dating from the 13th century, which was discovered in 1643 by Bishop Sveinsson of Iceland (the so-called *Elder or Poetic Edda*), and a treatise on the poetry of scalds written in 1179-1241 by Snorri Sturluson (the *Younger Edda*). "Ügisdrecka" is a song from the *Elder Edda* which is found among later texts of the collection. Engels quotes from stanza 32 and 36 of this song. p. 217

⁹¹ *Aesir* and *Vanir*—two groups of gods in Scandinavian mythology. The Ynglinga saga—the first saga in the book about Norwegian kings (from ancient times till the 12th century) entitled *Orb of the World*. It was written by the medieval Islandic poet and chronicler Snorri Sturluson in early 13th century on the basis of historical chronicles about Norwegian kings and Islandic and Norwegian tribal sagas. Engels quotes a passage from chapter 4 of this saga. p. 218

⁹² *Demagogues*—the name applied since 1819 by the reactionary circles of Germany to participants in the opposition movement from among the German intellectuals and students who, after the wars against the Napoleonic France, came out against the reactionary political system of the German states and organised manifestations to demand the unification of Germany. They were persecuted by the reactionary authorities. p. 219

⁹³ This refers to the amnesty granted to political prisoners in 1840 in connection with the coronation of Frederick William IV. p. 219

⁹⁴ *Restoration*—a period that set in when the Napoleonic Wars ended and the Bourbons dynasty was restored in France (1814, 1815-30). p. 219

⁹⁵ Engels refers to the collection *Rerum Hibernicarum Scriptores Veteres* ("Annalists of Ireland") published in four volumes in 1814, 1825 and 1826 by Charles O'Connor in Beckenham. p. 221

⁹⁶ This refers to the Irish uprising of 1798 in which Arthur O'Connor took part. p. 222

⁹⁷ *Senchus Mor*—a collection of ancient Irish laws which was published in 1865-73. Volume 3 of this publication (Dublin, 1873) was put out after Engels had written these pages. Engels was the first to appreciate the real significance of this code of ancient Irish laws as a historical source. p. 222

⁹⁸ These were two different types of land tenure in Ireland during the period of the consolidation of feudalism. They involved partial loss of personal freedom by the land-holder, the rank-and-file commoner,

NOTES 479

and his various duties to the nobleman who owned the land and cattle. These relations were reflected in *Senchus Mor.* Engels' "see below" refers to the section of his book on the history of Ireland which remained unwritten. p. 224

[99] Groups of the Celtic peoples who conquered ancient Ireland and Scotland. p. 225

[100] This item was written by Engels at the request of Marx's eldest daughter Jenny. It was intended as a preface to *Erins-Harfe*, a collection of songs to the words of Thomas Moore. It was then being prepared for publication. p. 225

[101] This refers to *The Poems of Ossian* written by the Scottish poet Macpherson who published them in 1760-65. He ascribed them to Ossian, the legendary Celtic bard. Macpherson wrote his poems on the basis of the ancient Irish epic in its later Scottish interpretation. p. 225

[102] This poem was composed as the death-song of Ragnar Lodbrôk, (9th century), a Danish Viking taken prisoner. According to the legend Krâka, Ragnar's wife, sang it to her children to inspire in them the desire to avenge their father's death. p. 227

[103] *Vulgate* is a canonised translation of the Bible into Latin. p. 232

[104] A religious sect that arose towards the close of the 12th century among the poor townspeople in southern France. They renounced private property, condemned accumulation of wealth by the Catholic Church and advocated the return to the traditions of early Christianity. The herecy of the Waldenses became particularly widespread among the country people of the mountainous districts of southwestern Switzerland and Savoie where it assumed the character of the defence of the survivals of the primitive communal system and patriarchal relations. p. 232

[105] This refers to "Perceval", "Willehalm..." and "Titurel" (the latter was not finished). p. 234

[106] This refers to the Treaty of Brétigny signed in 1360 between England and France (during the Hundred Years' War). p. 234

[107] Joseph von Görres, *Die deutschen Volksbücher*, Heidelberg, 1807.
p. 237

[108] *Eine wunderschöne Historie von dem gehörnten Siegfried.Was wunderliche Ebentheuer dieser theure Ritter ausgestanden, sehr denkwürdig und mit Lust zu Lesen.* Gedrückt in diesem Jahre, Cöln (n.d.).
p. 238

[109] The publication referred to is *Leben und Thaten des grossen Helden Heinrich des Löwen, Herzog zu Braunschweig*, Einbeck (n.d.). p. 238

[110] This refers to the decision passed by the German Federal Assembly on December 10, 1835, which banned the works by the Young Germany writers—Heine, Gutzkow, Laube, Wienbarg, and Mundt—some of whose works, such as Gutzkow's *Wally*, raised the question of women's emancipation.

The Federal Assembly (Diet)—the central authority of the German Confederation set up in 1815. It consisted of representatives of the German states; existed till 1866. p. 241

[111] *Young Germany* (Junges Deutschland)—a literary group that emerged in Germany in the 1830s and was under the influence of Heinrich Heine and Ludwig Börne. In their fiction and journalistic works, the writers of this group expressed the opposition sentiments of the petty bourgeois, advocated freedom of conscience and the press. Their political views were vague and inconsistent; many of them soon became ordinary bourgeois liberals. p. 241

[112] An allusion to Ludwig Tieck's comedy *Kaiser Octavianus*, which was based on a German popular book of the same name. p. 242

[113] This refers to *Tristan und Isolde*, a poem by Gottfried von Strassburg, which appeared in the early 13th century. p. 242

[114] L. Börne, *Briefe aus Paris*. p. 243

[115] This refers to K. Gutzkow's novel *Wally, die Zweiflerin* published in Mannheim in 1835. It was severely criticised by reactionary clericals. p. 243

[116] Engels refers to page 11 of his Notes, where the chronological table of inventions is quoted (Engels, *Dialectics of Nature*, Moscow, 1972, pp. 191-92). p. 247

[117] Engels is quoting Petrarch's 261st sonnet from his cycle *Rime in Vita e Morte di Madonna Laura*. p. 250

[118] The reference is to the 16th century (from the Italian "cinquecento"). p. 252

[119] These words were used in Ancient Rome to denote the world, the globe. p. 252

[120] Martin Luther's chorale "Ein' feste Burg ist unser Gott" became the Marseillaise of the rebellious peasants and other poor people during the Peasant War of 1524-25. p. 253

[121] In 1857, an arts exhibition was organised in Manchester, where Engels lived at that time. p. 254

NOTES 481

[122] *New York Daily Tribune*—an American progressive newspaper which, during the period between 1851 and 1862, carried many articles by Marx and Engels. p. 254

[123] Reference to a character from Terence's comedy *Eunuchus*, a vainglorious and silly warrior. p. 255

[124] *Salomon and Marcolf* (or Morolf)—characters from the German short satirical stories of the 14th and the 15th centuries; Salomon personifies a wise but impractical monarch and Marcolf, a sly peasant. p. 255

[125] K. Kautsky, *Thomas More und seine Utopie. Mit einer historischen Einleitung*, Stuttgart, 1888. p. 258

[126] In the Preface to the tragedy *Semirame* (1748), entitled "Disquisitions on the Ancient and Modern Tragedy", Voltaire wrote the following about Shakespeare's *Hamlet*: "One would think this work was created by the fantasy of a drunken savage. But amid these crude violations of form, which even now make the English theatre so absurd and barbarous, one finds in *Hamlet*, besides its still greater peculiarities, lofty thoughts worthy of a real genius." p. 259

[127] *Pantaloon* (Pantalone)—a character from the Italian folk comedy, a rich but stingy and silly Venetian merchant. p. 259

[128] This refers to the Crimean war of 1853-56, waged by Russia against the coalition of Britain, France, Turkey and Sardinia for domination in the Middle East. p. 259

[129] This refers to R. Benedix, *Die Schakespearomanie*. The book was directed against the Shakespearean influence on German drama.
p. 260

[130] A character from Shakespeare's comedy *Two Gentlemen of Verona*.
p. 260

[131] Shakespeare, *Timon of Athens*, Act IV, Scene 3. p. 261

[132] Shakespeare, *Love's Labour's Lost*, Act V, Scene 2. p. 262

[133] This refers to the Central Junta—the governmental authority in Spain during the period of the struggle against the Napoleonic domination. p. 262

[134] See Cervantes, *Coloquis de los perros Cipión y Berganza*. p. 264

[135] The *three unities* formed the cornerstone of the theory of drama in the period of French classicism of the 17th century, which demanded that action lasted only one day and night (unity of time), that it took place in one locality (unity of place) and was prompted by a single will (unity of action). p. 269

[136] François de la Rochefoucauld, *Reflexions ou sentences, et maximes morales* (Maxims and Moral Reflections). Marx quotes reflections Nos. 19, 93, 192, 257, 293, 304, 312, 509. p. 269

[137] G.W.F. Hegel, *Vorlesungen über die Philosophie der Geschichte, Werke*, Bd. IX, 2. Aufl., Berlin, 1840, S. 535-36. p. 271

[138] *Cartesianism*—the philosophy of Descartes (Cartesius in Latin); his followers drew materialist conclusions from it. p. 272

[139] Engels refers to the *Déclaration des droits de l'homme et du citoyen*, adopted by the Constituent Assembly in 1789. It set forth the political principles of the new, bourgeois system. p. 272

[140] The reference is to the book *Ludwig Feuerbach* by C. N. Starcke, Stuttgart, 1885. p. 279

[141] G.W.F. Hegel, *Phenomenologie des Geistes*; see *Werke*, Bd. II, Berlin, 1841, S. 381-85. p. 280

[142] Jules Gabriel Janin, *La fin d'un monde et du neveu de Rameau*. p. 280

[143] This refers to Rousseau's *Discours sur l'origine et les fondemens de l'inégalité parmi les hommes*, Amsterdam, 1755. p. 281

[144] The "Introduction" to *Anti-Dühring*. p. 284

[145] Th. Carlyle, *Past and Present*, London, 1843, p. 198. p. 285

[146] *Young England*—a group of Tory aristocrats (Disraeli, Borthwick, Lord Ashley and others) formed in the early 1840s. It expressed the discontent of the landed aristocracy with the increasing economic and political power of the bourgeoisie and sought to subject to its influence the working class in order to secure its support in its struggle against the bourgeoisie. p. 288

[147] The English physicist Matthew Tindal barred God from Nature, but conceded him a place in the sphere of emotions. p. 291

[148] *Congrès de Vérone*—a work by Chateaubriand. The Congress of Verona (1822)—the last meeting of the Holy Alliance, the coalition formed by Austria, Russia and Prussia in 1815 to suppress revolutionary movements and maintain feudal and monarchist regimes in power. The Congress of Verona was convened in connection with the upsurge of the revolutionary movement in Spain. Chateaubriand attended it as a diplomatic representative of France. p. 291

[149] Sainte-Beuve, *Chateaubriand et son groupe littéraire sous l'Empire*. p. 292

[150] The revolution of 1848. p. 294

[151] This refers to the counter-revolutionary coup d'état staged by Louis Bonaparte on December 2, 1851; on December 2, 1852, he proclaimed himself Emperor of the French under the name of Napoleon III. (See Marx's *The Eighteenth Brumaire of Louis Bonaparte.*) p. 295

[152] The reference is to the 1870-71 Franco-German war. p. 296

[153] Engels means Victor Hugo's appeal *Aux allemands* (To the Germans), published in the newspaper *Rappel* on September 10, and William I's letter to his wife, Auguste, published on September 7, 1870. p. 296

[154] Goethe, *Zahme Xenien*, IX. p. 311

[155] Paul Lafargue, *Socialism and Darwinism*, Progress, 1883, Vol. 2. p. 314

[156] Paul Lafargue's article "Le blé en Amérique" ("Corn in America"), *Journal des Économistes*, 1884, Vol. 27, Nos. 7 and 8. p. 314

[157] The novel, conceived by Paul Lafargue during his detention in the Sainte-Pelagie prison in Paris, was never written. p. 314

[158] This refers to Eduard Pindar, an emigrant from Russia who in the early 1850s helped Engels in his study of the Russian. p. 314

[159] Arthur Ranc, *Le roman d'une conspiration*, Paris, 1869. p. 315

[160] An ironic reference to Lassalle. p. 316

[161] Ernest Renan, *Histoire des origines du christianisme*, Paris, 1863-83. p. 316

[162] On January 31, 1887. p. 317

[163] In her letter to Engels of February 1, 1887, Laura Lafargue wrote about the conflict between the publisher of the newspaper *Le Cri du Peuple*, the Boulangist Caroline Séverine, and its editorial board, headed by Jules Guesde and other Socialists. p. 317

[164] *National-Zeitung*—a bourgeois daily published in Berlin from 1848 to 1915. p. 320

[165] The two lines are from the first book of Alexander Pope's satirical poem *Dunciad, an Heroic Poem in Three Books*. p. 320

[166] In 1745-46, the Scottish Highland clans rebelled against the repressions and evictions to which they were being subjected by the English and Scottish landed aristocracy and bourgeoisie. The Highlanders' discontent was taken advantage of by a section of the Scottish Highland nobility which was interested in preserving the feudal clan system and declared the restoration of the Stuarts on the English throne to be the aim of the rebellion. After several short-lived successes, the rebels' army was defeated. p. 321

[167] L. H. Morgan, *Ancient Society*, London, 1877, pp. 357, 358. p. 322

[168] *The Poor Law*, passed in 1834, forbade the relief of the poor except within poor-houses, in which a real prison regime was maintained. The people called the poor-houses Bastilles for the poor. p. 322

[169] This refers to Guizot's book *Pourquoi la révolution d'Angleterre a-t-elle réussi?* (Why the English Revolution Was Successful), Paris, 1850. p. 326

[170] *Pecksniff*—a character from Charles Dickens' book *Martin Chuzzlewit*, an unctuous hypocrite. p. 327

[171] *Illuminati*—members of a trend within the Freemason movement; the Illuminati were active mainly in Bavaria in the latter half of the eighteenth century.

Freemasons—a religious and philosophic movement which originated in Britain in the late seventeenth and the early eighteenth century, and became widespread in a number of countries. The Freemasons were organised in secret lodges and surrounded their activities with mystic rituals. p. 334

[172] *The Magic Flute (Die Zauberflöte)*—an opera by Mozart which in a naive, fairy-tale form suggests that he who has revealed the forces of Nature and abides by her laws is rewarded, while evil-doers are duly punished. p. 334

[173] *Laissez-faire, laissez-aller*—the motto of bourgeois economists advocating free trade and non-interference by the state in the economy. p. 336

[174] *In partibus infidelium* (literally, in the regions of infidels)—the formula added to the titles of Catholic bishops governing purely nominal dioceses in non-Christian countries. p. 337

[175] The *Social Democratic Federation*—an English socialist organisation founded in August 1884 and uniting diverse socialist elements, mainly intellectuals. For a long time the Federation was under the sway of reformists headed by Hyndman, who pursued an opportunist and sectarian policy. In opposition to this line, the revolutionary Marxists within the Federation (Eleanor Marx-Aveling, Edward Aveling, Tom Mann and others) worked for close ties with the mass labour movement.

After a split in the autumn of 1884 and the establishment of an independent organisation by the members of the Left wing (December 1889), the influence of the opportunists in the Federation became stronger. However, under the impact of the revolutionary sentiments of the masses, revolutionary elements dissatisfied with the opportunist leadership continued to germinate within the Federation.
p. 341

NOTES 485

[176] Here the word metaphysics is used in the sense of a philosophy treating of things lying beyond the sphere of experience. p. 347

[177] The 1791 Constitution, adopted by the bourgeois Constituent Assembly, established a constitutional monarchy in France. The constitution was abolished as a result of the popular uprising of August 10, 1792, which overthrew the king. p. 347

[178] The *Girondists*—a political group during the French Revolution. They expressed the interests of the moderate bourgeoisie, wavering between revolution and counter-revolution and compromising with the monarchy. p. 347

[179] The reference is to the Holy Roman Empire (962-1806), which comprised Germany (the dominant power) and numerous kingdoms, duchies and principalities. p. 348

[180] According to Kant, only such actions are moral as are performed not to satisfy any practical need but in the name of a purely moral ideal, at the prompting of an unconditionally binding moral obligation, which he called the "categorical imperative". p. 348

[181] A paraphrase of Mephistopheles' words from Goethe's *Faust* (Part I, Scene 3, "Faust's Study"). p. 350

[182] *Homunculus* (Lat., dim. of *homo*—man)—the manikin that was produced in a cucurbit by Wagner, Faust's pupil, in Goethe's *Faust* (Part II). p. 353

[183] True socialism—a teaching that became widespread in Germany in 1844; it expressed the reactionary ideology of the German petty bourgeoisie. The theorists of "true socialism" (Karl Grün, Moses Hess, Hermann Kriege and others) replaced socialist ideas with a sentimental preaching of love and fraternity and denied the need for a bourgeois-democratic revolution in Germany. p. 354

[184] In Goethe's comedy *Der Bürgergeneral*, satirising the French Revolution, the village barber Schnaps, who poses as a "Jacobin general", gets hold of a jug of milk and drinks the contents causing a scuffle among the peasants who claim ownership of it. p. 357

[185] Goethe, *Briefe aus der Schweiz*, Part I. This work, written after the publication of *Die Leiden des jungen Werthers*, consists of excerpts from letters that were supposedly found among Werther's papers.
p. 358

[186] *Frankfurter Gelehrte Anzeigen*—a journal published from 1772 to 1790 in Frankfort. In 1772, the editorial board included Goethe, Herder and other progressive-minded writers and scientists. p. 360

[187] From Goethe's cycle *Venezianische Epigramme*. p. 361

[188] The reference is to the short story *Unterhaltungen deutscher Ausgewanderten* (Conversations of German Emigrants). p. 362

[189] Goethe, *Hermann und Dorothea*, IX. Gesang. p. 363

[190] G.W.F. Hegel, *Vorlesungen über die Philosophie der Geschichte*, Einleitung. p. 363

[191] Goethe, *Über Naturwissenschaft im Allgemeinen, einzelne Betrachtungen und Aphorismen*. p. 364

[192] This refers to the reactionary majority in the French Chamber of Deputies which supported the Guizot government. p. 364

[193] The *Customs Union* of German states was founded in 1834 and was gradually joined by all German states, except Austria and a few other, small ones. Prussia played the leading role in the Union. Called into being by the need for creating an all-German market, the Union subsequently contributed also to Germany's political unification. p. 364

[194] Goethe, *Zahme Xenien*, IV. p. 367

[195] *Montagnards*—the group of revolutionary-democratic deputies in the Convention during the French Revolution. p. 369

[196] Goethe, *Faust*, Part I, Scene 1, "The Night". p. 370

[197] *Ghibellines*—the political party of the Italian feudal nobility from the 12th to the 15th centuries. In the struggle between the Popes and the German Emperors, the Ghibellines supported the latter. p. 371

[198] Paraphrase from Goethe's poem "Vanitas, vanitatum vanitas". p. 371

[199] From Goethe's quatrain "Warnung" (Zyklus *Epigrammatisch*). *Titania* and *Bottom*—characters in Shakespeare's play *A Midsummer Night's Dream*. p. 374

[200] This refers to Heine's statements about the philosophical revolution in Germany contained in his essays *Zur Geschichte der Religion und Philosophie in Deutschland*. Heine believed that the philosophical revolution, with Hegel's philosophy as its culmination, was the prelude to an imminent democratic revolution in Germany. p. 375

[201] Engels did the translation from an early version of Heine's poem. As distinct from the version first published in the newspaper *Vorwärts!* No. 55, of July 10, 1844, the first stanza of the translation has an extra line, the third. p. 375

[202] The reference is to the Afterword to *Romanzero*. p. 376

[203] Marx was expelled from France by the Guizot government for his

part in the editing of *Vorwärts!* The expulsion order was issued under pressure from the Prussian government, on January 16, 1845. Marx moved to Brussels on February 3, somewhat later than he originally planned. p. 377

[204] The annual *Rheinische Jahrbücher zur gesellschaftlichen Reform.* Two volumes of it appeared in 1845-46. p. 377

[205] The reference is to the book *Heinrich Heine über Ludwig Börne*, Hamburg, 1840. p. 377

[206] This refers to the July Revolution in France in 1830 and the uprisings that followed in its wake in Belgium, Poland, Germany and Italy. p. 378

[207] Ludwig Börne, *Briefe aus Paris*, 1.-2. Theile, Hamburg, 1832; 3.-6. Theile, Paris, 1833-1834. p. 380

[208] Friedrich Gottlieb Klopstock, *Der Messias*, Erster Gesang. p. 390

[209] The reference is to the sentimental trend in German literature typified by J. M. Miller's novel *Siegwart. Eine Klostergeschichte.* It was published in 1776 and was very popular in the late 18th century. p. 390

[210] The Maybug Club was founded by Gottfried Kinkel and Johanna Mockel and existed until 1848. p. 390

[211] Kinkel's speech at the military tribunal in Rastatt on April 4, 1849, was published in the bourgeois-democratic Berlin newspaper *Abend-Post* on April 6 and 7, 1850. Marx and Engels sharply criticised it in the *Neue Rheinische Zeitung*. p. 391

[212] On his way back from the Third Crusade (1190-92), King Richard I (Lionheart) of England was captured by Duke Leopold I of Austria. According to tradition, he managed to escape from captivity thanks to the assistance of the French troubadour Blondel, his court poet. p. 394

[213] The *Neue Rheinische Zeitung. Organ der Demokratie*—a daily newspaper edited by Marx. It appeared in Cologne from July 1, 1848, to May 19, 1849. p. 395

[214] *In partibus infidelium*—see Note 174. In this context the phrase means "non-existent". Engels is alluding to the poems "Die deutsche Flotte" (1841) by Georg Herwegh, and "Flotten-Träume" (1843) and "Zwei Flaggen" (1844) by Ferdinand Freiligrath, which sang the praises of the as yet non-existent German navy. p. 396

[215] *Moorish prince*—the hero of Freiligrath's poem of this title. Marx often applied the name to the poet himself. p. 397

[216] In his letter Weydemeyer relates an episode of the "war between mice and frogs" (Marx's phrase) which two German emigrant organisations in London—Arnold Ruge's Agitation Union and Gottfried Kinkel's Emigrant Club—waged against each other. Kinkel held that the main thing for the success of a revolution was "a small well-armed detachment abundantly provided with money". Kinkel went on a "revolutionary agitation and entertainment" tour of the United States with a view to obtaining a loan for organising a revolution in Germany. p. 397

[217] Shakespeare, *King Henry IV*, Part I, Act III, Scene 1. p. 401

[218] An allusion to the poem "An Wolfgang im Feld" ("To Wolfgang on the Battlefield") written by Freiligrath during the Franco-German war (August 12, 1870) and dedicated to his son, who had volunteered for the front. p. 401

[219] The reference is to the subscription organised by German petty-bourgeois democrats in Germany and New York in 1867 to enable Freiligrath to return from England to Germany. Nearly 60,000 talers was raised. Marx disapproved of Freiligrath's consent to the subscription on moral grounds. p. 401

[220] The first line of Freiligrath's poem "Hurra, Germania!" p. 401

[221] See Note 34. p. 405

[222] See Note 36. p. 406

[223] Vera Zasulich translated Engels' pamphlet *Socialism: Utopian and Scientific* into Russian in 1884. p. 409

[224] The collection of Czech heroic poetry mentioned by Marx was the *Rukopis Královédvorský*, translated into German in 1829 by Hanka and Swoboda, two prominent figures of the Czech national movement. The translators claimed that the manuscript was part of a lost 13th-century collection of Czech heroic songs. Actually, they had written the songs themselves. The poem "Zaboj a Slavoj" describes the liberation of the Czechs from the rule of an alien king by the heroes Zaboj and Slavoj. p. 410

[225] This text consists of notes made by Engels from the book of the English poet and translator John Bowring. p. 410

[226] Derzhavin, "On the Capture of Warsaw". p. 413

[227] Pushkin, *Eugene Onegin*. p. 413

[228] An inaccuracy in Engels' text. In 1867 Chernyshevsky was serving a term of hard labour at Alexandrovsky Zavod, east of Lake Baikal, whence he was transferred to Vilyuisk in 1872. p. 416

[229] See Marx's letter to the Editorial Board of the *Otechestvenniye Zapiski* (Fatherland Notes), November 1877. p. 418

[230] Marx and Engels refer to an article in the anonymous anarchist pamphlet published by Nechayev and Bakunin. p. 420

[231] The reference is to *Narodnoye Delo* (People's Cause), the journal of the Russian section of the International. It appeared in Geneva in 1868 and 1869 and upheld the programme and organisational integrity of the International. p. 420

[232] Intending to write an article about Chernyshevsky, Marx repeatedly asked Nikolai Danielson to send him the requisite biographical data. However, it was only on March 20 (April 1), 1873, that Danielson was able to send him a brief biographical note on Chernyshevsky. Danielson had not managed to obtain data on Chernyshevsky's literary work and political trial. The planned article therefore failed to materialise. p. 421

[233] Chernyshevsky's revolutionary activities are meant. p. 421

[234] The reference is to *Capital* by Karl Marx. p. 421

[235] Marx read Flerovsky's *Condition of the Working Class in Russia* in the language of the original (Russian). p. 422

[236] An allusion to the newspaper *Social-Demokrat* (founded in 1864), the organ of the General Association of German Workers. Controlled by Johann Baptist Schweitzer, a follower of Lassalle, the paper pursued a policy of compromise with the Junker monarchy. p. 427

[237] A hymn written by Martin Luther. Heine called it the Marseillaise of the Reformation. p. 431

[238] *Des Khaben Wunderhorn*—a collection of German folk songs published by the romanticist poets Clemens Brentano and Achim von Arnim in the period of 1806-08. p. 432

[239] The reference is to the song "Schleswig-Holstein meerumschlungen" (Schleswig-Holstein sea-embraced), written by M. F. Chemnitz in 1844, which became particularly popular at the time of the struggle for Schleswig-Holstein's liberation from Danish rule. p. 432

[240] The *Hecker Song*—a German revolutionary song, popular in 1848-49, about the April 1848 republican uprising in Baden. The uprising was led by Friedrich Hecker and Gustav Struve. p. 432

[241] The reference is to the revolutionary song "Das Blutgericht" (The Bloodbath), which was sung widely in Silesian textile districts on the eve of the weavers' uprising in 1844. p. 433

[242] Arnold Ruge contributed to the *Vorwärts!* under the pseudonym of "A Prussian". p. 433

[243] A theatre in Paris. p. 435

[244] The "Confessions" (1865) give Marx's answers to a questionnaire circulated at the time in England and Germany. Though formulated in a semi-facetious manner, the answers throw light on Marx's personality. p. 436

[245] Engels' "Confessions", humorous in character, are published according to the text contained in the album of Jenny, Marx's elder daughter. p. 437

[246] The following five reports appeared unsigned in the German democratic newspaper *Frankfurter Zeitung und Handelsblatt* on November 21, 1875, April 4, 1876, and January 3, February 8 and May 25, 1877. The reports were marked with the sign —·—. Even in those years only a few close friends knew that the reports were written by Jenny Marx, the wife and associate of Karl Marx. After the death of Marx and his relatives and friends, the fact of Jenny's authorship was forgotten.

The reports were discovered by the G.D.R. historians Louise Dornemann and Bernhard Doom and, after ninety years, reprinted in the journal *Beiträge zur Geschichte der deutschen Arbeiterbewegung* No. 6, 1966.

Jenny Marx's authorship has been proved beyond doubt on the basis of letters by Karl Marx and other members of his family. p. 449

[247] *The Daily News*—English liberal newspaper, organ of the industrial bourgeoisie; appeared under this title in London from 1846 to 1930. p. 452

[248] *The Standard*—an English Conservative daily, founded in London in 1827. p. 452

[249] *The Saturday Review of Politics, Literature, Science and Art*—British Conservative weekly, appeared in London from 1855 to 1938. p. 452

[250] The ruling party and the Opposition. p. 453

[251] *Queen Victoria* (1819-1901) was proclaimed Empress of India in 1876; she stayed in Coburg, Germany, from March 31 to April 20, 1876. p. 453

[252] The reference is to Albert Edward (1841-1910), the elder son of Queen Victoria, who was Prince of Wales and, from 1901, King of Great Britain, Ireland and the Dominions (Edward VII). From September 1875 to May 1876 he was travelling in India. p. 454

253 *Richmond*—a character from Shakespeare's chronicle *Richard III*, here in the sense of adversary, opponent. p. 456

254 The book of the English bourgeois economist William Stafford was signed with his initials, W. S. For a long time it was attributed to Shakespeare and in 1751 even appeared under his name. Marx analyses Stafford's economic views in the first volume of *Capital*. p. 457

255 The *Transactions of the New Shakespeare Society*. p. 458

256 Part of this article was translated into English by Eleanor Marx. p. 458

257 The international conference convoked on the initiative of Russia and Britain in Constantinople in December 1876 with a view to finding a peaceful solution to the Balkan problem. The conference failed of its purpose because of the intransigent attitude of Turkey. p. 461

258 *Pera*—the district of Constantinople where most Europeans lived. p. 461

259 Shakespeare, *Richard III*, Act I, Scene 1. p. 463

260 Ibid., Act IV, Scene 4. p. 464

261 Ibid., Act III, Scene 6. p. 464

262 *Le Courrier de Lyon*—a melodrama in 5 acts and 8 scenes by the playwright Louis Moreau (1806-1877), the author of vaudevilles Paul Siraudin (1813-1883) and the physician and author of vaudevilles Alfred Delacour. p. 466

263 The *Directory* (consisted of five members, with one re-elected every year)—the highest executive body in France established under the 1795 Constitution, which was adopted after the fall of the Jacobin revolutionary dictatorship in 1794. The Directory maintained a reign of terror against the democratic forces and protected the interests of the big bourgeoisie; it was abolished as a result of Bonaparte's coup d'état in 1799. p. 466

264 The reference is to the Third Republic, which was called a "republic without republicans". The struggle for its establishment began after the suppression of the Paris Commune in 1871. p. 467

265 *The Nineteenth Century*—a British liberal monthly journal; appeared under this title from 1877 to 1900. Irving's articles on Shakespeare were published in Issues 1 and 3, March and May 1877. p. 468

266 Chernyshevsky wrote two works directed against John Stuart Mill: *Addenda and Notes to the First Volume of John Stuart Mill's Political Economy* (Geneva, 1869) and *Studies in Political Economy (According to Mill)* in the 1870s Marx, who had learned Russian, read

them in the language of the original. The copies of these works preserved among Marx's books contain numerous marginal notes by Marx. p. 470

[267] *Sovremennik* (Contemporary)—a Russian literary and socio-political journal founded by Pushkin. Appeared in St. Petersburg from 1836 to 1866. Belinsky, Dobrolyubov and Chernyshevsky were among its contributors; in the 1860s the journal was virtually the organ of Russian revolutionary democracy. p. 470

Name Index

A

Abel, Karl (b. 1837)—German philologist and journalist, Berlin correspondent of *The Daily Telegraph.*—461

Aberdeen, George Gordon, Earl of (1784-1860)—English statesman, Tory; leader of the Peelites from 1850; Foreign Secretary (1828-30, 1841-46) and Prime Minister of the coalition government (1852-55).—259

Adam, Jean Victor Vincent (1801-1867)—French artist.—142

Aeschylus (525-456 B.C.)—Greek dramatist.—88, 95, 192-96, 436, 438

Alexander of Macedon (Alexander the Great) (356-323 B. C.)—king of Macedon (336-323 B. C.), general of antiquity.—79, 205, 221

Alexander I (1777-1825)—Emperor of Russia (1801-25).—292

Alexander II (1818-1881)—Emperor of Russia (1855-81).—416

Anacreon (c. 570-478 B. C.)—Greek lyrical poet.—215, 412

Anaxagoras of Clazomenae (c. 500-428 B.C.)—Greek materialist philosopher.—203

Anaxandridas (6th cent. B. C.)—King of Sparta.—197

Anne (Stuart) (1665-1714)—Queen of Great Britain (1702-14).—430

Annenkov, Pavel Vasilyevich (1812-1887)—Russian man of letters, liberal landowner; corresponded with Marx.—377

Appian of Alexandria (end of the 1st cent.—70s of the 2nd cent.—Roman historian, author of works on the history of Rome.—261

Arago, Dominique François (1786-1853)—French astronomer, mathematician and physicist.—178

Ariosto, Lodovico (1474-1533)—Italian poet of the Renaissance, author of *L'Orlando furioso.*—437

Ariston (6th cent. B. C.)—King of Sparta.—197

Aristophanes (c. 446-385 B. C.)—Greek dramatist, author of political satires.—88, 197

Aristotle (384-323 B. C.)—Greek philosopher and scholar.—202, 205, 269, 274

Auerswald, Hans Adolf Erdmann (1792-1848)—Prussian general, member of the Frankfurt National Assembly; killed by the people during the uprising in Frankfurt in September 1848.—403

Augustus, Octavianus (63 B.C.-A.D. 14)—Roman Emperor (27 B.C.-A.D. 14).—210, 242

Aveling, Edward (1851-1898)—English socialist, one of the founders of the Socialist League; writer.—89, 341

B

Babbedge, Charles (1792-1871)—English economist.—155

Bach, Johann Sebastian (1685-1750)—German composer.—344

Bachofen, Johann Jacob (1815-1887)—Swiss lawyer and historian, author of *Das Mutterrecht.*—192-94

Bahr, Hermann (1863-1934)—Austrian journalist, critic and dramatist.—75, 78

Bakunin, Mikhail Alexandrovich (1814-1876)—Russian revolutionary; writer; one of the ideologists of anarchism and an enemy of Marxism in the First International; for his splitting activities was expelled from it by the Hague Congress in 1872.—409, 414, 420

Ball, John (d. 1381)—English preacher, a leader of Wat Tyler's revolt.—234

Balzac, Honoré de (1799-1850)—French novelist.—91, 92, 313-15, 439, 442

Barrot, Odilon (1791-1873)—French politician, leader of the liberal dynastic opposition until February 1848; from December 1848 to October 1849 headed the ministry, which was supported by the counter-revolutionary bloc of monarchist parties.—261

Barth, Paul (1858-1922)—German sociologist and historian, opposed Marxism.—62, 65, 67

Bastide, Jules (1800-1879)—French politician and writer; an editor of the bourgeois-Republican newspaper *Le National* (1836-46); Foreign Minister (May to December 1848).—294

Bateman, Isabel—English actress popular in London in the 1870s.—460, 466, 467, 468

Bateman, Kate Josephine (1842-1917)—English actress popular in the 1860s and 1870s, performer of Shakespearian characters.—460, 464, 466

Bateman, Virginia—English actress of the 1870s.—460, 464, 465, 467

Batyushkov, Konstantin Nikolayevich (1787-1855)—Russian poet.—410

Bax, Ernest Belfort (1854-1926)—English socialist; historian, philosopher and journalist; one of the first propagandists of Marxism in England, a founder of the Socialist League and the British Socialist Party.—342

Bayle, Pierre (1647-1706)—French sceptic philosopher, critic of religious dogmatism.—256

Beau, Charles.—467

Beaumarchais, Pierre Augustin Caron de (1732-1794)—French playwright.—113

Bebel, August (1840-1913)—leader of the German and international working-class movement; one of the founders of the German Social-Democratic Party and the Second International, friend and comrade-in-arms of Marx and Engels.—405

Beck, Karl (1817-1879)—German poet; in the 1840s adhered to "true socialism".—387-89

Becker, Johann Philipp (1809-1886)—German Communist worker, participant in the 1848-49 revolution; after his emigration to Switzerland took part in organising the Geneva section of the First International; friend of Marx and Engels.—405, 406

Beethoven, Ludwig van (1770-1827)—German composer.—346

Benedix, Julius Roderich (1811-1873)—German playwright, director of the theatre in Elberfeld.—260

Benignus (d. 468)—Irish clergyman, Bishop of Armagh, one of the compilers of the collection *Senchus Mor*.—223

Bentham, Jeremy (1748-1832)—English politician, theoretician of utilitarianism.—165, 273

Béranger, Pierre Jean de (1780-1857)—French democratic poet, author of political satires.—148

Bernardin de Saint-Pierre, Jacques Henri (1737-1814)—French author.—263

Bernstein, Eduard (1850-1932)—German Social-Democrat; editor of the Social-Democratic newspaper *Der Sozial-demokrat* (1881-90); after Engels' death advocated revision of Marxism on the main questions of theory and tactics; subsequently leader and theoretician of opportunism.—119

Bessel, Friedrich Wilhelm (1784-1846)—German astronomer.—178

Bettziech, Heinrich (1813-1876)—German writer and journalist; petty-bourgeois democrat; emigrated to London.—400

Bismarck, Otto (1815-1898)—Chancellor of Prussia and of Germany, ideologist of reactionary Junkers; in the 1860s and 1870s effected unification of Germany "from above" under Prussian hegemony; author of Exceptional Laws against the Socialists.—67, 113, 115, 197

Blanc, Louis (1811-1882)—French petty-bourgeois socialist and historian; member of the Provisional Government in 1848.—95, 292, 314, 335

Blenker, Ludwig (Louis) (1812-1863)—German officer, participant in the Baden-Pfalz uprising in 1849; subsequently emigrated to the U.S.A.; fought in the American Civil War on the side of the Northerners.—432

Blondel de Néele—French troubadour of the end of the 12th and the beginning of the 13th century.—394

Blum, Robert (1807-1848)—German petty-bourgeois democrat, journalist; led the Left wing in the Frankfurt National Assembly.—432

Boccaccio Giovanni (1313-1375)

—Italian novelist and poet of the Renaissance.—248

Böhme, Jacob (1575-1624)—German handicraftsman; mystic philosopher.—344

Boleyn, Anne (c. 1507-1536)—second wife of Henry VIII of England (from 1533), mother of Queen Elizabeth I; was put to death by Henry VIII.—449

Bonald, Louis Gabriel Ambroise Vicomte (1754-1840)—French politician and writer; monarchist, one of the ideologists of the aristocratic and clerical reaction during the Restoration.—289

Börne, Ludwig (1786-1837)—German democratic writer and critic, ideologist of the Young Germany movement.—243, 355, 374, 377, 379-81

Bowring, John (1792-1872)—English politician, linguist and man of letters; follower of Bentham, free-trader.—411

Boz—see *Dickens, Charles.*

Brentano, Lujo (1844-1931)—German vulgar bourgeois economist, one of the chief exponents of Katheder-socialism.—113, 114

Brian Borumha (926-1014)—King of Ireland (1001-14), routed the Normans at Clontarf in 1014.—225

Broadhouse, John—see *Hyndman, Henry Mayers.*

Brontë, Charlotte (pen name *Currer Bell*) (1816-1855)—English realist writer.—339

Brutus, Marcus Junius (c. 85-42 B. C.)—Roman politician, republican; took part in the assassination of Julius Caesar.—81

Buchez, Philippe (1796-1865)—French politician and historian; subsequently ideologist of Christian socialism in France.—361

Burns, Mary Allen, "Pumps" (born c. 1860)—niece of Engels' wife.—89, 438

Byron, George Noel Gordon (1788-1824)—English poet, representative of revolutionary romanticism.—55, 162, 164, 320

C

Cabet, Étienne (1788-1856)—French utopian communist, author of the novel *Voyage en Icarie.*—274

Caesar, Gaius Julius (100-44 B. C.)—Roman general and statesman.—81, 190, 262

Cairnech (526-598)—Irish bishop.—223

Calderón de la Barca, Pedro (1600-1681)—Spanish poet and playwright.—262, 263, 443, 444

Calvin, Jean (1509-1564)—leader of the Reformation, founder of Calvinism, a trend of Protestantism.—52, 66

Campe, Julius (1792-1867)—German bookseller and publisher, head of the Hoffmann und Campe Publishing House in Hamburg; published works by Heine and other Left writers.—390, 403

Camphausen, Ludolf (1803-1890)—German banker, a leader of the Rhenish liberal bourgeoisie.—434

Capefigue, Jean Baptiste (1802-1872)—French writer and historian; monarchist.—314

Carleton, William (1794-1869)—Irish novelist.—340

Carlyle, Thomas (1795-1881)—English writer and historian; idealist philosopher; in his early works criticised the English bourgeoisie for its cruel exploitation of the working class, but after 1848 became a reactionary and an enemy of the working-class movement.—285, 325-27, 331, 332, 334, 336, 338, 339

Carolan (O'Carolan), Torlogh (1670-1738)—Irish bard, author of numerous folk songs.—225

Catherine II (1729-1796)—Empress of Russia (1762-96).—278, 412

Caussidière, Marc (1808-1861)—French Left-wing Republican, prefect of police in Paris after the February 1848 revolution.—95

Cavaignac, Louis Eugène (1802-1857)—French general and politician; moderate bourgeois Republican; Minister of War in May and June 1848; cruelly suppressed the June uprising of the Paris workers.—294

Cervantes Saavedra, Miguel de (1547-1616)—Spanish writer.—88, 264, 439, 444

Chamisso, Adelbert von (1781-1838)—German romantic poet.—442

Chamont, Céline.—454

Charlemagne (Charles the Great) (742-814)—Frankish king (768-800) and Roman Emperor (800-14).—231, 243

Charles Augustus (1757-1828)—grand duke of Saxe-Weimar; patronised Goethe who lived at his court.—344, 369

Charles II (1630-1685)—King of Great Britain (1660-85).—429

Charles V (1500-1558)—King of Spain as Charles I (1516-56) and Emperor of the Holy Roman Empire (1519-56).—100

Chateaubriand, François René, Vicomte (1768-1848)—French writer, reactionary statesman and diplomat; represented France at the Verona Congress in 1822.—263, 291, 292

Chaucer, Geoffrey (c. 1340-1400)—English poet.—235

Chernyshevsky, Nikolai Gavrilovich (1828-1889)—Russian revolutionary democrat, writer and critic.—408, 414-21, 469-70

Chester, Robert.—458

Cibber, Colley (1671-1757)—English actor, dramatist and poet.—462, 465

Cicero, Marcus Tullius (106-43 B. C.)—Roman orator and statesman; eclectic philosopher.—202, 205, 249

Cimbaoth (3rd cent. B. C.)—King of Ulster (Northern Ireland).—222

Cobbett, William (1762-1835)—English politician and publicist; championed democratisation of the English political system.—114-15, 321-23, 327, 438

Comte, Auguste (1798-1857)—French philosopher and sociologist, founder of positivism.—459

Constant de Rebecque, Henri Benjamin (1767-1830)—French liberal-bourgeois politician, journalist and writer.—81

Cooper, Fenimore (1789-1851)—American writer.—441

Corc (5th cent.)—King of Munster (Southern Ireland).—223

Cormac Mac Cuilennain (836-908)—King and Bishop of Cashel (901-08).—224

Courbet, Gustave (1819-1877)—French painter, a Communard.—169

Courier de Méré, Paul Louis (1772-1825)—French political writer of the Restoration.—113

Cousin, Victor (1792-1867)—French idealist philosopher, eclectic.—81

Craig, William.—458

Crassus, Marcus Licinius (115-53 B. C.)—Roman general and politician; in 71 suppressed the slave rebellion led by Spartacus; member of the 1st triumvirate (Julius Caesar, Pompey, Crassus).—262

Cromwell, Oliver (1599-1658)—leader of the bourgeoisie and the bourgeoisified nobility during the English revolution of the 17th century; Lord Protector of England, Scotland and Ireland from 1653.—81, 226, 327

D

Dacier, André (1651-1722)—French philologist, prepared an edition of Aristotle's *Poetica* supplied with commentaries.—269

Dagobert I—Frankish king (629-39).—410

Daire (5th cent.)—a chieftain in Ulster (Northern Ireland).—223

Dante, Alighieri (1265-1321)—Italian poet.—88, 247-49, 370, 438

Danton, Georges Jacques (1759-1794)—leader of the Jacobins' Right wing in the French Revolution.—80, 95, 327

Darwin, Charles Robert (1809-1882)—English naturalist, founder of scientific evolutionary biology.—438

Defoe, Daniel (c. 1660-1731)—English writer in the period of Enlightenment, author of *Robinson Crusoe*.—318

Delius, Nicolaus (1813-1888)—German philologist, Shakespearian.—456, 458

De Maistre, Joseph (1753-1821)—French writer, enemy of the French Revolution, an ideologist of the Restoration.—289

Demuth, Helene ("*Lenchen*", "*Nim*") (1823-1890)—housekeeper at Marx's, friend of the whole family; after Marx's death lived at Engels'.—89

Derby, Edward Geoffrey Smith Stanley, Earl (1799-1869)—English statesman.—457

Derzhavin, Gavriil Romanovich (1743-1816)—Russian poet, representative of classicism.—412

Descartes (Cartesius), René (1596-1650)—French philosopher, mathematician and naturalist.—272, 274

Desclée, Aimée (1836-1874)—French actress.—454

Desmoulins, Camille (1760-1794)—French writer; prominent in the French Revolution, Right-wing Jacobin.—80

Dézamy, Théodore (1803-1850)—French writer, representative of the revolutionary trend in utopian communism.—274

Dickens, Charles (pen-name *Boz*) (1812-1870)—English writer.— 297, 339, 455

Diderot, Denis (1713-1784)— French materialist philosopher, writer and critic; editor and publisher of *Encyclopaedia*.— 164, 256, 275, 278, 279, 280, 415, 436

Diodorus Siculus (c. 80-29 B. C.) —Greek historian.—45-46

Disraeli, Benjamin, Earl of Beaconsfield (1804-1881)—British statesman and author.—453

Dobrolyubov, Nikolai Alexandrovich (Ehrlieb) (1836-1861) —Russian revolutionary democrat, critic and materialist philosopher.—414, 415

Dowden, Edward (1843-1913)— Irish literary historian and critic; professor of English literature in Dublin University, author of works on Shakespeare, English romanticism and French literature.—460

Droste-Hülshoff, Annette Elisabeth (1797-1848)—German writer and poetess.—55-56

Dubthach—Irish lawyer and court poet of the first half of the 5th century.—223

Dühring, Eugen (1833-1921)— German eclectic philosopher and vulgar economist; pettybourgeois socialist.—281, 349

Dumas, Alexandre (Dumas père) (1803-1870)—French playwright.—292, 316, 439

Dumas, Alexandre (Dumas fils) (1824-1895)—French novelist and dramatist.—292, 316, 439

Dupont, Pierre (1821-1870)— French poet, author of songs popular among the workers.— 292, 316, 465

Dürer, Albrecht (1471-1528)— German painter of the Renaissance.—253

E

Ebner, Hermann (1805-1855)— German journalist; secret agent in the service of the Austrian Government in the 1840s and 1850s.—397

Echegaray y Eizaguirre, José (1832-1916)—Spanish playwright.—341

Ehrlieb—see *Dobrolyubov, Nikolai Alexandrovich*.

Eichhoff, Frédérick Gustave (1799-1875)—French philologist.—89, 409

Eichhoff, Karl Wilhelm (1833-1895)—German Socialist, friend of Marx and Engels.— 89

Elizabeth I (1533-1603)—Queen of England (1558-1603).—226, 458

Elizabeth Petrovna (1709-1761)— Empress of Russia (1741-61), daughter of Peter I.—411

Ella (d. 867)—King of Northumbria (North England) from 863. —227

Encke, Johann Franz (1791-1865) —German astronomer.—178

Epicurus (c. 341-270 B. C.)— Greek materialist philosopher. —201, 202, 204-05, 207, 303

Ernst, Paul (1866-1933)—German journalist, critic and playwright; in the 1880s was a Social-Democrat and contributed to the *Neue Zeit*; in the 1890s was one of the leaders of the anarchist Opposition of the "Young"; in his later years became a national-socialist.—75

Euripides (c. 480-406 B. C.)—Greek dramatist, author of classical tragedies.—198

F

Faucit, Helena (1817-1898)—English tragic actress.—460

Fauriel, Claude (1772-1842)—French historian and critic.—230-31

Favre, Jules (1809-1880)—French lawyer and politician; Foreign Minister (1870-71); butcher of the Paris Commune.—467

Fergus (5th cent.)—Irish bard, one of the compilers of the collection *Senchus Mor*.—223

Feuerbach, Ludwig (1804-1872)—German materialist philosopher of the pre-Marxian period.—110, 352, 354

Fichte, Johann Gottlieb (1762-1814)—German classical philosopher, subjective idealist.—66, 346

Fielding, Henry (1707-1754)—English novelist and playwright.—438, 442

Flerovsky, N. (Bervi, Vasily Vasilyevich) (1829-1918)—Russian writer; Narodnik; author of *Condition of the Working Class in Russia*.—408, 420, 422

Fletcher, John (1579-1625)—English playwright.—457-58

Fourier, Charles (1772-1837)—French utopian socialist.—110, 182

Frederick II (1712-1786)—King of Prussia (1740-86).—343, 404

Frederick, William (1620-1688)—elector of Brandenburg (1640-88).—67

Freiligrath, Ferdinand (1810-1876)—German revolutionary poet; an editor of the *Neue Rheinische Zeitung* and member of the Communist League; from 1851 to 1868 a refugee in London; in the 1850s withdrew from revolutionary activities.—51, 395-401, 404-05

Fries, Jakob Friedrich (1773-1843)—German idealist philosopher.—109

Froissart, Jean (1337-c. 1410)—French chronicler.—234, 458

Furnivall, Frederick James (1825-1910)—English philologist, Shakespearian, founder of the New Shakespeare Society.—457, 458

G

Gallenga, Antonio (pen name *Mariotti*) (1812-1895)—Italian journalist and writer, participant in the national liberation movement in Italy; from 1830 lived mainly in England; contributed to *The Times*.—461

Ganihl, Charles (1758-1836)—French economist, representative of New Mercantilism.—144

Garibaldi, Giuseppe (1807-1882)—Italian revolutionary, leader of the Italian people in the struggle for national liberation and unification of the country.—247, 248, 261

Garrick, David (1717-1779)—English actor, prominent as a performer of Shakespearian characters.—462

Gaskell, Elizabeth (1810-1865)—English writer.—339

NAME INDEX

Génin, François (1803-1856)—French philologist.—231

George, Henry (1839-1897)—American economist and writer.—118

Gerasimi (d. 475)—Palestine abbot, alleged author of *A Story of the Slave Andronicus*.—239

Gessner, Salomon (1730-1788)—Swiss poet and painter.—284

Gey, Johann Wilhelm (1789-1854)—German priest, author of fables and verses for children.—274

Gibson, Edward (1837-1913)—Irish statesman and historian; specialist in English literature; later Lord Chancellor of Ireland.—460

Gladstone, William Ewart (1809-1898)—English statesman.—453, 468

Gluck, Christoph Willibald (1714-1787)—German composer.—345

Godwin, William (1756-1836)—English writer; rationalist, one of the founders of anarchism.—165

Goethe, Johann Wolfgang von (1749-1832)—German writer and thinker.—99, 135, 218, 239, 263, 311, 345-47, 349-62, 364-67, 369-74, 405, 436-38, 442

Gogol, Nikolai Vasilyevich (1809-1852)—Russian writer.—439

Görres, Johann Joseph von (1776-1848)—German writer, philologist and historian.—237, 238, 243, 245

Gottfried von Bouillon (c. 1060-1100)—Duke of Lower Lorraine (1089-1100), one of the leaders of the first crusade.—238

Gottfried von Strassburg (born c. 1220)—German poet, author of the epic poem *Tristan und Isolde*.—242

Gottsched, Johann Christoph (1700-1766)—German writer and critic, representative of the early Enlightenment in Germany.—149

Gracchus, Gaius (153-121 B. C.) and his brother *Tiberius* (163-133 B. C.)—Roman tribunes; waged struggle for carrying out an agrarian reform in the interests of the peasants and plebeians.—81, 440

Green, Thomas (b. 1820)—English politician, Conservative M. P., Peelite.—235

Grimm, Jacob (1785-1863)—German philologist; author of folklore adaptations; historian of the German language.—50, 111, 244, 286

Grimm, Wilhelm (1787-1859)—German philologist; co-author of his brother Jacob's main works.—50

Grün, Karl (1817-1887)—German petty-bourgeois writer, prominent representative of "true socialism".—350-74, 386

Guizot, François Pierre Guillaume (1787-1874)—French liberal historian and politician.—81, 326

Gutzkow, Karl (1811-1878)—German playwright, novelist and journalist, member of the literary group "Young Germany".—377, 379-83

H

H.—See *Hermes, Carl Heinrich.*

Haeckel, Ernst Heinrich (1834-1919)—German naturalist, follower of Charles Darwin; materialist.—281

Händel, Georg Friedrich (1685-1759)—German composer.—345

Hanka, Václav (1791-1861)—Czech scholar and poet, a leader of the national liberation movement; well known as the publisher of the Zelenogradsky and Královédvorský manuscripts which he passed for the relics of ancient Czech poetry; later they were proved to be literary forgeries.—410

Hansemann, David (1790-1864)—big German capitalist, a leader of the liberal Rhenish bourgeoisie.—434

Harkness, Margaret (pen-name John Law)—English socialist writer of the 1880s.—89-92

Harrison, William.—457

Hartmann, Moritz (1821-1872)—Austrian poet; in the 1840s adhered to "true socialism".—109

Haussmann, Georges Eugène (1809-1891)—French politician, Bonapartist, prefect of the Seine department (1853-70); directed work on the reconstruction of Paris.—168

Hecker, Friedrich Karl (1811-1881)—German democrat, a leader of the Baden uprising in April 1848; subsequently emigrated to the USA; fought in the American Civil War on the side of the Northerners.—432

Hegel, Georg Wilhelm Friedrich (1770-1831)—German philosopher, objective idealist; elaborated idealist dialectics.—53, 59, 66, 95, 109, 110, 157, 271, 274, 276, 279-81, 327, 347-49, 352, 354, 363, 370, 375, 380, 382

Heine, Heinrich (1797-1856)—German revolutionary poet.—96, 112, 210, 374-76, 377, 381, 382, 388, 403-05, 438

Heinzen, Karl (1809-1880)—German writer, bourgeois democrat; opposed Marx and Engels; participated in the 1848-49 revolution; later emigrated to the U.S.A.—378, 410

Helvétius, Claude Adrien (1715-1771)—French materialist philosopher, Enlightener.—164, 273, 274, 275

Henry VIII (1491-1547)—King of England (1509-47).—258, 449

Henry the Lion (1129-1195)—Duke of Saxony (1139-81) and Bavaria (1156-81).—238

Herbart, Johann Friedrich (1776-1841)—German idealist philosopher, psychologist and pedagogue.—109

Herder, Johann Gottfried von (1744-1803)—German Enlightener, writer and philosopher.—345

Hermes, Carl Heinrich (H.) (1800-1856)—German reactionary writer.—206

Herodotus (c. 484-c. 425 B.C.)—Greek historian.—198

Herschel, William (1738-1822)—English astronomer.—178

Herwegh, Georg (1817-1875)—German revolutionary poet, petty-bourgeois democrat.—377

Herzen, Alexander Ivanovich (1812-1870)—Russian revolutionary democrat, materialist philosopher and writer.—416, 423

Hess, Moses (1812-1875)—German petty-bourgeois writer, ideologist of "true socialism".—352, 377

Hobbes, Thomas (1588-1679)—English philosopher, a founder of mechanistic materialism.—59, 275

Hoffmann—publisher in Hamburg, co-owner of the Hoffmann und Campe Publishing House, founded in 1818.—441

Hoffmann, Ernst Theodor Amadeus (1776-1822)—German romantic writer.—390, 403

Holbach, Paul Henri (1723-1789)—French materialist philosopher, atheist; an ideologist of the French revolutionary bourgeoisie of the 18th century.—162, 164, 275, 277

Hollinshed, Raphael (died c. 1580)—English chronicler; his *Chronicles of England, Scotland and Ireland* (1577) were used by Shakespeare in his historical dramas.—258

Homer—epic poet of Ancient Greece, author of *Iliad* and *Odyssey*.—190, 191, 196, 208, 240, 405, 441, 448

Horace (Quintus Horatius Flaccus) (65-8 B. C.)—Roman poet. 210, 405

Hugo, Victor (1802-1885)—French writer.—295, 296-97

Huxley, Thomas Henry (1825-1895)—English naturalist and philosopher.—468

Hyndman, Henry Mayers (penname *John Broadhouse*) (1842-1921)—English Socialist, Reformist.—120

I

Ibsen, Henrik (1828-1906)—Norwegian playwright.—75, 78, 341

Igor I Svyatoslavovich (1151-1202)—Prince of Novgorod-Seversky (from 1178) and of Chernigov (from 1198), hero of *The Lay of Igor's Host*.—409

Ingram, John Kells (1823-1907)—Irish economist and philologist.—460

Irving, Henry (John Henry Brodribb) (1838-1905)—English actor and stage manager; directed the Lyceum Theatre from 1878.—450, 452, 460-63, 465, 467-70

Itzstein, Johann (1775-1855)—German politician; Liberal.—364

J

Jackson, Charles Thomas (1805-1880)—U.S. physician and chemist; applied ether as an anaesthetic.—357

James I Stuart (1566-1625)—King of Great Britain and Ireland (1603-25).—226, 430, 458

James II Stuart (1633-1701)—King of Great Britain and Ireland (1685-88).—430

Janin, Jules (1804-1874)—French novelist, feuilletonist and critic.—280

Jean Paul—see *Richter, Johann.*

Joachim Joseph (1831-1907).—454

Johnstone, James (d. 1798)—collector and publisher of ancient

Scandinavian epics.—228
Julian the Apostate (c. 331-363)
—Roman Emperor (361-63).—
206
Jung, Alexander (1799-1884)—
German writer and literary
historian; was close to the
Young Germany literary
group.—379, 380, 381
Jung, Georg (1814-1886)—Lawyer and journalist; Young Hegelian; one of the founders of
the *Rheinische Zeitung* (1842);
in 1848 a democrat and later
National-Liberal.—377
Juvenal *(Decimus Junius Juvenalis)* (c.60-c.127)—Roman poet
and satirist.—405

K

Kant, Immanuel (1724-1804)—
founder of classical German
philosophy, idealist.—59, 66,
109, 345, 346, 348, 355
Kautsky, Karl (1854-1938)—
German Social-Democrat, editor of the *Neue Zeit* (1883-1917); in the 1880s adhered
to Marxism; subsequently adopted an opportunist stand and
was an ideologist of Centrism (Kautskianism).—89, 258
Kean, Charles (1811-1868)—
English actor and stage producer at the Princess Theatre
in London.—449
Kean, Edmund (1787-1833)—
English tragic actor.—450,
452, **462**
Keere, van den.—458
Kemble, John Philip (1757-1823)
—prominent English tragic
actor.—450

Kepler, Johannes (1571-1630)—
German astronomer.—344, 436
Kinkel, Johann Gottfried (1815-1882)—German poet; petty-bourgeois democrat; participant in the Baden uprising in
1849; was sentenced to imprisonment in a fortress, but escaped from prison, emigrated
and lived in London; opposed
Marx and Engels.—390, 391,
392, 393, 394-95, 397
Kinkel, Johanna (née *Mockel*)
(1810-1858)—German writer,
wife of Gottfried Kinkel.—
391, 392, 393
Klopstock, Friedrich Gottlieb
(1724-1803)—German poet.—
352
Knapp, Albert (1798-1864)—
German poet, author of church
hymns, pietist.—56
Kock, Paul de (c. 1794-1871)—
French writer.—439
Kokosky, Samuel (1838-1899)—
German Social-Democrat;
writer.—118
Kossuth, Lajos (Ludwig) (1802-1894)—leader of the Hungarian national liberation movement; headed the bourgeois-democratic forces in the 1848-49 revolution; after the
defeat of the revolution emigrated; in the 1850s sought
support among the Bonapartist circles.— 397
*Kotzebue, August Friedrich
Ferdinand* (1761-1819)— German reactionary writer and
journalist.— 280, 407
Krug, Wilhelm Traugott (1770-1842)—German idealist philosopher.—109
Kühne, Ferdinand Gustav (1806-1888)—German writer, mem-

ber of the Young Germany literary group.—379, 381, 382

L

Lacressonnière, Louis (1819-1893)—French dramatic actor; played two roles in the melodrama *Le Courrier de Lyon.*—467

Laeghaire (d. 458)—King of Ireland (428-58).—223

Lafargue, Paul (1842-1911)—a leader of the Marxist wing in the French working-class movement; member of the First International, one of the founders of the French Socialist Workers' Party (1880); author of historical and literary works.—141, 142, 314, 317, 438

Lamartine, Alphonse (1790-1869)—French poet, historian and bourgeois politician; in 1848 Foreign Minister in the French Provisional Government.—293, 294, 329, 394

Langland, William (c. 1332-c. 1400)—English poet.—234, 235

La Rochefoucauld, François, Duke (1613-1680)—French writer and politician of the period of Fronde.—269

Lasker, Eduard (1829-1884)—German politician, one of the founders and leaders of the National-Liberal Party.—113

Lassalle, Ferdinand (1825-1864)—German petty-bourgeois socialist; writer; one of the founders of the General Association of German Workers (1863); author of theoretical works which became a source of opportunism (Lassalleanism) in the working-class movement.—98-107.

Laube, Heinrich (1806-1884)—German writer, member of the Young Germany literary group.—50, 379, 381, 382

Laura—see Marx, Laura.

Lee, Jane.—458.

Lee, Jenny.—455.

Leibniz, Gottfried Wilhelm (1646-1716)—German mathematician; idealist philosopher.—344, 407

Lenchen—see Demuth, Helene.

Leonardo da Vinci (1452-1519)—Italian painter, scholar and engineer of the Renaissance.—177, 253.

Lermontov, Mikhail Yuryevich (1814-1841)—Russian poet.—443

Leske, Carl Wilhelm (died c. 1845)—publisher in Darmstadt.—377

Lessing, Gotthold Ephraim (1729-1781)—German writer, critic and philosopher; prominent Enlightener.—63, 64, 112, 141, 149, 345, 352, 414, 415, 437.

Lever, Charles James (1806-1872)—British novelist, Irish by birth.—340, 439

Leverrier, Urbain Jean Joseph (1811-1877)—French astronomer.—357

Lichnowski, Felix (1814-1848)—member of the Frankfurt National Assembly in 1848, Legitimist; was killed in September 1848 during the peasants' uprising.—263, 403

Liebknecht, Wilhelm (1826-1900)—member of the Communist League, participant in the 1848-49 revolution, one of the founders of the German Social-Democratic Party; friend of Marx and Engels.—118, 406

Littledale, Harold.—457, 458

Locke, John (1632-1704)—English philosopher and economist.—59, 81, 273, 275

Lomonosov, Mikhail Vasilyevich (1711-1765)—Russian scholar and poet; reformed the Russian literary language.—410, 411

Longus (A. D. 2nd-3rd cent.)—Greek writer, author of the pastoral novel *Daphnis and Chloë*.—215

Lopatin, Hermann Alexandrovich (1845-1918)—Russian revolutionary Narodnik, member of the First International; friend of Marx and Engels.—420

Lope de Vega Carpio (1562-1635)—Spanish writer.—444

Loria, Achille (1857-1943)—Italian sociologist and economist; falsified Marxism.—248

Louis XIV (1638-1715)—King of France (1643-1715).—263, 370

Louis XVIII (1755-1824)—King of France (1814-15 and 1815-24).—81

Louis Philippe I (1773-1850)—King of France (1830-48).—93, 280, 439

Lover, Samuel (1779-1868).—Irish novelist.—340

Lucian (c. 120-180)—Greek satirist.—95, 206, 211, 218, 412

Lucretius (Titus Lucretius Carus) (c. 95-55 B.C.)—Roman poet and materialist philosopher, author of the poem *De rerum natura*.—206, 208, 209

Lucullus, Lucius Licinius (c. 106-c. 57 B.C.)—Roman general; during his military campaigns against Greece and Asia amassed enormous riches.—261

Ludwig I of Bavaria (1786-1868)—King of Bavaria (1825-48).—352

Luther, Martin (1483-1546)—leader of the Reformation, founder of Protestantism (Lutheranism) in Germany; ideologist of the German burghers.—66, 80, 100, 253

M

Machiavelli, Niccolò (1469-1527)—Italian politician, writer and historian.—248, 253, 359

Macpherson, James (1736-1796)—Scottish poet, author of the poems *Fingal* and *Temora*.—225

Macready, William Charles (1793-1873)—English actor and stage producer.—450, 460, 462

Macrinus, Opellius (164-218)—Roman Emperor (217-18).—212

Malthus, Thomas Robert (1766-1834)—English clergyman and economist; author of the misanthropic theory of population.—111, 143, 161

Mandeville, Bernard de (1670-1733)—English moralist writer and satirist.—156, 273

Manning, Henry Edward (1808-1892)—head of the Catholic Church in England, Cardinal from 1875.—468

Marbach, Oswald (1810-1890)—German writer and poet; author of adaptations of German medieval epics and publisher of German popular books.—237, 238, 240, 241, 244

Marco Polo—see Polo.

Marryat, Frederick (1792-1848)—English naval officer and novelist; author of adventure novels.—441

Marstein—traditional ruler of Ireland.—227

Martin, Theodore (1816-1909)—British author and translator.—460

Marx, Eleanor (Tussy) (1855-1898)—youngest daughter of Karl Mark, representative of the English and international working-class movement; wife of Edward Aveling from 1884.—341

Marx, Laura (1845-1911)—daughter of Karl Marx, wife of Paul Lafargue from 1868; was active in the working-class movement in France.—113, 122

Maupassant, Henri René Albert Guy de (1850-1893)—French writer.—317

Mead, Edward—English worker poet; published his poems in the Chartist newspaper *The Northern Star*.—324

Mehring, Franz (1846-1919)—a Left-wing leader of the German Social-Democratic Party; one of the founders of the Communist Party of Germany in 1918-19; historian and critic; author of works on Marx and Engels.—63-69

Menke, Heinrich Theodor (1819-1892)—German geographer; revised *Handatlas für die Geschichte des Mittelalters und der neueren Zeit* by K. Spruner.—343, 344

Menzel, Wolfgang (1798-1873)—German reactionary writer and critic; nationalist.—365, 374

Michel, Francisque Xavier (1809-1887)—French philologist and literary historian.—231

Milde, Karl August (1805-1861)—big Silesian manufacturer; representative of the liberal German bourgeoisie.—434

Mill, John Stuart (1806-1873)—English economist and philosopher.—415, 470

Milton, John (1608-1674)—English poet, journalist and politician.—144, 449

Mithridates VI, the Great (132-63 B.C.)—King of Pontus (120-63).—261

Mockel, Johanna—see Kinkel, Johanna.

Mohammed (Muhammed) (570-682)—founder of the Moslem religion.—189, 459

Montalembert, Marc René (1714-1800)—French military engineer; worked out a new system of fortifications.—253

Monteil, Amans Alexis (1769-1850)—French historian.—422

Montesquieu, Charles Louis (1689-1755)—French sociologist, economist and writer; Enlightener.—66

More, Thomas (1478-1535)—English politician and humanist writer; an early representative of utopian communism, author of *Utopia*.—257, 258

Morgan, Lewis Henry (1818-1881)—American ethnographer, archaeologist and historian of the primitive society.—321

Morris, William (1834-1896)—English poet and artist; a leader of the Socialist League.—341, 342

Moschus (2nd cent. B.C.)—Greek poet.—200, 215

Motteler, Julius (1838-1907)—German Social-Democrat; during the Exceptional Laws Against the Socialists lived as a refugee in Zurich and subsequently in London.—406

Mozart, Wolfgang Amadeus (1756-1791)—Austrian composer.—177

Müllner, Adolph (1774-1829)—German writer and critic.—155

Mundt, Theodor (1808-1861)—German writer, member of the Young Germany literary group.—241, 379, 381, 382-83

Münzer, Thomas (c. 1490-1525)—German revolutionary, leader and ideologist of the peasant and plebeian masses during the Reformation and the Peasant War in Germany in 1524-25.—100

N

Napoleon I (Napoleon Bonaparte) (1769-1821)—Emperor of France (1804-14 and 1815).—58, 80, 262, 285, 345, 356

Napoleon III (Louis Napoleon) (1808-1873)—Emperor of France (1852-70).—96, 169, 403, 435, 439

Nechayev, Sergei Gennadievich (1847-1882)—Russian anarchist, organiser of students' conspiratorial groups in Russia; in 1872 was extradited by the Swiss authorities to the Russian Government; died in the Peter and Paul Fortress.—420

Necker, Jacques (1732-1804)—French banker and politician; Minister of Finance under Louis XVI.—328

Nero (37-68)—Roman Emperor (54-68).—210, 212

Newton, Isaac (1642-1727)—English physicist, astronomer and mathematician.—50

O

O'Clery, Michael (1575-1643)—Irish chronicler.—221

O'Connor, Arthur (1763-1852)—Irish revolutionary, one of the leaders of the United Irishmen Association in the 1798 uprising in Ireland.—222, 223

O'Connor, Charles (1764-1828)—Irish historian and archaeographer.—221

O'Connor, Feargus (1794-1855)—a Left-wing leader of the Chartist movement; founder and editor of *The Northern Star;* reformist after 1848.—114, 222

O'Connors—Irish royal dynasty in Connaught (Western Ireland).—222, 223

O'Donovan, John (1809-1861)—Irish philologist; studied Irish antiques.—221

Owen, Robert (1771-1858)—English utopian socialist.—90, 273, 274

P

Paganini, Niccolò (1782-1840)—Italian violinist and composer.—129

Paine, Thomas (1737-1809)—English radical writer; Republican; participant in the American War of Independence and in the French Revolution.—163

Painter, William (1540-1594)—author of *Palace of Pleasure*, a collection of short novels translated from Herodotus, Plutarch, Tacitus, Boccaccio and other authors, used by Shakespeare as plots for his works.—458

Paris, Paulin (1800-c. 1881)—French philologist and literary historian.—230

Parnell, Charles Stuart (1846-1891)—Irish politician and statesman, M.P., champion of Home Rule.—96

Parny, Evariste Désiré, Vicomte (1753-1814)—French poet.—373

Patrick (c. 384-c. 463)—Irish missioner, founder of the Catholic Church in Ireland.—323

Pericles (c. 490-429 B.C.)—Athenian statesman.—205

Persius (Aulus Persius Flaccus) (34-62)—Roman poet and satirist.—210

Peter I (1672-1725)—Russian Tsar from 1682; Emperor of all Russias from 1721.—411

Petrarch, Francesco (1304-1374) —Italian poet.—249

Phelps, Samuel (1804-1878)—English actor and manager in the Sadler's Wells Theatre in London.—449

Philip Augustus (1165-1223)—King of the French (1180-1223); took part in the third crusade.—66

Pieper, Wilhelm (b. 1826)—German philologist and journalist; member of the Communist League; emigrated to London; in the 1850s was close to Marx and Engels.—116, 117

Pius IX (1792-1878)—Pope (1846-78).—328.

Platen (Platen-Hallermünde), August (1796-1835)—German poet.—49

Plato (c. 427-c. 347 B.C.).—Greek idealist philosopher.—405

Plekhanov, Georgi Valentinovich (1856-1918)—Russian Marxist, in 1870s a Narodnik; organiser of the Emancipation of Labour group, the first Russian Marxist group, in Geneva in 1883; philosopher and propagandist of Marxism in Russia; after the Second Congress of the R.S.D.L.P. (1903) a Menshevik.—417

Plutarch (c. 46-c. 126)—Greek writer; idealist philosopher.—197, 202, 208, 209

Polo, Marco (1254-1324)—Italian traveller, in 1271-95 travelled to China.—247

Pompey (Gnaeus Pompeius Magnus) (106-48 B.C.)—Roman general and statesman.—262

Pope, Alexander (1688-1744)—English poet and satirist; author of the satirical poem *Dunciad*.—320

Prévost, Antoine François (1697-1763)—French writer.—291

Proudhon, Pierre Joseph (1809-1865)—French petty-bourgeois socialist; subsequently a founder of anarchism.—110, 164, 165, 283, 286, 295, 357, 367

Ptolemy (Claudius Ptolemaeus) (2nd cent.)—Greek astronomer and geographer, founder of the geocentric conception of the universe.—213

Publicola (Publius Valerius Publicola) (6th cent. B.C.)—traditional founder of the Roman Republic.—81

Pückler-Muskau, Hermann, Prince (1785-1871)—German writer.—380

"*Pumps*"—See *Burns, Mary Allen*.

Pushkin, Alexander Sergeyevich (1799-1837)—Russian poet.—413, 439, 445, 447

Q

Quintana, Manuel José (1772-1857)—Spanish poet and politician.—262

R

Radowitz, Joseph, von (1797-1853)—Prussian general and statesman; one of the Right-wing leaders in the Frankfurt National Assembly in 1848-49.—263

Ralston, William Ralston Shedden (1828-1889)—English writer; in the 1860s and 1870s several times visited Russia; author of works on Russian literature and history.—469, 470

Ranc, Arthur (1831-1908)—French politician and journalist.—315

Raphael (Raffaello Santi) (1483-1520)—Italian painter of the Renaissance.—93, 129, 177, 178

Razin, Stepan Timofeevich (d. 1671)—leader of the antifeudal rebellion of the peasants and Cossacks in Russia (1666-71).—428

Raumer, Friedrich (1781-1873) German reactionary historian and politician.—283

Reade, Charles (1814-1884)— English novelist and dramatist.—467

Rembrandt van Rijn (1606-1669) —Dutch painter.—92, 146

Renan, Ernest (1823-1892)— French theologian and historian, idealist philosopher, author of *Vie de Jésus*.—316

Reynouard, Antoine Augustin (1756-1853)—French literary historian and bibliographer.—232

Richter, Johann Paul Friedrich (1763-1825)—German writer.—327

Robespierre, Maximilien Marie (1758-1794)—a leader of the French Revolution; head of the Jacobin government.—80, 95

Roscher, Wilhelm (1818-1894)— German economist, founder of the Historical School.—154

Rose, Edward (1849-1904)—English playwright and critic.—341

Rossa (5th cent.)—Irish lawyer.—223

Rothschilds—dynasty of financiers; had banks in many countries.—387, 388

Rotteck, Karl (1775-1840)—German historian and politician; liberal.—434

Rousseau, Jean Jacques (1712-

1778)—French democratic writer and philosopher; Enlightener; ideologist of the petty bourgeoisie.—66, 162, 163, 271, 275, 278, 279, 281-283, 285

Royer-Collard, Pierre Paul (1763-1845)—French reactionary politician and philosopher.—81

Rückert, Friedrich (1788-1866)—German romantic poet, translator of Oriental poetry.—442

S

Šafařík, Pavel Josef (1795-1861)—Czech philologist and historian.—400

Sainte-Beuve, Charles Augustin (1804-1869)—French critic, poet and literary historian.—292

Saint-Just, Antoine (1767-1794)—prominent in the French Revolution; a Jacobin leader.—80

Saint-Simon, Claude Henri (1760-1825)—French utopian socialist.—90, 110, 334, 379

Saltykov, Mikhail Yevgrafovich (pen name *N. Shchedrin*) (1826-1889)—Russian satirist.—422, 439

Sancho—see Stirner, Max.

Sand, George (Dudevant, Aurore) (1804-1876)—French novelist.—56, 297

Sand, Karl Ludwig (1795-1820)—German student; participant in the liberal movement of German intelligentsia; was executed for the assassination of the reactionary writer Kotzebue.—297, 407

Sardou, Victorien (1831-1908)—French playwright.—451, 454, 465

Sax, Emanuel Hans (1857-1896)—Austrian economist, poet and journalist.—142

Say, Jean Baptiste (1767-1832)—French economist, disciple of Adam Smith.—81

Schiller, Friedrich von (1759-1805)—German writer.—88, 100, 105, 155, 345, 347, 348, 352, 355

Schlosser, Friedrich Christoph (1776-1861)—German liberal-bourgeois historian, author of *Weltgeschichte*—261

Schlözer, August Ludwig (1735-1809)—German historian.—344

Schmidt, Conrad (1863-1932)—German Social-Democrat; corresponded with Engels; subsequently a revisionist and Neo-Kantian.—317

Schömann, Georg Friedrich (1793-1879)—German historian and linguist, author of works on Greece.—197

Schopenhauer, Arthur (1788-1860)—German idealist philosopher.—109

Schubart, Christian Friedrich Daniel (1739-1791)—poet and writer; was imprisoned in a fortress for his works directed against feudal absolutism.—344

Schücking, Levin (1814-1883)—German writer and journalist.—55

Schumann, Clara.—454

Schurz, Karl (1829-1906)—German petty-bourgeois democrat, participant in the Baden-Pfalz uprising of 1849; in 1852 organised Kinkel's escape from prison; emigrated to the U.S.A.—394

Schütz, Christian Gottfried (1747-1832)—German philologist.—195

Schwab, Gustav (1792-1850)—German romantic poet, author of adaptations of German epics and classical myths.—238

Scott, Walter (1771-1832)—Scottish novelist.—321, 432, 442

Seneca, Lucius Annaeus (c. 4 B.C.-A.D. 65)—Roman stoic philosopher and dramatist.—210

Septimius Severus (146-211)—Roman Emperor (193-211).—212

Sertorius, Quintus (c. 123-72 B.C.)—Roman general.—261

Shakespeare, William (1564-1616)—English dramatist and poet.—54, 83, 100, 103-106, 135-37, 155, 259, 260, 262, 350, 436, 437, 438, 441, 442, 444, 449-54, 456-61, 465, 466, 468, 470

Shaw, George Bernard (1856-1950)—English playwright and politician; a leader of the Fabian Society from the late 1880s.—340

Shchedrin—See *Saltykov, M. Y.*

Shelley, Mary (1797-1851)—English novelist, second wife of Percy Bysshe Shelley.—56

Shelley, Percy Bysshe (1792-1822)—English poet.—48, 55, 162-64, 320

Shuvalov, Ivan Ivanovich (1727-1797)—Russian statesman, favourite of Empress Elizabeth Petrovna.—412

Siddons, Sarah (1755-1831)—English tragic actress.—450

Siebel, Carl (1836-1868)—German poet, a distant relative of Frederick Engels.—103, 400

Simrock, Karl Joseph (1802-1876)—German poet and philologist; translator of Medieval German poems and publisher of German popular books.—237, 240, 244

Sismondi, Jean Charles Léonard Simonde de (1773-1842)—Swiss petty-bourgeois historian and economist.—289

Smith, Adam (1723-1790)—British economist.—66, 142, 143, 161, 413, 445, 448

Socrates (469-399 B.C.)—Greek idealist philosopher.—203, 205

Soulouque, Faustin (c. 1782-1867)—President of the Republic of Haiti; in 1849 proclaimed himself emperor (Faustin I); was overthrown in 1859.—403

Spalding W.—professor.—457

Spartacus (d. 71 B.C.)—leader of the uprising of Roman slaves (73-71 B.C.).—261, 436

Spinoza, Baruch (Benedictus) de (1632-1677)—Dutch materialist philosopher, atheist.—274

Stafford, William (1554-1612)—English economist.—457

Stahr, Adolf Wilhelm (1805-1876)—German writer, author of historical novels and studies in the history of art and literature.—393

Starcke, Carl Nicolai (1858-1926)—Danish philosopher and sociologist.—279

Sterne, Laurence (1713-1768)—English writer, representative of sentimentalism.—269

Stirner, Max (Schmidt, Johann Caspar) (1806-1856)—German philosopher, Young Hegelian,

NAME INDEX

ideologist of petty-bourgeois anarchism.—177, 178

Stone, W.—458

Storch, Heinrich (Andrei Karlovich) (1766-1835)—Russian economist and statistician.—140, 141

Strauss, David Friedrich (1808-1874)—German theologian, Left Hegelian, author of *Das Leben Jesu* (1835).—162, 164, 327

Strodtmann, Adolph (1829-1879)—German writer, bourgeois democrat.—390, 393

Struve, Gustav (1805-1870)—German petty-bourgeois democrat, journalist; one of the leaders of the Baden and the Baden-Pfalz uprisings.—432

Stubbe, Philipp.—457

Sue, Eugène (1804-1857)—French novelist.—297, 298, 299, 300-04, 305, 306

Sulla, Lucius Cornelius (138-78 B.C.)—Roman general and statesman.—261

Sullivan, Barry—Irish actor.—450

Svoboda, Václac (1791-1849)—Czech poet and philologist, translated into German the *Rukopis Královédvorský.*—410

Swift, Jonathan (1667-1745)—English satirist.—319

Szeliga—see *Zychlinski, Franz.* —298, 299, 301, 312

T

Tacitus, Cornelius (c. 55-120)—Roman historian.—190, 212, 213

Taillefer—Norman jongleur.—231

Taylor, Thomas (1817-1880)—English dramatist and journalist.—454

Tennyson, Alfred (1809-1892)—English romantic poet.—468

Thackeray, William Makepeace (1811-1863)—English writer.—102, 339

Themistocles (c. 525-460 B.C.)—Greek statesman and general during the Greek-Persian wars.—207

Theocritus (3rd cent. B.C.)—Greek poet.—200, 215, 448

Thiers, Adolphe (1797-1877)—French historian and statesman; headed the Versailles goverment in 1871; butcher of the Paris Commune.—167, 168

Thiersch, Bernhard (1794-1855)—German pedagogue and poet. —50

Thorvaldsen, Bertel (1768-1844) —Danish sculptor.—129

Tiberius (Tiberius Claudius Nero Caesar) (42 B.C.-A.D. 37) Roman Emperor (14-37 A.D.). —212

Tieck, Ludwig (1773-1853)—German poet, novelist and playwright; representative of romanticism; author of adaptations of German popular books.—238, 242, 244, 245

Tirso de Molina (Téllez, Gabriel) (1571-1648)—Spanish playwright.—444

Titian (Tiziano Uecellio) (c. 1477-1576)—Italian painter of the Renaissance.—177, 254

Tkachov, Pyotr Nikitich (1844-1886)—Russian critic and journalist; revolutionary Narodnik. —114, 416

Triboni, Joachim—traveller from Genoa.—250

Trochu, Louis Jules (1815-1896) —French general and politician.—168

Tupper, Martin (1810-1889)—English poet.—436

Turgenev, Ivan Sergeyevich (1818-1883)—Russian writer.—443

Turgot, Anne Robert Jacques (1727-1781)—French statesman and economist; Physiocrat.—328

Turoldus—name frequently met in Norman chronicles; alleged author of the *Chanson de Roland.*—231

Türr, István (1825-1908)—Hungarian officer; participant in the 1848-49 revolution in Italy and Germany.—248

Tussy—see *Marx, Eleanor.*

Tyndall, John (1820-1893)—British physicist.—291

U

Uhland, Ludwig von (1787-1862) —German romantic poet, member of the Frankfurt National Assembly.—228, 229

Urquhart, David (1805-1877)— English diplomat and publicist. —459

V

Varnhagen von Ense, Karl August (1785-1858)—German writer and liberal critic.—380

Vaulabelle, Achille de (1799-1879)—French historian and politician, moderate bourgeois Republican.—314

Vernet, Horace (1789-1863)—French battle-painter.—178

Vezin, Germain—actress.—450

Vidocq, François Eugène (1775-1857)—French criminal, later a secret police agent.—299

Viereck, Louis (1851-1921)— German Social-Democrat, one of the Right-wing leaders of the Party during the operation of the Exceptional Law Against the Socialists; member of the Imperial Diet from 1884 to 1887; in 1896 emigrated to America and withdrew from the socialist movement.—115

Vincke, Ernst Friedrich Georg (1811-1875)—German liberal politician; member of the Frankfurt National Assembly and later of the Prussian Chamber of Deputies and of the Prussian Provincial Diet.—263

Vizetelly, Henry (1820-1894)— —English publisher and journalist.—89

Voltaire, François Marie Arouet de (1694-1778)—French philosopher, satirist and historian. Enlightener.—113, 150, 162, 163, 211, 256, 259, 277-79, 291

W

Wachsmuth, Ernst Wilhelm (1784-1866)—German historian.—67, 198

Wagner, Richard (1813-1883)— German composer.—217

Walther von der Vogelweide (c. 1170-1230)—German minnesinger.—122

Watts, John (1818-1887)—English writer, follower of Owen.—163

Weerth, Georg Ludwig (1822-

1856)—German proletarian poet, editor of the feuilleton section in the *Neue Rheinische Zeitung*; member of the Communist League; friend of Marx and Engels.—402-05

Weitling, Wilhelm (1808-1871) —prominent in the German working-class movement in its early period; an ideologist of utopian egalitarian communism; tailor by trade.—165, 166

Welcker, Karl Theodor (1790-1869)—German lawyer and writer; a leader of the German Liberals in the 1830s and 1840s.—364, 434

Weydemeyer, Joseph (1818-1866) —member of the Communist League; participant in the 1848-49 revolution in Germany; in 1851 emigrated to America; fought in the American Civil War on the side of the Northerners; friend and comrade-in-arms of Marx and Engels.—397, 407

Wheatley, Ch. B.—458

Wieland, Christoph Martin (1733-1813)—German writer of the Enlightenment.—345, 352

Wienbarg, Ludolf (1802-1872)— German writer and critic, member of the Young Germany literary group.—379, 381, 382

William I (1797-1888)—King of Prussia (1861-88) and Emperor of Germany (1871-88).—67, 96

William III of Orange (1650-1702)—Stadtholder of the Dutch Republic (1671-1702) and King of Britain (1689-1702).— 226, 430

Willich, August (1810-1878)— Prussian officer; retired from the army because of his political views; member of the Communist League; in 1853 emigrated to the U.S.A.; fought in the American Civil War on the side of the Northerners.—435

Wilton, Mary—actress.—454

Wladislaw IV Sigismund (1595-1648)—King of Poland (1632-48).—429

Wolff, Wilhelm ("Lupus") (1809-1864)—an organiser of the Communist League and member of its Central Committee; one of the editors of the *Neue Rheinische Zeitung*; friend of Marx and Engels.— 403

Wolfram von Eschenbach (c. 1170-1220)—German poet.— 234

Wright—English Sociaist, member of the Social-Democratic Federation.—342

Z

Zitz, Franz (1803-1847)—German lawyer, democrat; in 1848 member of the Frankfurt National Assembly; after the defeat of the 1848-49 revolution in Germany emigrated to the U.S.A.—432

Zola, Émile (1840-1902)—French writer.—91, 317

Zychlinski, Franz Zychlin von (Szeliga) (1816-1900)—Prussian officer, critic and journalist; Young Hegelian.—298, 299, 301, 302, 312

Index
of Literary
and Mythological Names

Achilles—great hero of the Trojan war according to Greek mythology.—84, 191, 196

Adam (Bib.)—156, 234

Aegisthus—character in Aeschylus' *Oresteia*.—192

Aegyptus—character in Aeschylus' *The Supplices*.—194

Aeneas—defender of Troy, the title character of Virgil's *Aeneid*.—221

Agamemnon—hero of Greek mythology, the main character in Homer's *Iliad* and Aeschylus' tragedies *Oresteia* and *Agamemnon*.—191, 192, 196

Ahasuerus—character in a medieval legend and the German popular book *Der ewige Jude*.—240

Andronicus—the title character in *A Story of the Slave Andronicus* attributed to Gerasimi, the abbot of a Palestinian monastery.—239

Antigone—the title character in Sophocles' and Aeschylus' tragedies.—460

Apollo (Gr. myth.)—Greek god of the arts.—193, 203

Arnold—character of Minna Kautsky's novel *Die Alten und die Neuen*.—87, 88

Arthur Grant—character in Margaret Harkness' novel *City Girl*.—90

Athena (Gr. myth.)—goddess of war and wisdom.—193, 207

Balthasar—character in Lassalle's drama *Franz von Sickingen*.—98, 100, 105

Brynhild—heroine of the *Nibelungenlied* and the *Edda*.—216, 342

Caesair—granddaughter of Noah according to the Irish annals.—221

Cassandra (Gr. myth.)—daughter of Priam endowed with the gift of prophesy; character in Aeschylus' tragedy *Agamemnon*.—196

Charles V—German Emperor, portrayed by Lassalle in *Franz von Sickingen*.—100, 105

Chloë—the title character in the novel *Daphnis and Chloë* by the Greek writer Longus.—215

Chourineur—character in Eugène Sue's *Les mystéres de Paris*.—299, 300, 303

Christ, Jesus (Bib.)—211, 359, 391, 392

Clarin—character in Calderón's drama *El Mágico prodigioso*.—263

Claudius—character in the German popular book *Kaiser Octavianus*.—242

INDEX OF LITERARY AND MYTHOLOGICAL NAMES 517

Clemens—character in the German popular book *Kaiser Octavianus*.—242
Clytemnestra (Gr. myth.)—the wife and murderess of Agamemnon; character in Aeschylus' *Oresteia*.—192
Cordelia—character in Shakespeare's *King Lear*.—450
Cyprian—character in Calderón's *El Mágico prodigioso*.—263

Danaides (Gr. myth.)—daughters of Danaus, the king of Argos.—194

Danaus (Gr. myth.)—king of Argos.—194
Daphnis—the title character in Longus' novel *Daphnis and Chloë*.—215
David—character in Eugène Sue's *Les mystères de Paris*.—300
Demodocus—character in Homèr's *Odyssey*.—191
Desdemona—the main character in Shakespeare's *Othello*.—450
Don Quixote—the title character in Cervantes' novel.—99, 242, 255, 265
Dorothea—the title character in Goethe's novel *Hermann und Dorothea*.—363
Dulcamara—character of the Italian puppet theatre.—248
Dunce I—character in Pope's Poem *Dunciad*.—320
Dunce II—character in Pope's *Dunciad*.—320

Else Barr—character in Minna Kautsky's novel *Die Alten und die Neuen*.— 88
Enceladus—character of Greek mythology.—388
Erinyes (Gr. Myth.)—Furies; characters in Aeschylus' *Eumenides*.—192
Etzel—character in the *Nibelungenlied*.—216
Eumaeus—character in Homer's *Odyssey*.—191
Eve (Bib.).—234

Falstaff—character in Shakespeare's *Merry Wives of Windsor* and *Henry IV*.—106
Fama (Rom. myth.)—the personification of Rumour.—83
Faust—the title character in a folk legend and Goethe's drama.—239, 263, 349, 354, 370
Fierabras—the title character in a German popular book.—243
Fingal—character in Macpherson's *Ossian*.—225
Finn Mac Cumhal—hero of Irish epics.—225
Fleur de Marie—the main character in Eugène Sue's *Les mystéres de Paris*.—299, 302, 304-13
Florens—character in the German popular book *Kaiser Octavianus*.—242
Fraçon—character in Terence's comedy *Eunuchus*.—255
Franz von Sickingen—the title character in Lassalle's drama.—98, 101, 104, 106
Freya (Norse myth.)—goddess of love and fruitfulnees.—217
Friday—character in Defoe's novel *Robinson Crusoe*.—318

Ganymede (Gr. myth.)—a beautiful boy, carried up to Olympus by Zeus; Zeus' cup-bearer.—198
Genovefa—the title character in a German popular book.—237, 241
Georges, madam—character in

Eugène Sue's *Les mystères de Paris*.—305, 307, 309
Germain—character in Eugène Sue's *Les mystères de Paris*.—301
Gobseck—the title character in Balzac's short novel.—313
Götz von Berlichingen—the title hero of Goethe's drama.—99, 354
Gretchen—the principal character in Goethe's *Faust*.—436
Grieux, de—character in Prévost's novel *Manon Lescaut*.—291
Griseldis—the title character in a German popular book.—241
Gudrun—the title character in a German epic.—217
Gunther—character in the *Nibelungenlied*.—216

Habakkuk (Bib.).—81
Hamlet—the title character in Shakespeare's drama.—450, 451, 453, 460, 468
Hartmut of Ormany—character in *Gudrun*, the German epic of the 13th century.—217
Heinrich von Ofterdingen—the title character in Novalis' novel.—391
Helena—the title character in a German popular book.—242
Hercules (Heracles)—hero of Greek mythology.—362, 365
Hermes (Gr. myth.)—a messenger and herald of the gods, patron of travellers, merchants and thieves.—83, 205
Herwig of Seeland—character in *Gudrun*, a German epic of the 13th century.—217
Hettel of Hegelingen—character in the 13th-century German epic *Gudrun*.—216

Hirlanda—the title character in a German popular book.—241

Io (Gr. myth.)—daughter of Inachus, the king of Argos, and Zeus' lover, whom Gera changed into a heifer.—194

Isolde—the main character in the medieval chivalry novel *Tristan und Isolde*.—242

Jesus—see *Christ, Jesus*.
Joss, Fritz—character in Lassalle's drama *Franz von Sickingen*.—105
Judas Iscariot (Bib.)—240
Jupiter (Rom. myth.)—supreme god of the Romans.—83, 211

Kriemhild—character in the *Nibelungenlied*.—216

Laporte—character in Eugène Sue's *Les mystères de Paris*.—306, 307, 309
Launce—character in Shakespeare's comedy *The Two Gentlemen of Verona*.—260
Lazarus (Bib.).—210, 316
Lear—he title character of Shakespeare's drama *King Lear*.—450
Loki—Norse god of fire; character in the old Scandinavian epic *Elder Edda*.—217
Lot (Bib.).—51
Lotte (Charlotte)—character in Goethe's *Die Leiden des jungen Werther*.—358

Macbeth—the title character in Shakespeare's drama.—450, 451, 452, 453
MacDuff—character in Shakespeare's *Macbeth*.—453
Maître d'école—character in Eu-

INDEX OF LITERARY AND MYTHOLOGICAL NAMES 519

gène Sue's *Les mystères de Paris.*—299, 301
Malvolio—character in Shakespeare's comedy *Twelfth Night.*—459
Manon Lescaut—the title character of Prévost's novel.—291
Marie—character in Lassalle's drama *Franz von Sickingen.*—100, 101
Mephistopheles—character in Goethe's *Faust.*—218, 354
Mercadet—character in Balzac's comedy *Le faiseur.*—315
Minos (Gr. myth.)—king of Crete, supreme judge in the underworld after his death.—357
Morgan le Fay (Celtic myth.)— a sorceress, one of the nine geniuses protecting the Celts.—220
Morolf (Marcolf)—the main character in the German popular book *Salomon und Morolf.*—255
Moscón—character in Calderón's drama *El Mágico prodigioso.*—263
Moses (Bib.).—221
Mulios—character in Homer's *Odyssey.*—191
Murph—character in Eugène Sue's *Les mystères de Paris.*—301
Njord (Norse myth.)—a god, protector of sailors.—218
Noah (Bib.).—221

Odysseus—the main hero of Homer's *Odyssey* and *Iliad.*—191
Oluf—the title character of old Danish ballad "Her Oluf".—228, 229
Ophelia—character in Shakespeare's *Hamlet.*—450, 453

Orestes—the main hero of Aeschylus' trilogy *Oresteia.*—102
Othello—the title character in Shakespeare's drama.—450, 454

Pan (Gr. myth.)—god of pastures and woods, protector of shepherds and cattle.—48
Pantaloon (Pantalone)—character in Italian folk comedy.—259
Paul (Bib.).—80
Pecksniff—character in Dickens' novel *Martin Chuzzlewit.*—327
Peg Woffington—the main character in the drama *Masks and Faces* by Tom Taylor and Charles Read.—454
Penelope—character in Homer's *Odyssey.*—454
Pontus—the main character in the German popular book *Pontus und Sidonia.*—243
Prometheus (Gr. myth.)—a titan who stole fire for men from the Olympus; character in Aeschylus' tragedy *Prometheus Bound.*—194, 203, 354
Prometheus—the title character in Goethe's poem.—354

Ragnar Lodbrôk—character in old Scandinavian epic *Krâkumâl.*—227
Rameau—character in Diderot's novel *Le Neveu de Rameau.*—281
Reinald—character in the German popular book *Die Haimonskinder.*—241
Rhadamanthus (Gr. myth.)— judge in the lower world.—337
Richard of Trier—character in Lassalle's drama *Franz von Sickingen.*—100

Robinson—the title character in Defoe's novel *Robinson Crusoe.*—318, 319

Roland—hero of the old French epic *Chanson de Roland.*—230

Rudolph, Prince of Geroldstein—character in Eugène Sue's *Les mystères de Paris.*—299, 300, 301, 302, 303, 304, 305, 306, 307, 308, 309

Salomon—the title character in the German popular book *Salomon und Morolf.*—255

Samuel (Bib.)—Hebrew prophet; character in Karl Gutzkow's drama *König Saul.*—233

Cancho Panza—character in Cervantes' novel *Don Quixote.*—255

Sganarelle—character of Italian puppet theatre.—248

Siegfried of Morland—character in the 13th-century epic *Gudrun.*—217, 218, 220, 241

Siegwart—the title character in J. M. Miller's novel.—390, 393

Sigebant of Ireland—character in the 13th-century epic *Gudrun.*—216

Sigurd—one of the main heroes of old Scandinavian epics.—342

Telamon—character in Homer's *Iliad.*—196

Telemachus—character in Homer's *Odyssey.*—196

Teukros—character in Homer's *Iliad.*—196

Tristan—the title character in the medieval chivalry novel *Tristan und Isolde.*—242

Ulrich von Hutten—character in Lassalle's drama *Franz von Sickingen.*—99, 100, 101, 105, 107

Ute the Norwegian—character in the 13th-century German epic *Gudrun.*—216

Volker—character in the *Nibelungenlied.*—406

Vulcan—Roman god of fire and metalworking.—83

Wagner—Faust's disciple in Goethe's *Faust.*—349

Walter, Markgraf— character in the German popular book *Griseldis.*—241

Werther—the title character in Goethe's *Die Leiden des jungen Werthers.*—358, 359

Wilhelm Meister—the title character of Goethe's novel *Wilhelm Meisters Lehr- und Wanderjahre.*—359, 367, 371

Zeus—the supremen Greek god.—349, 443